Exchange Rates and Inflation

Exchange Rates and Inflation

Rudiger Dornbusch

The MIT Press
Cambridge, Massachusetts
London, England

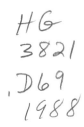
© 1988 Massachusetts Institute of Technology

This book was set in Palatino by Asco Trade Typesetting Ltd., Hong Kong and printed and bound by Halliday Lithograph in the United States of America.

Library of Congress Cataloging-in-Publication Data

Dornbusch, Rudiger.
  Exchange rates and inflation.

  Includes index.
  1. Foreign exchange.   2. Inflation (Finance)
I. Title.
HG3821.D69   1988   332.4'56   88-5367
ISBN 0-262-04096-4

For my father

Contents

Introduction

This collection of essays brings together much of my scholarly work of the past fifteen years. I have selected for inclusion those papers that clarify an issue of open economy macroeconomics or open a direction of research. I have also included some simply because I like them.

A collection of essays reaching back fifteen years is a curious matter, given the pace and passion with which our profession creates and destroys schools of thought. Younger readers will be unaccustomed to the near absence of the rituals of maximization. They will find that the analysis covers many of the same problems they study, and often the results are similar to those they are finding today. In turn, what was written in the 1970s on open economy macroeconomics finds its ancestry in some form in the literature of the interwar period and even the late nineteenth century. It helps to have that broad perspective to recognize that most sensible things have been said before simply because the problems are old and interesting.

Fifteen years is a long time. The length is marked by the profession's passage from global monetarism to the new classical economics. Over time my interests, and some beliefs, have changed very much. As a student, and early in my career, models and results were exciting, and there could not be enough of it. Today my interest is mostly in policy and policy-oriented research. The difference is subtle: in modeling, the main interest is in the structure and the implications; in policy-oriented research, by contrast, the central issue is to capture a problem, even if one does not write down the whole maximization problem. That is a weakness of the policy approach, and it might even be enough to reject it altogether. I do not think so. On the contrary, there is a broad complementarity between modeling and identifying and "painting" issues.

Although much of policy-oriented open economy macroeconomics stands unproved, I am impressed with near-complete sterility of the intertemporal approach in the face of actual policy issues. Perhaps, as it matures in the hands of some of the excellent scholars now working in that mode, it will come to yield a richer harvest.

I have accumulated in the past years more debts than the United States and all of Latin America combined. My students, at the University of Chicago, the University of Rochester, and since 1975 at MIT have been an unqualified pleasure. They have taught me, one way or the other, and they have given me the satisfaction of helping them learn and grow. There are many I would like to thank. I must also acknowledge among my own teachers and early colleagues some who have been especially important: Alexander Swoboda, Harry Johnson, Lloyd Metzler, Al Harberger, Ron Jones, Kark Brunner, and Michael Mussa. It is clear from my work that Robert Mundell has left his footprints all over it, and I will always be grateful for his teaching.

Since 1975 I have had the privilege to be part of MIT's Department of Economics. I cannot imagine a better place to do economics, and I must thank those of my senior colleagues who over the years shaped it into so civilized and excellent a place. Special thanks must go to Paul Samuelson and E. Cary Brown.

Special thanks go to Stan Fischer and Eliana Cardoso. Stan started as one of my thesis advisers and even today he occasionally rejects a draft. His warm friendship and support have been invaluable. Eliana has helped with love and advice and with almost unreasonable patience. I would finally like to acknowledge the generous editorial assistance of Carol McIntire who prepared the manuscript and saw this book through the publication process.

I

Exchange Rate Theory

Introduction to Part I

This first part of the collection brings together a number of essays that sought to clarify major issues or break new ground.

The first essay, which comes from my Chicago Ph.D. dissertation in the full bloom of the monetary approach to the balance of payments, had as its purpose to show what exactly is the role of money in the context of devaluation. Work by Kemp and Hahn had discussed the monetary economics of devaluation in as formal a manner as possible and demonstrated clearly the implications of homogeneity. But they had made a simple problem more obscure than necessary. The first essay might be accused of the opposite, but at least it shows starkly that under conditions of full employment and price flexibility, devaluation works only to the extent that money is not fully accommodating. Moreover it makes it clear that this is a short-run result. Over time, as money is being accumulated via the balance of payments, the economy returns to the initial real equilibrium.

The second essay discusses the role of real exchange rates in the context of international transfers. It is shown that the Robinson-Metzler-Bickerdike elasticity condition emerges as the criterion for the impact of a transfer on the terms of trade under special conditions. The model in which this occurs is one with traded goods, home goods, and income effects concentrated on the home goods market. The interest of the model is to highlight the "partial equilibrium" context in which elasticity formulas such as those derived by Bickerdike, Robinson, and Metzler do emerge.

The essay on the real and monetary effects of exchange rates integrates a broad range of approaches to devaluation. In the context of a model with home and traded goods, it is shown that a trade balance problem can be thought of as overspending, excessively high product wages in the traded goods sector, or an overvalued real exchange rate. By showing the general equilibrium of spending decisions, home goods market, and labor market equilibrium, these various perspectives appear as alternative facets of the same disequilibrium.

This model has been rediscovered several times over in various places: it dates back at least to the work of John E. Cairnes who used it in the late nineteenth century to discuss the influence of gold discoveries on Australia. It was well known in the interwar period in the work of R. G. Hawtrey or Bertil Ohlin, Carl Iversen, and Sir Roy Harrod. Since then it has been rediscovered as an Australian model, a Scandinavian model, and many times over as a Latin American model. The reason is that it captures a critical fact: an increase in absorption leads to trade problems and real appreciation, and a reduction in profitability in the traded goods sector. The fact is so common that not surprisingly the model keeps being rediscovered.

"Expectations and exchange rate dynamics" is the best-known paper in this collection. By combining sticky prices and instantly adjusting, forward-looking asset markets, it captured an essential feature of how live economies operate. The particular assumptions about the money supply process and all the details of the model are surely oversimplified, but the basic message that exchange rate volatility reflects the fact that exchange rates are determined in asset markets stands up well.

This first part concludes with a recent paper on exchange rates and prices. The impressive development of industrial organization, with ready to manipulate models such as those of Dixit and Stiglitz or Salop, could not leave open economy macroeconomics untouched. The obvious question was in the field of exchange rates: if some firms in an industry have a cost disturbance and others do not, what happens to the equilibrium price structure? That is in fact the question when, for reasons unrelated to a particular industry, the exchange rate changes but wages do not. The answer, as we see in this paper, is that the degree of substitution, the extent of oligopoly, market segmentation, and functional form of the demand curve are among the determinants. Among the interesting conclusions of this research is the idea that the typical model of a small country may be quite inappropriate: if "small country" means few distributors, then oligopoly models rather than perfect competition may be the appropriate framework for discussing tariffs or exchange rate effects. Of course, the model presented here only characterizes the short run. In the longer run there is entry and costs will become endogenous, and these considerations —via expectations and strategic pricing decisions—will already affect the short run. Work by Paul Krugman and by Giuseppe Bertola is fruitfully developing these broader ideas.

1   Devaluation, Money, and Nontraded Goods

This chapter develops a monetary approach to the theory of currency devaluation.[1] The approach is "monetary" in several respects. The role of the real balance effect is emphasized, and a distinction is drawn between the relative prices of goods, the exchange rate, and the price of money in terms of goods. Furthermore money is treated as a capital asset so that the expenditure effects induced by a monetary change are spread out over time and depend on the preferred rate of adjustment of real balances.[2] The latter aspect gives rise to the analytical distinction between impact and long-run effects of a devaluation.

The first part of this chapter develops a one-commodity and two-country model of devaluation. The simplicity of that structure is chosen quite deliberately to emphasize the monetary aspect of the problem as opposed to the derivative effects that arise from induced changes in relative commodity prices. Trade is viewed as the exchange of goods for money or a means of redistributing the world supply of assets. A devaluation is shown to give rise to a change in the level of trade and the terms of trade, the price of money in terms of goods.

In the second part the implications of the existence of nontraded goods are investigated, and induced changes in the relative prices of home goods enter the analysis.

1.1 Devaluation in a One-Commodity World

In this section we develop a purely monetary approach to devaluation in discussing a two-country, two-monies, and one-commodity model.[3] This stripped down model abstracts from the complexities of distribution and

Originally published in *American Economic Review*, vol. 63, no. 5 (December 1973), pp. 871–880.

substitution effects that may arise from changes in relative commodity prices and places primary emphasis on the real balance effect.

The Model

We assume that money is the only marketable asset and that real income (output) is in fixed supply in each country. The demand for nominal balances in each country is assumed to have the Cambridge form[4]

$$L = kP\overline{y};$$
$$L^* = k^*P^*\overline{y}^*,$$

(1)

where

$k, k^* =$ the desired ratios of money to income,

$\overline{y}, \overline{y}^* =$ real outputs,

$P, P^* =$ the money price of goods in terms of domestic and foreign currency,

and where an asterisk denotes the foreign country. Given the exchange rate, e, the domestic currency price of foreign exchange, arbitrage ensures that

$$P = P^*e.$$

(2)

With respect to monetary policy we assume that the nominal quantity of money in each country M, M^*, is initially given and that governments abstain from changing domestic money supplies except as it is necessary to maintain a pegged exchange rate. Accordingly the rate of increase in the domestic money supply is given by the trade balance surplus, B:

$$\dot{M} = B = -e\dot{M}^*.$$

(3)

Desired nominal expenditure in each country, Z, Z^*, is equal to money income less the *flow* demand for money, H, H^*, where the latter is assumed proportional to the *stock* excess demand

$$Z = P\overline{y} - H,$$
$$Z^* = P^*\overline{y}^* - H^*,$$

(4)

$$H = \pi(L - M) = H(P, M),$$
$$H^* = \pi^*(L^* - M^*) = H^*(P^*, M^*),$$

(5)

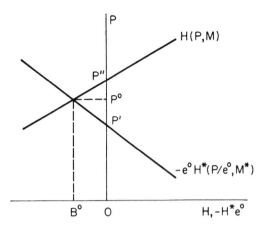

Figure 1.1

and where π and π^* are the domestic and foreign rates of adjustment. The expenditure functions in (4) imply a short-run marginal propensity to spend out of income smaller than unity while in the long run, when monetary stock equilibrium is attained, the average propensity to spend equals unity.

In figure 1.1 we show the domestic rate of hoarding, H, and the foreign rate of dishoarding, $-H^*$, as a function of P the domestic currency price of goods. The schedules are drawn for given nominal money supplies in each country and an exchange rate e^0. With the nominal quantity of money given, hoarding in the home country is an increasing function of the price level. An increase in the price level creates a stock excess demand for money and causes expenditure to decline relative to income as the community attempts to restore the real value of cash balances. It follows that we may view the hoarding schedule alternatively as the flow demand for money or the excess supply of goods (in nominal terms). By the same reasoning the foreign rate of dishoarding, given the exchange rate, is a decreasing function of the home price level. We note that the distribution of the money supplies underlying figure 1.1 is not compatible with balance of payments equilibrium. Foreign monetary stock equilibrium would obtain at P' while for domestic monetary equilibrium the price level would have to be equal to P''.

Consider now the conditions of short-run equilibrium. In order for the world goods market to clear, we require that world income equal world expenditure or equivalently that the home country's rate of hoarding equal the foreign country's rate of dishoarding.

$$H = -H^* e^0. \tag{6}$$

The equilibrium is shown in figure 1.1 at a domestic currency price of goods P^0; a higher price level would leave a world excess supply of goods and a lower price level a world excess demand for goods. We observe, too, that the short-run equilibrium at P^0 implies a trade balance deficit for the home country equal to B^0. That deficit, in the absence of sterilization, as we assume, redistributes money from the home country to the rest of the world. The reduction in the domestic nominal quantity of money reduces real balances at the initial price level and thereby causes planned hoarding to decrease and conversely abroad. In terms of figure 1.1 this implies that the hoarding and dishoarding schedules shift to the right, a process that continues over time until they intersect between P'' and P' on the vertical axis. At that time exchange of money for goods ceases since each country has achieved its preferred asset position and spends at a level equal to its income.

The Short-Run Effects of a Devaluation

Consider now the short-run or impact effect of a devaluation on the part of the home country. A devaluation changes the equilibrium relationship between price levels in the two countries. Differentiating equation (2), we obtain

$$\hat{P} = \hat{P}^* + \hat{e}, \tag{7}$$

where a $\hat{\ }$ denotes a relative change in a variable. Equation (7) informs us only about the relationship between changes in the price levels at home and abroad; we have to investigate the equilibrium condition in the world goods market in order to determine what the actual change in the price level in each country will be. For that purpose we turn to figure 1.2 where we show the world economy in initial long-run equilibrium at a domestic currency price of goods P^0.

The effect of a devaluation is shown in figure 1.2 by an upward shift in the foreign dishoarding schedule. For foreign monetary stock equilibrium to obtain, given the nominal quantity of money, the foreign currency price of goods would have to remain constant which in turn by (7) implies that the domestic price level would have to increase in the same proportion as the exchange rate, a price change equal to $(P'' - P^0)/P^0$. The domestic hoarding schedule, on the contrary, is unaffected, and domestic monetary stock equilibrium would continue to obtain at a domestic price level P^0. It

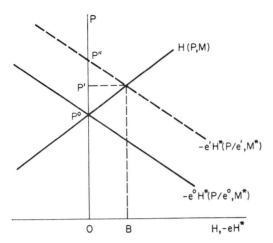

Figure 1.2

is observed from figure 1.2 that at an unchanged domestic price level there would be a world excess demand for goods due to the increase in foreign real balances and expenditure while at an unchanged foreign price level there would be a world excess supply of goods due to the decrease in domestic real balances and expenditure. It follows that in order for the world goods market to clear the price level, changes will have to be distributed in such a manner as to reduce domestic absorption and increase foreign absorption by an equal amount.

The equilibrium increase in the domestic price level is equal to $(P' - P^0)/P^0$, while the foreign price level declines in the proportion $(P'' - P^0)/P^0$. We note that both the domestic and foreign currency price of goods change less than proportionately to the rate of devaluation and that the distribution of price changes depends on the relative slopes of the hoarding schedules.

Given these price changes, foreign real balances have increased and the real value of domestic balances has decreased, thereby causing foreigners to dishoard in order to decumulate their capital gains and domestic residents to save in order to restore the real value of their cash balances. The home country's balance of payments surplus is equal to OB and causes a redistribution of the world money supply.

The formal criterion for the price changes and the balance of payments can be developed by differentiating the goods market equilibrium condition

$$\pi(k\overline{Py} - M) + e\pi^* \left(\frac{k^*P\overline{y}^*}{e - M^*} \right) = 0 \tag{6'}$$

with respect to P and e holding the nominal quantity of money constant in each country. The relative change in the domestic price level is

$$\hat{P} = \frac{\pi^* M^* e}{\pi M + \pi^* M^* e} \hat{e}. \tag{8}$$

Defining the world money supply, which is measured in terms of domestic currency $\overline{M}$,

$$\overline{M} = M + eM^* \tag{9}$$

and the domestic and foreign country's share in the money world supply, σ and σ^*, we can rewrite (8) as

$$\hat{P} = \frac{\pi^* \sigma^*}{\pi \sigma + \pi^* \sigma^*} - \hat{e} \geq 0. \tag{8'}$$

Substituting (8') in (7), we obtain the effect of a devaluation on the foreign price level:

$$\hat{P}^* = \frac{-\pi \sigma}{\pi \sigma + \pi^* \sigma^*} \hat{e} \leq 0. \tag{10}$$

Equations (8') and (10) show the distribution of price changes to depend on relative effective size where effective size is the product of the speed of adjustment and the share in the world money supply. In the small country case ($\pi \sigma / \pi^* \sigma^* = 0$), the home country price level increases in the same proportion as the exchange rate.

The home country's trade balance surplus is obtained by differentiating the flow demand function for money with respect to the price level and substituting (8) to yield

$$dB = dH = \pi M \left[\frac{\pi^* M^* e}{\pi M + \pi^* M^* e} \right] \hat{e} > 0. \tag{11}$$

Equation (11) confirms that the balance of payments unambiguously improves.

The Long-Run Effects of Devaluation

The long-run effects of devaluation on nominal money supplies and price levels may be interpreted with the help of figure 1.3. In quadrants II and IV

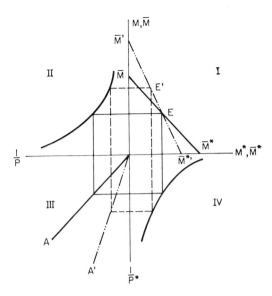

Figure 1.3

we show the domestic and foreign demand for real balances as hyperbolae; quadrant III shows the equilibrium price relationship $P^*e = P$ for the initial exchange rate as the ray OA. Lastly in quadrant I the world money supply at the initial exchange rate is given by $\overline{M}\,\overline{M}^*$, where $\overline{M}^* = \overline{M}/e$.

Initial long-run equilibrium is indicated by point E where the distribution of the world money supply is such that each country holds the desired quantity of real balances and where the equilibrium relationship between price levels is satisfied.[5]

A devaluation on the part of the home country affects both the price relationship and the world money supply. To each domestic price level corresponds now a lower equilibrium foreign price level; this is indicated in quadrant III by a rotation of the arbitrage line to OA'. Furthermore, given the initial nominal quantities of money in each country indicated by point E, the world money supply measured in terms of either currency changes: it decreases when measured in terms of foreign currency by the initial domestic quantity of money times the exchange rate change and it appreciates in terms of domestic currency by the initial foreign quantity of money times the exchange rate change. Accordingly the world monetary constraint rotates around point E—the initial endowment of currencies— to become $\overline{M}'\overline{M}^{*'}$.

It is readily verified from figure 1.3 that the initial distribution of money supplies at point E is no longer appropriate as a long-run equilibrium position since it would be inconsistent with the new price relationship. The new long-run equilibrium is shown by point E' indicating an increased domestic quantity of money and price level and a decreased foreign quantity of money and price level. Real balances obviously remain unchanged, between the new equilibrium and the old.

We should emphasize that our assumption about the absence of national money supply changes other than by the balance-of-payments mechanism is only one possible assumption about the behavior of money supplies. If we had assumed on the contrary that the home country accompanied the devaluation by an equiproportionate increase in its nominal quantity of money the only short- and long-run effect of the combination of policies would be an equiproportionate increase in the domestic price level and no effect whatsoever abroad.[6]

The latter monetary assumption would be appropriate if the home country wished to run a transitory budget deficit financed by money creation without impairing its foreign exchange position; the former assumption corresponds to the case where a country uses a devaluation to increase its foreign exchange holdings.

1.2 Devaluation and Nontraded Goods

In this section we consider an extension of the monetary model to introduce flexibility in relative prices. Following Jones (1972), Michael Michaely, Mundell, and Anne Krueger, we assume that there are two classes of goods produced and consumed in each country, traded goods and nontraded goods. Each class of goods itself is taken to be a composite commodity so that the relative prices of goods within each group are invariant. The aggregation chosen here places emphasis on the relative price of nontraded in terms of traded goods rather than on the terms of trade between internationally traded goods; it emphasizes the effects of changes in absorption on relative prices rather than the income effect of changes in the relative prices of traded goods.

This extension has two implications for the effects of a devaluation: changes in hoarding or equivalently changes in expenditure relative to income change the equilibrium relative price of home goods and these changes in relative prices in turn affect the equilibrium rates of hoarding.

We will show that in this more disaggregated structure the conclusions of the one-commodity model continue to hold for the effects of a devaluation on the balance of payments and the prices of traded goods; the additional element that arises is that the reduction in domestic absorption and the increase in foreign absorption cause the relative price of home goods to decline at home and to rise abroad. This result may be viewed as a special case of transfer analysis and arises in that perspective since each country's marginal propensity to spend on foreign home goods is by definition zero.[7]

The Model

Denoting traded and nontraded commodities as goods one and two, respectively, we assume that production takes place along a concave transformation curve and that supplies are a function only of the relative price:

$$X_i = X_i(q), \quad i = 1, 2, \tag{12}$$

where q is the relative price of nontraded goods—the ratio of the domestic currency prices of nontraded and traded goods, P_2 and P_1, respectively:

$$q = \frac{P_2}{P_1}. \tag{13}$$

Demand for the two commodities is assumed to depend on money prices and nominal expenditure or, using the homogeneity property and adopting traded goods as a numeraire, on relative prices and real expenditure measured in terms of traded goods, $\tilde{Z}$:[8]

$$C_i = C_i(q, \tilde{Z}), \quad i = 1, 2. \tag{14}$$

Real expenditure is defined as real income less real hoarding, all measured in terms of traded goods as a numeraire:

$$\tilde{Z} = \tilde{Y} - \tilde{H}, \tag{15}$$

where real income or the real value of output is defined as follows:

$$\tilde{Y} \equiv X_1 + qX_2 = \tilde{Y}(q). \tag{16}$$

Monetary considerations affect the goods markets via the expenditure function and in particular via the planned rate of hoarding. Maintaining our assumption that the demand for nominal balances is proportional to money income and that hoarding is proportional to the stock excess demand for money, we may write the desired real rate of hoarding, measured in terms of traded goods, as a function of the relative price and the real quantity of money measured in terms of traded goods:

$$\tilde{H} = \tilde{H}(q, \tilde{M}),$$ (17)

where

$$\tilde{M} = \frac{M}{P_1}.$$ (18)

Our assumptions about the stock demand for money ensure that an increase in either domestic currency price raises the desired rate of real hoarding so that the following properties hold:

$$q\frac{\partial \tilde{H}}{\partial q} \equiv \alpha > 0,$$

$$-\tilde{M}\frac{\partial \tilde{H}}{\partial \tilde{M}} \equiv \beta > 0.$$ (19)

The definition of real expenditure in (15) may be rewritten as the budget constraint in a manner that reveals the disaggregation of the model:

$$q(X_2 - C_2) + (X_1 - C_1) = \tilde{H}.$$ (20)

It is evident from the budget constraint that when the home-goods market clears ($X_2 = C_2$), the excess supply of traded goods identically equals the planned rate of hoarding.

Given a corresponding set of behavioral relations and constraints for the foreign country, we can now turn to the conditions of short-run equilibrium in this model. Short-run equilibrium obtains when for a given exchange rate and given money supplies, all goods markets clear, that is, when the market for nontraded goods clears in each country and when the world market for traded goods clears. Such an equilibrium, by the budget constraint in each country, implies that one country's planned rate of hoarding equals the other country's planned rate of dishoarding. Equations (21) formally state these equilibrium conditions of the model

$$E_2 \equiv X_2(q) - C_2(q, \tilde{Z}) = 0,$$

$$E_2^* \equiv X_2^*(q^*) - C_2^*(q^*, \tilde{Z}^*) = 0,$$ (21)

$$\tilde{H}(q, \tilde{M}) + \tilde{H}^*(q^*, \tilde{M}^*) = 0,$$

where

$$\tilde{M}^* \equiv \frac{M^*}{P_1^*},$$

$$q^* \equiv \frac{P_2^*}{P_1^*},$$

$$P_1^* e = P_1.$$

The first two conditions in (21) state that in equilibrium the excess demand for home goods is zero in each country, while the third equation is the market clearing condition in the market for traded goods.

The Impact Effect of a Devaluation

To examine the modifications in the effects of devaluation brought about by the introduction of nontraded goods, we consider first the relationship between the relative price of home goods and real hoarding. In particular, we want to show that an increase in real hoarding lowers the relative price of home goods. That result obtains since an increase in real hoarding represents a decrease in real expenditure relative to real income so that at constant relative prices and given a positive marginal propensity to spend on home goods the demand for home goods decreases. A decline in the relative price of home goods is required in order to eliminate the excess supply generated by an increase in hoarding. More formally, the relationship between the relative price of home goods and real hoarding may be derived by differentiating the first market equilibrium condition in (21) to obtain

$$\hat{q} = -\frac{m_2}{(\eta_2 + e_2)qC_2} d\tilde{H}, \tag{22}$$

where

$$m_2 \equiv q \frac{\partial C_2}{\partial \tilde{Z}} > 0,$$

$$\eta_2 \equiv -\frac{q}{C_2} \left[\frac{\partial C_2}{\partial q} + \frac{\partial C_2}{\partial \tilde{Z}} \frac{\partial \tilde{Y}}{\partial q} \right] > 0,$$

$$e_2 \equiv \frac{\partial X_2}{\partial q} \frac{q}{X_2} > 0.$$

The terms m_2, η_2, and e_2, denote, respectively, the marginal propensity to spend on home goods, the compensated elasticity of demand for home goods, and the elasticity of supply.

In figure 1.4 we show the market equilibrium schedule for the home

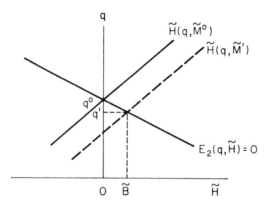

Figure 1.4

country's nontraded goods market as the locus $E_2 = 0$; to maintain market equilibrium, the expenditure-reducing effects of an increase in hoarding have to be offset by the substitution effects of a decrease in the relative price of home goods.

So far we have treated hoarding as the exogenous variable and have inquired into the relative price effects of changes in hoarding. We wish next to develop an expression that relates the rate of hoarding, given the nominal quantity of money, to price changes. Differentiating the hoarding function in (17), we obtain

$$d\tilde{H} = \alpha\hat{q} + \beta\hat{P}_1, \tag{23}$$

and substituting for the change in the relative price of home goods, $\hat{q}$, from (22), we obtain

$$d\tilde{H} = \gamma\beta\hat{P}_1, \tag{24}$$

where the terms

$$\gamma \equiv \frac{1}{1 + \alpha\delta} > 0,$$

$$\delta \equiv \frac{m_2}{(\eta_2 + e_2)qC_2} > 0,$$

are introduced for notational convenience. To gain further understanding of the relationship between hoarding, relative prices and the money price of traded goods derived in (24), we turn to figure 1.4 where we show the effect of an increase in the price of traded goods. In addition to the market equilibrium schedule for home goods we draw a hoarding schedule as an increasing function of the relative price of home goods, given the nominal quantity of money and the price of traded goods and hence the real quantity of money, $\tilde{M}^0$. The schedule is upward sloping since an increase in the price of home goods raises income and hence the demand for money, thereby increasing the desired rate of hoarding.

Initial equilibrium is shown at a relative price of nontraded goods, q^0. An increase in the price of traded goods reduces the real money supply and hence increases at constant relative prices the desired rate of hoarding. This is shown in figure 1.4 by a rightward shift of the hoarding schedule. Since at constant relative prices there is an excess supply of home goods, their relative price will decline to q', which in turn dampens the equilibrium rate of hoarding, $\tilde{B}$, relative to what it would have been at constant relative prices. The shift in the hoarding schedule corresponds to the term $\beta\hat{P}_1$ in (24), while the dampening effect shows in the term γ.

It will be recognized that in the composite commodity model analyzed earlier perfect substitutability ensured that $\delta = 0$. In the present formulation the absence of perfect substitution and the requirement that home-goods markets clear ensure that absorption changes are reflected in changes in relative prices; furthermore these induced changes in relative prices affect the equilibrium rate of hoarding, tending to reduce the hoarding response associated with a given change in the price of traded goods.

Having developed the basic relationships of the model, we can now proceed to investigate the effects of a devaluation. For that purpose we turn to figure 1.5. In the upper part of that figure we draw the domestic and foreign home goods market equilibrium schedules, where the latter is drawn as a function of the foreign rate of dishoarding and hence is negatively sloped. We assume, arbitrarily and without consequence, that initially the relative prices of home goods are the same in both countries. In the lower part of figure 1.5 we draw the domestic hoarding schedule and the foreign dishoarding schedule. It is important to note that along these hoarding schedules the relative price of home goods is allowed to adjust in order to clear the home-goods market so that by the budget constraint these hoarding schedules may alternatively be interpreted as the domestic excess supply of traded goods and the foreign excess demand for traded goods. Analytically, the schedules are defined by equation (24) and its counterpart for the foreign country.

Initial equilibrium obtains at a domestic currency price of traded goods P_1^0 and equilibrium relative prices of home goods $q^0 = q_0^*$. A devaluation by the home country may be analyzed in a manner similar to the composite

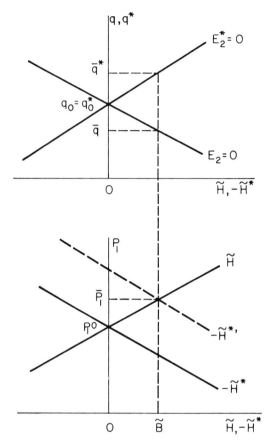

Figure 1.5

commodity model developed above. At an unchanged domestic currency price of goods foreign real balances increase causing foreigners to dishoard which is shown in figure 1.5 by a rightward shift of the foreign dishoarding schedule to $\tilde{H}^{*\prime}$. Short-run equilibrium will obtain at a domestic currency price of goods $\overline{P}_1$ where the world market for traded goods clears. The increase in the domestic price of traded goods causes the home country to reduce expenditure relative to income and run a trade balance surplus equal to $\tilde{B}$. Corresponding to the reduction in domestic absorption, we find a decline in the relative price of nontraded goods at home to $\overline{q}$, while the increase in foreign absorption raises the relative price of nontraded goods in that country to $\overline{q}^*$.

These results can be derived more formally by consideration of the equilibrium in the world market for traded goods. Recalling that (24) allows explicitly for market clearing in the home-goods market, that expression is identically equal to the excess supply of traded goods. Accordingly, we may use (24) and its counterpart for the foreign country to determine the effects of a devaluation on the domestic currency price of traded goods:

$$\beta\gamma\hat{P}_1 + \beta^*\gamma^*(\hat{P}_1 - \hat{e}) = 0 = d\tilde{H} + d\tilde{H}^*. \tag{25}$$

Solving for the relative change in the domestic currency price of traded goods yields

$$\hat{P}_1 = \frac{\beta^*\gamma^*}{\beta\gamma + \beta^*\gamma^*}\hat{e} \equiv \theta\hat{e}. \tag{26}$$

The solution for the effect of a devaluation on the domestic currency price of traded goods shows that this price will increase less than proportionately to the rate of devaluation ($0 < \theta < 1$). Differentiating the price relationship $P_1^* = P_1/e$ it is seen that the foreign currency price of traded goods will fall less than proportionately to the rate of devaluation. Substitution of (26) in (24) shows that the devaluing country's balance of payments unambiguously improves:

$$d\tilde{H} = \beta\gamma\theta\hat{e}. \tag{27}$$

So far our results correspond qualitatively to those obtained in the composite commodity model. The departure arises from the fact that changes in absorption in the two countries change the equilibrium relative prices of home goods. Substituting (27) in (22), we find that a devaluation lowers the relative price of nontraded goods in the home country and raises it abroad:

$$\hat{q} = -\delta\beta\gamma\theta\hat{e}; \quad \hat{q}^* = \delta^*\beta^*\gamma^*(1 - \theta)\hat{e}. \tag{28}$$

Although, as in the first part of this paper, short-run equilibrium is characterized by an exchange of traded goods for real balances and hence the absorption effects of a devaluation are emphasized, the role of the relative price of home goods is nevertheless crucial in the adjustment mechanism. Given imperfect substitutability between home goods and traded goods on the production side, it is the adjustment in the relative price of home goods that translates changes in absorption into an excess supply of traded goods at home and an excess demand for traded goods abroad.

1.3 Concluding Remarks

Rather than summarize here the conclusions of this chapter, we wish to emphasize some of the issues raised by the present formulation of devaluation analysis.

The first and primary issue concerns the role of money in models of devaluation. The stance taken here is that a devaluation is foremost a monetary phenomenon and that its effects derive from the reduction in the real value of money attendant upon a devaluation. If it is believed that the effects of a reduction of real balances on expenditure, by whatever transmission mechanism, are negligible, then it may stand to reason that the effects of a devaluation are negligible—not that there must be other powerful avenues through which it exerts its effects.

The second issue that deserves attention is that of aggregation. The formulation developed here suggests that it is helpful to view traded goods as a composite commodity and thus to highlight the distinction between money and goods and between classes of goods that are respectively traded and nontraded.

Notes

This chapter draws on my dissertation, and I am indebted to the members of my thesis committee, Harry Johnson, Stanley Fischer, and Robert Mundell. In revising the material, I had the benefit of comments from Karl Brunner, George Borts, Stanley Engerman, and Murray Kemp. I am particularly indebted to Ronald W. Jones and Michael Mussa with whom I enjoyed extended discussion of the topic.

1. This approach is by no means novel. For formal developments see Frank Hahn, Jones (1971), Kemp (1969, 1970), Mundell (1971), and Takashi Negishi (1972). Acceptance of that approach has nevertheless remained limited.

2. A "capital-theoretic" approach to the real balance effect is developed by Alvin Marty.

3. The notion of trade in one commodity may alternatively be interpreted as trade in a composite commodity, so that relative goods prices remain unchanged. Such conditions may obtain because of either perfect substitution or the absence of distribution effects.

4. The particular functional form of the demand for money obviously lacks generality. It is chosen here in order not to detract from the main line of argument. Alternative specifications would assume the demand for money proportional to expenditure as in Jones (1971) or else derive the demand for money from intertemporal utility maximization. Provided the underlying utility function is separable in consumption and real balances the qualitative conclusions of this paper carry over to such a formulation.

5. For a similar geometric treatment, see Arnold Collery (1971).

6. In terms of figure 1.3 the policy combination would imply that the world monetary constraint both rotates and shifts outward, passing through $\overline{M}^*$ since the world money supply measured in terms of foreign currency would remain unchanged. The conclusions in the text are readily verified from the fact that the new equilibrium point would lie vertically above point E.

7. The relationship between the transfer problem and devaluation is more extensively analyzed in Dornbusch (1973) and Jones (1971).

8. In the remainder of this paper a tilde will denote the fact that a quantity is measured in terms of traded goods. When these quantities are referred to as "real" this will not imply measurement in terms of a price index.

References

Collery, A. 1971. *International Adjustment, Open Economies and the Quantity Theory of Money*. Princeton Studies in International Finance. No. 28. Princeton.

Dornbusch, R. 1971. "Aspects of a Monetary Theory of Currency Depreciation." Unpublished doctoral dissertation. Univ. Chicago.

Dornbusch, R. 1973. "Currency Depreciation, Hoarding and Relative Prices." *J. Polit. Econ.* 81 (July/August): 893–915.

Hahn, F. 1959. "The Balance of Payments in a Monetary Economy," *Rev. Econ. Stud.* 26 (February): 110–125.

Jones, R. W. 1971. "A Role for Money in the Exchange Model." Unpublished. Univ. Rochester.

Jones, R. W. 1972. "Alternative Models of Devaluation." Unpublished. Univ. Rochester.

Kemp, M. 1970. "The Balance of Payments and the Terms of Trade in Relation to Financial Controls," *Rev. Econ. Stud.* 37 (January): 25–31.

Kemp, M. 1969. *The Pure Theory of International Trade and Investment*. Englewood Cliffs, N.J.: Prentice-Hall, ch. 14.

Krueger, O. A. 1971. "The Role of Home-Goods in Exchange Rate Adjustments." Unpublished.

Marty, A. 1964. "The Real Balance Effect: An Exercise in Capital Theory." *Can. J. Econ. Polit. Sci.* 30 (August): 360–367.

Michaely, M. 1960. "Relative-Prices and Income-Absorption Approaches to Devaluation: A Partial Reconciliation." *Amer. Econ. Rev.* 50 (March): 144–147.

Mundell, R. A. 1971. *Monetary Theory*. Pacific Palisades: Goodyear, ch. 9–11.

Negishi, T. 1972. *General Equilibrium Theory and International Trade*. Amsterdam: North-Holland, 15–17.

2

Exchange Rates and Fiscal Policy in a Popular Model of International Trade

This chapter develops a reinterpretation of the devaluation analysis in a popular model of international trade developed by Charles Bickerdike, Joan Robinson, and Lloyd Metzler. It has come to be known as the "elasticity approach."[1] That model, developed in terms of independent markets for imports and exports, has been criticized for its apparent lack of general equilibrium properties. The assumptions underlying the model have remained by and large implicit and vary across users, and the integration of this analysis with the "absorption approach" and macroeconomics has never been demonstrated. All this is very much recognized, and indeed application of the model is consistently accompanied by appropriate "partial equilibrium," "impact effect," or "upper bound" caveats. These shortcomings notwithstanding, the model continues to enjoy substantial popularity in policy discussions and interpretations of current events, in empirical work, and in recent textbooks in the field of international economics.[2]

The BRM model is likely to remain the preferred tool in the analysis of trade balance issues—along with the foreign trade multiplier model. It is therefore interesting and useful to enquire into its formal general equilibrium implications. This chapter is concerned with one such interpretation involving a nontraded goods sector and a well-defined government policy that makes the analysis consistent with the absorption approach. While it may well be possible to generate alternative interpretations, the present analysis would seem to have the advantage of simplicity while at the same time pointing out the essential properties that would have to be satisfied by alternative treatments.

In section 2.1 a brief review of the BRM approach is offered. In section 2.2 that approach is interpreted in terms of a simple model with nontraded goods and constant terms of trade. The implicit assumptions of the BRM

Originally published in *American Economic Review*, vol. 65, no. 5 (December 1975), pp. 859–871.

model are brought to the foreground by an explicit consideration of the market for home goods, the equilibrium conditions, and the role of the relative price of nontraded goods.[3] Following that analysis, section 2.3 considers the subsidiary issues that are raised by variable terms of trade. The notion of "total" elasticities is given an interpretation in section 2.4 where we return to the composite traded good model to explore alternative assumptions about absorption policies.

2.1 The Bickerdike-Robinson-Metzler Model

The BRM model discusses the effects of exchange rate changes in terms of separate markets for imports and exports. In each market, demand and supply depend only on the *nominal* price in terms of the importing or exporting country's currency, and cross-price effects between markets do not exist. The model is defined in equations (1) to (5):

$$M(P_m) = X^*(P_m^*),\tag{1}$$

$$X(P_x) = M^*(P_x^*),\tag{2}$$

$$B = P_x X - P_m M,\tag{3}$$

$$P_m = P_m^* e,\tag{4}$$

$$P_x = P_x^* e,\tag{5}$$

where[4]

$M, X =$ domestic imports and exports,
$M^*, X^* =$ foreign imports and exports,
$P_m, P_x =$ the domestic currency prices of (domestic) imports and exports,
$P_m^*, P_x^* =$ the foreign currency prices of imports and exports,
$e =$ the domestic currency price of foreign exchange.

Equation (1) is the equilibrium condition in the market for the home country's imports, and equation (2) is the equilibrium condition for the export market. Equation (3) defines the home country's trade balance surplus measured in terms of domestic currency. Equations (4) and (5) relate the domestic and foreign currency prices of goods via the exchange rate.

The initial equilibrium is shown in figure 2.1 at the intersection of the solid demand and supply schedules drawn for an exchange rate e^0. At that initial equilibrium the value of imports $P_m^0 M^0$ is equal to the value of exports $P_x^0 X^0$ so that the trade balance is in equilibrium.

Consider now a devaluation by the home country. The home demand

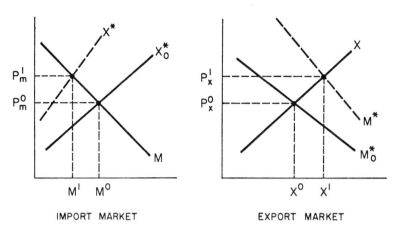

IMPORT MARKET   EXPORT MARKET

Figure 2.1

for imports and supply of exports, drawn against their domestic currency prices, will remain unaffected. The foreign supply and demand schedules, however, will shift. In order to maintain the foreign currency price of goods, by (4) and (5) the domestic currency price would have to rise in the same proportion as the exchange rate. It follows that both the foreign supply and demand schedules shift upward in the same proportion as the rate of devaluation. The new equilibrium obtains where both markets clear. The domestic price of imports and exports increases to P_m^1 and P_x^1, respectively; imports decline to M^1 and exports expand to X^1.

The effect of a devaluation on the trade balance in this model is ambiguous. While the value of exports increases, the value of imports may rise or fall depending on the elasticity of demand. A sufficient condition for trade balance improvement is provided by the familiar BRM condition.[5]

The disturbing features of this model arise primarily from its apparent disagreement with general equilibrium analysis. The particular questions that arise are the following:

Why should the behavioral equations depend on a single money price, rather than on relative prices and real income or real expenditure.

The budget constraint would imply that not all markets can be independent so that there must either be additional markets not accounted for explicitly in the model or else the model violates the budget constraint.

It is well known from the absorption approach that a trade balance surplus corresponds to an excess of income over expenditure; to the extent that a devaluation in this model generates a trade balance surplus, it must at the same time lower expenditure relative to income in a manner that is in no way explained in equations (1)–(5).

None of these question is particularly novel; indeed it is well understood by now that there are some things in the background and that some of these things are being held constant. Since these background stories are essential to the operation of the model, it is important to establish what exactly is implicitly assumed.

One interpretation takes a monetary view of the problem and assumes that there is another good in each country, money, and that the nominal quantity of money is fixed. The real effects of a devaluation derive in this formulation from the effect on expenditure of the reduction in the real value of money attendant upon a devaluation.[6]

An alternative and more accepted interpretation assumes that there is another commodity in each country, a nontraded good or home good, and that there is an active policy of maintaining constant some nominal quantity. Among the nominal quantities to be held constant, the following have been alternatively suggested: money income, money expenditure, wages, the price level, or the prices of a particular class of commodities.[7] It is this latter interpretation that we want to develop by an explicit consideration of the market for nontraded goods. That analysis will show that the formulation in figure 2.1 can be interpreted to assume the following.[8]

A nominal price of home goods that is maintained constant in each country by fiscal policy.[9]

A unit marginal propensity to spend on nontraded goods.[10]

Zero cross-price effects (substitution effects) between traded goods.

This set of assumptions, as will be shown below, ensures that there is no feedback effect from the "background" and that fiscal policy eliminates any market disequilibrium that arises in the nontraded goods market. It explains at the same time that the trade balance effects of a devaluation are due to the fiscal policy a devaluation brings into operation.

2.2 A Simple Model with Nontraded Goods

In this section a simple model is developed with nontraded goods. It is assumed that the relative price of traded goods is constant so that there is only one composite traded good in the world and one nontraded good in each country. The assumption of one composite traded good is a convenience that allows us to disregard terms of trade issues and instead focus consideration on the relative price of traded goods in terms of home goods and on absorption.[11]

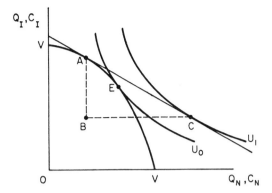

Figure 2.2

Figure 2.2 shows the Salter diagram with the full employment transformation curve VV between traded goods production Q_I and nontraded goods Q_N, as well as indifference curves. The shape of the indifference curves reflects the assumption that the marginal propensity to spend on home goods is unity so that the indifference curves are laterally parallel. Full equilibrium obtains at point E where income equals expenditure and where the demand and supply of traded and nontraded goods are respectively equal so that both the home-goods market clears and the trade balance is in equilibrium.

An increase in the relative price of traded goods moves the production equilibrium from E to A, while moving consumption from E to C; productive resources move into the traded goods industry while consumers substitute from traded to nontraded goods. At that higher relative price there is an excess demand for nontraded goods equal to BC, and an excess supply of traded goods equal to AB. We note too that the trade balance surplus AB, measured in terms of nontraded goods, is equal to the excess demand for nontraded goods. The latter equality is an implication of the assumption that income equals expenditure.

Consider now the operation of fiscal policy. We will assume that fiscal policy is used to maintain fixed the nominal price of home goods. This implies that any changes in the nominal prices of traded goods, as brought about by an exchange rate change, constitute changes in the relative prices of traded goods in terms of home goods. It implies too that the government has to levy income taxes whenever there is an excess demand for home goods; the increase in income taxes reduces private expenditure, thereby eliminating the excess demand and preventing the price of home goods from rising. Conversely, when there is an excess supply of nontraded goods so that their price would tend to decline, income transfers are required so as to raise private expenditure and eliminate the excess supply.

The assumption that the marginal propensity to spend on home goods is equal to one becomes important now, since it implies that the tax collection in response to an excess demand has to be identically equal to the excess demand. This can be seen from figure 2.2 by noting that in order to eliminate the excess demand for nontraded goods BC, consumption has to move to point B, which requires that the budget constraint facing consumers pass through that point, which in turn implies that disposable income declines by the distance BC due to the income taxes.

A further implication of the unit marginal propensity to spend on home goods is the fact that the fiscal policy will have no effect on the trade balance. The trade balance surplus will depend only on the nominal price of traded goods.

We conclude that we can represent the home country's real trade balance surplus $\bar{B}$ as an increasing function of the nominal price of traded goods P:

$$\bar{B} = \bar{B}(P). \tag{6}$$

By an identical line of argument the foreign country's real trade balance surplus $\bar{B}^*$ is an increasing function of the foreign nominal price of traded goods P^*:

$$\bar{B}^* = \bar{B}^*(P^*). \tag{7}$$

Finally the nominal prices of traded goods are related by the exchange rate e:

$$P = P^*e. \tag{8}$$

Given the policy of pegging the nominal prices of nontraded goods in both countries, an exchange rate change becomes a change in a real variable. Devaluation of the home currency raises the *relative* price of traded goods in terms of nontraded goods at home and lowers the relative price of traded in terms of nontraded goods abroad. In response to that change in relative prices, resources move into the traded goods sector at home while consumers substitute from traded goods to home goods. Abroad exactly the opposite move takes place: productive resources move to the home-goods sector while consumers substitute toward traded goods, thus generating a trade balance surplus for the home country. The magnitude of the surplus and the relative price changes will depend on the substitutability between goods.

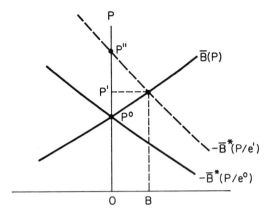

Figure 2.3

The equilibrium condition in the world traded goods market is that one country's excess supply of traded goods equal the other country's excess demand for traded goods. Using (6), (7), and (8), this equilibrium condition may be written as follows:

$$\bar{B}(P) = -\bar{B}^*\left(\frac{P}{e}\right). \tag{9}$$

Figure 2.3 shows the determination of the equilibrium in the traded goods market. The home country's excess supply of traded goods or trade balance surplus $\bar{B}(P)$ is drawn as an increasing function of the domestic currency price of traded goods. Similarly foreign excess demand for traded goods is shown as a decreasing function of the domestic price of traded goods for a given exchange rate e^0. Initial equilibrium obtains at a domestic price of traded goods P^0 where the world traded goods market is in equilibrium and trade is balanced. Returning to figure 2.2, this implies that income equals expenditure in each country and that the home-goods market clears in both countries.

A devaluation by the home country will change the relation between domestic and foreign prices. In terms of figure 2.3, the foreign excess demand schedule shifts upward in the proportion of the rate of devaluation. At the initial domestic currency price of traded goods P^0, there is a world excess demand for traded goods since the foreign price of traded goods has declined in the proportion as the exchange rate. In response to that excess demand the price of traded goods increases until the world market clears at a new domestic currency price P'. At that new price the home country has a trade balance surplus OB equal to the foreign country's deficit.

We note that the increase in the domestic price of traded goods $(P' - P^0)/P^0$ falls short of the rate of devaluation $(P'' - P^0)/P^0$ which implies that the foreign price of traded goods has declined in the proportion $(P'' - P')/P''$. It follows that a devaluation raises the domestic (relative) price of traded goods and lowers the foreign (relative) price of traded goods.

To appreciate why a devaluation exerts real effects, it is obviously necessary to go to the background of figure 2.3 and study the fiscal policies that are triggered off by these price changes. In the home country, as was shown in figure 2.2, the increase in the relative price of traded goods causes an excess demand for home goods which in turn is eliminated by an income tax collection equal to AB when measured in terms of traded goods. This implies that the counterpart of the trade balance surplus is an identically equal tax collection or budget surplus. It follows that the analysis is fully consistent with the absorption approach since it readily explains the decline in expenditure relative to income implied by the trade balance surplus. It follows too that in the absence of this fiscal policy the price of home goods would increase in response to the excess demand until relative prices returned to their initial position with no real effects persisting.

Consider next what happens in the foreign country. Abroad the nominal price of traded goods declines, and given the nominal price of home goods, the relative price of traded goods declines. In response to that relative price change, there will be an excess supply of nontraded goods triggering off income transfers in order to restore equilibrium in the nontraded goods market. Figure 2.4 shows the new equilibrium in the foreign country with

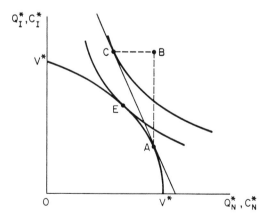

Figure 2.4

production at point A, consumption at point B, and a trade balance deficit equal to AB. The excess of expenditure over income or the income transfer measured in terms of traded goods is equal to the trade balance deficit.

Having shown that the domestic trade balance surplus is equal to income tax collections and that abroad the deficit equals the income transfers made by the government, it remains to infer from the equality of one country's deficit and the other country's surplus that a devaluation operates in the same manner as an international transfer from one country to another. Indeed, in this model a devaluation has exactly the same effects as a policy of transferring AB units of real income from the home country to the foreign country.

The preceding discussion can be formalized with the help of a few definitions. The real trade balance measured in terms of exportables is equal to the supply of exports less the demand for imports measured in terms of exportables:

$$\bar{B}(P) \equiv X(P_x) - \left(\frac{P_m}{P_x}\right)M(P_m), \tag{6'}$$

where we assume that P_m/P_x is constant so that by an appropriate choice of units we have $P_m = P_x = P$. Similarly the foreign trade balance surplus $\bar{B}^*$ is defined by

$$\bar{B}^*(P^*) \equiv \left(\frac{P_m^*}{P_x^*}\right)X^*(P_m^*) - M^*(P_x^*). \tag{7'}$$

Next we define the *compensated* elasticities of demand for imports and supply of exports:

$$\hat{M} = -\eta\hat{P}_m, \quad \hat{X} = \varepsilon\hat{P}_x,$$
$$\hat{M}^* = -\eta^*\hat{P}_x^*, \quad \hat{X}^* = \varepsilon^*\hat{P}_m^*, \tag{10}$$

where a $\hat{}$ denotes a proportional change in a variable.

Using these definitions, assuming initial trade balance equilibrium and constant terms of trade, we can define the elasticity of the trade balance surplus or the excess supply of traded goods with respect to the relative price of traded goods in terms of home goods:

$$\frac{d\bar{B}}{dP}\frac{P}{X} = \sigma \equiv \varepsilon + \eta,$$
$$\frac{d\bar{B}^*}{dP^*}\frac{P^*}{M^*} = \sigma^* \equiv \varepsilon^* + \eta^*. \tag{11}$$

We can now differentiate the equilibrium condition in (9), and using the definitions in (11), we derive the effect of a devaluation on the domestic (relative) price of traded goods:

$$\hat{P} = \frac{\sigma^*}{\sigma + \sigma^*}\hat{e}. \tag{12}$$

Differentiating equation (8) and substituting from (9) yields the effect of a devaluation on the foreign price:

$$\hat{P}^* = \frac{-\sigma}{\sigma + \sigma^*}\hat{e}. \tag{13}$$

We note from (12) and (13) that the distribution of price changes between countries will depend on the substitutability between traded goods and home goods in the two countries.

To determine the effect of the devaluation on the home country's trade balance, we differentiate (6'), and using (11) and (12), we have:

$$d\bar{B} = X\frac{\sigma\sigma^*}{\sigma + \sigma^*}\hat{e}. \tag{14}$$

Equation (14) shows that a devaluation unambiguously improves the trade balance of the devaluing country, and thus confirms the results derived in figure 2.3.

The fact that a devaluation cannot worsen the trade balance distinguishes this composite traded good version most fundamentally from the more general form of the BRM model. It points out that the possibility of a worsening of the trade balance is not due to a devaluation per se, but rather to the terms of trade changes that may accompany a devaluation. The model developed here emphasizes too that as long as the terms of trade remain unchanged the scope for "elasticity pessimism" is very limited. We note from (14) that at worst a devaluation will leave the trade balance unchanged, a circumstance that arises if in either country there is zero substitutability between home goods and traded goods.

In concluding this section, we remark that the essential elements of the BRM model are contained in the present version that maintains constant the terms of trade. These essential elements are that a devaluation changes the relative price of traded goods in terms of home goods, thereby generating a surplus in the devaluing country and a deficit abroad. The counterpart of the change in the trade balance arises in the home-goods markets: an excess demand at home and an excess supply abroad. It is essential to the success of a devaluation that there be an "internal balance" policy that validates the relative price changes by a reduction in absorption at home and an increase in absorption abroad.

The fact that terms of trade changes are "almost" secondary in their role in this context has been recognized by I. F. Pearce (1961) and June Flanders who emphasize both the requirement of absorption changes and the change in the relative price of traded goods in terms of home goods. Regrettably, the terms of trade may change, and therefore a more complicated analysis is called for.

2.3 The Terms of Trade, Transfers, and the Trade Balance

The preceding analysis showed that at constant terms of trade a devaluation has the same effects as an income transfer: it lowers domestic absorption and increases foreign absorption where the magnitude of the absorption change is identically equal to the trade balance surplus shown in (14). In deriving the equilibrium change in absorption, we have assumed that the world market for traded goods clears; we have not, however, shown that the market for each individual good will clear.

To determine whether the analysis in section 2.2 is in fact consistent with equilibrium in each individual traded-goods market, it is sufficient to consider equilibrium in one of these markets. This is so since the preceding analysis called for clearing of the world traded-goods market so that by implication the excess demand in any one market would be offset by the excess supply in the other market. Without loss of generality we can conduct the analysis in terms of the market for the home country's importable. We will use the results of section 2.2 to compute the change in domestic import demand and foreign export supply and to determine whether they are exactly equal so that no change in the terms of trade is called for.

The change in the equilibrium price of importables, at constant terms of trade, is given by (12). Using the definition of the elasticity of demand for imports in (10) and substituting for the price change from (12), we have:

$$\hat{M} = -\eta \hat{P}_m = -\eta \frac{\sigma^*}{\sigma + \sigma^*} \hat{e}. \tag{15}$$

The change in the foreign supply of exports is similarly derived by using the definition of the elasticity of supply in (10) and the equilibrium price change in (13), noting that $\hat{P}_m^* \equiv \hat{P}^*$:

$$\hat{X}^* = \varepsilon^* \hat{P}_m^* = -\varepsilon^* \frac{\sigma}{\sigma + \sigma^*} \hat{e}. \tag{16}$$

The world excess demand for importables, at constant terms of trade, is given by the difference between (15) and (16), which with some manipulation may be written as:

$$dM - dX^* = X\frac{\sigma\sigma^*}{\sigma + \sigma^*}\left[\frac{\varepsilon^*}{\varepsilon^* + \eta^*} - \frac{\eta}{\varepsilon + \eta}\right]\hat{e}. \qquad (17)$$

The home country's terms of trade will worsen or improve as there is at constant terms of trade a world excess demand or supply for importables, that is, depending on the familiar Robinson criterion:

$$\varepsilon\varepsilon^* - \eta\eta^* \gtreqless 0. \qquad (18)$$

Equation (17) has a ready interpretation in terms of the transfer problem. The term $X\sigma\sigma^*/(\sigma + \sigma^*)$ measures the change in absorption or the change in the trade balance that is induced by a devaluation at constant terms of trade. In the home country the trade balance surplus is achieved through a reduction in imports and an increase in exports. The fraction of the reduction in absorption or the improvement in the trade balance that is reflected in reduced imports is $\eta/(\varepsilon + \eta)$. Abroad the increased absorption and worsened trade balance is reflected in part in a decreased level of exports. The term $\varepsilon^*/(\varepsilon^* + \eta^*)$ measures the fraction of the increased absorption that is reflected in decreased exports. These fractions are not marginal propensities to spend that we ordinarily encounter in the discussion of the transfer problem, but they do play exactly the same role in that they indicate the effect of a change in absorption on individual commodity excess demands.[12] The channel here is not a direct expenditure effect measured by a marginal propensity, but rather a substitution effect that derives from the change in the equilibrium relative prices of home goods occasioned by the change in absorption that at constant relative prices falls entirely on these goods.

The preceding discussion shows that there is no presumption whatsoever about the direction in which a devaluation, or a transfer for that matter, will change the terms of trade. This point deserves emphasis since there continues to be the belief that a devaluation in and of itself changes the terms of trade. If a devaluation does, however, change the terms of trade, the effects on the trade balance are no longer described by (14) but have to be derived from the disaggregated model in (1) to (5). Differentiating equations (1), (2), (4), and (5) and using the definitions in (10) yields the effects of a devaluation on the domestic prices of importables and exportables:

$$\hat{P}_m = \frac{\varepsilon^*}{\varepsilon^* + \eta}\hat{e},$$

$$\hat{P}_x = \frac{\eta^*}{\varepsilon + \eta^*}\hat{e}. \tag{19}$$

Differentiating the trade balance equation in (3) and substituting the equilibrium price changes from (19) gives the trade balance effect of a devaluation:[13]

$$dB = P_x X\left[(1 + \varepsilon)\frac{\eta^*}{\varepsilon + \eta^*} - (1 - \eta)\frac{\varepsilon^*}{\varepsilon^* + \eta} \right]\hat{e}, \tag{20}$$

which with some manipulation may be rewritten in the more familiar BRM form:

$$dB = P_x X\left[\frac{\eta\eta^*(1 + \varepsilon + \varepsilon^*) - \varepsilon\varepsilon^*(1 - \eta - \eta^*)}{(\varepsilon + \eta^*)(\varepsilon^* + \eta)} \right]\hat{e}. \tag{20'}$$

Inspection of (20) shows that if the terms of trade remain unchanged or improve, $\eta^*/(\varepsilon + \eta^*) \geq \varepsilon^*/(\varepsilon^* + \eta)$, a devaluation will improve the trade balance. A worsening of the terms of trade, however, brings about the possibility of a worsening of the trade balance.[14] The interpretation of that possibility is as follows: The increase in the relative price of both traded goods in terms of home goods shown in (19) generates a substitution effect that induces a trade surplus and an excess demand for home goods. Against this substitution effect operates the income effect of a terms of trade deterioration which generates an excess supply of nontraded goods and a trade deficit. Similarly, abroad the decline in the relative price of traded goods generates an excess supply of home goods on account of the substitution effect, while the income effect of the foreign terms of trade improvement generates an excess demand. Whether the trade balance improves or worsens will depend on the relative size of the income and substitution effects. A more than sufficient condition is that in either country, the compensated elasticity of demand for imports be larger than unity —a condition that ensures that substitution effects dominate income effects.

The above argument shows too why a devaluation cannot worsen the trade balance when it improves the terms of trade. In this event both substitution effects and income effects operate in the same direction, generating an excess demand for nontraded goods and as its mirror image a trade surplus; abroad, similarly, both the income and substitution effects operate in the same direction to generate an excess supply of nontraded goods and a corresponding trade deficit. Furthermore, if the terms of trade remain unchanged there are only substitution effects and hence an unambiguous improvement in the trade balance.

The possibility that a devaluation worsens the trade balance cannot be ruled out on theoretical grounds. Before taking alarm at that contingency, however, it is worth noting what the implications for the nontraded goods markets are. If that should not be sufficient to discourage "elasticity pessimism," it should still be borne in mind that the model contains some assumptions that may be inordinately strong, in particular, the unit marginal propensity to spend on home goods and the zero cross elasticity between traded goods.

2.4 An Alternative Interpretation

In his discussion of the elasticity approach, Alexander pointed out that the import and export equations of the BRM model could be viewed as reduced forms that embody the effects of the absorption policies pursued in the background and where these effects are not necessarily limited to substitution effects as we have assumed so far. On this alternative interpretation the elasticities are no longer compensated elasticities but rather "total" elasticities, and it becomes important to know what effects they embody. One rather straightforward interpretation suggested by the analysis of section 2.2 is developed here. On the assumption that the terms of trade remain constant we can interpret the response to a change in the price of traded goods as composed of both a substitution effect and an expenditure effect. The expenditure effect derives now from the assumption that the marginal propensity to spend on traded goods is positive so that the fiscal policies pursued in the background exert a direct effect on the trade balance.

The trade balance surplus can now be written as a function of the (relative) price of traded goods and disposable income $Y - T$, where Y and T denote, respectively, the value of output and taxes both measured in terms of home goods:[15]

$$\tilde{B} = \tilde{B}(P, Y - T). \tag{21}$$

Differentiating (21) and using (11), we have:[16]

$$d\tilde{B} = \sigma X \hat{P} + \frac{(1 - \pi)dT}{P}, \tag{22}$$

where $(1 - \pi)$ denotes the marginal propensity to spend on traded goods.

As was shown in section 2.2, the trade surplus is equal to the change in absorption which in turn is equal to the change in taxes. We can therefore equate in (22) the terms $d\tilde{B} = dT/P$ to obtain the reduced form elasticity of the trade balance with respect to the relative price of traded goods:[17]

$$d\tilde{B}/X = \left(\frac{\sigma}{\pi}\right)\hat{P} \equiv \bar{\sigma}\hat{P}. \tag{23}$$

We note that (23) differs from (11) by the term in the denominator and reduces to (11) if the marginal propensity to spend on home goods, π, is unity. The direct expenditure effects on traded goods exerted by the fiscal policy raises the trade balance effects of a relative price change.

Proceeding in a similar manner for the foreign country, we derive the reduced form elasticity $\bar{\sigma}^* \equiv \sigma/\pi^*$. Substituting the terms $\bar{\sigma}$ and $\bar{\sigma}^*$ in (14) instead of the terms σ and σ^* yields the trade balance effect of a devaluation with positive marginal propensities to spend on traded goods:

$$d\tilde{B} = X\frac{\sigma\sigma^*}{\sigma\pi^* + \sigma^*\pi}\hat{e}. \tag{24}$$

Equation (24) shows that the trade balance effects of a devaluation are larger the smaller the marginal propensities to spend on home goods in each country. The reason is simply that if less of a tax change falls on home goods, then larger tax changes are required in order to maintain home-goods market equilibrium when the relative price of home goods is changed by an exchange rate change. Equation (24) therefore serves to highlight the role of the absorption policies in the BRM model.

So far the analysis has assumed that fiscal policy is used in each country to maintain constant the nominal price of home goods. This is certainly not the only interpretation of total elasticities. An alternative that has been widely referred to is the assumption that nominal income is maintained constant. This would require that an increase in the nominal price of traded goods be accompanied by a decline in the nominal prices of home goods. Assuming that fiscal policy maintains constant the nominal value of income, we have the following relationship between price changes:[18]

$$\hat{P}_N = -\left(\frac{1-\theta}{\theta}\right)\hat{P}, \tag{25}$$

where $\hat{P}_N$ denotes the proportional change in nominal home-goods prices, and where θ denotes the share of home goods in nominal income.

The trade balance effect of a change in the nominal price of home goods is now composed of three elements: The substitution effects induced by a rise in traded goods prices (relative to home-goods prices) and the accompanying decline in home-goods prices and the effect of the fiscal policy required to maintain home-goods market equilibrium at a constant nominal income. We can therefore rewrite the trade balance effect of a change in the nominal price of traded goods as:

$$\frac{d\tilde{B}}{X} = \bar{\sigma}(\hat{P} - \hat{P}_N) = \left(\frac{\sigma}{\pi\theta}\right)\hat{P}, \tag{26}$$

where we have substituted for the home-goods price change from (25).

Equation (26) shows that the trade balance effect of an increase in the nominal price of traded goods is inversely proportional to the share of home goods in nominal income. This is so because by (25) the smaller the share of home goods, the larger the change in the relative price of traded goods induced by a change in their nominal price, $\hat{P} - \hat{P}_N = (1/\theta)\hat{P}$. We can derive an expression analogous to (26) for the foreign country and substitute the reduced form or total elasticities, $\lambda \equiv \sigma/\pi\theta$ and $\lambda^* \equiv \sigma^*/\pi^*\theta^*$, in (14) to find that the effects of a devaluation on the trade balance are the larger the smaller the shares of home goods in nominal income, given a policy in each country of maintaining constant money income:

$$d\tilde{B} = X\frac{\sigma\sigma^*}{\sigma\pi^*\theta^* + \sigma^*\pi\theta}\hat{e}. \tag{27}$$

A comparison of equations (24) and (27) shows that the real effects of a devaluation depend crucially on what nominal variables are held constant. Thus a policy of maintaining constant the nominal prices of home goods generates a smaller trade surplus than one that maintains constant nominal income. Since exchange rate changes exert real effects because they constitute changes relative to some other nominal variable, it is indispensable to ask what that variable is in order to determine the nature and magnitude of the response to an exchange rate change.

2.5 Concluding Remarks

This chapter has developed an interpretation of the BRM model that gives emphasis to the general equilibrium context in which the analysis of the traded-goods markets has to be placed. Such a general equilibrium model will involve a market for home goods and an explicit policy of maintaining constant some nominal variable. That policy provides the link with the absorption approach. Comparison of alternative policies shows that the real effects of an exchange rate change depend critically on the choice of nominal variables to be pegged. It points out too that there is not much use in considering reduced form equations without making explicit the general equilibrium and macroeconomic system from which they are derived.

Notes

I am indebted to Ronald Jones and Michael Mussa for helpful discussions.

1. In this analysis it will be referred to as the BRM model.

2. See, for example, the articles by William Branson and Stephen Magee (1973, 1975); and the textbooks by Robert Heller, Mordechai Kreinin, and Robert Stern.

3. Throughout this chapter the terms home goods and nontraded goods are used interchangeably. This use differs from the Keynesian tradition where home goods are identified with exportables because the constancy of absolute and hence relative prices of domestically produced goods allows them to be aggregated.

4. All starred variables or quantities denote the foreign country.

5. See equation (20').

6. For such an interpretation, see Murray Kemp (1969), Takashi Negishi, and the author (1973).

7. See in particular the articles by Charles Kennedy, Sidney Alexander, Fritz Machlup, June Flanders, Gottfried Haberler, Ronald Jones (1961), and the book by James Meade.

8. Kemp (1962, 1969) provides an identical list.

9. The discussion in this chapter is developed in terms of fiscal policy, although what is essentially required is a policy that will control absorption so that alternatively the argument could be developed in terms of monetary policy. In the present context we assume (implicitly) that a Meade-type "neutral monetary policy" is pursued so as to maintain constant the rate of interest and thereby allow us to disregard the interrelationship between goods and asset markets. For a further discussion, see the author (1974).

10. An alternative view that interprets the behavioral equations as reduced forms and thereby allows for positive marginal propensities to spend on traded goods is developed in section 2.4. The assumption of a zero marginal propensity to spend on traded goods is obviously quite extraordinary, and the reader is reminded that I am not constructing the preferred model of the trade balance but rather seek to explain the BRM model.

11. The model developed here is a two-country version of W. E. G. Salter's "dependent economy" model.

12. For a discussion of the transfer problem in a more general model with nontraded goods, see Ian McDougall, Pearce (1961, 1970), and Jones (1974).

13. The reader will note that for the constant terms of trade case equation (20) reduces to (14) by using the substitution $\eta\eta^* = \varepsilon\varepsilon^*$.

14. Jones (1974) has developed the interpretation of the BRM condition in terms of the stability of the underlying commodity markets.

15. The value of output measured in terms of home goods is defined as $Y \equiv PQ_I + Q_N$.

16. A change in the relative price of home goods has no income effect since demand equals production. Accordingly (22) only reflects substitution effects and absorption effects of a tax change.

17. The equality of the change in the trade balance and in taxes is derived from the budget constraint. The value of expenditure equals the value of output less taxes: $PC_I + C_N = PQ_I + Q_N - T$ or $P(Q_I - C_I) + (Q_N - C_N) = T$. When the home-goods market clears, $Q_N = C_N$, the trade surplus is equal to taxes or $\tilde{B} = (Q_I - C_I) = T/P$.

18. From the definition of nominal income $Y = PQ_I + P_N Q_N$, we derive equation (25) by differentiation. A policy that maintains constant nominal income is equivalent to maintaining constant a price index $\bar{P} = P^{(1-\theta)} P_N^{\theta}$. For a further discussion, see the author (1974) and Pearce (1970). Since the nominal price of home goods now is flexible, P only denotes the nominal price of traded goods.

References

Alexander, S. 1959. "The Effects of Devaluation: A Simplified Synthesis of Elasticities and Absorption Approaches." *Amer. Econ. Rev.* 49 (March): 21–42.

Bickerdike, C. 1920. "The Instability of Foreign Exchange." *Econ. J.* 30 (March): 118–122.

Branson, W. 1972. "The Trade Effects of the 1971 Currency Realignments." *Brookings Papers*, Washington, 2, 15–69.

Dornbusch, R. 1973. "Currency Depreciation, Hoarding, and Relative Prices." *J. Polit. Econ.* 81 (July/August): 893–915.

Dornbusch, R. 1974. "Alternative Price Stabilization Policies and the Effects of Exchange Rate Changes." Unpublished paper. Univ. Chicago.

Flanders, J. 1963. "The Balance of Payments Adjustment Mechanism: Some Problems in Model Building." *Kyklos* 16, 395–412.

Haberler, G. 1949. "The Market for Foreign Exchange and the Stability of the Balance of Payments." *Kyklos* 3, 93–218. Reprinted in R. Cooper, ed. *International Finance.* Baltimore 1969.

Heller, R. 1974. *International Monetary Economics*. Englewood Cliffs, N.J.: Prentice-Hall.

Jones, R. W. 1961. "Stability Conditions in International Trade: A General Equilibrium Analysis." *Int. Econ. Rev.* 2 (May): 199–209.

Jones, R. W. 1974. "Trade with Nontraded Goods: The Anatomy of Interconnected Markets," *Economica* 41 (May): 121–138.

Kemp, M. 1962. "The Rate of Exchange, the Terms of Trade and the Balance of Payments in Fully Employed Economies." *Int. Econ. Rev.* 3 (September): 314–327.

Kemp, M. 1969. *The Pure Theory of International Trade*. Englewood Cliffs, N.J.: Prentice-Hall.

Kennedy, C. 1950. "Devaluation and the Terms of Trade." *Rev. Econ. Stud.* 18, no. 1, 28–41.

Kreinin, M. 1971. *International Economics*, New York: Harcourt Brace Jovanovich.

Machlup, F. 1955. "Relative Prices and Aggregate Expenditure in the Analysis of Devaluation." *Amer. Econ. Rev.* 45 (June): 255–279.

Magee, S. 1973. "Currency Contracts, Pass-Through and Devaluation," *Brookings Papers*, Washington, 3, 303–323.

Magee, S. 1975. "Prices, Incomes and Foreign Trade." In P. B. Kenen, ed., *International Trade and Finance: Frontiers for Research*. Cambridge Univ. Press.

McDougall, I. A. 1970. "Non-Traded Goods and the Pure Theory of International Trade." In I. A. McDougall and R. N. Snape, eds., *Studies in International Economics*. Amsterdam: North-Holland.

Meade, J. E. 1951. *The Theory of International Policy*. Vol. I: *The Balance of Payments*. Oxford Univ. Press.

Metzler, L. A. 1949. "The Theory of International Trade." In H. Ellis, ed., *A Survey of Contemporary Economics*. Philadelphia, 210–214. Reprinted in his *Collected Papers*, Cambridge, Mass., 1973, 1–49.

Negishi, T. 1968. "Approaches to the Analysis of Devaluation," *Int. Econ. Rev.* 9 (June): 218–227.

Pearce, I. 1961. "The Problem of the Balance of Payments." *Int. Econ. Rev.* 2 (January): 1–28.

Pearce, I. 1970. *International Trade*. New York: Norton.

Robinson, J. 1950. "The Foreign Exchanges." In H. Ellis and L. A. Metzler, eds., *Readings in the Theory of International Trade*. Homewood, Ill.: Glencoe, 83–103.

Salter, W. 1959. "Internal and External Balance: The Role of Price and Expenditure Effects." *Econ. Rec.* 35 (August): 226–238.

Stern, R. M. 1973. *The Balance of Payments*. Chicago: Aldine.

3

Real and Monetary Aspects of the Effects of Exchange Rate Changes

This chapter investigates the role and effects of exchange rate changes in a simple general equilibrium model of a small open economy. The purpose of the analysis is to combine two strands of literature that, respectively, view the sources of balance-of-payments difficulties and the effects of devaluation as "monetary" and "real." A monetary view of devaluation would emphasize the role of the real value of cash balances, while the alternative approach would place primary emphasis on relative prices and real wages—a divergence of views not entirely unlike the earlier debate over "elasticity" and "absorption" approaches.[1]

The model in which we propose to develop the analysis has three special features: It adopts the emphasis on the distinction between traded and nontraded goods as developed in the "dependent economy" model in the work of Corden, Meade, Salter, and Swan. On the production side, that model receives some underpinnings by a distinction between mobile and immobile factors. Last, on the demand side the model is supplemented with an expenditure function linking the real and the monetary sectors of the economy in a manner suggested by Prais.

The first four sections of the chapter develop in some detail the formal structure of the model. In section 3.5 the effects of devaluation are analyzed under conditions of wage and price flexibility. In the last section the scope of devaluation is discussed for an economy where wages and prices are inflexible.

3.1 Internal and External Balance

In this section we develop the notion of internal and external balance in the "dependent economy" model. That model has been formally developed in

Originally published in R. Z. Aliber (ed.), *National Monetary Policies and the International Financial System* (University of Chicago Press, 1974), pp. 64–81. © 1974 by The University of Chicago. All rights reserved.

a sequence of articles by Corden (1960), Meade (1956), Salter (1959), and Swan (1960, 1963) and is familiar in the form of the Salter and Swan (1960, 1963) and is familiar in the form of the Salter and Swan diagrams shown in figures 3.1, 3.2, and 3.3, respectively.[2]

The basic features of the model are the following: The home country produces and consumes two classes of commodities, traded goods and nontraded goods. Each class of goods is viewed as a composite commodity, which implies that the relative prices of goods within each group are fixed. In particular, the terms of trade are assumed given and independent of the home country's actions, so that production and consumption of traded goods, respectively, can be conveniently treated as an aggregate. The emphasis of the model bears on the relation between aggregate expenditure and the relative price of home goods in terms of traded goods.

In figure 3.1 we show, following Jones (1972) and Salter (1959), the transformation curve AA between the production of traded goods (X_T) and nontraded goods (X_N), respectively; points on the transformation curve correspond to full employment of the given stock of resources. The slope of the tangent to the transformation curve represents the relative price of nontraded goods in terms of traded goods, $\tilde{P}$, and the intercept with the vertical axis measures the real value of output in terms of traded goods, $\tilde{I}$:

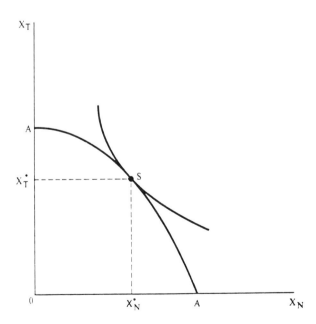

Figure 3.1

$$\tilde{I} = X_T + \tilde{P}X_N. \tag{1}$$

Demand conditions are represented by indifference curves and for diagrammatic convenience preferences will be assumed homothetic. Corresponding to the measurement of real output we measure real expenditure in terms of traded goods, $\tilde{Z}$, by the intercept of the tangent to an indifference curve with the vertical axis:

$$\tilde{Z} = D_T + \tilde{P}D_N. \tag{2}$$

We define *external* balance by the equality of demand and supply of traded goods and *internal* balance by the equality of demand and (full employment) supply of home goods. At point S in figure 3.1 both internal and external balance obtain since demand for each good equals supply and accordingly income equals expenditure.[3] From the construction of figure 3.1 it is apparent that the joint occurrence of internal and external balance is unique to point S. At any other point at least one of the equilibria will fail to obtain.

Next we propose to consider combinations of relative prices and levels of real expenditure that will maintain internal or external balance, respectively.[4] For that purpose we consider a decrease in the relative price of nontraded goods moving production from point S to point C in figure 3.2. At this new relative price, real income has decreased relative to point

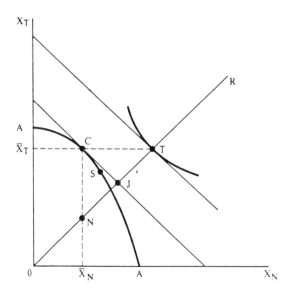

Figure 3.2

S, production of traded goods has increased to $\bar{X}_T$, and production of home goods has decreased to $\bar{X}_N$. The preferred composition of consumption at this new relative price is indicated by the slope of the ray OR, the expenditure-consumption line.

At point J, income equals expenditure, but there is an excess supply of traded goods and an excess demand for home goods. In order for the home goods market to clear, real expenditure would have to decline to a level indicated by the budget line passing through point N. At that level of expenditure, however, there would be an excess supply of traded goods or a trade balance surplus equal to CN. To achieve trade balance equilibrium, real expenditure would have to increase to a level indicated by the budget line through point T. At that point, demand equals the supply of traded goods, but there is an excess demand for home goods equal to CT. More generally, a decrease in the relative price of home goods causes a substitution effect toward home goods on the demand side and a substitution effect away from home goods on the supply side; the income effect of the price change at a constant level of real expenditure raises the demand for both goods. Assuming that the income effect does not dominate, the net effect of a decrease in the relative price of nontraded goods is to generate—at a constant level of real expenditure—an excess demand for nontraded goods and a trade balance surplus.[5] To achieve trade balance equilibrium, expenditure has to increase relative to income while equilibrium in the home goods market requires a reduction in expenditure relative to income.

In figure 3.3 we show the market equilibrium schedules NN and TT, along which the home goods market and the trade balance, respectively, are in equilibrium; we draw too the locus $\tilde{II}$, showing the real value of output measured in terms of traded goods associated with each relative price. Full equilibrium obtains at point S where we have both internal and external balance and where accordingly income equals expenditure. Points above the NN schedule correspond to an excess supply of home goods, and conversely points below the schedule reflect an excess demand for home goods. Points above the TT schedule correspond to a trade balance deficit while points below correspond to a surplus. Last, points to the right of the $\tilde{II}$ schedule imply an excess of expenditure over income while points to the left involve an excess of income over expenditure.

Formally, the NN, TT, and II loci are, respectively, defined by equations (3), (4), and (5):

$$X_N(\tilde{P}) = D_N(\tilde{P}, \tilde{Z}), \tag{3}$$

$$X_T(\tilde{P}) = D_T(\tilde{P}, \tilde{Z}), \tag{4}$$

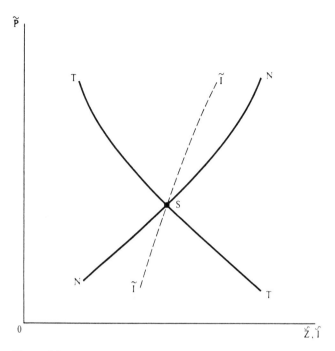

Figure 3.3

$$I \equiv X_T(\tilde{P}) + \tilde{P}X_N(P) = \tilde{I}(\tilde{P}), \tag{5}$$

where supplies are a function of the relative price of home goods, and demands are a function of the relative price and real expenditure.[6]

We can make use of the definitions of income and expenditure to show that when the home goods market clears, the excess of expenditure over income equals the trade balance deficit,

$$\tilde{Z} - \tilde{I} = (D_T - X_T) + \tilde{P}(D_N - X_N), \tag{6}$$

and that when income equals expenditure, the trade balance deficit equals the excess supply of home goods.

The preceding analysis suggests two alternative sources of disequilibrium: one arises from disequilibrium relative prices and may be identified with points on the $\tilde{I}\tilde{I}$ schedule; alternatively, trade imbalance may obtain because of a disparity between expenditure and income as is the case for points along the NN schedule. Correction of such a disequilibrium requires in all instances both a change in relative prices and an adjustment in real expenditure.

3.2 Factor Endowments, Factor Returns, and Relative Prices

In this section we develop the relation between the given supplies of factors of production, relative prices, and factor rentals. We depart from the standard treatment of production models in assuming that the stock of capital in each industry is given, specific to that industry and *immobile* between industries. The (homogeneous) labor force on the contrary is mobile between sectors and ensures thereby the equalization of money wages between industries. These assumptions are made for three reasons. First, they possess a compelling realism for short-run analysis and yield conclusions for the effects of policy changes on income distribution that agree with observed behavior. Next, they yield a specific relation between wages and the relative price of home goods, independently of factor intensity assumptions. Last, they allow flexibility in the relative price of home goods, given the terms of trade, in the absence of specialization.[7] The formal properties of a model with one mobile factor and a specific factor in each industry have been extensively developed in Jones (1971) and are exploited in a dynamic context in Mussa (1972).

We assume linear homogeneous production functions, competition, and a given stock of capital in both the traded and nontraded goods sectors. Furthermore the aggregate supply of labor is assumed fixed and equal to L. The demand for labor in each sector is given by the marginal product of labor schedule. Full employment requires that the demand for labor of the respective sectors add up to the aggregate labor supply. That equilibrium condition is expressed in equation (7):

$$L_T(\tilde{w}) + L_N\left(\frac{\tilde{w}}{\tilde{P}}\right) = L, \tag{7}$$

where L_T and L_N are the demand functions for labor in the traded and nontraded goods sector and where $\tilde{w}$ and $\tilde{w}/\tilde{P}$ are the real wages measured in terms of traded and nontraded goods, respectively. Figure 3.4 shows the allocation of labor between sectors as a function of the real wage measured in terms of traded goods, $\tilde{w}$, and the relative price of home goods, $\tilde{P}$. Given a relative price, $\tilde{P}^0$, an increase in the real wage reduces employment in both industries and requires an increase in the relative price of nontraded goods in order to maintain full employment; in particular, the relative price has to increase more than proportionally to the increase in real wages so that wages measured in terms of nontraded goods decline and thus encourage increased employment in the home goods industry. Accordingly, the competitive profit conditions together with the full em-

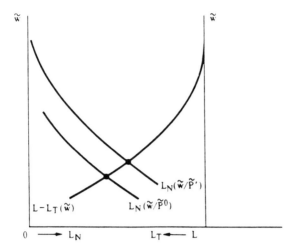

Figure 3.4

ployment constraint imply a relation between real wages measured in terms of traded goods and the relative price of home goods. An increase in the real wage requires a more than proportionate increase in the relative price of nontraded goods in order to maintain full employment. That relationship is shown in the left-hand panel of figure 3.9, where points to the left of the schedule correspond to unemployment and points to the right to an excess demand for labor.

A further set of relations that we need to discuss is that between income distribution and relative prices. It follows from the previous analysis that an increase in the relative price of home goods causes real wages, measured in terms of traded goods, to increase, and wages measured in terms of nontraded goods to decrease. Furthermore, since an increase in the relative price of nontraded goods causes labor to move toward that industry, it follows that the return to capital in that industry, measured in terms of either commodity, increases, while the return to capital in the traded goods sector decreases in terms of both commodities.

3.3 Money, Hoarding, and the Expenditure Function

The expenditure function provides the link between the monetary and the real aspects of the model. It will be recalled that in section 3.1 we treated expenditure as an exogenous variable and inquired into the relative prices that in combination with various levels of expenditure yielded internal and external balance. We now introduce expenditure as a behavioral relationship, a function of income and the stock excess demand for money, and thereby close the model.

We assume that money is the only asset and that the stock demand for nominal balances is proportional to money income, Y:

$$M^d = kY. \tag{8}$$

When monetary stock equilibrium obtains, we assume that all income is spent. In the presence of a stock excess demand for money, expenditure falls short of income as the community hoards in order to attain the desired asset position, and the converse occurs in the presence of a stock excess supply of money. Assuming that hoarding is proportional to the stock excess demand for money, and measuring real income and the real money supply both in terms of traded goods, we may write real hoarding as a function of the relative price of nontraded goods and the real money supply:

$$\tilde{H} = \tilde{H}(\tilde{P}, \tilde{M}), \tag{9}$$

where the real money supply is defined as the ratio of the nominal money supply to the domestic currency price of traded goods,

$$\tilde{M} = \frac{M}{P_T e}, \tag{10}$$

and where the latter is the product of the given foreign currency price of traded goods, P_T, and the exchange rate, e.

An increase in the relative price of nontraded goods, given the price of traded goods, raises hoarding since it increases money income and thereby the demand for money. In the same manner an increase in the domestic currency price of traded goods increases hoarding, while an increase in the nominal quantity of money lowers hoarding.

Given the hoarding function in (9), we may write the expenditure function as follows:[8]

$$\tilde{Z} = \tilde{I} - \tilde{H}, \tag{11}$$

and using the definitions of income and expenditure in (1) and (2), we can rewrite (11) as the budget constraint:

$$(X_T - D_T) + \tilde{P}(X_N - D_N) = \tilde{H}. \tag{12}$$

From the budget constraint we observe that when the home goods market clears, the trade balance surplus, $B \equiv X_T - D_T$, equals the planned rate of hoarding.

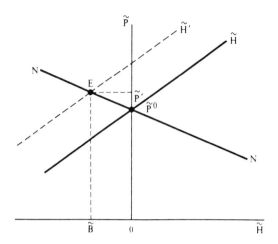

Figure 3.5

3.4 Short-Run Equilibrium and the Monetary Mechanism

The expenditure function developed above together with the market clearing condition gives rise to an analytical distinction between short-run and long-run equilibrium. Short-run equilibrium obtains when the home goods market clears, and accordingly, the trade balance surplus equals the planned rate of hoarding. In long-run equilibrium, in addition to the above equilibrium condition, planned and actual hoarding are zero so that the trade balance is in equilibrium and the money supply is constant.

Short-run equilibrium is illustrated in figure 3.5. The schedule NN is the home goods market equilibrium schedule. The schedule is negatively sloped, since an increase in hoarding creates an excess supply of home goods at constant relative prices and thus requires a decrease in the relative price of home goods, generating substitution effects that will clear the market.

The hoarding schedule $\tilde{H}'$ is drawn as a function of the relative price of home goods for a given exchange rate and hence the price of traded goods for a given nominal quantity of money. It is positively sloped since an increase in the price of home goods raises money income and hence the demand for money.

Short-run equilibrium obtains at point E, where the home goods market clears and the planned rate of hoarding equals the actual rate of hoarding. That equilibrium, however, is not compatible with trade balance equilibrium and, indeed, corresponds to a deficit $\tilde{B}$. The deficit in turn implies that the domestic quantity of money is decreasing. The decrease in the nominal quantity of money, at a given exchange rate, in turn implies that the hoarding schedule shifts down and to the right over time until long-run equilibrium is attained with trade balance equilibrium and the home goods market clearing at a relative price $\tilde{P}^0$.

This description of the adjustment process presupposes two features of the economy that are worth emphasizing. On the one hand, we assume flexibility of prices and wages so that the reallocation of resources can be achieved under conditions of full employment. On the other hand, we assume that the government abstains from neutralizing the effects of the trade imbalance on the domestic quantity of money. We will subsequently discuss the manner in which relaxation of these assumptions affects the analysis.

3.5 The Effects of Devaluation under Conditions of Price Flexibility and Full Employment

In this section we investigate the effects of a devaluation on the assumption that the flexibility of factor rentals and home goods prices ensures full employment and continuous equilibrium in the market for home goods. This set of assumptions is designed to highlight the monetary aspects of a devaluation, and resembles the treatment by Krueger (1971), Kemp (1970), Michaely (1960), and Mundell (1971).

We assume that initially the economy is in full equilibrium such that the home goods market clears and the public holds the desired quantity of money; accordingly, hoarding is zero and so is the trade balance. That equilibrium is shown in figure 3.6 at the equilibrium relative price $\tilde{P}^0$. Consider now the effects of a devaluation, given the nominal quantity of money. At unchanged relative prices the devaluation increases the price level thereby reducing the real value of the quantity of money in existence. The excess demand for money would at constant relative prices cause an increase in real hoarding, represented in figure 3.6 by a shift of the hoarding schedule to the right. At point Q, however, the increase in real hoarding, or equivalently the reduction in real expenditure relative to real income, causes an excess supply of nontraded goods; that excess supply causes the relative price of nontraded goods to decline until short-run equilibrium is attained at point E, where the home goods market clears and the trade balance surplus equals $\tilde{B}$.

The adjustment in the price of home goods is important in two respects. First, the change in relative prices translates a reduction in expenditure

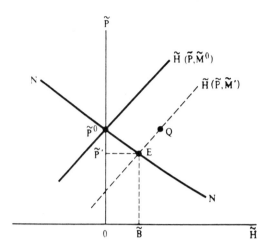

Figure 3.6

relative to income into an equal trade balance surplus by encouraging productive resources to move to the traded goods sector and inviting substitution on the demand side toward home goods. Second, the adjustment in the price of home goods affects the equilibrium rate of hoarding itself; in particular, the decline in the relative price of home goods makes the rate of hoarding lower than in a situation where relative prices remained constant.

Over time the trade balance surplus gives rise to an increase in the domestic nominal quantity of money, thereby reducing the incentive to hoard, until the initial real equilibrium is reattained. The only long-run effects are an increase in the nominal quantity of money and money prices proportional to the rate of devaluation.

While the homogeneity properties of the system and the assumed price flexibility inevitably yield long-run Quantity Theory results, in the short run a devaluation has considerable real effects. In the short run a devaluation changes expenditure relative to income, or it reduces absorption thereby changing equilibrium-relative prices and the allocation of resources between traded and nontraded goods. The reallocation of resources in turn implies that the distribution of income is affected. In particular, the decline in the relative price of home goods and the transfer of labor toward the traded goods sector causes the return on capital in the home goods industry to decline in terms of both goods while the return on capital in the traded goods sector increases in terms of both goods. The real wage increases in terms of nontraded goods, and declines in terms of traded goods.

Our model suggests that the monetary mechanism provides an automatic adjustment to trade disequilibrium and that a devaluation does not yield any long-run real effects. The question may reasonably be asked why a country should ever wish to devalue. Disregarding for the moment issues arising from the inflexibility of prices and wages, there remain several objectives that are furthered by a devaluation. A country may use a devaluation to increase its stock of reserves or to adjust its trade balance in a situation where the reserve holdings are inadequate to allow the monetary mechanism to operate. Alternatively, a government may wish to finance a transitory budget deficit by money creation without incurring balance-of-payments problems; in this case a devaluation would reduce private real expenditure, and thus free resources for public programs, while the increase in the price level would encourage the public to add to their cash holdings the money issue with which the government finances itself. This capital levy aspect of a devaluation that is central to the monetary analysis of devaluation was particularly emphasized by Keynes, as a means to reduce the real burden of the public debt, and by Mundell, as a means to increase real tax liabilities in the presence of progressive income taxation.

The effects of a devaluation, as developed in this section, derive from the fact that a currency depreciation lowers the real value of a given nominal quantity of money and thereby affects the desired rate of absorption. It follows that the real effects of a devaluation could be readily negated by a concurrent expansion in the nominal quantity of money. The fact that monetary aspects of a devaluation are deemphasized in many models of currency depreciation, and in particular in Keynesian variants, follows from one of two assumptions: either it is assumed that the country is completely specialized in the production of its exportable good, which is supplied at a fixed price in terms of domestic currency, and that the demand for money is independent of the price of importables; or else it is assumed that a "neutral" monetary policy is pursued such as to maintain interest rates constant. In either case a devaluation has no effect via the monetary sector on expenditure, but rather deploys its effects by changing relative prices.

3.6 Wage and Price Rigidity, Employment, and the Exchange Rate

So far we have entertained the assumption that the flexibility of nominal wages and the money price of home goods ensures full employment irrespective of the level or pattern of aggregate demand. A reduction in aggregate expenditure would cause a decline in the price of home goods and the money wage rate, thereby lowering the real wage in terms of

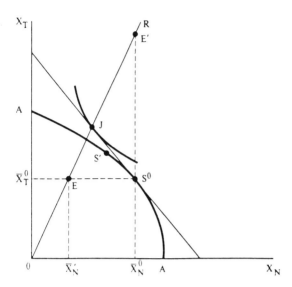

Figure 3.7

traded goods, and would encourage employment in that industry—an industry that by assumption faces a perfectly elastic world demand. Now we introduce the assumption that money wages and the money price of home goods are inflexible in a downward direction, so that the choice of the exchange rate determines both the real wage in terms of traded goods and the relative price of home goods in terms of traded goods. In this context devaluation becomes an instrument for attaining full employment.

Consider an economy that is in initial equilibrium, with home goods market clearing and trade balance equilibrium at point S^0 in figure 3.7, and assume that we have a shift in demand from home goods to traded goods. The shift in demand leaves the economy at initial relative prices in a disequilibrium, since production remains at point S^0, while the preferred composition of consumption is indicated by point J and the ray OR. At point J the value of output equals the value of expenditure, but there is an excess demand for traded goods and an excess supply of nontraded goods; the trade balance deficit is equal to the involuntary accumulation of inventories in the home goods industry.

With flexible prices the economy would move to a new equilibrium at point S', where internal and external balance obtain. Given, however, the fixed exchange rate and the rigidity in the money price of home goods, the relative price of home goods is fixed and two alternatives are open to the government. If the government does not intervene in any manner, long-run unemployment equilibrium will be attained at point E, where the home goods market clears and the trade balance is in equilibrium. That equilibrium is characterized by a reduction in the production of home goods to the level X_N' and a corresponding unemployment; the output of traded goods is unaffected. Since the equilibrium level of home goods production is entirely demand-determined, the reduction in the equilibrium level of output is the larger the greater the initial shift away from home goods and the larger the marginal propensity to spend on home goods.

An alternative to the equilibrium with unemployment and trade balance equilibrium is for the government to pursue an expansionary policy, such as to raise expenditure relative to income sufficiently to maintain full employment and home goods market equilibrium at point E'. While at that point all resources are fully used and the demand for home goods equals the initial supply, there is a trade balance deficit equal to $E'S^0$. That deficit is the larger the initial shift in demand and larger the marginal propensity to spend on traded goods.[9]

Furthermore, to the extent that the trade balance deficit at E' implies that the domestic quantity of money—and hence expenditure—is decreasing, we need continuously to sterilize the balance-of-payments effects on the money supply, a policy that is obviously infeasible in the long run. Rather than suffer the unemployment equilibrium at point E, the authorities might contemplate an expenditure-switching policy that would offset the initial shift in demand. One possibility is a consumption subsidy on home goods. Such a policy, by distorting the relative prices faced by consumers, would permit internal and external balance to be attained at the initial equilibrium S^0 as is shown in figure 3.8. Furthermore, in terms of welfare, this policy would clearly dominate the unemployment equilibrium at point E.

A devaluation is a superior way of restoring full employment. It raises the domestic currency price of traded goods and, given the money wages and money prices of home goods, lowers the real wage in terms of traded goods and the relative price of home goods. The lowering of the real wage encourages employment and production in the traded goods industry, while the lowering in the relative price of home goods invites substitution on the demand side toward home goods so that full equilibrium can be attained in the long run at point S'. Corresponding to that equilibrium, we have a reduction in the real wage in terms of traded goods and an increase in the real wage in terms of nontraded goods, so that money wages rise relative to the price of home goods.[10]

The manner in which long-run equilibrium at point S' is attained depends essentially on the behavior of the monetary authorities. Assume we

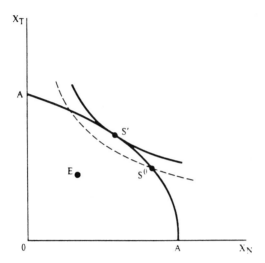

Figure 3.8

were initially in underemployment equilibrium at point E, with income equal to expenditure. The devaluation would reduce the real value of money, while the expansionary effect of the devaluation on production would raise the demand for real balances. Without an expansion in the nominal quantity of money, the devaluation would tend to have a defla-tionary effect on aggregate demand and yield a trade balance surplus with residual unemployment in the short run. An appropriate monetary policy would be to accompany the devaluation with an expansion in the nominal quantity of money. Such a policy would permit expenditure to remain at the level of income, so that the increase in real output is accompanied by an increase in aggregate demand.

The interrelations between the monetary and real aspects of balance-of-payments problems and the effects of a devaluation are further emphasized by the following hypothetical situation. Assume the economy is initially in equilibrium at point S in figure 3.9, with internal and external balance. Assume next an increase in aggregate demand such as would arise from an increase in the nominal quantity of money, a reduction in the demand for money, or a budget deficit financed by money creation. The increase in aggregate demand causes expenditure on both traded and nontraded goods to increase, thereby leading directly to a balance-of-payments deficit and an increase in the money price of home goods at a point such as Q. The trade balance deficit at point Q has three sources. One is the increase in expenditure at constant prices. Another is the reduction in output of

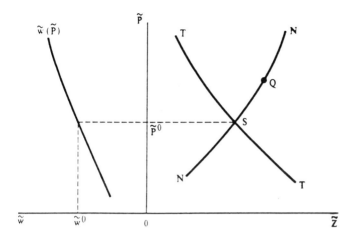

Figure 3.9

traded goods that occurs as the expansion of the home goods industry leads to an increase in money wages, thereby raising costs in the traded goods industry relative to market prices given by the world economy. Last, there is the substitution from nontraded goods to traded goods that occurs as the relative price of home goods increases.

The short-run equilibrium at point Q cannot be sustained over an extended period, since it implies a trade balance deficit. But the adjustment via the monetary mechanism, given downward inflexibility of wages, would lead to an unemployment equilibrium, and accordingly a devaluation would be called for to reduce real wages in terms of traded goods.

The policy problem we described started off with an increase in aggregate demand, causing a deficit directly and indirectly via an increase in money wages. An alternative description of the move to point Q would be to assume an increase in money wages. Such an increase in money wages would directly deteriorate the trade balance via its cost effects on the traded goods industry and would also give rise to unemployment. To avoid unemployment, the government could entertain an expansionary policy sustaining aggregate demand and short-run equilibrium at point Q. Again a devaluation would be called for to restore the initial real equilibrium.

The conclusion that emerges from this section is that there is no conflict whatsoever between three alternative views of the nature of balance-of-payments problems and the effects of a devaluation. Point Q represents a trade balance disequilibrium because (a) the community spends more than its income and the effects of the trade balance on the money supply are neutralized, (b) the relative price of nontraded goods is too high, (c) the real wage in terms of traded goods is too high for the traded goods sector to be competitive. Obviously the three sources of trade disequilibrium are not independent.

A devaluation will cure all three sources of disequilibrium simultaneously: it reduces real expenditure relative to income by the deflationary effects of an increase in the price of traded goods on the real money supply, and it reduces directly the relative price of home goods and the real wage in terms of traded goods. Furthermore, to the extent that money wages are inflexible downward, a devaluation is superior to deflation since it allows full employment to be maintained. For that effect to operate, however, we require, as Meade and Mundell have emphasized, that there be money illusion, so that a reduction in real wages via an increase in the price level is preferred to a reduction in nominal wages.

Notes

I wish to acknowledge helpful comments from R. N. Cooper, R. W. Jones, J. Marquez, M. Mussa, and C. Wilson.

1. A recent assessment of both the theory and evidence on currency depreciation is provided in Cooper (1971).

2. Earlier use of this model may be found in the work of Hawtrey (1931). Harberger (1966) considered alternative policy goals in the model, while McKinnon (1963) and Mundell (1971) discussed the issue of optimum currency areas in this framework. Extensions to two countries are developed in Pearce (1961), McDougall (1970), and more recently Amano (1972).

3. This equilibrium was characterized by Salter (1959) as "a rare and delicate creature" at "the kissing-tangency point."

4. "Real" throughout this chapter refers to a measurement in terms of the numeraire traded goods, not to a measurement in terms of some price index.

5. A necessary condition for the income effect not to dominate is that the elasticity of supply plus the compensated elasticity of demand exceed the marginal propensity to spend on traded goods.

6. The relation between price and expenditure changes that will satisfy external and internal balance, respectively, are given by

$$\frac{d\tilde{P}}{\tilde{P}} = -\frac{m}{\varepsilon + \eta - m} \frac{d\tilde{Z}}{\tilde{P}D_N}$$

and

$$\frac{d\tilde{P}}{\tilde{P}} = \frac{1 - m}{\varepsilon + \eta + 1 - m} \frac{d\tilde{Z}}{\tilde{P}D_N},$$

where ε is the elasticity of supply along the transformation curve, η is the compensated elasticity of demand defined positive, and m is the marginal propensity to spend on traded goods.

7. On this point see Komyia (1967).

8. The particular approach to the expenditure function adopted here was developed by Prais (1961). See also Dornbusch (1973), and Johnson (1958).

9. The analysis assumes that the government either pursues policies that increase private aggregate demand or that the government has the same marginal spending pattern as the private sector.

10. We should note that a tariff, an equal rate tax on imports and subsidy on exports, would serve the same purpose as a devaluation, since its effect would be confined to raising the price level without distorting choices between consumers and producers.

References

Amano, A. 1972. "Nontraded Goods and the Effects of Devaluation." *Economic Studies Quarterly* (August): 1–9.

Cooper, R. N. 1971. *Currency Devaluation in Developing Countries*. Essays in International Finance, no. 86, June. Princeton University Press.

Corden, M. 1960. "The Geometric Representation of Policies to Attain Internal and External Balance." *Review of Economic Studies* 28: 1–22.

Dornbusch, R. 1973. "Devaluation, Money, and Nontraded Goods." *American Economic Review* 73, no. 5 (December): 871–880.

Harberger, A. 1966. "The Case of the Three Numeraires." Paper presented at the Econometric Society, December.

Hawtrey, R. G. 1931. *Trade Depression and the Way Out*. London: Longmans.

Johnson, H. G. 1958. "Toward a General Theory of the Balance of Payments." In *International Trade and Economic Growth*, edited by H. G. Johnson. London: Unwin.

Jones, R. W. 1972. "Alternative Models of Devaluation." Unpublished manuscript, University of Rochester.

Jones, R. W. 1971. "A Three-Factor Model in Theory, Trade, and History." In *Trade, Balance of Payments, and Growth*, edited by J. Bhagwati et al. Amsterdam: North-Holland.

Kemp, M. 1970. "The Balance of Payments and the Terms of Trade in Relation to Financial Controls." *Review of Economic Studies* 37 (January): 25–31.

Komiya, R. 1967. "Nontraded Goods and the Pure Theory of International Trade." *International Economic Review* 8 (June): 132—152.

Krueger, A. 1971. "The Role of Home-Goods in Exchange Rate Adjustments." Unpublished manuscript, University of Minnesota.

McDougall, I. 1970. "Nontraded Goods and the Pure Theory of International Trade." In *Studies in International Economics,* edited by I. A. McDougall and R. N. Snape. Amsterdam: North-Holland.

McKinnon, R. 1963. "Optimum Currency Areas." *American Economic Review* 53: 717—724.

Meade, J. 1956. "The Price Adjustment and the Australian Balance of Payments." *Economic Record* 32 (November): 239—256.

Michaely, M. 1960. "Relative-Prices and Income-Absorption Approaches to Devaluation: A Partial Reconciliation." *American Economic Review* 50 (March): 144—147.

Mundell, R. A. 1961. "A Theory of Optimum Currency Areas." *American Economic Review* 51 (September): 657—665.

Mundell, R. A. 1971. *Monetary Theory.* Pacific Palisades, Calif.: Goodyear.

Mussa, M. 1972. "A Simple General Equilibrium Model of the Balance of Payments." Unpublished manuscript, University of Chicago.

Pearce, I. 1961. "The Problem of the Balance of Payments." *International Economic Review* 2, no. 1 (January): 1—28.

Prais, S. J. 1961. "Mathematical Notes on the Quantity Theory of Money in an Open Economy." *IMF Staff Papers* 8 (May): 212—226.

Salter, W. E. 1959. "Internal and External Balance: The Role of Price and Expenditure Effects." *Economic Record* 35 (August): 226—238.

Swan, T. 1960. "Economic Control in a Dependent Economy." *Economic Record* 36 (March): 51—66.

Swan, T. 1963. "Longer-Run Problems of the Balance of Payments." In *The Australian Economy: A Volume of Readings,* edited by H. W. Arndt and M. W. Corden. Melbourne: Cheshire Press.

4   Expectations and Exchange Rate Dynamics

This chapter develops a simple macroeconomic framework for the study of exchange rate movements. The purpose is to develop a theory that is suggestive of the observed large fluctuations in exchange rates, while at the same time establishing that such exchange rate movements are consistent with rational expectations formation. In developing a formal model, we draw on the role of asset markets, capital mobility, and expectations that have been emphasized in recent literature.[1] We draw too on the fact of differential adjustment speeds in goods and asset markets. In fact, the dynamic aspects of exchange rate determination in this model arise from the assumption that exchange rates and asset markets adjust fast relative to goods markets.

The adjustment process to a monetary expansion in this framework serves to identify several features that are suggestive of recent currency experience. In the short run, a monetary expansion is shown to induce an immediate depreciation in the exchange rate and accounts therefore for fluctuations in the exchange rate and the terms of trade. Second, during the adjustment process, rising prices may be accompanied by an appreciating exchange rate so that the trend behavior of exchange rates stands potentially in strong contrast with the cyclical behavior of exchange rates and prices. The third aspect of the adjustment process is a direct effect of the exchange rate on domestic inflation. In this context the exchange rate is identified as a critical channel for the transmission of monetary policy to aggregate demand for domestic output.

The effect of monetary policy on interest rates and exchange rates is significantly affected by the behavior of real output. If real output is fixed, a monetary expansion will, in the short run, lower interest rates and cause

*Originally published in Journal of Political Economy, vol. 84, no. 6 (December 1976), pp. 1161–1176. © 1976 by The University of Chicago. All rights reserved.

the exchange rate to overshoot its long-run depreciation. If output, on the contrary, responds to aggregrate demand, the exchange rate and interest rate changes will be dampened. Although the exchange rate will still depreciate, it may no longer overshoot, and interest rates may actually rise.

In section 4.1 we develop a formal model in terms of explicit functional forms. That development allows us to derive an analytical solution for the time path of variables and, in section 4.2, for the expectations that generate the perfect foresight path. In section 4.3, the model is used to investigate the effects of a monetary disturbance. While the major part of the analysis is developed for the case of fixed output, an extension to variable output is introduced in section 4.4.

4.1 The Model

We will assume a country that is small in the world capital market so that it faces a given interest rate. Capital mobility will ensure the equalization of expected net yields so that the domestic interest rate, less the expected rate of depreciation, will equal the world rate. In the goods market we will assume that the world price of imports is given. Domestic output is an imperfect substitute for imports, and aggregate demand for domestic goods, therefore, will determine their absolute and relative price.

Capital Mobility and Expectations

Assets denominated in terms of domestic and foreign currency are assumed to be perfect substitutes given a proper premium to offset anticipated exchange rate changes. Accordingly, if the domestic currency is expected to depreciate, interest rates on assets denominated in terms of domestic currency will exceed those abroad by the expected rate of depreciation. That relationship is expressed in (1), where r is the domestic interest rate, r^* is the given world rate of interest, and x is the expected rate of depreciation of the domestic currency, or the expected rate of increase of the domestic currency price of foreign exchange:

$$r = r^* + x. \tag{1}$$

Equation (1) is a representation of perfect capital mobility, and it is assumed that incipient capital flows will ensure that (1) holds at all times.

Consider next expectations formation. Here we distinguish between the long-run exchange rate, to which the economy will ultimately converge, and the current exchange rate. Denoting the logarithms of the current and long-run rate by e and $\bar{e}$, respectively, we assume that

$$x = \theta(\bar{e} - e). \tag{2}$$

Equation (2) states that the expected rate of depreciation of the spot rate is proportional to the discrepancy between the long-run rate and the current spot rate. The coefficient of adjustment θ is for the present taken as a parameter. The long-run exchange rate is assumed known, and an expression for it will be developed below. We note further that, while expectations formation according to (2) may appear ad hoc, it will actually be consistent with perfect foresight, as shown in section 4.2.

The Money Market

The domestic interest rate is determined by the condition of equilibrium in the domestic money market. The demand for real money balances is assumed to depend on the domestic interest rate and real income and will, in equilibrium, equal the real money supply. Assuming a conventional demand for money, the log of which is linear in the log of real income and in interest rates, we have[2]

$$-\lambda r + \phi y = m - p, \tag{3}$$

where m, p, and y denote the logs of the nominal quantity of money, the price level, and real income. For the remainder of this section we will take the nominal quantity of money and the level of real income as given.

   Combining (1), (2), and (3) will give us a relationship between the spot exchange rate, the price level, and the long-run exchange rate, *given* that the money market clears and net asset yields are equalized:

$$p - m = -\phi y + \lambda r^* + \lambda\theta(\bar{e} - e). \tag{4}$$

Equation (4) can be simplified by noting that with a stationary money supply long-run equilibrium will imply equality between interest rates, because current and expected exchange rates are equal. This implies that the long-run equilibrium price level, $\bar{p}$, will equal

$$\bar{p} = m + (\lambda r^* - \phi y). \tag{5}$$

Substituting (5) in (4) gives us a relationship between the exchange rate and the price level:[3]

$$e = \bar{e} - \frac{1}{\lambda\theta}(p - \bar{p}). \tag{6}$$

Equation (6) is one of the key equations of the model. For given long-run values of exchange rates and prices, it serves to determine the current spot price of foreign exchange as a function of the current level of prices. Given the level of prices, we have a domestic interest rate and an interest differential. Given the long-run exchange rate, there is a unique level of the spot rate such that the expected appreciation, or depreciation, matches the interest differential. An increase in the price level, because it raises interest rates, gives rise to an incipient capital inflow that will appreciate the spot rate to the point where the anticipated depreciation exactly offsets the increase in domestic interest rates.

The Goods Market

The demand for domestic output depends on the relative price of domestic goods, $e - p$, interest rates, and real income. The demand function is assumed to have the form

$$\ln D = u + \delta(e - p) + \gamma y - \sigma r, \tag{7}$$

where D denotes the demand for domestic output and where u is a shift parameter.[4] From (7) we note that a decrease in the relative price of domestic goods raises demand, as does an increase in income or a reduction in interest rates. The rate of increase in the price of domestic goods, $\dot{p}$, is described in (8) as proportional to an excess demand measure:

$$\dot{p} = \pi \ln \frac{D}{Y} = \pi[u + \delta(e - p) + (\gamma - 1)y - \sigma r]. \tag{8}$$

We note that the long-run equilibrium exchange rate implied by (8) is[5]

$$\bar{e} = \bar{p} + \frac{1}{\delta}[\sigma r^* + (1 - \gamma)y - u], \tag{9}$$

where $\bar{p}$ is defined in (5). From (9) it is apparent that the long-run exchange rate depends with the conventional homogeneity properties on monetary variables, though obviously on real variables too.

The price equation in (8) can be simplified by using the definition of the long-run rate in (9) and the fact that interest differences equal expected depreciation, $r - r^* = \theta(\bar{e} - e)$, to become[6]

$$\dot{p} = -\pi \left(\frac{\delta + \sigma\theta}{\theta\lambda + \delta} \right)(p - \bar{p}) = -v(p - \bar{p}), \tag{10}$$

where

$$v \equiv \pi \left(\frac{\delta + \sigma\theta}{\theta\lambda + \delta} \right). \tag{11}$$

The price adjustment equation in (10) can be solved to yield

$$p(t) = \bar{p} + (p_0 - \bar{p}) \exp(-vt), \tag{12}$$

which shows that the price of domestic output will converge to its long-run level at a rate determined by (11). Substitution of (12) in (6) gives the time path of the exchange rate

$$e(t) = \bar{e} - \frac{1}{\lambda\theta}(p_0 - \bar{p}) \exp(-vt)$$

$$\tag{13}$$

$$= \bar{e} + (e_0 - \bar{e}) \exp(-vt).$$

From (13) the exchange rate will likewise converge to its long-run level. The rate will appreciate if prices are initially below their long-run level and, conversely, if prices initially exceed their long-run level.

Equilibrium Exchange Rates

The adjustment process of the economy can be described with the help of figure 4.1. At every point in time the money market clears and expected yields are arbitraged. This implies a relationship between prices and the spot exchange rate shown in (6) and reflected in the QQ schedule in figure 4.1. The positively sloped schedule $\dot{p} = 0$ shows combinations of price levels and exchange rates for which the goods market and money market are in equilibrium.[7] Points above and to the left of that schedule correspond to an excess supply of goods and falling prices. Conversely, points to the right and below the schedule correspond to an excess demand. The $\dot{p} = 0$ schedule is positively sloped and flatter than a $45°$ line for the following reason.[8] An increase in the exchange rate creates an excess demand for domestic goods by lowering their relative price. To restore equilibrium, domestic prices will have to increase, though proportionately less, since an increase in domestic prices affects aggregate demand, both via the relative price effect and via higher interest rates.

For any given price level the exchange rate adjusts instantaneously to clear the asset market. Accordingly, we are continuously on the QQ schedule with money-market equilibrium and international arbitrage of

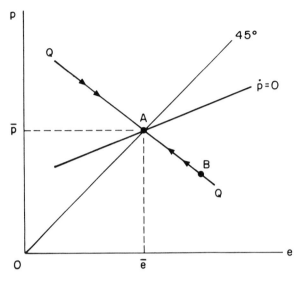

Figure 4.1

net expected yields. Goods-market equilibrium, to the contrary, is only achieved in the long run. Conditions in the goods market, however, are critical in moving the economy to the long-run equilibrium by inducing rising or falling prices. Specifically, an initial position such as point *B*, with a price level below the long-run level and, correspondingly, an exchange rate in excess of the long-run equilibrium, implies an excess demand for goods because domestic output commands a low relative price and because the interest rate is low. Accordingly, prices will be rising, thereby inducing over time a reduction in excess demand. The path of rising prices is accompanied by an appreciation of the exchange rate. As interest rates rise, as a consequence of declining real balances, the spot rate will approach the long-run rate. Once the long-run equilibrium at point *A* is attained, interest rates are equal internationally, the goods markets clear, prices are constant, and expected exchange rate changes are zero.

4.2 Consistent Expectations

So far we have placed no restrictions on the formation of expectations other than the assumption that the expected rate of depreciation, as shown in (2), is proportional to the discrepancy between the long-run and the current exchange rate. From (12) and (13) we note that the rate at which prices and the exchange rate converge to equilibrium is given by v. From (11) it is apparent that the rate of convergence is a function of the expectations coefficient, θ.

Clearly, for the expectations formation process in (2) to correctly predict the actual path of exchange rates it must be true that $\theta = v$. Accordingly, the expectations coefficient, θ, that corresponds to perfect foresight, or, equivalently, that is consistent with the model is given by the solution to the equation

$$\theta = v \equiv \pi\left(\frac{\delta + \sigma\theta}{\theta\lambda + \delta}\right). \tag{14}$$

The consistent expectations coefficient, $\tilde{\theta}$, obtained as the solution to (14), is a function of the structural parameters of the economy[9]

$$\tilde{\theta}(\lambda, \delta, \sigma, \pi) = \frac{\pi(\sigma/\lambda + \delta)}{2} + \left[\frac{\pi^2(\sigma/\lambda + \delta)^2}{4} + \frac{\pi\delta}{\lambda}\right]^{1/2}. \tag{15}$$

Equation (15) gives the rate at which the economy will converge to long-run equilibrium along the perfect foresight path. If expectations are formed according to (2) and (15), exchange rate predictions will actually be borne out.[10] The characteristics of the perfect foresight path are that the economy will converge faster the lower the interest response of money demand and the higher the interest response of goods demand and the price elasticity of demand for domestic output. The reason is simply that with a low interest response a given change in real balances will give rise to a large change in interest rates which, in combination with a high interest response of goods demand, will give rise to a large excess demand and therefore inflationary impact. Similarly, a large price elasticity serves to translate an exchange rate change into a large excess demand and, therefore, serves to speed up the adjustment process.

4.3 The Effects of a Monetary Expansion

In this section we will study the adjustment process to a monetary expansion. The analysis serves to derive substantive results but also to highlight the manner in which expectations about the future path of the economy affect the current level of the exchange rate. This link is embodied in consistent expectations and makes the impact effect of a monetary disturbance depend on the entire structure of the economy.

In figure 4.2 we show the economy in initial full equilibrium at point A,

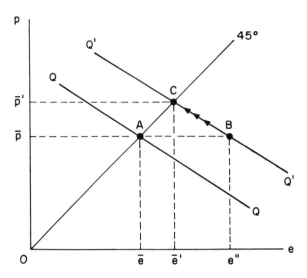

Figure 4.2

with a long-run price level $\bar{p}$ and a corresponding long-run exchange rate $\bar{e}$ where the level of prices is determined, according to (5), by the nominal quantity of money, real income, and the interest rate. The long-run exchange rate by (9) will depend on the level of domestic prices and characteristics of the demand for domestic goods. The asset-market equilibrium schedule QQ that combines monetary equilibrium and arbitrage of net expected yields is drawn for the initial nominal quantity of money.

An increase in the nominal quantity of money that is expected to persist will cause a goods and asset market disequilibrium at the initial exchange rate and price. To maintain asset-market equilibrium, the increased quantity of money would have to be matched by higher prices and/or a depreciation in the exchange rate. The asset-market equilibrium schedule will shift out to $Q'Q'$, a shift that is (proportionately) equal to the increase in the nominal quantity of money.

It is immediately obvious that the new long-run equilibrium is at point C, where both goods and asset markets clear and exchange rate and price changes exactly reflect the increase in money.[11] This long-run homogeneity result is not surprising, since there is no source of money illusion or long-run price rigidity in the system.

Consider next the adjustment process. At the initial level of prices, the monetary expansion reduces interest rates and leads to the anticipation of a depreciation in the long run and, therefore, at the current exchange rate, to the expectation of a depreciating exchange rate. Both factors serve to reduce the attractiveness of domestic assets, lead to an incipient capital outflow, and thus cause the spot rate to depreciate. The extent of that depreciation has to be sufficient to give rise to the anticipation of appreciation at just sufficient a rate to offset the reduced domestic interest rate. The impact effect of a monetary expansion is therefore to induce an immediate depreciation in the spot rate and one that exceeds the long-run depreciation, since only under these circumstances will the public anticipate an appreciating exchange rate and thus be compensated for the reduced interest on domestic assets. This is shown in figure 4.2 by the move from point A to the short-run equilibrium at point B.

From (4), noting that $d\bar{e} = dm = d\bar{p}$, we obtain a formal expression for the impact effect of a monetary expansion on the spot exchange rate:

$$\frac{de}{dm} = 1 + \frac{1}{\lambda\theta}. \tag{16}$$

Equation (16) confirms that in the short run the exchange rate will overshoot. The extent of the overshooting will depend on the interest response of money demand and the expectations coefficient.

A high interest response of money demand will serve to dampen the overshooting because it implies that a given expansion in the (real) quantity of money will only induce a small reduction in the interest rate. A small reduction in the interest rate in turn requires only a small expectation of appreciation to offset it and therefore, given the coefficient of expectations and the long-run rate, only a small depreciation of the spot rate (in excess of the long-run rate) to generate that expectation. A similar interpretation applies to the coefficient of expectations in (16).

It is quite obvious from the preceding explanation that the short-term effects of a monetary expansion, in this model, are entirely dominated by asset markets and, more specifically, by capital mobility and expectations. This feature places in sharp relief the assumption that asset markets and exchange rates adjust fast relative to the goods market and the price of domestic output. It is under these circumstances that a change in the nominal quantity of money is, in fact, a change in the real quantity of money, and the spot rate adjustment serves to achieve equilibrium in the asset markets by creating the expectation of appreciation of just sufficient an extent to balance the reduced interest rate on domestic assets.

The interpretation of (16) has not so far used the restriction that expectations be rational. That restriction is introduced by substituting (15) in (16) to obtain

$$\frac{de}{dm} = 1 + \frac{1}{\lambda\tilde{\theta}} = 1 + \frac{1}{\pi(\sigma + \delta\lambda)/2 + [\pi^2(\sigma + \delta\lambda)^2/4 + \pi\delta\lambda]^{1/2}}. \tag{17}$$

Equation (17) has two implications that cannot be derived from (16). The first is that with an interest response of money demand that approaches zero the initial depreciation remains finite and, in fact, approaches $de/dm = 1 + 1/\pi\sigma$. This result reflects the fact that for the large interest rate changes that would result in these circumstances, the subsequent path of prices and the exchange rate is governed by the effect of interest rates on aggregate demand.

A second implication of (17) is the fact that the short-run overshooting of the exchange rate is inversely related to the speed of adjustment of the system, $\tilde{\theta}$. That fact is particularly obvious for the case where the speed of adjustment of prices, π, becomes infinite and where, accordingly, the economy jumps instantaneously to the new long-run equilibrium at point C.[12] More generally, those factors that serve to speed up the adjustment process, in particular high interest rate responsiveness of money demand, or aggregate spending, or high price elasticities, will therefore serve to dampen the impact effect of a monetary expansion on the exchange rate. This effect relies entirely on expectations about the subsequent path of the economy, rather than on *current* interaction between goods and asset markets.

Consider next the adjustment process from the short-run market equilibrium at point B to long-run equilibrium at point C. We note from figure 4.2 that at point B there is an excess demand for goods. That excess demand arises both from the decline in domestic interest rates and from the depreciation in the exchange rate that lowers the *relative* price of domestic goods. Each factor by itself is sufficient to account for this excess demand and, in fact, they constitute independent channels through which monetary changes affect demand for domestic output.

The exchange rate channel has been identified by Fleming and Mundell as an important avenue for monetary policy to act on aggregate demand.[13] In the present context the depreciation of the spot rate that is induced by the conditions of asset-market equilibrium serves to reduce the relative price of domestic goods, and thereby to raise aggregate demand and give rise to inflationary pressure as opposed to an increase in output. The importance of this channel is larger, the higher the price elasticity of demand relative to the interest response of aggregate spending.

The lower interest rates and a lower relative price of domestic goods, that are characteristics of the impact effect, will cause domestic prices to rise and therefore be reflected in falling real money balances, rising interest rates, and an appreciating exchange rate. The adjustment process of rising prices over time restores the economy to the initial real equilibrium. An important feature of that adjustment process is the fact that rising prices are accompanied by an appreciating exchange rate. In terms of figure 4.2, this is described by the move along $Q'Q'$ from B to C. This result is due to the fact that rising prices cause the real money supply to be falling and interest rates to be rising. The rising interest rate, in turn, gives rise to an incipient capital inflow that appreciates the exchange rate at the same rate as interest rates are rising and thus maintains expected net yields in line. The model therefore confirms the link between interest rates and exchange rates that is emphasized in popular interpretations of foreign exchange events. The observation is correct, in the present circumstances, because rising interest rates are accompanied by the expectation of an appreciating exchange rate.

In summarizing this part we note that the ultimate effect of a monetary expansion is an equiproportionate increase in prices and the exchange rate. In the short run, however, the monetary expansion does exert real effects on interest rates, the terms of trade, and aggregate demand. The details of the adjustment process will depend on the economic structure. In particular, terms of trade changes will be both larger and more persistent the lower the speed of adjustment, $\hat{\theta}$.

A key role in this analysis is played by the sluggish adjustment of prices as compared with asset markets. There is no very persuasive theoretical support for the slow adjustment of goods markets, but the facts clearly point in this direction. While the differential adjustment speed lacks theoretical backing, it implies, nevertheless, a behavior of exchange rates that is suggestive of recent experience.[14]

4.4 Short-Run Adjustment in Output

So far we have assumed that output is fixed at the full-employment level, $\bar{y}$. In the present part, the analysis is extended to allow for short-run adjustments in output in response to changes in aggregate demand. Therefore we replace equation (8) by an equilibrium condition in the domestic goods market,

$$y = \ln D \equiv u + \delta(e - p) + \gamma y - \sigma r. \tag{18}$$

where y is the log of the actual level of output that in the short run is demand determined. In addition to (18), we require a price adjustment equation which is shown in (19):

$$\dot{p} = \pi(y - \bar{y}). \tag{19}$$

According to (19) the rate of inflation is proportional to the discrepancy between actual and full employment, or "potential" output, $\bar{y}$. This price adjustment equation is a combination of a relationship between wage and price inflation, a relation between wage inflation and unemployment as in a Phillips curve, and a relation between unemployment and the departure from potential output, $y - \bar{y}$, as described by Okun's law.

It is shown in the appendix that the extension that incorporates (18) and (19) in place of (8) leaves most of the analysis of adjustments to a monetary increase unchanged. In particular, the price adjustment will continue to be exponential although the speed of adjustment will depend now also on the income elasticities of demand for domestic goods and real balances, γ and ϕ.

In the present framework it continues to be true that in the short run an increase in the nominal quantity of money is an increase in the real quantity of money. Accordingly, a monetary expansion has the conventional effect of increasing in the short run the level of output and inducing inflation. Since the inflation that is induced by the expansion in real output serves to raise over time the price level, real balances will decline back to their initial level until in the long run the expansion in money is fully matched by increased prices and output has returned to the full-employment level.

The impact effect of a monetary expansion on exchange rates and interest rates may, however, differ significantly from the analysis in section 4.3. The new possibility that arises from the expansion in output in the short run is that the exchange rate depreciation will fall short of the monetary expansion rather than exceed it as in (16). That possibility arises because, in the short run, the income expansion raises money demand and may do so sufficiently to actually increase interest rates. If the output expansion were sufficiently strong to raise interest rates, equalization of net yields internationally would require the expectation of a depreciation and therefore a spot rate that falls short of the long-run equilibrium rate. Since the long-run equilibrium rate increases in the same proportion as the nominal quantity of money, it follows that the spot rate would increase less than the quantity of money. The condition that gives rise to this case is

$$1 - \frac{\phi\delta}{1 - \gamma} < 0. \tag{20}$$

The term $\delta/(1 - \gamma)$ is the elasticity of equilibrium output with respect to the exchange rate. That term multiplied by the income elasticity of demand gives the increase in money demand due to a depreciation in the spot rate. Accordingly, (20) tells us whether at constant interest rates, and allowing the exchange rate to depreciate in the same proportion as the increase in money, we have an excess demand or supply of money and, accordingly, an increase or decrease in interest rates. The possibility of an excess demand and therefore an increase in interest rates is associated with a high income elasticity of money demand, high price elasticity, and a high income elasticity of demand for domestic goods.

The time path of exchange rates and the interest rate therefore depends on income and price elasticities, and the short-run overshooting of exchange rates is no longer a necessary feature of the adjustment process. In fact, if in the short run the interest rate rises and the exchange rate therefore depreciates less than proportionately to the increase in money, the adjustment process will be one of rising prices and a depreciating exchange rate. In this event, therefore, terms of trade fluctuations will be dampened as compared with the case described earlier where the exchange rate overshooting introduces large terms of trade variations in the adjustment process.

The analysis of a monetary expansion in this part confirms once more the Mundell-Fleming result that under conditions of capital mobility and flexible rates a small country can conduct, in the short run, an effective monetary policy. More important, the exchange rate proves a critical channel for the transmission of monetary changes to an increase in aggregate demand and output. That channel may, in fact, prove to be the only channel since, as was shown above, the interest rate may actually rise in the transition. Unlike in the Mundell-Fleming world, extension of the analysis to the long run shows that the effects of a monetary expansion are only transitory, since the inflation that is induced by the output expansion serves to reduce real balances and thereby return interest rates, relative prices, and real income to their initial level.

The possibility of short-run output adjustment has been shown to dampen exchange rate movements and possibly reverse the interest rate effects of a monetary expansion. It is appropriate, therefore, to ask which of the assumptions, fixed or variable output, is a more relevant characteristic of the adjustment process. The answer no doubt is that the fixed output adjustment is a suitable characterization of the very short run. In the very short run we would not expect output to adjust instantaneously to meet an increase in aggregate demand and, accordingly, the adjustment will be primarily confined to the asset markets and will be characterized by a decline in interest rates and overshooting of exchange rates. In the intermediate run, on the contrary, the present analysis gains relevance, since here we would expect an adjustment of both output and prices in response to increased aggregate demand. On balance, therefore, the fixed output case retains relevance, and particularly so if output adjusts sluggishly to changes in aggregate demand.

4.5 Appendix

This appendix extends the model to include short-run supply responses. For that purpose we replace the price adjustment equation in (8) by a goods-market equilibrium condition (A1) and a price equation (A2):

$$y = \mu[u + \delta(e - p) - \sigma r],$$

$$\mu \equiv \frac{1}{1 - \gamma} > 0; \tag{A1}$$

$$\dot{p} = \pi(y - \bar{y}), \tag{A2}$$

where $\bar{y}$ denotes the full-employment level of output and where the price adjustment equation can be thought of as arising from a Phillips-curve relation between wage inflation and unemployment combined with an Okun's-law relation between the deviation from potential output, $y - \bar{y}$, and unemployment.[15]

The specification of the money market and exchange rate expectations remains unchanged, and equation (4) that represents these relations is repeated here for convenience:

$$p - m + \phi y = \lambda r^* + \theta\lambda(\bar{e} - e). \tag{A3}$$

Noting that in long-run equilibrium we have $y = \bar{y}$ and $r = r^*$, we obtain from (A1) the long-run goods-market relationship

$$\bar{y} = \mu[u + \delta(\bar{e} - \bar{p}) - \sigma r^*], \tag{A4}$$

and subtracting (A4) from (A1), we obtain the goods-market equilibrium condition expressed in terms of deviations from long-run equilibrium,

$$y - \bar{y} = \mu(\delta + \sigma\theta)(e - \bar{e}) + \mu\delta(\bar{p} - p), \tag{A5}$$

where we have used the fact that $r^* - r = \theta(e - \bar{e})$.

Next we proceed in a similar manner for the money market and rewrite the equilibrium condition as

$$\phi(y - \bar{y}) + (p - \bar{p}) = \lambda\theta(\bar{e} - e). \tag{A6}$$

Equations (A5) and (A6) can be simultaneously solved to yield the spot exchange rate and the level of output as a function of the existing price level. These solutions are, respectively,

$$y - \bar{y} = -w(p - \bar{p}), \tag{A7}$$

where

$$w \equiv \frac{\mu(\delta + \theta\sigma) + \mu\delta\theta\lambda}{\Delta},$$

$$\Delta \equiv \phi\mu(\delta + \theta\sigma) + \theta\lambda,$$

and

$$e - \bar{e} = -\left(\frac{1 - \phi\mu\delta}{\Delta}\right)(p - \bar{p}). \tag{A8}$$

Substitution of (A7) in (A2) yields the equilibrium rate of inflation as a function of the price level:

$$\dot{p} = -\pi w(p - \bar{p}). \tag{A9}$$

Following the procedure in section 4.2, rational expectations require that the expectations coefficient, θ, equal the rate at which exchange rates actually adjust, πw:

$$\theta = \pi w, \tag{A10}$$

which can be solved for the rational expectations coefficient of adjustment, $\tilde{\theta}$.

Consider next the impact effect of a monetary expansion. Remembering that in the long run an increase in money causes an equiproportionate increase in prices and the exchange rate, we have $d\bar{e} = d\bar{p} = dm$. Therefore from (A8) we obtain the impact effect of a monetary expansion on the exchange rate as

$$\frac{de}{dm} = 1 + \frac{1 - \phi\mu\delta}{\Delta} > 0. \tag{A11}$$

Whether the exchange rate increases more or less proportionately than the nominal quantity of money depends on the condition

$$1 - \phi\mu\delta \gtrless 0, \tag{A12}$$

which determines too whether the interest rate declines or increases.

By (A7) the impact effect on real output is unambiguously positive and equal to $dy/dm = w$. The increase in the rate of inflation is given by $d\dot{p}/dm = \pi w$.

Since from (A9) the inflation rate converges monotonically to the long-run level, we know that output declines monotonically back toward the level of full employment. The exchange rate, following the impact effect, will appreciate, or depreciate, depending on (A12).

Notes

I am indebted to Stanley Black, Franco Modigliani, and Edward Tower who provided the stimulus for this chapter. In revising various drafts I have had the benefit of many comments. I wish, in particular, to acknowledge the helpful suggestions I have received from Wilfred Ethier, Stanley Fischer, Jacob Frenkel, and the thoughtful remarks of two anonymous referees. Financial support was provided by a grant from the Ford Foundation.

1. For recent work on flexible exchange rates that shares some of the present emphasis, see Black (1973, 1975), Henderson (1975), Niehans (1975), Dornbusch (1976a, 1976b), Frenkel (1976), Kouri (1976), and Mussa (1976). The classics remain Fleming (1962) and Mundell (1964, 1968).

2. Equation (3) is obtained by taking the logarithm of the money market equilibrium condition $M/P = Y^\phi \exp(-\lambda r)$.

3. In (3) we assumed that the appropriate deflator for money balance is the price of domestic output. An alternative is provided by a deflator that is a weighted average of domestic and import prices. In such a formulation the "price level," q, could be written as $q = \alpha p + (1 - \alpha)e$, where α and $(1 - \alpha)$ are the expenditure shares of domestic goods and imports. With such a formulation (6) would be amended to the following equation: $e = \bar{e} - \beta(p - \bar{p})$, where $\beta \equiv \alpha/[\lambda\theta + (1 - \alpha)]$. None of the qualitative results described below would be affected by this extension.

4. The complete relative price argument in (7) is $(e + p^* - p)$ where p^* is the logarithm of the foreign price level. Setting the foreign price level equal to unity implies that $p^* = 0$.

5. Equation (9) is obtained by setting $\dot{p} = 0$ and $r = r^*$ as is appropriate for the long run where markets clear and exchange rates are constant.

6. In (8) aggregate demand depends on the nominal interest rate. An alternative formulation allows aggregate demand to depend on the real interest rate, $r - \dot{p}$. Such a formulation requires that we substitute $\rho \equiv \pi/(1 - \sigma\pi) > 0$ in place of π in (11) and the equations below. The restriction that $\rho > 0$ is required for stability.

7. The $\dot{p} = 0$ schedule represents combined goods- and money-market equilibrium. Setting $\dot{p} = 0$ in (8) and substituting for the domestic interest rate from (3) yields the equation of the goods-market equilibrium schedule:

$$p = \left(\frac{\delta\lambda}{\delta\lambda + \sigma}\right)e + \left(\frac{\sigma}{\delta\lambda + \sigma}\right)m + \left(\frac{\lambda}{\delta\lambda + \sigma}\right)\left(u + (1 - \gamma)y - \frac{\phi\sigma y}{\lambda}\right).$$

8. The 45° line in figure 4.1 is drawn through the origin on the assumption that by appropriate choice of units, the prices of both goods are initially equal.

9. In (16) we have taken the positive and therefore stable root of the quadratic equation implied by (14).

10. Perhaps a remark about the perfect foresight path is in order here. Why should that path command our interest rather than being a mere *curiosum*? The reason is that it is the only expectational assumption that is not arbitrary (given the model) and that does not involve persistent prediction errors. The perfect foresight path is obviously the deterministic equivalent of rational expectations.

11. We have not drawn in figure 4.2, the $\dot{p} = 0$ schedule. It is apparent, however, from the homogeneity properties of the model that the $\dot{p} = 0$ schedule will pass through point C.

12. The slope of the QQ schedule is $dp/de = -\tilde{\theta}\lambda$, and the schedule becomes vertical as $\tilde{\theta}$ approaches infinity.

13. In the Mundell-Fleming model with prices and interest rates fixed, the depreciation by worsening the terms of trade creates the necessary increase in aggregate demand to support the higher level of income required by monetary equilibrium (for a further discussion, see Niehans 1975 and Dornbusch 1976).

14. An extension of this paper would draw in an explicit manner on stochastic elements to provide a rationale for the short-run stickiness of prices. At the same time, such an extension would have interesting implications for the manner in which expectations are formed. Exchange rate determination in a stochastic setting has been studied by Black (1973), Kouri (1975), and Mussa (1976). Fischer (1976) has used a stochastic framework to evaluate fixed versus flexible exchange rate systems.

15. To deal with steady-state inflation, we would have to add in (A2) the long-run rate of inflation which is given by the rate of monetary growth, which in the present treatment is assumed equal to zero.

References

Black, S. 1973. *International Money Markets and Flexible Exchange Rates.* Princeton Studies in International Finance, no. 32. Princeton, N.J.: Princeton Univ. Press.

Black, S. 1975. "Exchange Rate Policies for Less Developed Countries in a World of Floating Rates." Mimeographed. Vanderbilt Univ.

Dornbusch, R. 1976a. "Exchange Rate Expectations and Monetary Policy." *J. Internat. Econ.*, forthcoming.

Dornbusch, R. 1976b. "The Theory of Flexible Exchange Rate Regimes and Macroeconomic Policy." *Scandinavian J. Econ.* 2 (May): 255–275.

Fischer, S. 1976. "Stability and Exchange Rate Systems in a Monetarist Model of the Balance of Payments." In *The Political Economy of Monetary Reform,* edited by R. Aliber. London: Macmillan.

Fleming, M. 1962. "Domestic Financial Policies under Fixed and Floating Exchange Rates." *I.M.F. Staff Papers* 9 (November): 369–379.

Frenkel, J. A. 1976. "A Monetary Approach to the Exchange Rate." *Scandinavian J. Econ.* 2 (May): 200–221.

Henderson, D. 1975. "Monetary, Fiscal and Exchange Rate Policy in a Two-Country, Short-Run Macroeconomic Model." Mimeographed. Board of Governors, Federal Res.

Kouri, P. 1975. *Essays on the Theory of Flexible Exchange Rates*. Ph.D. dissertation, Massachusetts Inst. Tech.

Kouri, P. 1976. "The Exchange Rate and the Balance of Payments in the Short Run and in the Long Run." *Scandinavian J. Econ.* 2 (May): 280–304.

Mundell, R. A. 1964. "Exchange Rate Margins and Economic Policy." In *Money in the International Order*, edited by C. Murphy. Dallas: Southern Methodist Univ. Press.

Mundell, R. A. 1968. *International Economics*. New York: Macmillan.

Mussa, M. 1976. "The Exchange Rate, the Balance of Payments and Monetary and Fiscal Policy under a Regime of Controlled Floating." *Scandinavian J. Econ.* 2 (May): 229–248.

Niehans, J. 1975. "Some Doubts about the Efficacy of Monetary Policy under Flexible Exchange Rates." *J. Internat. Econ.* 5 (August): 275–281.

5   Exchange Rates and Prices

The large appreciation of the U.S. dollar over the 1980–85 period and the subsequent depreciation open important areas of research. The fact of a large and persistent real appreciation poses a challenge for equilibrium theorists to uncover the change in fundamentals. For those who explain medium-term macroeconomics in terms of Fischer-Taylor long-term wage contracts, the episode provides a striking example of the differential speeds of adjustment of wages and goods and assets prices. I adopt this perspective here to explain the determinants of relative price changes of different groups of goods. Specifically, I advance hypotheses about those sectors where an exchange rate change should lead to large relative price changes, and others where the relative price effects should be negligible.

The approach is to draw on models of industrial organization to explain price adjustments in terms of the degree of market concentration, the extent of product homogeneity and substitutability, and the relative market shares of domestic and foreign firms. Models of industrial organization have, of course, been fruitfully applied in trade theory; their application to macro-pricing issues, however, has been surprisingly slow.[1] There is a long-standing questioning of purchasing power parity (PPP), especially in the work of Irving Kravis and Robert Lipsey (1978, 1984).[2] But so far there seems to exist little formal analysis of price-setting behavior in this context.[3]

This chapter adopts a partial-equilibrium approach in that it assumes throughout a given exogenous movement in the nominal exchange rate. The exchange rate movement and the less-than-fully flexible money wage interact to produce a cost shock for some firms in an industry—foreign firms in the home market and home firms abroad—and thus bring about the need for an industry-wide adjustment in prices. Although the assump-

Originally published in *American Economic Review*, vol. 77, no. 1 (March 1987), pp. 93–106.

Table 5.1
Relative costs and prices in manufacturing (cumulative percentage change)

	1976–80	1980–85:I	1980–85:IV
Relative value-added deflator	− 14.7	49.3	27.0
Relative unit labor cost	− 12.6	59.8	22.0

Source: *International Finance Statistics*, Yearbook 1985 and August 1986.

tion of exogenous exchange rate movements and sticky wages is open to criticism, it is a useful working hypothesis for the purpose of investigating relative price issues.

Section 5.1 reviews some facts. Section 5.2 offers a stylized view of the link between exchange rates and prices, and the third section studies the behavior of equilibrium prices.

5.1 Some Facts

The large dollar movements are reflected both in absolute and relative prices. Table 5.1 shows two measures of the change in U.S. relative costs and prices: relative unit labor costs and the relative value-added deflator in manufacturing. In each case, the U.S. series is deflated by the corresponding time-series for the trade-weighted average in dollars of our trading partners. The large magnitude of the change in relative costs and prices arises from the fact that unit labor costs and prices abroad (in national currencies) were rising at a lower rate than in the United States. But at the same time, the dollar, rather than offsetting the divergent trend by a depreciation, further reinforced that divergence by a strong appreciation. The depreciation since mid-1985 has not been sufficient to eliminate the change in competitiveness.

Figure 5.1 shows absolute prices measured by the U.S. GNP deflator and the deflators for imports. Prior to 1980 import prices increase more rapidly than the deflator and, to a lesser extent, so do export prices (not shown). During this period the dollar was depreciating. After 1980, however, the dollar appreciation gets underway, and import price increases slow down and ultimately import prices fall in absolute terms. Export prices track the GDP deflator more closely, though the pattern of divergences is similar to that for imports. At this broad level it is clear then that import prices fell relative to the deflator and relative to export prices.

In the absence of comprehensive price series, table 5.2 shows unit values for different export and import groups. The table brings out that the

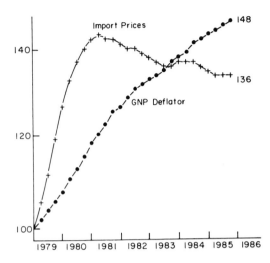

Figure 5.1
The impact of dollar appreciation

Table 5.2
Unit values of imports and exports (index 1980:I = 100)

	Foods		Materials		Semi-manufactures		Finished manufactures	
	E	M	E	M	E	M	E	M
1979:II	87	82	92	60	71	77	95	91
1980:I	100	100	100	100	100	100	100	100
1985:I	94	87	91	97	86	82	139	106

Note: E = exports, M = imports. For definition and source, see the appendix.

absolute decline in import prices must be primarily attributed to the first three groups, and not to finished manufactures. Oil price increases in 1979 easily explain the divergent pattern of export and import unit values for crude materials. The interesting comparison therefore is between the relatively homogeneous commodity groups—food and semimanufactures—and finished manufactures where price setting and product differentiation are likely to be important. For the former group, export and import unit values move roughly in line, while for finished manufactures, exports follow the domestic price trend and imports show a much smaller increase.

5.2 Standard Models

There are two extreme models of price relationships in the open economy literature. One assumes that the "law of one price" holds. Prices of goods are geographically arbitraged and, adjusted for tariffs and transport costs, they are equalized in different locations. Homogeneity, information and perfect competition assure this result.[4] Let p_i, p_i^*, and e denote the price of good i in the home country and currency, the foreign price, and the home-currency price of foreign exchange. Arbitrage then implies

$$p_i = e p_i^*. \tag{1}$$

In this form, or in the first-difference version of Gustav Cassel, the law of one price is asserted in the PPP literature. The law of one price has been applied in the monetary approach to exchange rates in combination with the quantity theory of money and the assumption of full-price flexibility to obtain a theory of the exchange rate. An important implication of complete spatial arbitrage, not only for commodities but for all goods, is the idea that relative national price levels in a common currency are independent of the exchange rate, since exchange rate movements merely reflect, passively, divergent national price trends. That is of course an application of the homogeneity postulate which holds when money is fully neutral.

The alternative model might be called "Keynesian." Here it is assumed that each country is fully specialized in the production of "its own" good. Domestic and foreign goods are less than fully homogeneous or substitutable. Wages are fixed in national currencies or at least sticky.

Letting P and P^* be the national GDP deflators, the relative price of domestic and foreign goods or the real exchange rate then is

$$\lambda = \frac{P}{eP^*}. \tag{2}$$

If the markup of prices over unit labor costs is constant, then for given unit labor costs, prices will also be given. Hence in this model, exchange rate movements change relative prices one for one. Exchange-rate-induced changes in the relative price affect the world distribution of demand and employment. This approach tends to be used in open economy versions of the IS-LM model in the Meade-Mundell tradition.

Equation (1) would be a useful model of international price relations for materials—say sisal, copper, tea—whereas (2) more nearly describes what happens with manufactures. But the assumption of a constant markup is no longer justified as we shall now see when domestic and foreign firms have strategic interactions in their pricing.

5.3 Equilibrium Pricing Models

Table 5.1 gave evidence of large, persistent fluctuations in exchange rate-adjusted relative prices in manufacturing. In this section I explore theoretical models that would explain these price movements as the result of changes in relative unit labor costs.

The basic assumption I make is that firms in any industry have a linear technology, with labor as the only input. Unit labor costs, w and w^*, are given in home and foreign currency, respectively. This assumption about costs is combined with a model of pricing to yield predictions about the behavior of relative prices. The experiment is simply this: the exchange rate change, say a dollar appreciation, lowers foreign unit labor costs in dollars. As a result the market equilibrium is disturbed in each industry, and price and output adjustments must occur. What these adjustments look like depends on three factors:[5]

Market integration or separation. Is a particular commodity traded in an integrated world market, or are there significant barriers to restrict spatial arbitrage?

Substitution between domestic and foreign variants of a product. The extent of substitution influences price setting and the output effects of cost and price changes.

Market organization. Is the market perfectly competitive, in which case firms are price takers, or is the market imperfectly competitive or oligopolistic, in which case firms are price setters and may interact in strategic ways?

Two models lend themselves in a straightforward fashion to formulating the price response to cost shocks of part of the industry. The Cournot model assumes perfect substitution between alternative suppliers and places more emphasis on the extent of oligopoly. It allows in principle more variation in the markup in response to cost shocks, and thus has the potential for a richer pattern of response to cost shocks. The Dixit-Stiglitz (1977) model by contrast emphasizes imperfect substitution between alternative suppliers and in its predictions looks very much like the Keynesian model discussed above. An alternative to the Dixit-Stiglitz model, again emphasizing product differentiation, is the Salop (1979) model of competition on a circle.

The Cournot Model

In the Cournot formulation, the analytical focus is on a homogeneous commodity sold in an oligopolistic market. Each seller assumes that other sellers defend their sales volume. I assume that there is an effective spatial separation between the home market and foreign markets, and discuss the pricing in the U.S. market.

For expository purposes, I start with the case of a linear demand function:

$$Q_d = a - bp, \tag{3}$$

where all nonprice determinants are captured in the constant. There are n domestic suppliers and n^* foreign firms with respective sales of q and q^* per firm. Aggregate sales of these firms, Q, have to sum to market demand:

$$Q = nq + n^*q^*. \tag{4}$$

Each firm maximizes profits taking the sales of other firms as given. Profits of the representative domestic and foreign firm in the home market are

$$\pi_i = (p - w)[a - bp - (n - 1)q - n^*q^*],$$

$$\pi_j = \left(\frac{p}{e} - w^*\right)[a - bp - nq - (n^* - 1)q^*]. \tag{5}$$

Maximization gives rise to the reaction functions shown in figure 5.2. The home country's reaction function is JJ, while J^*J^* represents the foreign country. They yield the Cournot-Nash equilibrium shown at point A which gives the equilibrium quantity allocation between representative domestic and foreign firms. The common equilibrium price in the industry

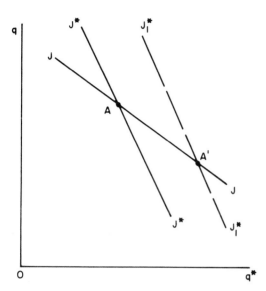

Figure 5.2
The Cournot equilibrium

is given by

$$p = \frac{nw + n^* ew^*}{N} + \frac{a}{bN},$$

$$N \equiv n + n^* + 1.$$

(6)

A dollar appreciation shifts the J^*J^* schedule out and to the right, thus leading to increased foreign sales and reduced domestic sales. At the initial level of sales for every other supplier, the individual foreign firm faces a given marginal revenue schedule in dollars but experiences a reduction in its dollar marginal cost, and hence wishes to increase output. In the new equilibrium at point A', foreign firms increase their output while home firms contract. The industry price declines, as seen from (6).

We are now interested in the extent to which exchange rate movements (or movements in relative unit labor costs) affect the equilibrium price. The elasticity of the equilibrium price with respect to the exchange rate is

$$\varphi = \left(\frac{n^*}{N}\right)\left(\frac{ew^*}{p}\right).$$

(7)

The elasticity formula has two determinants: the relative number of foreign firms (or the relative number of firms with wages not fixed in dollars), and the ratio of marginal cost to price of foreign suppliers. Since both terms are fractions, it is immediately clear from (7) that a dollar appreciation will lower price less than proportionally. The decline in the dollar price is larger the more competitive the industry (i.e., the smaller the markup of price over marginal cost) and the larger the share of imports in total sales. This latter term is represented by n^*/N on the assumption of symmetry and initially equal wages between countries.

Equation (7) is interesting because it stretches all the way from the "small country" case to the case where exchange rates have virtually no impact on home pricing. The small country case, in the trade literature, is the case where a country is a price taker in world markets. In that case, a currency depreciation will raise prices in the same proportion. This is, of course, the limiting case for perfect competition *and* a large number of foreign firms relative to the number of home firms.

The other extreme case where exchange rates have no influence on home prices results when there are few firms in the industry, most of which are domestic. In that case, foreign firms absorb the dollar appreciation primarily in the form of extra profits rather than increased sales.

The Cournot model thus potentially explains both unchanging prices and steep price declines. The market structure—import share and concentration—are the key parameters that explain the outcome.

Consider next U.S. export firms competing in a foreign market. A dollar appreciation will lower their marginal revenue in dollars. With unchanged marginal dollar cost, these firms will contract. In terms of figure 5.2 applied to the foreign market, our schedule *JJ* shifts down and to the left. The common foreign currency price rises, but in dollars it declines, though less than proportionately to the appreciation. Using the same model for the foreign market, we find that the elasticity of foreign price with respect to the exchange rate is

$$\varphi^* = -\left(\frac{n'}{N^*}\right)\left(\frac{w}{ep^*}\right), \tag{8}$$

where n' is the number of domestic firms in the foreign market and N^* the total number of firms. With φ^* a negative fraction, the dollar price of exports, p^*e, has an elasticity $1 + \varphi$, and hence must decline in response to a dollar appreciation.

Remembering that the markets are separated, let us look at the price of U.S. exports relative to the price of imports p/ep^*. In the case of a dollar appreciation, dollar export prices rise relative to import prices if the following condition holds:

$$\varphi > 1 + \varphi^*. \tag{9}$$

In principle, the condition can go either way. In the small country case, export and import prices in dollars fall in the same proportion as the currency appreciates ($\varphi = 1$, $\varphi^* = -1$), so that the relative price p/ep^* remains constant. In general, the outcome depends on the relative oligopolistic structure of the two markets. Export prices will rise relative to import prices in the appreciation case, if at-home import competition is pervasive and foreign markets are strongly affected by U.S. suppliers as well as highly competitive.

Jesus Seade (1983) and Avinash Dixit (1986) have shown that the price effects of disturbances in oligopoly models are highly sensitive to the functional form. It is therefore interesting to ask what happens with a more general functional form. For example, with a constant elasticity demand function $D = Ap\exp(-\beta)$, the elasticity of equilibrium price with respect to the exchange rate becomes $\varphi = (n^*/N)(ew^*/W)$, where $N = n + n^*$ and $W = (n/N)w + (n^*/N)ew^*$. The exchange rate impact thus depends no longer on cost-price markup and, when costs are initially equal between countries, is only a function of the relative number of firms.

In general the elasticity of price with respect to the exchange rate is[6]

$$\varphi = \left(\frac{n^*}{N - \theta}\right)\left(\frac{ew^*}{p}\right) > 0, \tag{9'}$$

where θ is the elasticity of the slope of the inverse demand curve which, for stability, is less than N. In the linear case, the formula reduces to (9) since $\theta = 0$. But, since θ is positive (or zero), there is no upper bound on φ. From public finance applications, it is known that tax disturbances may lead to magnified price adjustment under oligopoly. I find the same possibility here for the exchange rate effect on prices.

The Dixit-Stiglitz Model

The representative consumer in this model maximizes a utility function V with consumption of two commodities z and x as arguments:

$$V = U(z, x),$$
$$x = (\Sigma x_i^a)^{1/a}, \quad 0 < a < 1. \tag{10}$$

I focus on commodity x which is an index of consumption of different brands of the same good. It is assumed that there are n domestic firms supplying some variant each, and n^* foreign firms doing the same.

Maximization yields the demand for each individual brand, as well as the utility-based price index for commodity x:

$$x_i = x \left(\frac{P}{p_i} \right)^c,$$

(11)

$$c = \frac{1}{1-a},$$

$$P = [(\Sigma p_i^h + \Sigma p_j^h)]^{1/h},$$

(12)

$$h = -\frac{a}{1-a}.$$

In equation (12) p_i denotes the price of a brand produced in the home country, p_j is the price of an imported brand, and P is the industry price.

We are now interested in the response of prices to cost shocks. The individual imperfectly competitive firm faces a demand curve as in (11) with the relative price of its product p_i/P as the determinant. The firm assumes it is sufficiently small so that its own price changes leave the industry price, P, unchanged. The representative firm's profits are

$$\pi_i = (p_i - w)x_i.$$

(13)

Maximization yields the familiar constant markup pricing equation:

$$p_i = \alpha w,$$

(14)

$$\alpha = \frac{1}{1 - 1/c},$$

where α depends inversely on the elasticity of substitution among variants. Since the industry structure is symmetric, each domestic firm will follow the same pricing rule with an equal markup.

Now assume again markets are separated and we can thus meaningfully discuss the price set by a foreign firm for our market. Foreign firms in the home market face the same form of demand curve as home firms and hence they also follow the same pricing rule, with the same markup, but with foreign wages in dollars, ew^*, as the base of their pricing:

$$p_j = \alpha e w^*.$$

(15)

From (14) and (15), we have two strong predictions: First the relative price of domestic and foreign variants in the home market depends just on relative unit labor costs in a common currency:

$$\frac{p_i}{p_j} = \frac{w}{ew^*}. \tag{16}$$

Second, it is readily shown that the relative price of a domestic variant in terms of the industry price index (p_i/P) is just a function of the relative wage, w/ew^*. The elasticity of the relative price will be

$$\varphi = \frac{n^* z}{n + n^* z},$$

$$z = \left(\frac{w}{ew^*}\right)^{1/h}. \tag{17}$$

If wages are initially equal between countries, the effect of an exchange rate change on the industry price and on the relative price depends merely on the fraction of firms that has wages fixed in foreign currency, and hence experiences a reduction of its costs in dollars when the dollar appreciates.

Given the wages in home and foreign currency, the Dixit-Stiglitz model provides strong predictions about the impact of dollar appreciation:

The prices of imported variants fall in proportion to the decline of dollar unit labor costs of foreign firms and the prices of domestic variants would remain unchanged.

Exporting firms at home, although they have to compete in foreign markets, still follow their markup pricing on dollar wages. Accordingly, a change in the dollar does not affect their dollar export price. Of course, it does affect their sales and profits. A dollar appreciation will raise their foreign currency price in the same proportion and hence raise their relative price in the foreign market.

The strong prediction of the model is to look for a sharp fall in import prices relative to domestic prices and to see export prices stay constant relative to domestic prices of the same variant. This is, of course, the exact specification of the fixed-price Keynesian model which is derived here as an implication of given labor costs and an invariant markup.

An Extended Dixit-Stiglitz Model

The Dixit-Stiglitz model assumes Chamberlinian imperfect competition and hence each supplier assumes that he does not affect industry price. Strategic interaction with other firms is therefore excluded. But the same structure of differentiated products can easily be adapted to introduce strategic interaction by way of a conjectural variation. Assume, contrary to the preceding section, that the individual firm is sufficiently large to affect industry price. Assume, too, that firms respond to changes in the industry price, and let the conjectural variation be the parameter σ, a fraction between zero and one. Thus a one-percentage-point rise in the industry price is assumed to cause each firm to raise its price by σ percent. Assuming a given conjectural variation rather than deriving it from a dynamic game-theoretic framework is obviously a shortcut. Nor is there any concern here with consistent conjectural variations.

With this adaptation, the individual firm's price policy no longer is a constant markup over unit labor costs but rather becomes

$$p_i = \alpha' w,$$

$$\alpha' \equiv \frac{1}{1 - 1/c(1 - \varepsilon)},$$ (18)

where the term $\varepsilon \equiv (dP/P)/(dP_i/P_i)$ captures the strategic interaction between firms as perceived by the individual price-setting firm. The term is a function of relative prices and the conjectural variation:[7]

$$0 < \varepsilon\left(\sigma, \frac{p_i}{p_j}\right) \pi \equiv \left[\sigma + (1 - \sigma)\left\{n + n^*\left(\frac{p_j}{p_i}\right)^h\right\}\right]^{-1} < 1.$$ (19)

From (18) and (19), it is clear that pricing decisions are now interdependent. We can represent each firm's pricing policy in terms of a price reaction function:

$$p_i = F\left(\frac{p_j}{p_i}, \sigma, c\right) w,$$

$$p_j = F^*\left(\frac{p_i}{p_j}, \sigma, c\right) ew^*.$$ (20)

Figure 5.3 shows the impact of a dollar appreciation in this setting. The schedules HH and H^*H^* are the reaction functions and A is the initial equilibrium.

An appreciation will shift the foreign reaction function up and to the left while leaving the home country's reaction function in place. The magnitude of the shift in H^*H^* at given relative prices (e.g., along the OR ray) is proportional to the appreciation. Thus AB/AO represents the percentage appreciation. The new equilibrium is therefore at A'.

Note that this equilibrium at A' differs from the Dixit-Stiglitz one and resembles more nearly the Cournot model. Foreign firms reduce their price

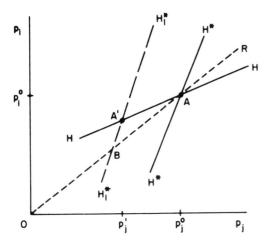

Figure 5.3
The extended Dixit-Stiglitz model

proportionally less than the reduction in dollar unit labor costs and home firms cut their price. But at A', the *relative* price of domestic products has increased compared to A as can be seen by the slope of a ray through A' compared to OR.

Competition on the Circle

I conclude the discussion of manufactures prices with a sketch of a third model of pricing for differentiated products. In the Dixit-Stiglitz model, consumers buy some of each brand of a product. Applied to toothpaste, that is an implausible model; we should therefore look for an alternative model where consumers buy only one brand. A particularly manageable version is the Salop model where consumers' tastes (defined by preferences for the attributes or characteristics of goods) are uniformly spread over the unit circle. Since domestic and foreign firms have potentially different costs, a symmetric equilibrium does not necessarily exist.

I simplify matters by assuming that there is an even number of firms, that domestic and foreign firms alternate along the circle, and that each consumer buys a unit from one or the other of the firms adjacent to his (her) preferred location. This is a very strong simplifying assumption because it implies a very different competition pattern from a circumstance where two foreign firms are adjacent.

Producers have constant unit labor costs and, other than entry costs, there are no fixed costs. With these assumptions, we can derive equilibrium prices and study the impact of dollar cost changes for foreign suppliers. Each consumer is located at a point on the circle. The significance of the location on the circle is that firms may not supply precisely the most preferred product. Accordingly, the consumer is forced to chose between the alternatives offered by the most adjacently located brands. Following Salop, consumers' surplus derived from buying a good that is a distance τ from the best location (on the circle) depends on the price and on the distance and the relationship is assumed linear:

$$h = v - c\tau - p, \tag{21}$$

where v is a constant, c denotes the utility cost per unit distance from the best location, and p is the price of a particular firm. Consumers will be indifferent between the brands offered by two competing firms on either side of their preferred location if the consumers' surplus is the same, $h_i = h_j$. Taking the case of n firms that are equally spaced on the circle, the condition for indifference between a domestic and a foreign supplier is

$$v - c\tau - p^* = v - c\left(\frac{1}{n - \tau}\right) - p. \tag{22}$$

Hence the distance served by a foreign firm is an increasing function of the price charged by domestic firms and a declining function of its own price:

$$\tau = \frac{p + c/n - p^*}{2c}. \tag{22'}$$

Profits for the foreign firm are equal to $2Lx$ times the excess of price over marginal cost:

$$\pi^* = \frac{(p^* - ew^*)2L(p + c/n - p^*)}{2c}, \tag{23}$$

where L denotes the total number of consumers and hence L also represents the density per unit distance served by the firm. Since the firm serves both sides of its location, $2L\tau$ is the total number of units sold. Maximization taking domestic price as given yields the foreign reaction function:

$$p^* = \frac{p + c/n + ew^*}{2}. \tag{24}$$

The typical domestic firm's reaction function is derived in the same manner:

$$p = \frac{p^* + c/n + w}{2}. \tag{25}$$

From (24) and (25), we obtain the solution for the prices charged by home and foreign firms:

$$p = \frac{c}{n} + \frac{ew^* + 2w}{3},$$

$$p^* = \frac{c}{n} + \frac{2ew^* + w}{3}. \tag{26}$$

From (26), we can calculate the elasticity of prices with respect to the exchange rate in this model:

$$\varphi = \left(\frac{1}{3}\right)\left(\frac{ew^*}{p}\right),$$

$$\varphi^* = \left(\frac{2}{3}\right)\left(\frac{ew^*}{p^*}\right). \tag{27}$$

Note that these elasticities once again are fractions. If wages and hence prices are initially equal, $w = ep^*$, the elasticities simplify to the following expressions:

$$\varphi = \frac{\psi}{3},$$

$$\varphi^* = \frac{2\psi}{3}, \tag{27'}$$

$$\psi \equiv \frac{1}{1 + c/nw}.$$

The elasticities show that the relative price of imported goods declines and that the change in the relative price $\psi/3$ is smaller, the smaller the number of firms in the industry, and the lower the substitutability as measured by the term c. Along with the change in relative prices, there will be a shift in demand from home firms to foreign firms as consumers trade off the reduction in price for a larger distance from their most-preferred brand location.

At this point, it is worth commenting on the properties of the equilibrium when there is not an alternating pattern between domestic and foreign firms. Specifically, suppose that there are five firms, two domestic and three adjacent foreign firms. It is apparent that the middle foreign firm competes only with foreign firms, and hence will cut its price more than the outlying foreign firms that compete with home firms which have not experienced a cost reduction. Hence there will be three prices.

The same model can be applied to the foreign market. In terms of foreign exchange, the prices will rise and the relative price of our export brands abroad will rise. But, because it rises proportionally less than the currency appreciates, the export price in dollars changes in the proportion:

$$\varphi' = 1 - \frac{2\psi^*}{3},$$

$$\psi^* = \frac{1}{1 + c/n^*w},$$

(28)

where n^* is the total number of firms serving the foreign market. We can therefore find the change in the relative price of domestic exports in terms of imports and in terms of home brands:

$$\varphi' - \varphi^* = 1 - \frac{2(\psi + \psi^*)}{3},$$

$$\varphi' - \varphi = 1 - \frac{2\psi^*}{3} - \frac{\psi}{3}.$$

(29)

The first point to note is that export prices may rise or fall in terms of import prices as a result of appreciation. But the fewer the number of firms in each country, the more likely that an appreciation leads to a *fall* in the relative price of exports. By contrast, as the number of firms increases (and hence ψ and ψ^* tend to unity), the relative price of exports *must* rise, reflecting the increase in the relative unit labor cost at home which sets competitive relative prices.

The second point is that export prices may decline relative to domestic prices as a result of an appreciation. This must be the case if the number of firms in the two markets is the same ($\psi = \psi^*$). As the number of firms increases, the relative price tends to remain unchanged. This result arises because price gets competed down to marginal cost which is the same for home and export production. It is apparent from (29) that the change in the relative price in terms of importables will always be larger than that in terms of domestic goods.

Summary

We have now seen common features of a number of models: they all predict that appreciation should lead to a decline in the price of imports. In the case of homogeneous goods, domestic firms of course fully match the decline in price. If products are differentiated, it will always be the case that the relative price of the imported brands declines in response to an appreciation. The extent of the decline depends on a measure of competition and on the relative number of home and foreign firms.

The empirically testable hypotheses concern price-marginal cost markups and the behavior of relative prices. For differentiated products, it is always the case that export and domestic prices will stay closer in line than import and domestic prices. In the Dixit-Stiglitz model, imports fall in terms of domestic goods and the relative price of export goods stays unchanged in terms of home goods. In other models the export price can in principle even decline in terms of imports.

5.4 Some Evidence

Econometric testing of the hypotheses is unfortunately precluded by the absence of a comprehensive matched data set of export, import, and domestic prices. The BLS now publishes transactions prices for exports and imports that are disaggregated to the 4-digit level and classified on the SIC basis. But few of the series go back beyond the early 1980's. Where they do, the revisions of the SIC-based U.S. producer prices in most cases are either not all available yet, or only go back very few years. A complete overlap between export, import, and domestic prices for more than two years apparently only exists for fewer than a handful of cases, and overlap between any two series is limited to less than a dozen.

At a more informal level there are interesting patterns to observe. First, consider a comparison of U.S. export prices in dollars with those of Germany and Japan. Table 5.3 shows the percentage loss in U.S. competitiveness over the period 1980:IV to 1984:IV, using as a sample all available data at a highly disaggregated level. In the U.S.-Germany comparison, there are 36 different matched time-series, in the U.S.-Japan comparison, there are 20. Typical items in the list of commodities are "gears and gear units," or "household electrical space heating."

The data do not allow us to tell whether these are prices of the same products sold in the same third market (say France), or whether they represent exports to different markets (say U.S. sales to France and German

Table 5.3
Changes in relative prices: United States vs. Germany and Japan (percentage change in relative export prices: 1980:IV−1984:IV)

	United States−Germany	United States−Japan
Mean	39.3	24.9
Standard deviation	6.1	8.3

Source: See the appendix.

Table 5.4
Cumulative price change: 1980:IV−1985:I

	Export prices	Import prices
Nonelectrical machinery	18.0	−10.1
Scientific instruments	18.0	−13.4

Source: See the appendix.

sales in the United States). Accordingly, we cannot tell from these data whether they reflect market segmentation or imperfect substitution. They are consistent with markets being segmented, but goods being perfect substitutes and having a common price in the same market independent of supply source. But they are also consistent with markets being integrated —a common world market—but goods being imperfect substitutes so that the relative price of different suppliers can change.

Consider next a comparison of the transactions prices of U.S. exports and U.S. imports in the same commodity group. There is overwhelming evidence that, virtually without exception, the dollar appreciation of 1980– 85 has been accompanied by an increase in the price of exports relative to imports. Evidence in this direction comes from export-import price comparisons at the more narrow 2- and 4-digit level. An example is provided in table 5.4 which shows data for two 2-digit industries.

Figure 5.4 shows the ratio of export prices to import prices for telecommunications equipment and for nonelectrical machinery. The figure also shows the index of the *nominal* dollar exchange rate index. The dollar appreciation since 1980 gives rise to an increase in the relative price of exports in terms of imports. Table 5.4 shows indexes of the relative export-import prices for all series where comparable SIC data exist. The same pattern would be obtained by comparing U.S. to German and Japanese export prices in these individual commodity groups. The first finding then is, that across industries, virtually without exception, export prices have

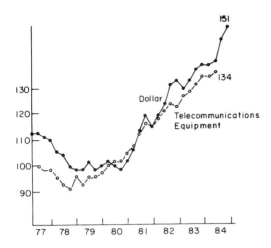

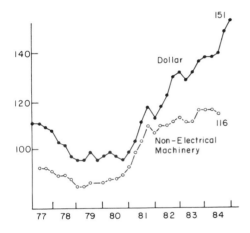

Figure 5.4

Table 5.5
The ratio of export to import prices (index 1980:I = 100)

	2,011	301	35	353	356	3,569	357	3,643	38
1979:IV	105	103	—	100	95	96	—	91	92
1981:IV	108	105	112	118	119	121	106	115	108
1985:I	126	104	131	135	152	143	110	152	136

Note: The headings as SIC codes. For definitions and source, see the appendix.

Table 5.6
The ratio of export to domestic prices (index 1980:IV = 100)

	3,546	3,555	3,674	3,533	3,523	3,519	3,494	2,011	3,537
1979:IV	101	101	109	99	99	103	99	110	97
1981:IV	100	104	91	100	100	103	103	93	99
1985:I	95	107	93	100	102	105	108	108	100

Note: See table 5.5.

Table 5.7
The ratio of import to domestic prices (index 1980:IV = 100)

	2,311	2,033	3,651	3,143	3,531	2,435	2,011	3,312	3,313
1979:IV	100	108	—	96	98	120	105	101	88
1981:IV	101	92	100	95	90	114	92	98	88
1985:I	110	90	92	88	76	102	85	84	74

Note: See table 5.5.

increased relative to import prices. This is true at the level of individual commodities, but also, as shown at the outset of the paper, for aggregate export and import unit values.

This result would obtain strictly only in the Dixit-Stiglitz model. In the other formulations, it is a possibility though it need not occur. Tables 5.5 through 5.7 look at the price of exports and imports relative to each other and relative to domestic producer prices in the commodity group. Export prices change little relative to domestic prices, even though there is no clear pattern of decline in all industries. By contrast, most import prices decline in terms of domestic prices. But the order of magnitude of the decline remains relatively small compared to the change in relative unit labor costs. With a change in relative unit labor costs of more than 40 percent, the decline in the relative price is in most cases less than 20 percent. That is not at all out of line with the theory once some degree of "pricing to the American market" is taken into account, just as the price-setting models above suggest.

It is worth noting that, at the retail level, this effect would obtain even more strongly. The reason is that here distribution costs come into play, so that even with the full pass-through of cost reductions on imported goods, the proportional decline in the price of imported goods would be much less than the exchange rate appreciation.

5.5 Concluding Remarks

The models reviewed in this chapter focus on a relatively short time perspective. The wage rate is assumed not to react to changes in output and profitability, and the number and location of firms in an industry is unaffected. These assumptions are plausible in the short term, but it is clear that a sustained real appreciation will ultimately show its effects in wage cuts in those industries where the loss in competitiveness causes unemployment and wage increases in the expanding sectors. Firms will close in high-wage areas and entry into an industry will take place in areas where labor costs are low. These longer-term adjustments are also part of the macroeconomics of adjustment to exchange rate movements. They imply that the absolute and relative numbers of firms (n and n^*) will be endogenous as well as the location of firms on the product circle.

It is clear from the analysis offered here that for these issues, a microeconomic perspective will also be helpful. In particular, it will be interesting to see how pricing decisions are affected by entry and relocation possibilities at an international level, and by the anticipated persistence of disequilibrium exchange rates.

The analysis developed here has application not only to the exchange rate question but also to the short-term effect of trade liberalization. The common argument is that a small country by opening up can take advantage of the world markets, enjoying price reductions in proportion to the tariff reduction. That clearly assumes perfect competition. If markets are less than fully competitive, the analysis offered here becomes relevant to the trade liberalization issue.

5.6 Data Appendix

The data in table 5.2 are unit values obtained from Data Resources, Inc., U.S. Central Data Bank.

The data in table 5.3 are compiled by the Bureau of Labor Statistics, Division of International Prices. The unpublished data are from a compilation entitled "Comparisons of U.S., German and Japanese Export Price Indices," dated May 1985. The data for export and import prices in tables 5.4—5.7 are SIC-based price data compiled by the Branch of Export and Import Price Indexes of the Bureau of Labor Statistics. The data are from a printout, dated July 1985. The domestic price index for SIC-based producer prices is obtained from Data Resources, Inc. In table 5.4 the data refer to SIC codes 34 and 38, respectively. In tables 5.5—5.7, the following are the definitions of the SIC codes shown in the table heading:

Table 5.5: 2011—Meat and Meat Packing Products; 301—Tires and Inner Tubes; 35—Machinery, except electrical; 353—Construction, Mining Equipment; 3569—General Industrial Machines; 357—Office, Computing and Accounting Machinery; 3643—Current-Carrying Wiring Devices; 38—Scientific Instruments, Optical Goods, Clocks.

Table 5.6: 3546—Power-Driven Hand Tools; 3555—Printing Trades Machines, Parts; 3674—Semiconductor Devices; 3533—Oil and Gas Field Equipment; 3523—Farm Machinery and Equipment; 3519—Internal Combustion Engines; 3494—Metal Valves, Pipe Fittings; 2011—Meat and Meat-Packing Products; 3537—Industrial Trucks, Portable Elevators.

Table 5.7: 2311—Men's or Boy's Suits & Coats, except Raincoats; 2033—Canned and Preserved Fruits, Vegetables, Jams, Juices; 3651—Video and Audio Equipment; 3143—Men's Footwear except Athletic; 3531—Construction Machinery; 2435—Hardwood Veneer and Plywood; 2011—Meat and Meat-Packing Products; 3311—Rolling Mill Products; 3313—Electrometallurgical Products.

The index of the nominal dollar exchange rate in figure 5.4 is the Morgan Guaranty trade weighted index of the dollar. The series was obtained from Data Resources, Inc. The series for telecommunications equipment and nonelectrical machinery are unpublished, SITC-based prices of exports and imports obtained from the Division of International Prices, Bureau of Labor Statistics.

Notes

I am indebted to Olivier Blanchard, Stanley Fischer, Paul Krugman, Michael Rothschild, Julio Rotemberg, Sergio Sanchez, Lawrence Summers, and Jean Tirole. Avinash Dixit provided especially valuable suggestions. An earlier version of this chapter was presented at the 1985 NBER Summer Workshop and the NBER Meeting on Business Fluctuations, and I acknowledge helpful comments received on those occasions. David Wilcox provided valuable research assistance.

1. See Avinash Dixit (1984) and Elhanan Helpman and Paul Krugman (1985) for extensive work on and references to trade applications. In the macro context, see Olivier Blanchard (1985), Oliver Hart (1982), and N. Gregory Mankiw (1985).

2. For a review of the PPP literature, see my papers (1985, 1986).

3. Joshua Aizenman (1985, 1986) and Alberto Giovannini (1985) investigate price-setting behavior in the context of exchange rate movements. Their focus, however, is on short-term issues of transactions costs and uncertainty rather than on

the large, persistent movements in the real exchange rate. See, too, the more recent papers by Catherine Mann (1986), Robert Feinberg (1986), and Eugene Flood (1986).

4. For a review of PPP, see my paper (1985).

5. A fourth item of relevance is the functional form of the demand curve. See Jesus Seade (1983) and Dixit (1986).

6. Let $p = F(Q)$ be the inverse market demand curve. The elasticity of the slope of the inverse demand curve then is $\theta = -QF''(Q)/F'(Q)$. The derivation of (9') is as follows: The individual firm maximizes profits $\pi = F(Q)q - wq$ and $\pi = (F(Q)/e)q^* - w^*q^*$. The first-order conditions are $F(Q) + qF'(Q) = w$ and $F(Q) + q^*F'(Q) = ew^*$. Multiplying the first-order conditions respectively by n and n^* and adding them yields: $(n + n^*)F(Q) + QF'(Q) = nw + n^*ew^*$. Differentiating this expression, using $dp = F'(Q)dQ$, yields the expression for θ in (9').

7. The derivation is as follows: maximization of profits for a domestic firm k in (13) yields $1 + (p_k - w)c\,(\varepsilon - 1)/p_k = 0$ which yields the markup equation in (18). The elasticity ε of the aggregate price level with respect to a variation in an individual domestic price p_k is derived as follows: from (12) we have $p^h = p_k^h + \Sigma p_{i \neq k}^h + \Sigma p_j^h$. Now assuming that $\sigma = d\ln p_i/d\ln P$ for all firms i and j other than k, we obtain the elasticity of aggregate price with respect to a variation in p_k.

References

Aizenman, Joshua. 1985. "Monopolistic Competition and Deviations from PPP." Unpublished manuscript. University of Chicago.

Aizenman, Joshua. 1986. "Testing Deviations from Purchasing Power Parity (PPP)." *Journal of International Money and Finance* 5 (March): 25–35.

Blanchard, Olivier. 1985. "Monopolistic Competition, Small Menu Costs, and Real Effects of Nominal Money." Unpublished manuscript. MIT.

Dixit, Avinash. 1984. "International Trade Policy for Oligopolistic Industries." *Economic Journal* 94, suppl. 1–16.

Dixit, Avinash. 1986. "Comparative Statics for Oligopoly," *International Economic Review* 27 (February): 107–122.

Dixit, Avinash, and Stiglitz, Joseph. 1977. "Monopolistic Competition and Optimum Product Diversity." *American Economic Review* 67 (June): 297–308.

Dornbusch, Rudiger. 1983. "Flexible Exchange Rates and Interdependence." *IMF Staff Papers*, March. Reprinted in *Dollars, Debts and Deficits*. Cambridge: MIT Press, 1986.

Dornbusch, Rudiger. 1985. "Purchasing Power Parity." NBER Working Paper No. 1591. In *Palgrave's Dictionary of Economics*. London: Macmillan, forthcoming.

Dornbusch, Rudiger. 1986. "Inflation, Exchange Rates and Stabilization." *Essays in International Finance*, International Finance Section. Princeton University.

Giovannini, Alberto. 1985. "Exchange Rates and Traded Goods Prices." Unpublished manuscript, Columbia University.

Feinberg, Robert M. 1986. "The Interaction of Foreign Exchange and Market Power Effects on German Domestic Prices." *Journal of Industrial Economics* (September): 61—70.

Flood, Eugene, Jr., 1986. "An Empirical Analysis of the Effects of Exchange Rate Changes on Goods Prices." Unpublished manuscript, Stanford University.

Hart, Oliver. 1982. "A Model of Imperfect Competition with Keynesian Features," *Quarterly Journal of Economics* 97 (February): 109—138.

Helpman, Ephanan, and Krugman, Paul. 1985. *Market Structure and Foreign Trade*. Cambridge: MIT Press.

Kravis, Irving, and Lipsey, Robert. 1978. "Price Behavior in the Light of Balance of Payments Theories." *Journal of International Economics* 8 (May): 193—246.

Kravis, Irving, and Lipsey, Robert. 1984. "Prices and Terms of Trade for Developed Country Exports of Manufactured Goods." In B. Csikos-Nagy et al., eds., *The Economics of Relative Prices*. New York: Saint Martin's Press.

Krugman, Paul. 1986. "Pricing to Market when the Exchange Rate Changes." NBER Working Paper No. 1926. May.

Mankiw, N. Gregory. 1985. "Small Menu Costs and Large Business Cycles: A Macroeconomic Model of Monopoly." *Quarterly Journal of Economics* 100 (May): 529—537.

Mann, Catherine. 1986. "Prices, Profit Margins and Exchange Rates." *Federal Reserve Bulletin* 72 (June): 366—379.

Seade, Jesus. 1983. "Prices, Profits and Taxes in Oligopoly." Working Paper, University of Warwick.

Salop, Steven. 1979. "Monopolistic Competition with Outside Goods," *Bell Journal of Economics* 10 (Spring): 141—156.

II

Special Topics in Exchange Rate Economics

The lowest common denominator for the essays in this part is that they deal with exchange rate problems. The first essay in this part is the first article I wrote on flexible exchange rates. In writing on exchange rate determination, I was struck with the fact that the asset market (or the stock market) was where exchange rates were determined, not in the balance of payments. Of course, the Mundell-Fleming model had just that property, but it took me a while to see that point. In other respects the essay is of interest in that it signals a direction the literature does not in fact take, namely an emphasis on money versus real assets rather than the money–bond model of the Mundell-Fleming model. Only recently, with the work of Mike Gavin and Maurice Obstfeld, is there an interest in the money–capital model.

The next essay deals with exchange risk and represents an attempt to deal with the issue of imperfect asset substitution. The portfolio balance model of flexible exchange rates emphasizes that home and foreign bonds are imperfect substitutes. In this model imperfect substitution is derived from the combination of risk-averse speculators and less than full correlation of real rates of return. When the paper was written, it drew on the work of Pentti Kouri and Jeffrey Frankel. I would note with hindsight that the integration of money in the model is even less satisfactory today than it was at the time. But I am not certain that cash in advance variations, even though they would be formally more satisfying, offer a much better solution.

The next two essays deal with dual exchange rates. Dual exchange rates address a simple problem: how to have control over monetary policy and yet not suffer the instability of the exchange rate and price level that might result from flexible exchange rates. It is not clear that in practice a dual exchange rate system offers significant room for policy independence, but the papers set out how such a system works and what basic relationships would hold. The topic remains an important one as many countries do rely, rightly or wrongly, on dual rates at least to offer a shock absorber role. Yet, though there may be macroeconomic advantages, there are also issues of resource allocation, and on that count multiple rates may be troublesome. The present essays cannot answer the question of welfare economics, but important work by Aaron Tornell suggests that there may be a rather strong case even in rigorous, new classical models.

The paper on the black market for the U.S. dollar in Brazil grew out of an examination question I gave at the Getulio Vargas Foundation in Rio de Janeiro. The coauthors all passed the exam. The paper is interesting in that it shows that the portfolio balance model, applied in a partial equilibrium setting, stands up well to empirical testing. Interestingly, even the predicted seasonal pattern of the black-market premium follows the path predicted by the model. At an analytical level the main interest of the model is the integration of stock and flow elements of exchange rate determination. In this model of rational, forward-looking speculators, the determinants of the current account matter as much as the existing stock of assets. This part of the analysis draws on earlier work with Stanley Fischer.

The article on exchange rate rules places exchange rate economics in the context of Fischer-Taylor overlapping long-term wage contracts. In addition to the wage rule there are an exchange rate rule and a rule of monetary accommodation. The model shows that a rule of maintaining relatively constant the real exchange rate, accommodating price disturbances by depreciation, may increase the variability of output. The reason is that real balances will tend to be more unstable.

This point is of interest in view of the strongly accepted view that maintaining constancy of the real exchange rate is sound policy in the context of an economy with high and variable inflation. The implicit assumption, in advocating a stable real exchange rate, is that fluctuations of the real exchange rate hurt trade performance. But it is also true that accommodating price level disturbances by exchange depreciation makes for more unstable inflation, which is costly.

The concluding essay in this part offers a broad overview of exchange rate economics. The review claims that the Mundell-Fleming model does well in predicting the impact of monetary and fiscal policies under flexible exchange rates. Among current issues of research the paper highlights primarily two: the adjustment of traded goods prices to exchange rate changes, and the possibility that exchange markets are inefficient. The adjustment of traded goods prices is a central new issue in balance of payments economics: the old-fashioned view that exchange rate movements change one for one a country's competitiveness no longer stands up. Models that take into account strategic pricing decisions seem much more appropriate in the aftermath of the dollar experience of the 1980s. This experience, and others before, also raise the question of whether asset markets are efficient. The hypothesis of short-horizon speculation, and of bubbles that lead to excess volatility, is being discussed, though not supported. The next step is to ask whether in such circumstances dual exchange rates or some other form of market segmentation enhances micro- and macroeconomic efficiency.

6

Capital Mobility, Flexible Exchange Rates, and Macroeconomic Equilibrium

This chapter develops a formal two-country model with flexible exchange rates and capital mobility. The model departs from some of the recent literature, and, in particular, Mundell (1968), in three respects: we assume continuous full employment and price flexibility, the government's policies are subject to a budget constraint that is explicitly recognized, and the effect of capital movements on asset positions and income is used to generate the equilibrium path of the economies over time.

The basic model is developed in section 6.1 and has as its key elements a wealth-saving relationship as well as a portfolio-balance relation. Both these elements obviously derive from Metzler (1951, 1968). In section 6.2 we study the equilibrium properties of the model for given policy parameters. Short-run equilibrium is defined as of a given distribution of equity in the world. Associated with the short-run equilibrium is a rate of capital movement that generates the dynamics of the system.[1] The long-run equilibrium is characterized by desired wealth and long-run demand functions for equity as well as the world supply of assets. After the study of equilibrium we turn in section 6.3 to some comparative static applications to determine the short- and long-run effects of various combinations of government policies. In section 6.4 the behavior of the exchange rate is discussed in some detail, while in section 6.5 the model is extended to accommodate inflationary finance and the interdependence between national inflation rates is discussed.

6.1 The Model

In this section we lay out the structure of the model as well as the assumptions about exogenous variables and government policy. We will

Originally published in E. Classen and P. Salen (eds.), *Recent Developments in International Monetary Economics* (Amsterdam: North-Holland, 1976), pp. 261–278. © North-Holland Publishing Company.

assume that there is a single homogeneous good, the output of which is given in each country; along with the quantity of output income distribution is predetermined. The production of output, y, gives rise to income from labor y^0 and income from capital v,

$$y = y^0 + v. \tag{1}$$

With trade in assets we have to distinguish income accruing to domestic residents from the value of output; the difference arises from a net creditor or debtor position. Denoting disposable income by z, we have

$$z = y^0 + a - T, \tag{2}$$

where a denotes the number of permanent real income streams owned by domestic residents and where T denotes real lump-sum taxes.

Asset preferences between money and equities are characterized by the demand for real balances, L,

$$L = \delta(r)w, \quad \delta_r < 0. \tag{3}$$

According to (3) the demand for real balances is a fraction δ of real wealth where the fraction is a function of the rate of interest and where real wealth is defined as the sum of real balances, m, and real equity holdings, a/r,

$$w \equiv m + \frac{a}{r}. \tag{4}$$

Saving is assumed to be proportional to the excess of target wealth, $\bar{w}$, over actual wealth,

$$S = \gamma(\bar{w} - w), \tag{5}$$

and target wealth is proportional to labor income less lump-sum taxes,

$$\bar{w} = \phi(r)(y^0 - T), \quad \phi_r > 0. \tag{6}$$

It will be convenient to rewrite actual real wealth as a function of security holdings assuming portfolio balance equilibrium. Given the equality of the demand and supply of real balances subject to the budget constraint in (4), we have

$$m = \frac{\delta(a/r)}{1 - \delta}, \tag{7}$$

and after substitution in (4), we obtain

$$w = \frac{a/r}{1 - \delta}. \tag{8}$$

Substitution of (6) and (8) in the saving function (5) yields the (reduced form) rate of saving as an increasing function of the rate of interest and a decreasing function of security holdings and taxes,

$$S = \gamma \left[\phi(r)(y^0 - T) - \frac{a/r}{1 - \delta} \right] = \tilde{S}(r, a, T). \tag{9}$$

The government spends at the rate G on goods and the budget is balanced. The government income derives from lump-sum taxes, T, and from the government's holdings of real income streams, g, where the latter may be negative if the government is a net issuer of debt and where it is assumed that government real consols are perfect substitutes for equities,

$$G = T + g. \tag{10}$$

Furthermore the government determines the nominal quantity of money, M. The exchange rate is flexible and links the domestic and foreign currency prices of goods in a manner familiar from purchasing-power-parity theory,

$$P = P^*e, \tag{11}$$

where P and P^* are the domestic and foreign price levels and where e is the domestic currency price of foreign exchange.[2]

We define next the trade balance and current account surplus. The trade balance surplus, B, is equal to the excess of domestic output over domestic absorption,

$$B \equiv y - (z - S) - G = (v - g - a) + S + (T + g - G). \tag{12}$$

The current account surplus, C, is equal to the trade surplus plus the service account surplus, $a + g - v$, or

$$C \equiv B + (a + g - v) = S + (T + g - G). \tag{13}$$

From (13) the current account surplus is equal to the rate of saving plus the government budget surplus which is assumed to equal zero. Noting that under flexible exchange rates the current account surplus equals the capital account deficit we appreciate that the rate of capital outflow is fully specified by the saving function and does not require an ad hoc "capital flow function".

A last point concerns the world supply of securities, Q. This is equal to the number of claims to income from capital in each country, v and v^*, respectively, less the respective governments' holdings of claims, g and g^*, where the latter may be negative,

$$Q \equiv v + v^* - g - g^*. \tag{14}$$

Finally we will assume that the foreign country is characterized by a similar system of behavioral equations and government policies. This completes the description of the model, and we can turn now to the study of the equilibrium of the system.

6.2 Equilibrium

In this section we study the equilibrium properties of the model. First the equilibrium is studied for a given distribution of equities. Next we turn to the dynamics that describe the rate at which equities are redistributed in the world and finally we consider the steady state of the model.

Short-Run Equilibrium

At a point in time the distribution of equities between countries is given since under flexible exchange rates it is not possible for a country in the aggregate to sell money for securities.[3] This fact will permit us to use the distribution of securities as a state variable contingent upon which short-run equilibrium is defined. Over time the distribution is endogenous since saving or dissaving allows a country to add to or subtract from its holdings of securities. It is that process of redistribution that moves the system over time and connects the short run to the steady state.

The equilibrium conditions at any point in time are that the demand for money equals the real money supply in each country and that the *world* goods market clears.[4] These equilibrium conditions are stated in

$$m = \left(\frac{\delta}{1 - \delta}\right)\left(\frac{a}{r}\right), \tag{15}$$

$$m^* = \left(\frac{\delta^*}{1 - \delta^*}\right)\left(\frac{a^*}{r}\right), \tag{16}$$

$$S(r, w) + S^*(r, w^*) = 0, \tag{17}$$

where in writing (17) we have assumed given taxes and a balanced budget so that equilibrium in the world goods market implies that one country's rate of saving has to equal the other country's rate of dissaving.

Given each country's security holdings, a_0 and a_0^*, real balances by equation (7) will be a function of the number of securities and so will be wealth by equation (8) so that we can rewrite the world goods market equilibrium condition in (17) in terms of the reduced-form saving functions that embody the conditions of portfolio balance in each country as developed in (9). Deriving an equation analogous to (9) for the foreign country, we have as an equilibrium condition of the system of equations (15)–(17),

$$\tilde{S}(r, a, T) + \tilde{S}^*(r, a^*, T^*) = 0. \tag{18}$$

The determination of the equilibrium interest rate and along with it the equilibrium rate of saving and the equilibrium stock of real balances is shown in figure 6.1.

In the left-hand figure we show the reduced-form saving rate, for a given level of a, as an increasing function of the rate of interest. The foreign rate of *dis* saving in turn is shown as a decreasing function of the rate of interest. Equilibrium in the world goods and asset markets obtains at point A, where the home country's rate of saving equals the foreign country's rate of dissaving.[5] In the right-hand panel we show the home country's money market equilibrium schedule LM. Associated with the equilibrium interest rate, r_0, and given the number of equities, a_0, the equilibrium stock of real balances is m_0.

Dynamics

The short-run equilibrium in figure 6.1 is defined for a given stock of securities a and a^*. Given government holdings and in view of (14), we can take domestic holdings, a, to characterize the distribution of equities. Associated with the equilibrium in figure 6.1 is an equilibrium interest rate,

$$r = \tilde{r}(a), \tag{19}$$

and an equilibrium saving rate,

$$S = \tilde{S}(\tilde{r}(a), a). \tag{20}$$

Furthermore we note that the rate of increase in domestic holdings of equities is equal to the rate of saving times the rate of interest or the rate of saving divided by the price of equities,

$$\dot{a} = \tilde{r}(a)\tilde{S}(\tilde{r}(a), a). \tag{21}$$

Equation (21) governs the behavior of the system over time, and we will assume that a solution exists and is unique. It is important to note that the dynamics described here correspond to a continuous sequence of short-run

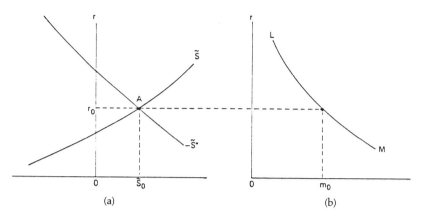

Figure 6.1

equilibria as defined in figure 6.1 so that all the time markets clear and the behavioral equations are satisfied.

The dynamics may be studied in terms of figure 6.1. An increase in the domestic holdings of equities, a, shifts the domestic LM schedule to the right since it generates at the initial interest rate an excess demand for real balances. The reduced-form saving schedule, similarly, is affected and will shift to the left since at the initial interest rate target wealth is unaffected while actual wealth increases from both the increase in equity holdings and the accompanying increase in the equilibrium quantity of real balances. Abroad the opposite is true so that the foreign *dis* saving schedule shifts to the left, too. The net result is a decrease in the *equilibrium* rate of saving, S, and an increase or decrease in the rate of interest. Provided the system is stable the process of redistribution will continue shifting both saving schedules leftward until they intersect on the vertical axis. At that time saving and hence capital flows are zero and each country has attained its steady state equilibrium.

For the stability of the process described by (21) we require that in the neighborhood of the steady-state level of domestic security holdings, $\bar{a}$, an increase in domestic security holdings causes a net capital inflow or de-cumulation of assets by domestic residents. It is shown in the appendix that this stability condition is satisfied at the point of long-run equilibrium.

Long-Run Equilibrium

In this section we study the properties of the long-run equilibrium. In addition to the equilibrium conditions in (15) to (17) the long-run equilib-

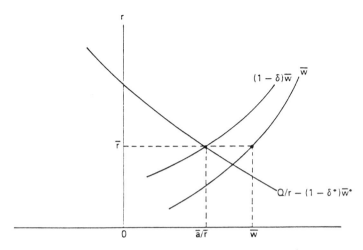

Figure 6.2

rium must satisfy the restriction that saving be zero in each country so that $w = \bar{w}$ and $w^* = \bar{w}^*$. Furthermore, since in the long run the distribution of the world supply of equities is endogenous, it must be true that the world demand for equities equals the world supply. That equilibrium condition is written as[6]

$$(1 - \delta)\bar{w} + (1 - \delta^*)\bar{w}^* = \frac{Q}{r}. \tag{22}$$

We note that in (22) we have, by the definition of long-run equilibrium, constrained actual wealth equal to long-run wealth. The determination of the long-run equilibrium interest rate and wealth is shown in figure 6.2. The negatively sloped schedule represents the supply of equities to the home country; it is negatively sloped since a decrease in the interest rate raises the value of the stock outstanding, Q/r, and reduces the foreign demand. The domestic long-run wealth and the part of it to be held in securities are shown as upward sloping schedules. The equilibrium obtains where the domestic demand of securities equals the supply to the home country. The corresponding rate of interest is $\bar{r}$. In that equilibrium position the home country will hold $\bar{a}/\bar{r}$ of securities and $\bar{w} - \bar{a}/\bar{r}$ of real balances.

Associated with the equilibrium described in figure 6.2 is a composition of the trade balance that will depend on the domestic holdings of securities relative to the number of claims issued domestically. The trade balance surplus in the long run equals

$$\overline{B} = v - g - \overline{a}, \tag{23}$$

and is equal to the service account deficit.

6.3 Some Comparative Static Applications

In this section we consider some of the comparative static properties of the model. For that purpose we note that both the short- and long-run equilibrium are defined relative to a set of exogenous variables in particular the nominal quantity of money in each country as well as lump-sum taxes and central bank holdings of securities. Furthermore the government budget constraint implies restrictions on the independence of the parameters since changes in government expenditure have to be financed by either tax changes or changes in the government's net holdings of securities.

A Tax-Financed Increase in Government Expenditure

Consider now the effects of an increase in government spending financed by an increase in lump-sum taxes. Assuming an initial position of long-run equilibrium the impact effect is to reduce, by (6), the level of target wealth and accordingly, by (5), domestic saving. It follows that at the initial equilibrium interest rate there will be a *world* excess demand for goods forcing up the equilibrium interest rate until enough "crowding out" has been generated for *world* consumption to decline by the increase in government expenditure.

Associated with that higher interest rate is a current account deficit for the home country and a lower level of real balances. Given the nominal quantity of money this implies that the domestic price level will have risen. In the foreign country the increase in the world interest rate similarly causes desired real balances to decline and the price level to increase.

Consider next the long-run effects allowing the distribution of equities to be endogenous. In terms of figure 6.2 the long-run effects of the increase will be reflected in a leftward shift of both the target wealth function and the long-run demand for securities function. The world excess supply schedule will be unaffected and accordingly we obtain in the long run an increase in the world interest rate, an increase in foreign wealth and security holdings, and a reduction in domestic wealth and security holdings. The increase in foreign security holdings implies an increase in foreign steady state consumption and a worsening in the foreign trade balance. Domestic private consumption will be reduced by the increase in taxes and the reduction in security holdings.

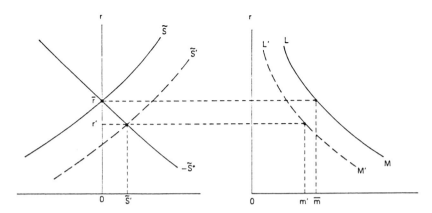

Figure 6.3

An Increase in Government Spending Financed by Income from Securities

The government budget constraint in (10) suggests that an increase in government spending can be financed by government income from securities. Accordingly we consider now a combination of policies: A once-and-for-all open-market purchase of securities and a permanent increase in government spending so that $dG = dg$ and $dM = (P/r)dg$.

Consider now the short-run effect of that policy combination. The increase in the domestic nominal quantity of money and the corresponding reduction in security holdings generate at the initial interest rate and price level an excess supply of money and an excess demand for securities. In the aggregate attempt to sell money for securities the price level is bid up proportionately more than the nominal quantity of money so that real balances decline. This is shown in figure 6.3 by a leftward shift of the LM schedule. Corresponding to the reduction in real balances, we have a decline in real wealth that shifts the home country's saving schedule to the right and thus generates a world excess supply of goods at the initial interest rate. The equilibrium interest rate will decline to r' and the home country will be running a current account surplus and be a net importer of securities.

The long-run equilibrium is characterized by the fact that the supply of securities to the private sector, Q, is reduced by the government's purchases. In terms of figure 6.2 we have a leftward shift of the excess supply schedule facing the home country and accordingly a decline in the equilibrium interest rate, in real wealth and in security holdings in both countries. The corresponding reduction in disposable income and private absorption is obviously the manner in which the government expenditure is financed.

It is interesting to note that in the long run the effect of increased government spending is to reduce private absorption in *both* countries, while in the short run it lowered domestic absorption while increasing foreign absorption thereby allowing domestic residents to partially restore their security holdings.

An Increase in Government Security Holdings Accompanied by Tax Reductions

A third policy combination is a government purchase of securities accompanied by a tax reduction. The impact effect of the policy resembles that of the previous section since the open-market operation is the same. There is a difference, however, that arises from the reduction in taxes. The latter raises target wealth and therefore adds to the shift in the domestic saving function in figure 6.3. It follows that the impact effect is to raise the domestic equilibrium rate of saving and yield a current account surplus along with a decrease in the rate of interest.

The long-run equilibrium, viewed in terms of figure 6.2, is characterized by a reduction in the excess supply of debt facing the home country and an increase in the domestic target wealth function as well as in the long-run demand function for securities. The net effect of these changes is to generate a reduction in the equilibrium interest rate and a reduction in foreign wealth and security holdings. In the home country wealth may rise or decline since the decrease in the equilibrium interest rate and the increase in target wealth operate in opposite directions.

6.4 The Exchange Rate

In this part we discuss in some detail the determination of the equilibrium exchange rate. For that purpose we use the relationship between price levels and the exchange rate in (11), repeated here for convenience,

$$P = P^*e.$$

To relate the exchange rate to the general equilibrium model discussed above we introduce the definition of real balances,

$$m \equiv \frac{M}{P},$$

$$m^* \equiv \frac{M^*}{P^*}, \tag{24}$$

and substitute from these definitions into (11) to obtain the following equation for the exchange rate:

$$e = \left(\frac{M}{M^*}\right)\left(\frac{m^*}{m}\right). \tag{25}$$

Equation (25) shows that the equilibrium exchange rate depends on nominal money supplies and real balances in each country. Differentiating (25) and denoting a proportional change by a ^, we have

$$\hat{e} = (\hat{M} - \hat{M}^*) + (\hat{m}^* - \hat{m}). \tag{26}$$

For a given stock of real balances in each country the rate at which the exchange rate depreciates is equal to the difference in the rates of change in nominal money supplies.[7] For given nominal money supplies the exchange rate will depend on equilibrium real balances in the two countries and is therefore related to the general equilibrium of the system. The dependence of the exchange rate on the general equilibrium of the system accounts for the ambiguity that arises in determining the effects of various policies on the exchange rate. To clarify this point, we define the elasticity of real balances in (7) with respect to the interest rate as α and similarly for the foreign country.[8] Given that definition, we can rewrite (26) as

$$\hat{e} = (\hat{M} - \hat{M}^*) + (\alpha^* - \alpha)\hat{r} + (\hat{a}^* - \hat{a}). \tag{27}$$

Any policy combinations such as those analyzed in section 6.3 will affect in the short run each term in (27). Consider, for example, a domestic open-market purchase of securities combined with an increase in government spending. This will increase domestic nominal balances while reducing security holdings and, therefore, on both counts, will tend to depreciate the exchange rate. The decline in the equilibrium world interest rate, however, would seem to introduce some ambiguity that is captured in the second term in (27). This is not the case, however, and it can readily be shown that the exchange rate must depreciate. Considering figure 6.3, we note that at the lower equilibrium interest rate the foreign country is dissaving while the home country is saving. Abroad the demand for real balances increases, and therefore the foreign price level will decline. In the home country the reduced interest rate by itself would lower target wealth and raise actual wealth, and therefore lead to dissaving. This tendency is, however, more than outbalanced by an increase in the price level that contributes to lowering real wealth, both absolutely and relative to target wealth, and, therefore, leads to saving as shown in figure 6.3. Since the foreign price level declines while the domestic price level rises, there must be by (11) an unambiguous depreciation in the exchange rate. The extent of that depreciation will in turn depend on the differences in size and liquidity preference between countries as well as the responsiveness of saving to the rate of interest. These same factors will determine whether in the home country prices rise more or less than proportionately to the nominal quantity of money. Specifically, we note the "small" country case where the interest rate will remain unchanged and the exchange rate and the price level rise proportionally more than the quantity of money.

For other applications it may be convenient to assume away outright any ambiguities that may arise from differences in liquidity preference between countries. Given that these differences are neglected and that, therefore, the second term in (27) vanishes, we obtain rather strong results for the effects of parametric changes on the exchange rate. In particular, a shift out of money into securities will cause the equilibrium exchange rate to depreciate. The same result would follow from a wealth transfer from the home country to the rest of the world or an open market purchase of securities at home. More generally the country where the nominal quantity of money is increased or the demand for real balances is reduced will find its exchange rate depreciated.

The view of exchange rate determination developed here differs significantly from an approach where the exchange rate is determined by the balance between imports and exports. The present view is likely to be a much better approximation in all those circumstances where monetary disturbances or shifts in the demand for money predominate. The present approach is, however, too aggregative to cope with issues of relative prices or relative asset yields. To answer questions about the effect of shifts in relative commodity demands on the exchange rate or questions about the effect of shifts in demand between securities, a more disaggregated model is required and the present simplicity would be lost. The loss of simplicity notwithstanding, one would, however, expect such more extended models to carry the key feature of the present approach, namely, that the equilibrium exchange rate is such that asset markets clear.

6.5 Inflation, Deficit Financing, and Interdependence

In this section we extend the earlier framework to allow for money creation as a means of financing budget deficits. To accommodate such a policy, we require several alterations in our model. The government budget constraint will reflect the income from money creation, $\dot{M}/P$,

$$G - g - T = \frac{\dot{M}}{P}. \tag{10'}$$

To the extent that money creation by the government will, at least in the steady state, involve inflation, the behavioral equations will have to reflect this element as an opportunity cost of holding money. We will make two rather strong assumptions. First, the expected rate of inflation is equal to the equilibrium rate of inflation obtaining in the steady state. Second, the target wealth defined in (6) is independent of the rate of inflation so that only the division of wealth between money and securities is affected.

Defining the steady-state rate of inflation as $\bar{\pi}$, we rewrite disposable income as

$$z = y^0 + a - T - \bar{\pi}m, \tag{2'}$$

the demand for real balances as

$$L = \delta(r + \bar{\pi})w, \tag{3'}$$

and the steady-state value of real balances, $\bar{m}$, as

$$\bar{m} \equiv \delta\bar{w} = \bar{m}(r, \bar{\pi}), \quad \bar{m}_r < 0, \bar{m}_\pi < 0. \tag{3''}$$

The impact effect of inflationary expectations together with increased government expenditure is to create a stock excess supply of real balances and an increase in the price level as the community attempts to shift out of money. The resulting decline in real wealth causes the saving function to shift to the right, thus reducing the equilibrium rate of interest and generating a current account surplus. Thus the short-run effects are similar to those discussed in figure 6.3 for the case of increased expenditure accompanied by an open-market operation.

In the long run, the equilibrium rate of interest and the equilibrium rate of inflation are jointly determined. The appropriate system of equations is given by the equilibrium condition in the world capital market, (22), repeated here for convenience,

$$(1 - \delta)\bar{w} + (1 - \delta^*)\bar{w}^* = \frac{Q}{r},$$

and the government budget constraint with the long-run inflation tax base, $\bar{m}$, introduced as an argument,

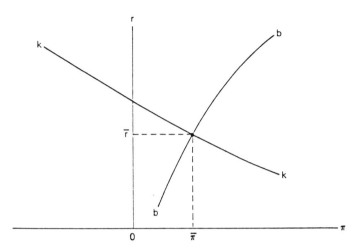

Figure 6.4

$$G - g - T = \bar{\pi}\bar{m}(r, \bar{\pi}). \tag{28}$$

In figure 6.4 we show the determination of the long-run equilibrium interest and inflation rates. The schedule kk shows combinations of interest and inflation rates such that the world capital market is in equilibrium. It is negatively sloped since an increase in the rate of inflation creates, by the substitution effect, an excess demand for securities and thus has to be accompanied by a reduction in the rate of interest to maintain market equilibrium.[9] The bb schedule shows combinations of interest and inflation rates such that the budget remains balanced. It is drawn on the assumption that an increase in the rate of inflation raises the inflation tax revenue and that an increase in the rate of interest lowers the long-run demand for real balances.

The equilibrium rate of inflation and interest are $\bar{\pi}$ and $\bar{r}$ given the remaining parameters, namely, G, g, T and the foreign policy variables.

Figure 6.4 can be used to enquire into the steady-state effects of changes in domestic or foreign parameters. Thus an increase in government spending, given g and T, shifts the bb schedule to the right and results in a higher equilibrium rate of inflation and a reduction in the rate of interest. An increase in government expenditure financed by increased government holdings of securities will leave the bb schedule unaffected and shift the kk schedule to the left thereby reducing both the rate of interest and the rate of inflation.

The interdependence between countries is emphasized by enquiring into the effects on the domestic rate of inflation of an increase in foreign money financed government spending. For that purpose we can parametrize the foreign equilibrium rate of inflation along the foreign b^*b^* schedule as a function of the rate of interest and the foreign budget deficit,

$$\pi^* = \pi^*(r, G^* - T^* - g^*), \quad \pi_r^* > 0, \pi_{G^*}^* > 0, \tag{29}$$

and substitute that relation in the foreign demand for securities in (22). An increase in foreign government expenditure financed by money creation will, at a constant interest rate, increase foreign inflation, increase the foreign demand for securities and thus lead, in figure 6.4, to a leftward shift of the kk schedule and hence to a decrease in the domestic rate of inflation.

This interdependence between national inflation rates is well worth noting in view of the well publicized case for flexible exchange rates as a means of obtaining "monetary sovereignty." The interdependence that arises in the present analysis is due to two factors. First, we assume that money creation and inflation are endogenous to the extent that a specified real budget deficit is financed by money issue. Second, perfect capital mobility implies that each country by its choice of budget affects via the world capital market the other country's real balances or inflation tax base, and thereby the equilibrium rate of inflation.

This interdependence is not surprising once it is understood that the inflation rate is a real variable and that variations in a real variable ought, in any general equilibrium model, to affect all other real variables everywhere. It suggests too that the view of flexible exchange rates as a means of isolating a country from monetary disturbances originating abroad must be one that centers on once and for all changes in the nominal quantity of money in an environment of static expectations such as that developed in the earlier parts of this chapter.

Rather than summarize our results here, we want to draw attention to some aspects of the foregoing discussion that should generalize beyond the particulars of our model. The first is the determination and role of the exchange rate. We noted that the model determines at each point in time an equilibrium level of real balances in each country which together with a specification of nominal balances allowed us to determine national price levels and hence by (11) the exchange rate. The view of the exchange rate that emerges is accordingly that it is such that the existing quantity of nominal balances be willingly held, or, to put the same point a bit more forcefully, the exchange rate is determined in the asset market. Such a view would differ considerably from an alternative characterization of exchange rate determination as arising in the market for foreign exchange with an emphasis on the financing of current trade flows. It is important to recognize the stock-market aspect of exchange rate determination since what governs in the short run the equilibrium price of money is the stock demand and the stock supply.

Such a view of the determination of flexible exchange rates emerges from much of the discussion of flexible exchange rates and capital mobility in the interwar period and in particular Nurkse (League of Nations, 1944) and Kindleberger (1937, p. 106) who notes: "The fact that the French Franc is weak when the chamber of Deputies is sitting or when an unbalanced budget is announced is due to the fact that the French public fears uncontrolled inflation and begins to export capital."[10] The relationship between the budget, inflation and the exchange rate was emphasized, too, in the literature on the German hyperinflation in particular by Graham (1930) and Bresciani-Turroni (1937), while the role of capital mobility in earlier Austrian and Russian experiences is emphasized by Yeager (1969).

A second aspect that deserves emphasis is the view of capital mobility that is developed here. That view rather than specifying an ad hoc "capital flow function" derives the equilibrium rate of capital flow or the current account surplus as part of the macroeconomic equilibrium. A counterpart of that equilibrium rate of capital flow is the time path of the economy and the distinction between short-run equilibrium where the distribution of assets is given and long-run equilibrium where it is fully endogenous.[11]

A last aspect we wish to mention concerns the interdependence between countries that arises from capital mobility and that is reflected in a common interest rate. That integration implies that all policies have repercussion effects throughout the world and that, flexible rates notwithstanding, even inflation rates are interdependent.

Appendix

This appendix shows the local stability of the linearized system. We start from the reduced form savings function,

$$S = \tilde{S}(r, a),$$
$$S^* = \tilde{S}^*(r, a^*),$$
(A1)

and the fact that short-run equilibrium requires that *world* saving be equal to zero,

$$\tilde{S}(r, a) + \tilde{S}^*(r, a^*) = 0. \tag{A2}$$

Differentiating that market equilibrium condition and noting that $da = -da^*$, we have

$$\frac{dr}{da} = -\frac{\tilde{S}_a - \tilde{S}_a^*}{\tilde{S}_r + \tilde{S}_r^*}. \tag{A3}$$

The equilibrium rate of change in domestic security holdings equals

$$\dot{a} = \tilde{r}\tilde{S}(\tilde{r}, a). \tag{A4}$$

Linearizing that equation around the equilibrium value $S = 0$, $a = \bar{a}$ yields

$$\dot{a} = \left[\tilde{S}_r \left(\frac{dr}{da} \right) + \tilde{S}_a \right] \tilde{r}(a - \bar{a}), \tag{A5}$$

and substituting from (A3), we obtain

$$\dot{a} = \left(\frac{\tilde{S}_r \tilde{S}_a^* + \tilde{S}_r^* \tilde{S}_a}{\tilde{S}_r + \tilde{S}_r^*} \right) \tilde{r}(a - \bar{a}). \tag{A6}$$

Since $\tilde{S}_r$, $\tilde{S}_r^* > 0$ and $\tilde{S}_a$, $\tilde{S}_a^* < 0$, the system is stable.

Notes

I am indebted to Michael Mussa for discussions on the issues raised in this chapter. I should like to acknowledge, too, helpful suggestions and comments I have received from John Pomery, Michael Schmid and Juan Urrutia.

1. I have used a similar approach in two earlier papers (see Dornbusch 1973, 1975).

2. Throughout this chapter an asterisk * denotes a foreign quantity or variable.

3. It is assumed that residents of neither country hold the other country's currency for speculative purposes or otherwise. Central banks are assumed not to intervene by open-market or foreign exchange market operations to stabilize the exchange rate. With these assumptions money is a nontraded asset. The counterpart is that securities can only be traded via a current account surplus so that at a point in time the existing distribution of the stocks of securities is predetermined.

4. The *stock* budget constraint implies that the excess demand for real balances in each country is equal to the stock excess supply of securities in each country. It follows therefore that when both countries' money markets clear so will the world capital market.

5. The asset markets clear at point A since, by construction, the reduced-form savings function embodies the conditions of equilibrium in the money markets.

6. Throughout this chapter a bar over a variable will denote its steady-state value.

7. The relationship between money creation, inflation and currency depreciation is further developed in section 6.5.

8. The elasticities are defined as $\alpha \equiv [d \ln \delta/(1 - \delta)]/d \ln r$ and $\alpha^* \equiv [d \ln \delta^*/(1 - \delta^*)]/d \ln r$ and are both negative.

9. In drawing figure 6.4, the foreign rate of inflation is assumed to equal zero. Alternatively, the foreign demand for securities must be interpreted as a reduced form embodying the response of the foreign equilibrium rate of inflation to the changes in the rate of interest.

10. Kindleberger in characterizing contemporary theory notes: "The French psychological theory of the exchanges, connecting the budget with the rate of exchange can be reduced to the simple proposition that the rate of exchange can be directly affected by capital flight." See Kindleberger (1937, p. 106).

11. A similar view is suggested in McKinnon and Oates (1966, p. 19) although their argument is presented in a Keynesian framework.

References

Bresciani-Turroni, C. 1937. The Economics of Inflation. Allen & Unwin, London.

Dornbusch, R. 1973. Macroeconomics in an Open Economy: Some Comments. Unpublished manuscript. University of Rochester, Rochester, N.Y.

Dornbusch, R. 1975. A Portfolio Balance Model of the Open Economy. Journal of Monetary Economics 1 (Jan): 3—20.

Graham, F. 1930. Exchange, Prices and Production in Hyper-Inflation: Germany, 1920—23. Princeton University Press, Princeton, N.J.

Kindleberger, C. 1937. International Short-Term Capital Movements. Columbia University Press, New York.

League of Nations. 1944. International Currency Experience. Princeton University Press, Princeton, N.J.

McKinnon, R., and W. Oates. 1966. The Implications of International Financial Integration for Monetary, Fiscal and Exchange-Rate Policy. Princeton Studies in International Finance, no. 16. Princeton University, Princeton, N.J.

Metzler, L. A. 1968. The Process of International Adjustment under Conditions of Full Employment: A Keynesian View. In R. Caves and H. G. Johnson, eds., Readings in International Economics. Irwin, Homewood, Ill.

Metzler, L. A. 1951. Wealth, Saving and the Rate of Interest. Journal of Political Economy 59 (April).

Mundell, R. A. 1968. International Economics. Macmillan, New York, ch. 18.

Yeager, L. 1969. Fluctuating Exchange Rates in the Nineteenth Century: The Experiences of Austria and Russia. In R. A. Mundell and A. K. Swoboda, eds., Monetary Problems of the International Economy. University of Chicago Press, Chicago, Ill.

7

Exchange Rate Risk and the Macroeconomics of Exchange Rate Determination

This chapter addresses the question of what contribution finance theory can make to an explanation of exchange rate movements. It is an attempt to integrate ideas of finance theory such as portfolio diversification, efficiency, rationality, and use of information in a reasonably eclectic macroeconomic model and to study in that broadened context the determination of exchange rates.

There have been traditionally two views of exchange rates. One holds that the exchange rate is the relative price of two monies, the other that it is the relative price of domestic and foreign goods. A third view, suggested by Fischer (1976), takes into account portfolio considerations to suggest that the exchange rate is the relative price of nominal assets. There is of course little sense in any of these partial equilibrium slogans; and it becomes readily apparent that in most instances real, monetary, and financial considerations interact in the determination of exchange rates. Real and monetary aspects of exchange rate determination have been extensively modeled, but this has not been the case for portfolio considerations until the very recent interest in current-account-oriented exchange rate theory. This chapter attempts to contribute to the integration of the various approaches by providing an integrated statement of the various elements of portfolio theory that are relevant and by modeling these elements in a macroeconomic context.

The chapter proceeds as follows: section 7.1 develops the basic portfolio model for an abstract economy. In section 7.2 the model is made "international" by a specification of the international inflation process. In that context we discuss the role of exchange risk in portfolio selection and the

Originally published in R. Hawkins, R. Levich, and Clas G. Wihlborg (eds.), *The Internationalization of Financial Markets and National Economic Policy*, Vol. 3 (Greenwich, CT: JAI Press, 1983), pp. 3–27.

determinants of the forward premium. Many of the ideas here are well established, and the sections dealing with them may be looked at primarily as an exposition.

In section 7.3 the portfolio demands are integrated in a macroeconomic model. The model is one with rational expectations and focuses on the determination of inflation, depreciation, and the level of the exchange rate. In studying various real and financial disturbances we point out the role of portfolio considerations in a macro setting. The section concludes with a discussion of the critical role played by the particular formulation of money demand.

7.1 Portfolio Selection, Market Equilibrium, and Risk Premia

This section lays out, for review and integration, the basic analytical framework of portfolio selection, market equilibrium, and risk premia. This field, in the finance literature, is of course already commonplace. The application to the open economy has been slow or late. Nevertheless, a relatively complete statement has now emerged from the writing of Solnik (1973), Kouri (1975, 1978a, 1978b), Wihlborg (1978), Roll and Solnik (1977), Adler and Dumas (1976), Jeffrey Frankel (1979), Kouri and Macedo (1978), Stulz (1979), and Fama and Farber (1979).

Portfolio Selection

The model is one of two-period expected utility maximization for an individual faced with two securities with random *real* returns. (We lack the macho for *n*.) The random returns on these securities are characterized in terms of their means and variances-covariances. The portfolio composition, derived from expected utility maximization, can be stated in terms of the parameters of risk aversion and the structure of returns. We now briefly sketch the derivation. Let w, r, r^*, and x be the initial level of real wealth, the random returns on home and foreign securities, and the portfolio share of foreign securities. End of period wealth then is random and equal to $\bar{w} = w(1 + r) + xw(r^* - r)$.

Utility is a function of the mean and variance of end period wealth:

$$U = U(\bar{w}, s_w^2). \tag{1}$$

The mean and variance of wealth are defined as

$$\bar{w} = w(1 + \bar{r}) + xw(\bar{r}^* - \bar{r}),$$

$$s_w^2 = w^2[(1-x)^2 s_r^2 + x^2 s_{r^*}^2 + 2x(1-x)s_{rr^*}], \tag{2}$$

where a bar denotes a mean. Maximizing equation (1) with respect to x yields the optimal portfolio share:

$$x = \frac{(\bar{r}^* - \bar{r}) + \Theta(s_r^2 - s_{rr^*})}{\Theta s^2},$$

$$\tag{3}$$

$$s^2 \equiv (s_r^2 + s_{r^*}^2 - 2s_{rr^*}),$$

and where $\Theta \equiv -U_2 w/U_1$ is the coefficient of risk aversion.

Equation (3) shows the conventional result that portfolio selection depends on yield differentials, risk aversion, and the return structure. To gain some further understanding, we can separate the portfolio share into two separate components. The first is a speculative component and the other share corresponds to a minimum variance portfolio, as pointed out in Kouri (1978a):

$$x = \frac{(\bar{r}^* - \bar{r})}{\Theta s^2} + \alpha,$$

$$\tag{3'}$$

$$\alpha \equiv \frac{s_r^2 - s_{rr^*}}{s^2}.$$

It is readily shown that α is the share of the foreign security in a portfolio chosen to minimize the variance of wealth. The minimum variance portfolio is independent of risk aversion, of course, and its composition depends only on the relative riskiness of the two securities. The first term in equation (3') represents the speculative portfolio share. This one depends on yield differentials, risk aversion, and risk. It is readily recognized that speculative holdings of the other security are $-(\bar{r}^* - \bar{r})/\theta s^2$ so that across assets the speculative portfolio sums to zero. Investors thus allocate their wealth to a minimum variance portfolio and issue one of the securities using the proceeds to hold another as a speculative portfolio.

Market Equilibrium

The optimal portfolio share in equation (3') is that for an individual investor. To proceed from here to the condition of market equilibrium, we have to aggregate across investors, all of whom share the same information, but may differ in their wealth or risk aversion. Nominal demand for asterisk-type securities (there is no sense, as yet, in which they are foreign) of the typical investor is $x_j W_j$. Here x_j depends on the investor's risk aversion and W_j denotes her nominal, nonmonetary wealth. Denoting the nominal supply of asterisk-type securities V^*, the market equilibrium condition becomes: $V^* = \sum x_j W_j$. Using the definition of aggregate nonmonetary wealth, $\overline{W} = \sum W_j$, the equilibrium condition can be expressed in the form:

$$\left(\frac{r^* - r}{\Theta s^2} + \alpha \right) \overline{W} = V^*,$$

$$\Theta = \sum \frac{\Theta_j}{W_j / \overline{W}}.$$

(4)

In equation (4) Θ now denotes the market coefficient of relative risk aversion, being a wealth-weighted average of the individual coefficients.

Equation (4) can be solved for the market equilibrium real yield differential:

$$\bar{r}^* - \bar{r} = \Theta s^2 \left(\frac{V^*}{\overline{W}} - \alpha \right).$$

(5)

The yield differential in equation (5) has three determinants. The higher risk aversion, Θ, the larger the yield differential. In the same direction works an increase in relative yield variability, s^2. The third determinant is the relative asset supply. It takes the interesting form of a yield differential proportional to the difference between the actual relative supply, $V^*/\overline{W}$, and the share of the asset in the minimum variance portfolio, α. The yield differential is therefore positive or negative depending on whether the relative supply of the security exceeds or falls short of its share in the minimum variance portfolio.[1]

Figure 7.1 shows the equilibrium yield differential. The upper schedule represents the variance of wealth, achieving a minimum at $x = \alpha$. The lower schedule shows the yield differential as a function of the discrepancy between actual relative supplies and the minimum variance portfolio. The slope of the schedule is the coefficient Θs^2. For a relative security supply $V^*/\overline{W}$, we show at point A the equilibrium risk premium.

The result is intuitive, as all market participants will want to hold the minimum variance portfolio and need compensation to bear more than the minimum risk. Relatively more risk averse market participants will hold more nearly the minimum variance portfolio than is available in the aggregate. The more risk neutral participants will issue the lacking securities and hold the excess ones, charging a yield differential for bearing the speculative role.

Risk is thus defined in terms of divergences from the minimum variance

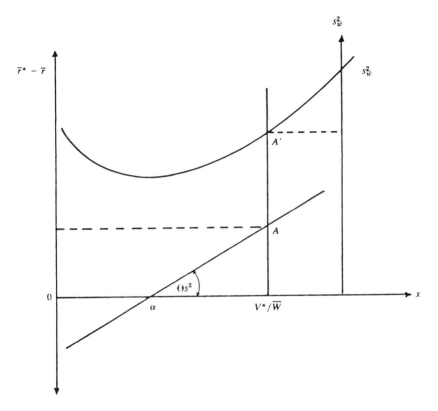

Figure 7.1

portfolio. Given this interpretation, it is clear that an increase in the relative supply of a security will change the yield differential; the yield differential will rise or decline absolutely as $V^*/\overline{W} - \alpha \gtrless 0$.

So far the model is in no particular way "international." In the next section we apply it to a two-country context by specifying the sources of real yield variability.

7.2 Inflation, Depreciation, and Real Returns

In this section we develop a model of the process that generates real returns. With the model of real returns supplementing the equations of portfolio choice and yield differentials we can answer a number of questions. First, what is the role of exchange risk in portfolio selection and in risk premia? Second, what are the determinants of the forward premium for foreign exchange? Third, what roles do distribution effects play in asset markets, or to what extent do differences in consumption patterns get reflected in asset markets?[2]

A Model of Real Returns

We assume that there are only two securities. Both are bonds with nominal payoffs in the currencies of the home country and the foreign country. The nominal interest rates on these short-term securities are known, but the real returns are random because of uncertain inflation rates and uncertain exchange rate behavior. A first task now is to specify the rate of inflation in terms of the consumption basket.

This is a two-commodity world, each country being specialized in the production of one commodity. The rates of inflation of the local currency prices of the two commodities are π and π^*, respectively. All portfolio holders, domestic and foreign alike, consume the two commodities in the same proportions. This assumption of common tastes, maintained until the appendix, implies that all portfolio holders face a common dollar rate of inflation, $\tilde{\pi}$:

$$\tilde{\pi} = a\pi + (1 - a)(\pi^* + d), \tag{6}$$

where d is the random rate of depreciation of the dollar relative to the foreign currency. The "world" rate of inflation relevant in assessing real security returns is thus simply a weighted average of the dollar inflation rates of the two commodities, the weights corresponding to the budget shares.

The rate of depreciation is a random variable, assumed to follow purchasing power parity, but with a random component reflecting real exchange rate variability:

$$d = \pi - \pi^* + u, \tag{7}$$

where the real exchange rate variation u for the present has a zero mean.

Equations (6) and (7) in combination with the nominal interest rates, i and i^*, define the real returns on the two securities:

$$r = i - \tilde{\pi} = i - \pi - (1 - a)u,$$
$$r^* = (i^* + d) - \tilde{\pi} = i^* - \pi^* + au. \tag{8}$$

We note, once more, that the assumption of a common consumption basket across countries implies that investors face the same "real" return structure and therefore will choose the same portfolio composition. Equation (8) shows that real returns are affected not only by random variations in the inflation rates but also by real exchange rate variations or deviations of the exchange rate from purchasing power parity. For given inflation rates a positive u implies that the home currency depreciates beyond the PPP path, raising in home currency the price of foreign goods and thus lowering the real return to home currency bonds. The real return to foreign currency bonds of course rises, as in foreign currency domestic goods prices decline.

We now define the variances and covariances of the real returns and the real return differentials:

$$s_r^2 \equiv s_\pi^2 + (1 - a)^2 s_u^2,$$

$$s_{r^*}^2 \equiv s_{\pi^*}^2 + a^2 s_u^2,$$

$$s_{rr^*} \equiv s_{\pi\pi^*} - a(1 - a)s_u^2,$$

$$s_d^2 \equiv s_\pi^2 + s_{\pi^*}^2 - 2s_{\pi\pi^*} + s_u^2 \equiv s^2,$$

(9)

where we have assumed that deviations from PPP are uncorrelated with inflation rates. It is interesting to note from the expression for the covariance of real returns, s_{rr^*}, that real exchange rate variability contributes a negative correlation to the real return structure, while raising the variance of real returns. In equation (9) we define the variance of the real yield differential which, by equations (7) and (8), is also the variance of the rate of depreciation, s_d^2.

The variance of real returns in equation (9) shows that for dollar bonds the real return variability depends on the U.S. inflation variability, s_π^2, and on the variability of PPP deviations, s_u^2. The latter is more significant the larger the foreign country, as measured by its share in world inflation, $1 - a$. Note that the foreign rate of inflation has no impact on the real return variability of dollar bonds as it is fully offset by exchange depreciation. Only deviations from PPP matter. For foreign currency bonds the real return variability depends on the variance of foreign currency inflation and again on the variability of deviations from PPP.

Portfolio Composition and Exchange Risk

Replacing the formula for return variance in equation (9) into equation (3) yields an interesting expression for the portfolio and in particular for its minimum variance component:

$$x = \frac{(\bar{r}^* - \bar{r})}{\Theta s_d^2} + \frac{s_\pi^2 - s_{\pi\pi^*} + (1 - a)s_u^2}{s_d^2}.$$

(10)

The hedging portfolio or minimum variance portfolio will now depend on the structure of the world inflation process. Suppose, first, that inflation rates are deterministic so that $s_d^2 = s_u^2$. In that case the portfolio share reduces to

$$x = \frac{\overline{r}^* - \overline{r}}{\Theta s_u^2} + (1 - a).\tag{11}$$

The equation states that, with exchange risk as the only source of real return variability, hedging can be complete. Investors will allocate their wealth to the two securities in a proportion determined by the relative inflation shares $(1 - a)/a$. With that allocation, because of the perfect negative correlation of real returns, the minimum variance portfolio is actually risk free. The speculative portfolio of course still depends on risk, return, and risk aversion. The first striking result then is that with deviations from PPP the only source of real return variability, the individual can fully hedge, although in the aggregate that may not be possible, as we note below.

The alternative case assumes that there is no variability in the real exchange rate, $s_u^2 = 0$, and the variance of exchange depreciation only depends on national inflation variance. Now the portfolio share is:

$$x = \frac{\overline{r}^* - \overline{r}}{\Theta s_d^2} + \frac{s_\pi(s_\pi - \rho s_{\pi^*})}{s_d^2},\tag{11}$$

where ρ is the coefficient of correlation of inflation rates. Thus, without real exchange rate variability, the allocation of portfolios depends on the inflation variances and covariances. With inflation rates uncorrelated, investors favor the securities of the country with the more stable inflation rate. The minimum variance portfolio share is inversely proportional to the ratio of the inflation variance to the variance of exchange depreciation, s_π^2/s_d^2.

In the general case the portfolio share, as shown in equation (10), will depend on both exchange rate and inflation variability. Even here, though, it remains true that portfolio shares in the minimum variance portfolio are positively related to country size as measured by $(1 - a)$, although the coefficient on that size variable is the fraction that indicates the *relative* importance of exchange risk.

Yield Differentials and Risk Premia

We return now to the yield differential in equation (5) and state it in terms of the more specific structure. Replacing α by the minimum variance portfolio share in equation (10), we have:

$$\bar{r}^* - \bar{r} = \Theta s^2 \left[\frac{V^*}{\overline{W}} - \frac{s_\pi^2 - s_{\pi\pi^*}}{s^2} - \frac{(1-a)s_u^2}{s^2} \right]. \tag{5'}$$

Consider first again the case where deviations from PPP are the only source of real rate variability. In that event equation (5') reduces to

$$\bar{r}^* - \bar{r} = \Theta s_u^2 \left[\frac{V^*}{\overline{W}} - (1-a) \right]. \tag{5''}$$

There will be a yield differential to induce the public to bear positive risk. The risk is proportional to the deviation of relative asset supplies from the zero variance portfolio share, $1 - a$. Again the price of that risk is higher the higher risk aversion and *real* exchange rate variability. We have thus established that in a world where exchange rate uncertainty is the only source of real return variability there is a yield differential or risk premium if asset supplies are out of line with minimum variance portfolios, where the latter replicate the relative importance of countries in world inflation and thus, roughly, relative country size.

In the case of pure exchange risk, risk premia emerge therefore only if relative asset supplies are out of line with relative country size.

Consider now the more general case. What characterizes the risk premium, and how does it respond to changes in the stochastic structure? From equation (5') we can write the change in the risk premium induced by a change in the stochastic structure, dv:

$$\frac{d(\bar{r}^* - \bar{r})}{dv} = \Theta \left(\frac{V^*}{\overline{W}} - \alpha \right) \frac{ds^2}{dv} - \Theta s^2 \frac{V^* \, d\alpha}{W \, dv}. \tag{12}$$

There are thus two channels. The first is a change in the premium due to a change in the variability of relative real yield differentials. The second channel is the change in the minimum variance portfolio induced by a shift in the stochastic structure.

By the first channel a higher variability of yield differentials raises the risk premium. Variability would increase as a consequence of increased home inflation variance, if inflation variances are negatively correlated. Increased correlation of inflation rates, by contrast, reduces variability of relative returns and thus tends to reduce the premium due to this first channel. The second channel captures the effect on the risk premium due to changes in the minimum variance portfolio. The effects of changes in inflation variance or correlation are ambiguous here.

The implications of higher real exchange rate variability are particularly interesting. From equation (5') we obtain the expression:

$$\frac{d(\bar{r}^* - \bar{r})}{ds_u^2} = \Theta\left[\frac{V^*}{W} - (1 - a)\right] \qquad (12')$$

Accordingly, the effect of increased real exchange rate variance depends only on the relative size of asset supplies and countries.

The Forward Premium and Excess Depreciation

In this section we review several implications of the portfolio balance model that are of interest from a macroeconomic perspective. They concern, respectively, the risk premium on forward foreign exchange, homogeneity, and the relation between the level of exchange rates and the anticipated rate of depreciation.

There is a direct link between the risk premium in equation (5') and the risk premium in the foreign exchange market. Nominal interest differentials are equal to the forward premium, $i - i^* = f$, as has been amply documented. From equations (7) and (8) the mean or anticipated real yield differential is $\bar{r}^* - \bar{r} = i^* - i + \bar{d}$, where $\bar{d}$ is the anticipated rate of depreciation. Thus $f - \bar{d} = -(\bar{r}^* - \bar{r})$, or the difference between the anticipated rate of depreciation and the forward rate equals the equilibrium real yield differential. Using the substitution in equation (5') yields:

$$f = \bar{d} - \Theta s^2\left(\frac{V^*}{\bar{w}} - \alpha\right). \qquad (13)$$

Accordingly, the forward premium exceeds the anticipated rate of depreciation if the relative supply of foreign securities falls short of their minimum variance portfolio share. The theory thus supports the view that there is a negative relationship between the foreign exchange risk premium and relative asset supplies as shown in figure 7.2. The interpretation of the forward exchange premium is simply that with excessive relative supplies of foreign assets some speculators will borrow in the home currency, thus issuing domestic securities that are relatively scarce, and hold foreign securities that are relatively plentiful. Their expected return must exceed the interest differential in order to warrant the above minimum risk position.

The forward exchange premium in equation (13) and figure 7.2 warrants three observations. First, we observe that its determinants are those of the real yield differentials and that accordingly our earlier analysis applies. Second, the slope of the premium schedule with respect to a change in

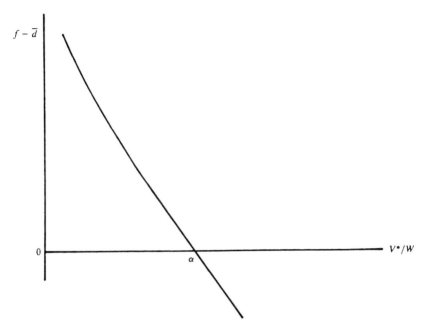

Figure 7.2

relative asset supplies is determined by both the stochastic structure and risk aversion.

A third point has been particularly emphasized by Jeffrey Frankel (1979b). It is that the risk premium is a function of the relative supplies of outside assets, *not* a function of net foreign assets as has been suggested in earlier discussions. The point is particularly important because it implies that there is no direct link between the current account and the related changes in net foreign assets and the risk premium. We return to this point below when we discuss differences in national consumption patterns and the resulting portfolio preferences.[3]

The discussion of the relation between the forward premium and the expected rate of depreciation leads naturally to a second question: What is the relation between actual depreciation, d, and the forward premium? To answer that question, we use the identity $d - f = d - \bar{d} + \bar{d} - f$ to write

$$d - f = d - \bar{d} + \Theta s^2 \left(\frac{V^*}{W} - \alpha \right), \tag{14}$$

or

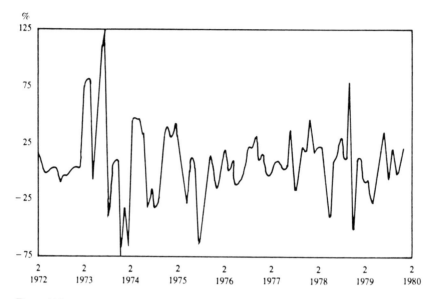

Figure 7.3
Excess dollar-DM depreciation (monthly, at annual rates)

Excess depreciation = "News" + Risk premium.

The decomposition in equation (14) suggests that we can break up "excess depreciation" or depreciation in excess of the forward premium into two components. One is the risk premium; the other is unanticipated depreciation or "news." How much of the actual excess depreciation, as defined by the left-hand side, do we believe to be due to "news," and how much can be attributed to the risk premium?

Figure 7.3 shows the excess depreciation of the dollar, monthly at annual rates. It is quite apparent that this excess depreciation displays a substantial randomness. The "news" component is therefore likely to be an important item in explaining the excess depreciation. In Dornbusch (1980) unanticipated current account and cyclical developments are shown to explain a large part of the excess depreciation. Cumby and Obstfeld (1979) have shown that on weekly data all major currencies show serial correlation in the excess depreciation, thus making a case that the risk component, in addition to news, is an important and systematic component of excess depreciation. This remains an active area of research as shown in the work of Frenkel (1980) or Isard (1980).

In the appendix we discuss a more general model that allows for differences in national consumption patterns. It is shown there that portfolio preferences will differ only to the extent that there is real exchange rate risk, $s_u^2 > 0$. With real exchange rate risk, countries will tend to hold relatively more of their own currency securities, thus hedging against the impact of exchange rate deviations from PPP exerting adverse effects on their real returns. Interestingly, the quantative importance of these local habitat effects may be small. Indeed, the local habitat component of the risk premium is the product of three fractions.

Further Implications

A further implication of the portfolio model is the homogeneity of degree zero of the risk premium, Patinkin-like, in nominal money, nominal outside bonds, and the exchange rate. The point is immediately appreciated by writing the relative supplies of bonds in the form:

$$\frac{V^*}{\overline{W}} = \frac{\overline{V}^* E}{V + \overline{V}^* E},$$

where $\overline{W} = V + E\overline{V}^*$ is world nominal, nonmonetary wealth measured in home currency and $\overline{V}^*$ is the foreign currency value of foreign currency bonds, E being the home currency price of foreign exchange. An exchange depreciation, accordingly, will change relative asset supplies, and therefore the equilibrium real rate differential, unless it is accompanied by an equi-proportionate rise in home currency bonds.

Another point, particularly stressed by Dooley and Isard (1979), is that the portfolio balance model is not a complete model of exchange rate determination. Indeed, it only establishes a relation between nominal interest differentials, anticipated depreciation, and the level of the exchange rate. This is apparent from rewriting equation (13) in the form:

$$i - i^* = \overline{d} - \Theta s^2 \left(\frac{\overline{V}^* E}{\overline{V}^* E + V} - \alpha \right), \tag{15}$$

where we have substituted $V^* = E\overline{V}^*$ to show the domestic currency value of foreign assets as the product of the exchange rate and the given nominal stock of foreign currency denominated securities, $\overline{V}^*$. For given nominal interest rates the portfolio balance model thus implies a positive relation between the level of the exchange rate, E, and the rate of depreciation. To close the model, we need further equations that determine the nominal interest differential and that restrict the exchange rate dynamics. Accordingly, the portfolio model must be embedded in a broader macroeconomic model. This is the task of the next section.

7.3 Portfolio Balance in a Macro Model

In this section we develop a rational expectations macroeconomic model in which the portfolio balance equation in equation (15) is one of the key equations. The macroeconomic model determines the nominal interest differential from conditions of monetary equilibrium and portfolio balance. Inflation is determined by trend money growth and the state of aggregate demand, which in turn depends on the real exchange rate. In that setting there will be a unique path of the level and rate of depreciation of the exchange rate—and thus rates of inflation and rates of change of the terms of trade—such as to be consistent with expectations *and* ensure convergence to the steady state. We first develop the macroeconomic model and then apply it to investigate the adjustment process to a variety of real and financial disturbances. The analysis will establish that the portfolio balance relation is central to determining the exchange rate implications of various shocks.

The Macro Model

In money markets we assume that real money demand is a function of real income and the expected nominal yields on domestic and foreign securities. For ease of manipulation we assume unit real income elasticities and a semilogarithmic functional form. With these assumptions, and imposing money market equilibrium at home and abroad, we have

$$m - y = -bi - c(i^* + \bar{d}),$$
$$m^* - y^* = -bi^* - c(i - \bar{d}),$$

(16)

where m, y, m^* denote home and foreign logs of nominal money and nominal income. Note in passing that each country's money demand depends on the alternative cost of holding that particular currency as measured by the nominal interest in home currency and the exchange depreciation-adjusted return on foreign securities. There is an explicit assumption here that the alternative to holding each currency is to hold securities, not other monies. Currency substitution therefore is not recognized as a possibility.

Now subtracting one equilibrium condition from the other and collecting terms yields an expression for the interest differential:

$$i - i^* = -\frac{1}{b - c}(z + 2c\bar{d}\,),$$

$$z \equiv m - y - (m^* - y^*), \quad b - c > 0, \tag{17}$$

where the term z denotes relative money income ratios and where we assume that $b - c > 0$. Money market equilibrium, as shown in equation (17), thus implies that a rise in domestic money relative to income will lower the interest differential, as will a rise in anticipated depreciation.

Both portfolio balance and money market equilibrium establish relations between interest differentials and anticipated depreciation. We combine these now by equating equation (15) and equation (17) to solve for the equilibrium rate of depreciation consistent with full asset market equilibrium:

$$\bar{d} = \beta\left(\frac{v^*}{v^* + v/\sigma} - \alpha\right) - \gamma z, \tag{18}$$

where we define the coefficients:

$$\beta \equiv \frac{b - c}{b + c}\Theta s^1 \geq 0 \quad \text{and} \quad \gamma \equiv \frac{1}{b + c} > 0,$$

and use the definitions of the terms of trade and real security supplies:

$$\sigma \equiv \frac{EP^*}{P},$$

$$v \equiv \frac{V}{P},$$

$$v^* \equiv \frac{V^*}{P^*}.$$

Equation (18) describes full equilibrium in the asset markets and will be used below in our diagrams as the asset market equilibrium schedule QQ. In asset market equilibrium the rate of depreciation is higher the higher the real supplies of foreign securities or the real exchange rate, σ, and the lower the real supply of home securities. There is thus clearly a link among the relative supplies of financial assets, the terms of trade, and the rate of depreciation. Monetary factors enter in the term z that proxies relative money market conditions. Depreciation is higher the higher the ratio of money to income is at home and the lower it is abroad.

We note that the relative substitutability of monies with home and foreign bonds affects the equilibrium rate of depreciation in equation (18). The closer the substitutability, the more nearly b equals c, so that β tends toward zero. This implies that security markets are relatively unimportant in comparison with monetary conditions in the determination of the rate of depreciation.

In the following analysis we assume that the home country is sufficiently small so that foreign repercussions can be ignored. Accordingly, foreign inflation is taken as given, as are the real values of foreign securities, employment abroad, and real balances. We concentrate thus on the home economy.

In the home goods market we assume that the rate of inflation is equal to the rate of trend money creation, $\dot{m}$, plus an increasing function of the terms of trade:[4]

$$\pi = g(\sigma) + \dot{m}. \tag{19}$$

The price adjustment mechanism reflects the assumption that goods prices adjust only slowly to imbalance in the goods market and that goods demand is determined by relative prices. Output is assumed throughout to be at the full employment level. The model thus corresponds to that shown in Dornbusch (1976), although the asset market specification is, of course, different.

The expected rate of depreciation, $\bar{d}$, is determined by the inflation differential and the anticipated rate of adjustment in the terms of trade along the equilibrium path, $\dot{\sigma}$. We assume that along the rational expectations path the rate of adjustment in the terms of trade is proportional to the discrepancy between the long-run equilibrium terms of trade and the current actual level:

$$\bar{d} = g(\sigma) + \dot{m} + h(\bar{\sigma} - \sigma),$$

$$g' - h < 0, \tag{20}$$

$$g(\bar{\sigma}) = 0,$$

where we already impose a restriction on h required for the stability of the rational expectations path, as will become apparent below.

In figure 7.4 we show the whole system in steady-state equilibrium. The model is conveniently studied in terms of rates of depreciation and inflation relative to the growth rates of nominal assets, $\dot{m}$, and by reference to the terms of trade, or real exchange rate, σ. In steady state equilibrium at point A the real values of money and bonds are constant, inflation equals depreci-

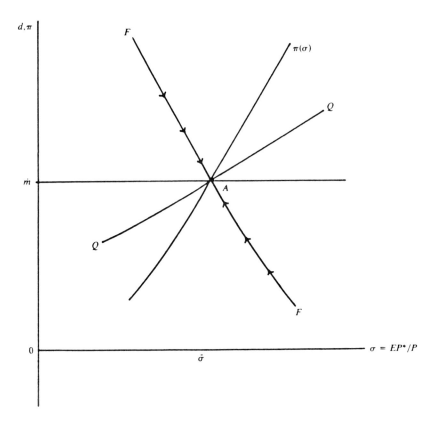

Figure 7.4

ation, and actual and anticipated depreciation are equal. The figure shows as upward sloping the schedule QQ that reflects the equilibrium in assets markets defined by equation (18). The schedule is flatter, the lower the term β. That implies that a low coefficient of risk aversion or a low variability of relative asset returns tends to reduce the slope; if home and foreign securities tend to be equally close substitutes for monies, this will tend to reduce the slope, as will a high level of substitutability between money and securities, $b + c$.

The inflation schedule corresponding to equation (19) is also shown upward sloping, by assumption steeper than the QQ schedule. The slope reflects the effect of changes in the real exchange rate on aggregate demand and the resulting effect of excess demand on the rate of inflation. The schedule thus represents a standard expectations-augmented Phillips curve.

The rational expectations path is shown as FF and represents equation

(20). The path shows the actual rate of depreciation as a function of money growth and the terms of trade. The coefficient h in equation (20) depends of course on the structural coefficients of the entire model[5].

Real and Financial Disturbances

Long-run equilibrium is shown at point A, where inflation and depreciation equal the rates of expansion of nominal assets. At A real asset supplies and relative asset supplies are accordingly constant. Consider now how that economy is affected by real and financial disturbances. We start with the effects of a permanent fall in demand for domestic goods.

The current account worsening or fall in demand implies that the long-run equilibrium terms of trade will deteriorate to $\bar{\sigma}'$ in figure 7.5. Accordingly, the inflation schedule will shift out and to the right as will the

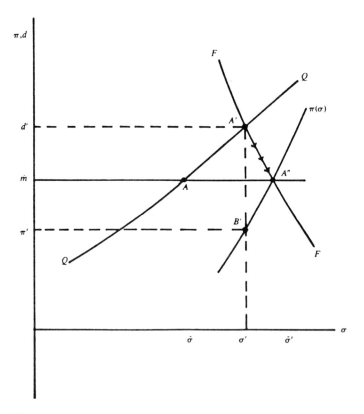

Figure 7.5

schedule describing the depreciation rate along the perfect foresight path. The new shortrun equilibrium is determined by point A'. There is thus an immediate depreciation of the exchange rate and an immediate terms of trade deterioration. This is a result well in line with current account-oriented models of the exchange rate. Associated with the terms of trade deterioration we have an increase in the rate of depreciation and a reduction in the rate of inflation.

At point A' the reduced rate of inflation implies that real balances are rising, thereby inducing a tendency for the rate of depreciation in equation (18) to decline. At the same time the rate of depreciation exceeds the rate of creation of bonds so that $v/\sigma = V/E$ declines, thus tending to raise the rate of depreciation through the risk premium effect. We assume that money market effects dominate the risk premium effect so that the asset market equilibrium shifts down and to the right. The economy adjusts accordingly with a further deterioration in the terms of trade that raises competitiveness and thus narrows the gap between depreciation and inflation. The process continues until the new long-run equilibrium at A'' is reached.

In figure 7.6 we consider the effect of a once-and-for-all, unanticipated rise in the nominal money stock. From equations (18) to (20) it is apparent that only the asset market equilibrium schedule QQ will shift and that it shifts down and to the right. Long-run equilibrium terms of trade consistent with goods market equilibrium remain unchanged at $\bar{\sigma}$.

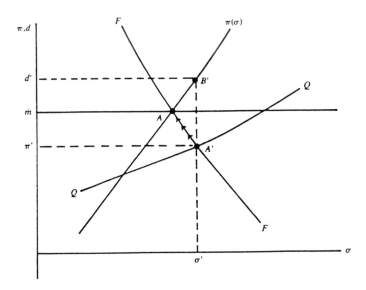

Figure 7.6

The short-run effect of the money disturbance is a depreciation of the exchange rate and a deterioration in the terms of trade. At point A' the rate of depreciation has declined while the rate of inflation associated with the gain in competitiveness has risen. Accordingly the terms of trade are improving.

In short-run equilibrium inflation exceeds money growth, and the creation of debt exceeds the rate of depreciation. Accordingly real balances are rising but the relative supply of foreign assets is declining. Again assuming that the monetary effect dominates, we have an upward shifting asset market equilibrium schedule. The economy moves toward the steady state with continuing terms of trade improvement and a narrowing of the gap between inflation and depreciation.

What about the steady state? The long-run homogeneity in money prices, bonds, and the exchange rate cannot be satisfied here because only money increased. Therefore money rises relative to debt, while exchange rates remain unchanged relative to prices.

Next we study a shift in asset demands. Suppose the public recognizes increased real exchange rate variability. Then by equation $(12')$ asset demand shifts will change the equilibrium risk premium. Particularly if initially foreign relative asset supplies fell short of the foreign size, $V^*/W - (1 - a) < 0$ the risk premium on foreign securities will fall. In terms of figure 7.6 this implies a downward shift of the asset market equilibrium schedule. Accordingly the exchange rate will depreciate, and we go through the adjustment process already described. An alternative is a market intervention. The appropriate policy here is to issue Carter bonds—an issue of foreign currency denominated bonds—with the proceeds serving to recover domestic securities. This is equivalent to a sterilized exchange market intervention in support of the home currency. The intervention policy would preserve the initial real equilibrium as the change in the relative supply of nominal assets is achieved by trading nominal assets rather than through valuation changes. The risk of the operation of course is that we do not know when we are facing portfolio shifts and when the source of the disturbance is a change in the equilibrium terms of trade.

A last application of the model is the effect of a currently anticipated future disturbance. In different models this question has been addressed by Wilson (1979), Rogoff (1979), Dornbusch and Fischer (1980), and others. We take here the case of a currently anticipated future increase in the nominal money stock. Suppose it becomes known that T years into the future there will be a once-and-for-all increase in nominal money. How will

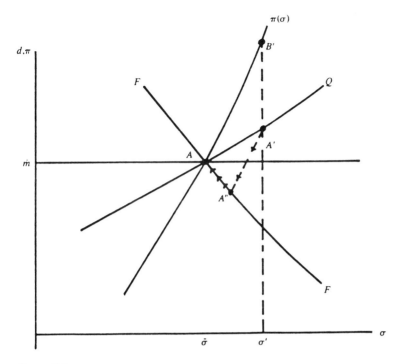

Figure 7.7

that expectation affect the current exchange rate, inflation, and rate of depreciation?

In figure 7.6 we showed that an unanticipated increase in current money leads to a transitory depreciation, increased inflation, and reduced rates of depreciation. The expectation of a future increase in money of course leads the public to contemplate that future course of events, leads to the expectation of a capital gain on foreign exchange holdings, and thereby forces an immediate depreciation of the spot exchange rate.

In figure 7.7 we show the impact effect of currently anticipated future money. The spot exchange rate immediately depreciates and leads to a terms of trade deterioration from $\bar{\sigma}$ to σ. In that short-run equilibrium we have increased inflation and depreciation and thus falling real money and security holdings. Furthermore with inflation in excess of depreciation the terms of trade are improving. This implies that there is an initial exchange rate overshooting. Over time now with falling real asset holdings the QQ schedule is shifting upward while the real exchange rate continues to appreciate. Only at the time when the money does actually arrive does the

QQ schedule shift back down, as in figure 2.6, and lead to an equilibrium at point A" on the perfect foresight path. From here the economy returns to the initial steady state.

A Let-Down?

A central part of our macro model was the specification of the monetary sector in equation (16), where nominal yields on home and foreign currency securities had a differential effect on money demand. Suppose, alternatively, that money demand depends on the average nominal return on the portfolio, measured in terms of the respective currencies. Then the money market equilibrium conditions become

$$m - p = -b'\lambda,$$
$$m^* - p^* = -b'\lambda^*,$$
(16')

where $\lambda = \omega i + (1 + \omega)(i^* + \bar{d})$ and $\lambda^* = \omega(i - \bar{d}) + (1 + \omega)i^*$ are the alternative costs of holding home and foreign monies.

It is immediately apparent that this specification is equivalent, in terms of equation (18), to the case where $b = c$ or $\beta = 0$. The asset market equilibrium condition representing the QQ schedule reduces to

$$\bar{d} = -\gamma z.$$
(18')

The striking implication of this case is that security markets have no relevance now to the macroeconomics of exchange rate determination, inflation, and depreciation. The relative supplies of securities affect only interest rate differentials. The rate of depreciation and the average level of interest rates are determined by the conditions of monetary equilibrium.

None of our earlier analysis is substantially affected—because we already assumed the dominance of monetary considerations in the QQ schedule—except in three respects. First, the QQ schedule now is flat and security markets have no role in determining the extent of exchange rate adjustment in response to a disturbance. Second, adjustment to a real disturbance such as a permanent terms of trade change is now immediate and full rather than a drawn-out process. Finally, as already noted, the relative supplies of securities and sterilized intervention policy become irrelevant to exchange rates. Moreover these observations remain true when a broader specification of the goods market allows the real interest rate to affect aggregate demand.

Whether portfolio considerations are relevant to the macroeconomics of exchange rate determination depends then critically on the precise way in which home and foreign interest rates enter the demand for money. This suggests of course that more attention must be paid to the derivation of money demand. In particular it may be quite frivolous to assume a money demand equation such as equation (16') rather than to derive it jointly with the portfolio equations from maximization considerations. The force of that consideration is strengthened by an observation due to Kouri (1975, 1978b). He notes that domestic money and home currency bonds have the same stochastic characteristics, as they are both assets fixed in nominal terms. This implies an interdependence of money holdings and bond holdings, as investors can effectively rent their money rather than own it. In Kouri's work the joint derivation of money and portfolio equations leads to a money demand equation that depends only on home interest rates and wealth, rather than income. In terms of our model that would imply that the term $c = 0$ and that portfolio considerations do play a role in exchange rate determination. Clearly, then, money demand properties remain the key issue in integrating portfolio balance and exchange rate determination.

7.4 Appendix: Local Habitats

Suppose that, unlike in section 7.2, we assume different consumption patterns across countries. Then the relevant inflation rates will differ as the composition of consumption baskets varies across countries. Maintaining for the home country the definition of dollar inflation of the consumer price index as in equation (6), we have a parallel equation for the foreign consumer:

$$\pi^* = a^*\pi + (1 - a^*)(\pi^* + d). \tag{6'}$$

Accordingly, the real rates of return faced by foreign consumers will be

$$j = i - \pi - (1 - a^*)u, \quad j^* = i^* - \pi^* + a^*u, \tag{8'}$$

where j and j^* are the real returns to foreign consumers on home and foreign securities, respectively. It is immediately apparent from the real return equations that both variances and covariances of real returns will be different for home and foreign consumers but that the variance of the rate of depreciation will be the same. This point is apparent from inspection of equation (9).

The foreign portfolio holders' share of foreign securities can now be written as

$$x^* = \frac{\overline{r}^* - \overline{r}}{\theta s_d^2} + \frac{s_\pi^2 - s_{\pi\pi^*} + (1 - a^*)s_u^2}{s_d^2}, \tag{10'}$$

where we have used the fact that mean real yield differentials are equal across countries. The foreign portfolio share differs only in the minimum variance component and does so only to the extent that there is real exchange rate variability.

In particular, with real exchange rate variability foreigners will hold a larger share of their portfolio in terms of foreign securities if their expenditure share of foreign goods, $1 - a^*$, exceeds our expenditure share for those commodities, $1 - a$. Differences in tastes do *not* affect the speculative portfolio.

The condition of market equilibrium is obtained from aggregation: $xW + x^*W^* = V^*$, or using (10) and (10'),

$$\bar{r}^* - \bar{r} = \theta s_d^2 \left[\frac{V^*}{V^* + V} - \alpha \right] + \theta s_u^2 (a^* - a) \frac{W^*}{W + W^*}, \tag{5''}$$

where α was defined in (3') and where W and W^* are aggregate home and foreign, nonmonetary nominal assets: $W + W^* = \overline{W} = V + V^*$.

Country-specific consumption patterns thus introduce a real interest differential or risk premium. The extent of the premium depends on the difference in tastes, $a^* - a$, the coefficient of risk aversion, the variance of the *real* exchange rate depreciation, and wealth distribution $W^*/(W + W^*)$.

The role of differences in consumption patterns is to introduce distribution effects into the determination of the risk premium. An international redistribution of wealth toward the foreign country, with $a > a^*$, will lower the real yield differential on foreign securities. In terms of excess depreciation we now obtain the following relation:

$$d - f = (d - \bar{d}) + \theta s_d^2 \left[\left(\frac{V^*}{V^* + V} - \alpha \right) + (a^* - a) \frac{s_u^2}{s_d^2} \frac{W^*}{W^* + W} \right]. \tag{14'}$$

Accordingly, differences in consumption patterns induce an extra term in the risk premium that causes a divergence between the forward premium and the rate of depreciation. A redistribution of wealth toward the foreign country, through a cumulative current account deficit of the home country, would reduce the rate of excess depreciation, as $a^* - a < 0$.

Equations (5'') and (14') are interesting in that they point to the difference in the quantitative importance of the relative supply and the relative wealth effects. The latter has a coefficient $(a^* - a)s_u^2/s_d^2$ that is a fraction of the other coefficient. Thus empirically we would expect relative supply effects to be more important, unless current account imbalances dominate budget imbalances that give rise to the issue of outside debt. In much of the literature on the risk premium, in particular in the work by Dooley and Isard (1979), the wealth distribution effect is singled out, and rejected, as an explanation for the large excess depreciation of exchange rates in the 1970s. For a further discussion, see Dornbusch (1980).

Notes

I wish to acknowledge helpful comments from E. Cardoso, R. Cumby, and S. Fischer. Financial support was provided by a grant from the National Science Foundation.

1. Equation (5) can of course be directly derived using the conventional result that the yield differential over the risk-free rate is proportional to the covariance with

the market. Forming the respective expressions, we find that $r^* - r = \theta(s_{rR} - s_{r^*R})$, where $R = (1 - x)r + xr^*$ is the return on the market portfolio. Calculating the expression and using $x = V^*/W$ and the definition of α yields equation (5).

2. This last question is addressed in the appendix.

3. Throughout this chapter we abstract from differences in risk aversion as a source of distribution effects. Thus θ is assumed constant and independent of the distribution of wealth. We also assume away the possibility of default.

4. More extensively we can write equation (19) as $\pi = \Psi(q - y) + m$, where q and y are actual demand and full employment output. Actual demand is a function of output and the terms of trade: $q = vy + \mu\sigma$. Accordingly, the equilibrium terms of trade are $\sigma = y(1 - v)/\mu$. Using the definition, we can write the inflation equation as $\pi = \mu\psi(\sigma - \bar{\sigma}) + \dot{m}$.

5. The saddle point properties of the model, as is conventional for rational expectations problems, can be seen by looking at the real balance and terms of trade space, plotting the schedules corresponding to constant real balances (and real bonds) and to constant terms of trade, respectively.

References

Adler, M., and Dumas, B. 1976. "Portfolio Choice and the Demand for Forward Exchange." *American Economic Review* (May).

Branson, W. et. al. 1977. "Exchange Rates in the Short Run." *European Economic Review* (December).

Cumby, R., and Obstfeld, M. 1979. "Exchange Rate Expectations and Nominal Interest Differentials: A Test of the Fisher Hypothesis." Unpublished manuscript, MIT.

Dooley, M., and Isard, P. 1979. "The Portfolio Balance Model of Exchange Rates." Unpublished manuscript, Federal Reserve Board.

Dornbusch, R. 1976a. "Capital Mobility, Flexible Exchange Rates and Macroeconomic Equilibrium." In Claassen, E. and Salin, P. (eds.), *Recent Developments in International Monetary Economics*. North-Holland.

Dornbusch, R. 1976b. "Expectations and Exchange Rate Dynamics." *Journal of Political Economy* (December).

Dornbusch, R. 1978. "Monetary Policy under Exchange Rate Flexibility." In Federal Reserve Bank of Boston. Conference Series. *Managed Exchange Rate Flexibility*.

Dornbusch, R. 1979. "Intervention, Monetary Stabilisation and Real Appreciation." Unpublished manuscript, MIT.

Dornbusch, R. 1980. "Flexible Exchange Rates and the Capital Mobility Problem." Unpublished manuscript, MIT.

Dornbusch, R., and Fischer, S. 1980. "Exchange Rates and the Current Account." *American Economic Review* (December).

Fama, E., and Farber, A. 1979. "Money, Bonds and Foreign Exchange." *American Economic Review* (September).

Fischer, S. 1976. "Comment." *Scandinavian Journal of Economics* 2.

Frankel, J. 1979a. "On the Mark: A Theory of Floating Exchange Rates Based on Real Interest Differentials." *American Economic Review* (September).

Frankel, J. 1979b. "The Diversifiability of Exchange Risk." *Journal of International Economics* (September).

Frenkel, J. 1980. "Flexible Exchange Rates in the 1970s." Unpublished manuscript, University of Chicago.

Harris, R., and Purvis, D. 1979. "Equilibrium Theories of the Forward Exchange Rate." Unpublished manuscript. Queens University.

Henderson, D. 1979. "The Dynamics of Exchange Market Intervention." Unpublished manuscript, Federal Reserve Board.

Isard, P. 1980. "Expected and Unexpected Exchange Rate Changes." Unpublished manuscript, Federal Reserve Board.

Kouri, P. 1975. *Three Essays on the Theory of Flexible Exchange Rates.* Unpublished Ph.D. dissertation, MIT.

Kouri, P. 1978a. "The Determinants of the Forward Premium." Unpublished manuscript, University of Stockholm.

Kouri, P. 1978b. "International Investment and Interest Rate Linkages under Flexible Exchange Rates." In Aliber, R. (ed.). *The Political Economy of Monetary Reform.* New York: Macmillan.

Kouri, P., and Macedo, J. 1978. "Exchange Rates and the International Adjustment Process." *Brookings Papers,* 2.

Levich, R. 1979. "On the Efficiency of Markets for Foreign Exchange." In Dornbusch, R. and Frenkel, J. (eds.). *International Economic Policy.* Baltimore, MD: Johns Hopkins University Press.

Longworth, D. 1979. *Essays on the Canadian Dollar.* Unpublished Ph.D. dissertation, MIT.

Mussa, M. 1976. "The Exchange Rate and the Balance of Payments." *Scandinavian Journal of Economics,* 2.

Mussa, M. 1979. "The Empirical Regularities in the Behavior of Exchange Rates and Theories of the Foreign Exchange Market." *Carnegie Rochester Conference Series,* Vol. 11.

Obstfeld, M. 1979. *Portfolio Balance, Monetary Policy and the $/DM Rate.* Unpublished Ph.D. dissertation; MIT.

Porter, M. 1979. "Exchange Rates, Current Accounts and Economic Activity." Unpublished manuscript, Federal Reserve Board.

Rogoff, K. 1979. *Essays on Expectations and Exchange Rate Volatility.* Unpublished Ph.D. dissertation, MIT.

Roll, R., and Solnik, B. 1977. "A Pure Foreign Exchange Asset Pricing Model." *Journal of International Economics* (May).

Stulz, R. 1979. "An Essay on the Theory of International Asset Pricing." Unpublished manuscript, MIT.

Tryon, R. 1979. *Essays on Exchange Rates in the 1920s.* Unpublished Ph.D. dissertation, MIT.

Solnik, B. 1973. *European Capital Markets: Toward a General Theory of International Investment.* Lexington Books.

Wihlborg, C. 1978. *Currency Risks in International Financial Markets.* Princeton Studies in International Finance. No. 44.

Wilson, C. 1979. "Anticipated Disturbances and Exchange Rate Dynamics" *Journal of Political Economy* (September).

8

The Theory of Flexible Exchange Rate Regimes and Macroeconomic Policy

This chapter is concerned with some issues in theory of flexible exchange rates. Specifically, we study the determinants of the exchange rate, both in the short and long run, the role of capital mobility and speculation in that context, and the scope for the international transmission of disturbances. In discussing the transmission of disturbances, particular emphasis is given to the idea that in the short run monetary and price disturbances are not offset by matching exchange rate changes and, for that reason, are spread internationally.

The issues raised in this chapter have been, to a large extent, discussed in the literature. We note here, in particular, Mundell (1964, 1968) and Fleming (1962) in their discussion of stabilization policy under flexible exchange rates as well as the subsequent work of Argy and Porter (1972) that formalizes the role of expectations in this context. Work by Black (1973, 1975) has emphasized the role of asset markets in exchange rate determination and a paper by Niehans (1975) has explored the interaction of exchange rate expectations and relative price responses to question the effectiveness of monetary policy under flexible rates.

The present study adds to that strand of literature in that it distinguishes short-run effects of policies, sustained in part by price rigidities and expectational errors, from the longer-run effects where relative prices and homogeneity are given emphasis. The aggregation departs from the standard Keynesian model of complete specialization and two traded goods in distinguishing traded goods as a composite commodity and nontraded goods. Such an aggregation is preferred since it breaks the identification of the exchange rate with the terms of trade, introduces scope for a monetary interpretation of the exchange rate and leaves room at the same time for intersectoral considerations.

Originally published in *Scandinavian Journal of Economics*, vol. 78 (1976), pp. 255–275.

In section 8.1 we lay out a general equilibrium framework for the discussion of exchangé rates from a long-run perspective. The critical assumptions of that theory are purchasing power parity for traded goods and monetary equilibrium. In section 8.2 the assumption of purchasing power parity is relaxed to yield a short-run or "money-market" theory of the exchange rate. In section 8.3 we return to purchasing power parity and investigate the role of speculation in affecting the scope for the international transmission of monetary disturbances and for the operation of monetary and fiscal policy. In section 8.4 the discussion is extended to a dual exchange rate system.

8.1 A General View of Exchange Rate Determinants

In this section we outline a fairly general and eclectic view of the determinants of exchange rates. Such a view links monetary and real variables as jointly influencing the equilibrium level of the exchange rate. The view is appropriate to full equilibrium or the 'long run' and is a benchmark from which to judge departures and alternatives.

A critical ingredient of this approach is purchasing power parity, in the narrow sense of goods arbitrage for internationally traded goods, so that the exchange rate equates the prices of traded goods in alternative currencies:[1]

$$P_T = eP_T^*, \tag{1}$$

where P_T and P_T^* represent the domestic and foreign currency prices of traded goods and where e is the domestic currency price of foreign exchange.[2]

The prices of traded goods can be related to the price levels, P and P^*, respectively. The appropriate relationship is given by the equilibrium *relative* price of traded goods in terms of the price levels, θ and θ^*:

$$P_T = \theta P; \quad P_T^* = \theta^* P^*. \tag{2}$$

The determinants of the equilibrium relative price structure, denoted here by θ and θ^*, will be discussed later. For the present it suffices to note that an increase in the equilibrium price of traded goods by x percent raises their relative price θ by $(1 - \gamma)x$ percent, where γ and $(1 - \gamma)$, respectively, denote the shares of traded goods and nontraded goods in the price index.

Using (2) in equation (1), we can express the exchange rate in terms of price levels and relative prices:

$$e = \left(\frac{P}{P^*}\right)\left(\frac{\theta}{\theta^*}\right). \tag{3}$$

The next step is to link up the discussion with the monetary sector. This is achieved by multiplying and dividing (3) by the domestic and foreign nominal quantity of money, M and M^*.[3] Futhermore, imposing the conditions of of monetary equilibrium,

$$\frac{M}{P} = L(\ ),$$

$$\frac{M^*}{P^*} = L^*(\ ), \tag{4}$$

where L and L^* represent the domestic and foreign demand for real balances, we arrive at (5):[4]

$$e = \left(\frac{M}{M^*}\right)\left(\frac{L^*}{L}\right)\left(\frac{\theta}{\theta^*}\right). \tag{5}$$

Equation (5) collects the principal determinants of exchange rates. These are, respectively, the nominal quantities of monies, the real money demands, and the relative price structure. It can be viewed as an *equilibrium* exchange rate since in its derivation we have used the conditions of goods arbitrage, money market equilibrium and, implicitly in using (2), home goods market equilibrium. The usefulness of (5) is enhanced by considering the logarithmic differential denoting a percentage change by a $\hat{}$:

$$\hat{e} = (\hat{M} - \hat{M}^*) + (\hat{L}^* - \hat{L}) + (\hat{\theta} - \hat{\theta}^*). \tag{6}$$

The first term in (6) captures the effects of monetary changes on the exchange rate. Other things equal, the country with the higher monetary growth will have a depreciating exchange rate. This particular term captures the effect of differences in long-run inflation rates between countries and their reflection in exchange rates.

The effect of changes in real money demand is captured in the second term in (6). The country that experiences a (relative) increase in real money demand will have an appreciation in the exchange rate. Among the factors that exert an influence on real money demand, we note here, in particular, interest rates, expected inflation, and real income growth. The real money demand term in (6) constitutes one of the links between the exchange rate, the monetary sector and the real sector. This term helps explain how changes in productivity, for example, get reflected in exchange rate changes.

The last term in (6) collects the effect of changes in the relative price structure on the exchange rate. This term arises entirely from real considerations and, in fact, has been identified in some literature as the "real exchange rate"[*][5] Given the nominal quantity of money and the demand for real balances, and therefore the price level, an increase in the equilibrium relative price of traded goods will be reflected in a depreciation in the exchange rate. Changes in absorption, shifts in demand, or biased output growth, *given* a monetary policy that sustains the price level, will therefore directly affect the exchange rate.

An example will show how equation (6) can be applied. Assume that in the home country we have an increase in spending that falls entirely on traded goods, while abroad everything remains unchanged. Assume further that because of the absence of capital mobility the exchange rate adjusts to maintain trade balance equilibrium. In figure 8.1 we show the equilibrium in the home goods market along the NN schedule. At higher interest rates, and hence lower real spending, we require a higher relative price of traded goods to clear the home goods market. An increase in interest rates has an expenditure reducing effect that has to be offset by the expenditure and production switching effects of a relative price change. Along the $T = 0$ schedule, we have trade balance equilibrium. At lower interest rates and hence higher aggregate real spending, we require a higher relative price of traded goods to maintain trade balance. The initial equilibrium is at point A_0.

An increase in spending that falls on traded goods creates at the initial equilibrium an excess demand for traded goods and therefore requires higher interest rates and/or a higher relative price of traded goods to maintain trade balance. The $T = 0$ schedule accordingly shifts to $T' = 0$, and our new equilibrium is at point A' with an increase in both interest rates and the relative price of traded goods. The higher interest rate is required to restore balance between income and spending. At that higher interest rate, spending on home goods has declined and we accordingly require a reduction in their relative price.

Consider next the implications of this disturbance for the exchange rate. The higher equilibrium interest rate lowers the demand for real balances and therefore contributes, via an increase in the price level, to a depreciation of the exchange rate. This effect is further enhanced by the required increase in the relative price of traded goods so that the net result is an unambiguous depreciation of the exchange rate.[6]

The example features several aspects of exchange rate determination that are worth spelling out in more detail. First, and perhaps foremost, the exchange rate is determined in a general equilibrium framework by the interaction of all markets (and countries). A particularly important feature is that the equilibrium obtains in *both* the flow and stock markets so that the exchange rate is in no manner determined by the current flow demands and supplies of foreign exchange.[7]

Next we give emphasis to the role of *monetary* considerations in the context of exchange rate determinations. As has been emphasized by J. Robinson (1935), the exchange rate is proximately determined by the balance between money supply and real money demand. The fact that the approach taken here is "monetary" in no manner precludes the role of "real" factors since these must be expected to enter as determinants of the demand for real balances and thus exert an effect on the exchange rate. Mussa (1974) has emphasized this point for the analysis of the balance of payments and has noted the obvious extension to a flexible rate regime.

Since the exchange rate is determined as part of the general, real and monetary equilibrium of the system, there is no relevant sense in which one would want to assert that the exchange rate is an exclusively monetary phenomenon. Indeed, the equilibrium exchange rate can change without any accompanying change in the money supply, or the real money demand. Such would, for example, be the case if there were a change in the composition of production between home goods and traded goods. Having noted the role of real considerations in this context, it is important, however, to recognize that organizing thought about the exchange rate around the monetary sector is likely to be a direct and informative approach. To appreciate this point, consider the alternative of a "wage approach."

A wage approach can be formulated by using in (3) the definition of real wages, $w = W/P$ and $w^* = W^*/P^*$, to obtain an equation similar to (6):

$$\hat{e} = (\hat{W} - \hat{W}^*) + (\hat{w}^* - \hat{w}) + (\hat{\theta} - \hat{\theta}^*). \tag{6}'$$

Provided the general equilibrium structure is used to fill in the details of (6)', we arrive at the same answer as we would obtain from (6). The choice then must lie in an assumption about the stability of the relevant behavioral equations and, perhaps, an assumption about the dominant source of disturbances.

A third feature of this approach is the *long-run* or *equilibrium* nature of exchange rate determination. This view is implicit in the fact that we allow all markets to clear and that we explicitly impose the condition of monetary stock equilibrium, goods market equilibrium and purchasing power parity for traded goods. Either of these conditions may not hold in the short run, and, therefore, exchange rates can depart from the prediction in (6)'.

For short-run purposes, we will assume that the exchange rate is altogether dominated by the asset markets and more specifically by capital mobility and money market equilibrium. Arbitrage of traded goods prices and goods market equilibrium is attained only over time.[8] Within such a perspective, we could assume that the price level and real income, at a point in time, are given and that the interest rate is determined by the quantity of money along with elements that shift the demand for real balances. Interest arbitrage for given expected future spot rates, determined by speculators, will then set the spot rates. Such a view is explored in the next section.

8.2 Short-Run Determination of Exchange Rates

In the short run, the scope for goods arbitrage may be limited, and accordingly purchasing power parity as in (1) may only obtain for a limited set of commodities. Under these conditions, it is useful to abstract altogether from the details of goods markets and rather view exchange rates as being determined entirely in the asset market. Such a view will assume capital mobility and indeed assign a critical role to it. Exchange rates in this perspective are determined by interest arbitrage together with speculation about future spot rates. To provide an example of this approach, we consider the effects of an increase in the nominal quantity of money in a "small country."

Given real income and other determinants of the demand for real balances, the equilibrium interest rate, at which the existing quantity of money is willingly held, will be a function of the real quantity of money:[9]

$$r = r(M/P, \ldots). \tag{7}$$

Interest arbitrage, assuming that on a covered basis domestic and foreign assets are perfect substitutes, requires that the domestic interest rate, less the forward premium on foreign exchange, λ, be equal to the foreign interest rate, r^*:[10]

$$r - \lambda = r^*, \tag{8}$$

where the forward premium is defined as the percentage excess of the forward rate, $\bar{e}$, over the current spot rate:

$$\lambda \equiv \frac{\overline{e} - e}{e}.$$

Substituting (7) and λ in (8), we have a relationship between the real money supply, the spot rate and the forward rate:

$$r\left(\frac{M}{P}, \dots\right) = r^* + \frac{\overline{e}}{e} - 1. \tag{8'}$$

Differentiating (8)' and denoting the interest responsiveness of money demand by σ we obtain:[11]

$$\hat{e} = \hat{\overline{e}} + \left(\frac{1}{\sigma}\right)\hat{M}, \tag{9}$$

where by assumption the foreign interest rate and the price level are held constant. Equation (9) suggests that a change in the forward rate induces an equiproportionate change in the spot rate, while an increase in the money supply causes a depreciation in the spot rate that is inversely proportional to the interest responsiveness of money demand. Since the interest responsiveness of money demand is of the order of $\sigma = 0.5$, a monetary expansion will be matched by a significantly more than proportionate depreciation.

So far we have assumed that the forward rate is exogenous. The next step is therefore to link the forward rate to the analysis. For the point to be made, it is sufficient to assume that the forward rate is set by speculators in a perfectly elastic manner at the level of the expected future spot rate and that expectations about the latter are formed in an adaptive manner. With these assumptions we have

$$\overline{e} = \pi e + (1 - \pi)e_{-1}, \quad 0 < \pi < 1. \tag{10}$$

The impact effect of a change in the spot rate is therefore to raise the forward rate but proportionately less, so the price of foreign exchange is at a forward discount. Substituting from (10), the expression $\hat{\overline{e}} = \pi\hat{e}$ in (9) yields the total impact effect of a monetary expansion on the spot rate:

$$\hat{e} = \frac{1}{(1 - \pi)\sigma}\hat{M}. \tag{9'}$$

We note that the adaptive expectations serve to increase the impact effect of money on the exchange rate. In fact, the more closely the forward rate is determined by the current spot rate, the closer π is to unity, the larger the exchange rate fluctuations induced by a variation in money.

In interpreting the effect of a monetary expansion on the exchange rate, three considerations stand out: First domestic and foreign assets are assumed perfect substitutes on a covered basis as is reflected in (8). This implies that independently of any particular assumptions about expectations, a reduction in domestic interest rates has to be matched by a forward discount on foreign exchange in order to equalize the net yields on domestic and foreign assets. The next two considerations are dependent on the particular expectations assumption in (10) and concern, respectively, the direction and magnitude of the change in the spot rate. A reduced domestic interest rate, for asset market equilibrium, has to be matched by an expected appreciation of the exchange rate. The expectations mechanism in (10) implies that a depreciation in the spot rate will give rise to such an expectation, since the elasticity of expectations, π, is less than unity. With an elasticity of expectations less than unity, a depreciation of the spot rate is accompanied by a less than proportionate depreciation of the expected future spot rate, or an anticipated appreciation. Finally, the magnitude of the depreciation in the spot rate that is required depends on both the interest response of money demand, σ, and the elasticity of expectations, π. The smaller the interest responsiveness of money demand, the larger the interest rate change that is brought about by a monetary expansion and therefore, the larger the expected appreciation that has to be brought about by a depreciation in the spot rate. Furthermore a given depreciation of the spot rate will give rise to an expected appreciation of the future spot rate that is smaller, the larger the elasticity of expectations. Accordingly, large exchange rate changes will arise in circumstances where the interest response of money demand is small and the elasticity of expectations is large.

The short-run determination of exchange rates is entirely dominated by the conditions of equilibrium in the asset markets and expectations. The *liquidity* effect of money on the interest rate has a counterpart in the immediate depreciation of the spot rate that has to be sufficient to cause the existing stock of domestic assets to be held. It is in this sense that in the short run the exchange rate is determined in the asset markets.

Over time the exchange rate is determined by the interaction between goods markets and asset markets. This is so because the price level will rise to match the expansion in the nominal quantity of money until, in the long run, the monetary expansion is exactly matched by a price increase so that real balances and interest rates are unchanged and the spot and forward rates depreciate in the same proportion as the increase in the nominal quantity of money. The exact dynamics of that adjustment process will depend on the speed with which prices respond as compared to expectations. The response of prices will be due, in part, to the traditional effect of a reduced interest rate on aggregate spending. There will be in the present framework an additional channel that serves to speed up the responsiveness of prices to a monetary expansion. The impact effect of a monetary expansion on the spot rate, as of a given price level, will cause a departure from goods arbitrage. Domestic goods will become relatively cheap as compared to foreign goods and therefore induce a substitution of world demand toward domestic goods. This additional channel implies that even if domestic aggregate spending were unresponsive to the interest rate, or slow to adjust, there remains a subsidiary channel, the arbitrage effect, that serves to drive up domestic prices and causes the real effects of a monetary expansion to be transitory.

8.3 Speculation, Macroeconomic Policies, and the Transmission of Disturbances

In the present section we go beyond the impact effect of disturbances and consider the behavior over time of the economy in response to policy-induced or speculative disturbances. In particular, we want to show that speculation that is not guided by "rational expectations" allows monetary changes to be transmitted internationally even under circumstances where prices are fully flexible. For the purposes of the present section, we continue to assume that the home country is small and therefore faces given world prices of traded goods and a given world rate of interest. We furthermore assume that goods arbitrage is continuously maintained. In addition to internationally traded commodities, the home country produces and consumes nontraded goods. Price and factor cost flexibility ensure that markets clear all the time and full employment is maintained.

   The analysis focuses on the equilibrium conditions in the markets for home goods and in the asset market. Consider first the home goods market. The excess demand for home goods will depend on the relative price of traded goods in terms of the price level, P_T/P, the interest rate that determines absorption for a given level of real income, and the level of government spending on nontraded goods, g:

$$N\left(\frac{P_T}{P}, r, g\right) = 0, \quad N_{P_T/P} > 0, N_r < 0, N_g = 1. \tag{11}$$

An increase in the relative price of traded goods creates an excess demand as consumers substitute toward home goods, while productive resources

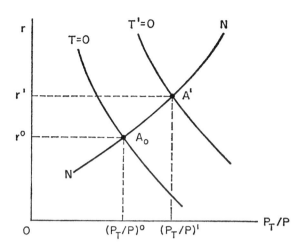

Figure 8.1

move into the traded goods sector, thus reducing the supply of home goods. An increase in the interest rate reduces absorption, part of which falls on home goods and to that extent creates an excess supply. Finally, an increase in government spending directly adds to home goods demand. We can solve the equilibrium condition in (11) for the equilibrium relative price of traded goods in terms of the interest rate and government spending:

$$\frac{P_T}{P} = \theta(r; g), \quad \theta_r > 0, \theta_g < 0. \tag{11}'$$

Equation (11)′ is plotted in figure 8.1 as the NN schedule.[12]

Consider next the condition of equilibrium in the money market. With a demand for real balances that depends on interest rates and real income, we can solve the money market equilibrium condition for the equilibrium interest rate as a function of the real money supply and real income:

$$r = r\left(\frac{M}{P}; y\right), \quad r_{M/P} < 0, r_y > 0. \tag{12}$$

Next we substitute the equilibrium interest rate in (11), and noting that purchasing power parity obtains with a given price of foreign goods, $P_T = eP_T^*$, we can write the home goods market equilibrium condition as:

$$\bar{N}\left(\frac{eP_T^*}{P}, r\left(\frac{M}{P}\right), g\right) = 0, \tag{13}$$

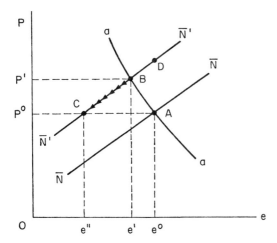

Figure 8.2

where $\bar{N}$ denotes the reduced form that embodies the condition of money market equilibrium and where the constant level of real income is suppressed as an argument.

In figure 8.2 we show the home goods market equilibrium schedule $\bar{N}\bar{N}$. The schedule is positively sloped and flatter than a ray through the origin. The reason is as follows. At a higher price level, we have lower real balances, higher interest rates, and therefore reduced real spending. Part of the reduction in real spending falls on home goods and creates an excess supply that has to be eliminated by a decline in their *relative* price, that is, by an increase in the exchange rate or the price of traded goods relative to the price level.[13] The $\bar{N}\bar{N}$ schedule is drawn for a given nominal quantity of money and a given foreign currency price of traded goods.

We again assume that covered interest arbitrage ensures that interest rates are linked internationally so that (8) continues to hold. The forward rate is set by speculators, according to the adaptive expectations scheme in (10). Substituting the expression for the forward rate in (8), and using the equilibrium interest rate in (12), we obtain the condition for money market equilibrium together with covered interest arbitrage:

$$r\left(\frac{M}{P}\right) - (1 - \pi)\left(\frac{e_{-1}}{e - 1}\right) = r^*, \tag{14}$$

A critical property of the speculative behavior is that an increase in the spot rate creates a forward discount, since it will cause the forward rate to rise less than proportionately. To maintain interest parity, a forward discount on foreign exchange has to be accompanied by a reduction in domestic relative to foreign interest rates. Given the nominal quantity of money, such a decline in interest rates would arise if the domestic price level declined. The asset market equilibrium schedule aa in figure 8.2 reflects equation (14) for a given foreign interest rate, a given nominal quantity of money, and a given past spot rate e_{-1}. The initial equilibrium obtains at point A with all markets clearing and the forward rate at par so that no revision of expectations is required.

Consider next the effect of an increase in the foreign price level. We note from (14) that there is no direct effect on the asset market and therefore the aa schedule remains unaffected. Consider next the home goods market. At an unchanged exchange rate, the increase in the foreign price level raises the domestic currency price of traded goods and hence their relative price, so that an excess demand for home goods would arise. To eliminate the excess demand, the exchange rate would have to appreciate to fully offset the foreign price increase. This is represented in figure 8.2 by a leftward shift of the $\overline{N}\,\overline{N}$ schedule to $\overline{N}'\,\overline{N}'$ in the proportion of the foreign price increase.

The short-run effect of the price increase is to move the economy to point B with an appreciation in the exchange rate that falls short of the foreign price increase and an increase in the domestic price level. Furthermore, the *relative* price of traded goods rises, and the increase in the price level reduces real balances and therefore raises interest rates with a matching premium on forward exchange.

Quite obviously, the foreign price change in the short run exerts real effects in the home country. The flexible exchange rate, in this formulation, fails to isolate the home country from foreign nominal disturbances. The explanation for this nonneutrality lies in the behavior of speculators.

The adjustment process from the initial equilibrium at point A to the short-run position of equilibrium can be viewed in the following manner: The increase in the foreign currency price of traded goods, at the initial exchange rate, raises the domestic currency price of traded goods, the price level and therefore the rate of interest. Such a position is shown at point D where the home goods market clears and the price level has risen, although proportionately less than the price of traded goods. At that point covered interest arbitrage is not satisfied, since the increased interest rate is not compensated by an offsetting forward premium on foreign exchange. Therefore an *incipient* capital inflow develops that causes the spot rate to appreciate until the appropriate premium has been generated. This is the move from point D to the short-run equilibrium at point B.[14]

In the short run the failure of exchange rates to fully offset the foreign price increase implies that the domestic nominal and real equilibrium is affected by a foreign nominal disturbance. The domestic price level rises as do interest rates. Domestic absorption declines and real spending on home goods falls so that a deflationary effect is exerted on that sector. The reduction in absorption and the induced increase in the relative price of traded goods imply an expansion in the production of traded goods and a trade balance surplus. The trade surplus in turn is financed by a capital outflow.

The equilibrium at point B is only transitory, since it is sustained by expectational errors. Speculators underpredict the actual appreciation of the exchange rate and therefore will revise their forecast. That revision causes at each current rate the premium to decline and therefore to create a covered differential in favor of the home country that leads to continued appreciation of the exchange rate. That process moves the economy from point B to C over time. The process will continue until the exchange rate has sufficiently appreciated to fully offset the increase in foreign prices. This is true at point C, where the domestic price level and hence interest rates have returned to their initial level.[15]

The lack of homogeneity that the system exhibits in the short run applies similarly to an increase in the domestic money stock. In the short run, price flexibility notwithstanding, the price level and the exchange rate increase proportionately less than the money supply, and accordingly, the interest rate decreases while the forward rate goes to a discount. The change in the spot rate induced by a monetary expansion in the short run is given by:

$$\hat{e} = \frac{\delta}{\delta + \sigma(1 - \pi)} \hat{M}, \quad 0 < \delta < 1, \tag{15}$$

where δ is the elasticity of the price level with respect to the price of traded goods along the $\bar{N}\bar{N}$ schedule. We note that in the present context, and unlike in section 8.2, the exchange rate changes proportionately less than the nominal quantity of money. This is entirely due to the adjustment in prices that is permitted here and that serves to lower the increase in real balances associated with a given increase in the nominal quantity of money.

Over time, as expectations are revised, the system will converge to neutrality in the sense that the monetary change leaves all real variables

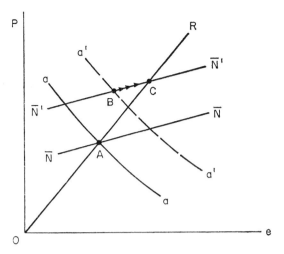

Figure 8.3

unchanged. The short run real effects of a monetary change are again due to expectational errors, or more precisely, to the fact that speculators use irrelevant information and therefore affect the real equilibrium. If instead the equilibrium exchange rate in (5) were used as a basis of prediction, the system would be homogeneous, even in the short run.

The adjustment process to a monetary disturbance is illustrated in figure 8.3. Initial equilibrium obtains at point A, with a relative price structure indicated by the slope of the ray OR. The increase in the nominal quantity of money at the initial equilibrium exchange rate and prices lowers interest rates and therefore creates an excess demand for home goods and a departure from covered interest arbitrage. For home goods equilibrium to obtain, the exchange rate and prices would have to increase in the same proportion as the nominal quantity of money. This is indicated by an upward shift of the $\bar{N}\bar{N}$ schedule in the proportion $AC/OA = \hat{M}$. The asset market equilibrium in the short run does not possess homogeneity properties, since the elasticity of exchange rate expectations is less than unity, which is equivalent to saying that expectations are sticky. Accordingly, the aa schedule shifts upward in a smaller proportion. Short-run equilibrium will obtain at point B with an increase in the exchange rate and prices that are proportionately smaller than the increase in money. In that short-run equilibrium, the relative price of home goods will be higher compared to A, which is a reflection of the fact that in the short run the interest rate declines and absorption expands. The adjustment of expectations over time will shift the

$a'a'$ schedule up and to the right until the long run real equilibrium is restored at point C, where expectational errors have subsided and prices and exchange rates fully reflect the monetary change.

In discussing stabilization policy under flexible exchange rates, Mundell (1964, 1968) notes that with perfect capital mobility monetary policy exerts strong effects on nominal income, while fiscal policy has no effect. The reason is that in the absence of forward market considerations, the given interest rate in the world determines the domestic interest rate and hence velocity. Given velocity, fiscal policy has no effect on nominal income, while monetary policy becomes most powerful. The present framework, following Mundell (1964) and Wonnacott (1972), notes that the short-run changes in forward premia allow interest rate and hence velocity changes that tend to dampen the effect of monetary policy. In the short run, monetary policy causes a depreciation of the exchange rate accompanied by a premium on forward exchange and a decline in interest rates. The decline in interest rates lowers velocity and therefore dampens in the short run the nominal income expansion. Over time the revision of expectations eliminates the premium and therefore restores interest rates and velocity to their initial level and thus causes monetary changes to be reflected in equiproportionate changes in nominal income.

In concluding this section, we return to the transmission of foreign price disturbances and ask what policies the government could pursue to offset the transmission process. Here the choice has to be made between price level stability, or stability of the real equilibrium, that is, of interest rates, absorption and relative prices. If the preference is for stability of the real equilibrium, then the government should peg the interest rate, or the exchange rate, and therefore increase the domestic nominal quantity of money in the same proportion as the foreign price increase. If such a policy is followed, domestic prices move along with foreign prices at constant exchange rates and without any real effects. The alternative of a constant domestic price level will require a reduction in the nominal quantity of money in the short run and will involve larger relative price fluctuations. Noting that a constant price level policy will require in the adjustment process first a decline in the nominal price of home goods and an increase in the nominal price of traded goods with a subsequent reversal, any downward rigidity of prices will make such a policy costly. The same argument applies to the automatic adjustment process associated with a constant nominal quantity of money. These remarks accordingly provide support for a policy of pegging interest rates and exchange rates in the case of foreign nominal disturbances.

8.4 Speculative Disturbances and Dual Exchange Rates

In the present section, we will investigate the effects of exogenous speculative disturbances and proceed from there to a discussion of a dual exchange rate system that has been advocated as a remedy against the influence of speculation on the real sector.

To allow for an exogenous change in the expected future spot rate, we modify (10) to

$$\bar{e} = \pi e + (1 - \pi)e_{-1} - eu, \tag{16}$$

where u denotes a current shift term in expectations. Specifically, an increase in u implies that given the current and past spot rates, we have an expected appreciation in the exchange rate and therefore a forward discount. Using the present form of the forward rate in the asset market equilibrium condition yields:

$$r\left(\frac{M}{P}\right) - (1 - \pi)\left(\frac{e_{-1}}{e} - 1\right) + u = r^*. \tag{17}$$

Consider now the implication of an anticipated appreciation of the exchange rate. In figure 8.4 we have the initial full equilibrium at point A. An increase in the expected future spot rate will shift the asset market equilibrium schedule down and to the left to $a'a'$. At the initial equilibrium interest rate and prices, the anticipated appreciation creates a covered

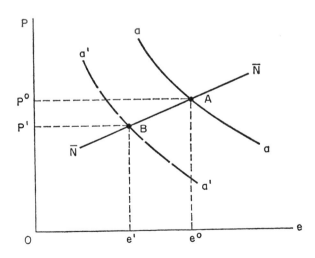

Figure 8.4

differential in favor of the home country and therefore causes an incipient capital inflow that appreciates the exchange rate.

Short-run equilibrium obtains at point B. The anticipated increase in the future spot rate is reflected in an appreciation in the current spot rate, a discount on forward exchange, and a decline in the domestic interest rate. More important, the decline in traded goods prices that is implied by the appreciation and the decline in the relative price of traded goods imply a deflationary influence in that sector. Traded goods prices decline relative to costs, and for that reason, the speculative attack imposes a real cost on the traded goods sector. This is very much the problem currently experienced by strong currency countries and, in particular, Switzerland.[16]

The short-run equilibrium at B is sustained by expectations that will prove erroneous and, to that extent, will over time give rise to revision of expectations and a return to the initial equilibrium. More likely, however, the sectoral problems caused by the speculative pressure on the exchange rate will give rise to some form of intervention. There would seem to be a case for dual exchange rates that isolate the current account transactions from speculative attacks; alternatively, and this has been a solution favored by the Swiss, to join a strong currency area and thereby share the burden of a speculative attack.

A dual or two-tier exchange market can be readily introduced in the preceding analysis. Under such a regime, we distinguish the official rate, $\bar{e}$, applicable to current account transactions, from the free rate that applies to capital account transactions.[17] In the following, we will assume that interest earnings can be converted at the free rate, e. The latter assumption implies that the analysis underlying the asset market equilibrium schedule aa in figure 8.5 remains unchanged. Equilibrium in the asset market continues to require that covered interest arbitrage obtains where the forward rate continues to be formed by an adaptive expectations mechanism.[18] The home goods market equilibrium schedule $\bar{N}\bar{N}$ is drawn as a function of the official rate $\bar{e}$. Initial equilibrium obtains at point A, where the official rate, $\bar{e}^0$, happens to coincide with the free rate.

To illustrate the working of the system, now consider again in figure 8.5 the problem of a speculative attack in the form of an increase in the expected future spot rate. The incipient capital flow will immediately bid up the free rate to e', where the spot rate has appreciated sufficiently to offset the expected appreciation. There is no effect at all on the equilibrium price level, relative prices, or interest rate because the relevant rate for the determination of relative prices is the fixed official rate $\bar{e}^0$. Under these circumstances the economy is entirely shielded from the effects of specula-

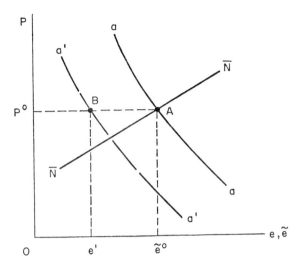

Figure 8.5

tion on the real sector. How does the system differ from a unified free rate? Under the latter the appreciation of the exchange rate would have put downward pressure on traded goods prices and the price level, while here the international price connection via the official rate remains undisturbed.

How does a dual exchange rate system affect the scope of domestic policies? Consider an increase in government spending or a cut in taxes that gives rise to an expansion in aggregate real spending. In figure 8.6, we show that, as a consequence of higher real spending, we have an excess demand for home goods and therefore the market equilibrium schedule shifts up to $\bar{N}'\bar{N}'$. With the official rate fixed at $\tilde{e}^0$, the increased spending causes an increase in the domestic price level and in the relative price of home goods, to P'. The increased price level, in turn, implies higher interest rates. To maintain asset market equilibrium in the face of higher domestic interest rates, we experience an appreciation in the spot free rate to e'. At that rate the spot rate has sufficiently fallen relative to the forward rate to generate a premium that offsets the higher domestic interest rate.

The equilibrium at point B implies that fiscal policy under a dual exchange rate system exerts a stronger effect on interest rates and the price level and that the same increase in spending gives rise to a smaller increase in the relative price of home goods. The latter point can be appreciated by noting that under a unified free rate we would be at point D. The explanation is simply that under a dual system we have larger increases in interest

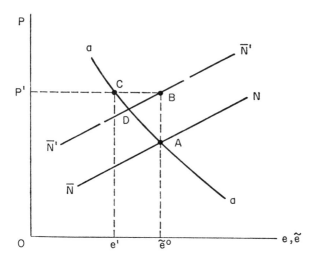

Figure 8.6

rates and therefore more of a dampening of the increased spending and for that reason require only smaller *relative* price changes. The counterpart of the smaller relative price changes is, however, a larger change in nominal income. To the extent that sectoral considerations are relevant, and they most assuredly are, the question of relative prices and intersectoral resource allocation is important. From that perspective, the dual rate system is more nearly neutral than a system with a free unified rate.

8.5 Concluding Remarks

This chapter has developed models of the determination of exchange rates and of the operation of a flexible exchange rate system. Among the conclusions two deserve emphasis here. First, that the exchange rate, as a first approximation, is determined in the asset markets. This implies that expectations and changes in expectations as much as changes in money supplies dominate the course of the exchange rate in the short run.

The second conclusion that we wish to retain here concerns the lack of homogeneity that a flexible rate system is likely to exhibit in the short run. With prices sticky, or exchange rate expectations sticky, monetary changes as much as foreign price disturbances will be transmitted internationally and thus destroy the argument that a flexible rate system provides isolation from and for monetary disorder.

8.6 Appendix

In this appendix we will derive some of the results presented in section 8.3 and discuss the stability of the adjustment process. We start with the equation for the $\bar{N}\bar{N}$ schedule that embodies equilibrium in the home goods market, given monetary equilibrium:

$$\bar{N}\left(\frac{eP_T^*}{P}, r\left(\frac{M}{P}\right), g\right) = 0. \tag{A1}$$

We can solve that equation for the equilibrium price level, $\bar{P}$, as a function of the money supply, traded goods prices in terms of foreign currency, and the exchange rate:

$$P = \bar{P}(eP_T^*, M, g). \tag{A2}$$

Nothing that the excess demand in (A1) is homogeneous of degree zero in all prices and the quantity of money it follows that the equilibrium price level in (A2) is homogeneous of degree one in the quantity of money and the domestic currency price of traded goods. Accordingly, we can write the logarithmic differential of (A2) as follows:

$$\hat{P} = \delta(\hat{e} + \hat{P}_T^*) + (1 - \delta)\hat{M}, \quad 0 < \delta < 1, \tag{A3}$$

where government spending is held constant.

Taking similarly the differential of the asset market equilibrium condition

$$r\left(\frac{M}{P}\right) = r^* + (1 - \pi)\left(\frac{e_{-1}}{e - 1}\right), \tag{A4}$$

we obtain

$$\hat{M} - \hat{P} = -\sigma(1 - \pi)(\hat{e}_{-1} - \hat{e}), \tag{A5}$$

where the foreign interest rate is held constant. Combining (A3) and (A5) yields an expression for the change in the spot rate as a function of the disturbances:

$$\hat{e} = \frac{\delta}{\delta + \sigma(1 - \pi)}(\hat{M} - \hat{P}_T^*) + \frac{\sigma(1 - \pi)}{\delta + \sigma(1 - \pi)}\hat{e}_{-1}. \tag{A6}$$

In the short run $\hat{e}_{-1} = 0$, and the first term in (A6) indicates the impact effect of a monetary or foreign price disturbance. In the long run $\hat{e} = \hat{e}_{-1}$, and therefore nominal disturbances are reflected in corresponding exchange rate changes.

Consider next the stability question.[19] Substituting the equilibrium price level, $P(\ )$ in (4) yields a final reduced form equation that relates the current spot rate to the past spot rate for given money and foreign prices:

$$r\left(\frac{M}{\bar{P}}(eP_T^*, M, g)\right) - (1 - \pi)\left(\frac{e_{-1}}{e - 1}\right) = r^* \tag{A7}$$

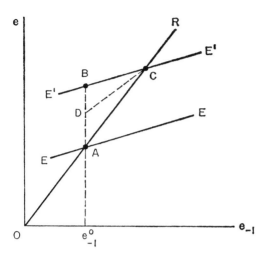

Figure 8.7

Equation (A7) is a difference equation in the exchange rate. To determine stability, we differentiate (7) and evaluate at equilibrium the derivative to obtain:

$$\frac{de}{de_{-1}} = \frac{\sigma(1 - \pi)}{\delta + \sigma(1 - \pi)} < 1, \tag{A8}$$

which ensures stability.

In figure 8.7 we show equation (A7) for an initial nominal quantity of money as the upward sloping line EE with a slope less than unity. An increase in the nominal quantity of money shifts the schedule upward in the same proportion to $E'E'$. From the initial equilibrium at A, the spot rate immediately jumps to point B and then moves along $E'E'$ until the new equilibrium at point C is reached. We have inserted, too, in figure 8.7 the path of the forward rate ADC. The forward rate by (10) will always lie between the current and past spot rates and therefore consistently underpredict the actual exchange rate. This departure from rational expectations forms the basis of the transitory real effects of a monetary disturbance.

Notes

I wish to acknowledge helpful comments on an earlier draft from Stanley Black, Stanley Fischer, Jacob Frenkel, and Dwight Jaffee. Financial support was provided by a grant from the Ford Foundation.

1. We abstract here from tariffs and transport costs that introduce obvious modifications in (1).

2. All starred variables refer to the foreign country.

3. The choice of monetary aggregate in (4) is presumably that for which real money demand is most stable. Furthermore, we do not require that in (4) the same monetary aggregate be used for both countries.

4. For a similar equation that concentrates on traded goods, see Collery (1971).

5. See, for example, Corden (1971, chapter 5) and Dornbusch (1974b). Much of the partial equilibrium literature concerned with real trade questions uses implicitly (3) together with the assumption that monetary or fiscal policies maintain constant the level of prices, P and P^*. Under these assumptions the exchange rate can be identified with the relative price structure.

6. If the increased spending had fallen entirely on home goods, the required relative price adjustment would have been a fall in the relative price of traded goods, and therefore ambiguity in the net effect of the disturbance on the exchange rate.

7. There is a peculiar tradition in the discussion of the markets for both bonds and foreign exchange, and unlike in the discussion of equity prices, that associates price formation with the rate at which funds flow, rather than with the conditions required for the existing stocks to be held. The "tradable funds" approach in the foreign exchange market has a "loanable funds" equivalent in the bond market. This issue is not new. See, for example, Pollak (1944) and Laursen (1955). The latter raises the issue quite explicitly and opts for a stock approach. See, also, Dornbusch (1974a, 1975), Johnson (1975), and, in particular, Black (1973).

8. Magee (1974) has presented information on the adjustment time for purchasing power parity, or arbitrage, to be achieved. The evidence suggests a significant lag and a substantial dispersion across commodities.

9. Equation (7) is obtained by solving the money market equilibrium condition, $M/P = L(r, \ldots)$.

10. For recent evidence on covered interest arbitrage, see Frenkel and Levich (1975).

11. From the conditions of money market equilibrium $M/P = L(r, \ldots)$, we have $dr = \dot{M}(M/P)/L_r \equiv -(1/\sigma)\dot{M}$. The interest responsiveness of money demand, that is, the semilogarithmic derivative $\sigma \equiv -L_r/L$, is for the short run significantly less than unity. Econometric models such as the MPS model estimate a short run elasticity of $-rL_r/L = 0.05$, so that with an interest rate of $r = 0.1$ we obtain a value $\sigma = 0.5$.

12. The trade balance is given by $T = T(P_T/P, r)$, where the relative price term again reflects substitution between home goods and traded goods and the interest rate term reflects absorption or the level of spending. Accordingly, an increase in the relative price of traded goods worsens the trade balance, while an increase in the interest rate improves the trade balance.

13. For a given foreign currency price of traded goods, the ratio e/P represents the domestic relative price of traded goods in terms of the price level.

14. The effect of a foreign price increase on the exchange rate at point B is given by $\hat{e} = [-\delta/(\delta + \sigma(1 - \pi))]\hat{P}_T^*$, where δ is the elasticity of the price level with respect to the price of traded goods along the $\overline{N}\overline{N}$ schedule. Unless $\pi = 1$, the exchange rate change does not fully offset the increase in foreign prices. See the appendix.

15. The dynamics and stability of the adjustment process are studied in the appendix.

16. Under the heading, "Are the Swiss Enjoying Their Strong Currency? No, Not in the Least," the *Wall Street Journal* of February 27, 1975 notes: "And what is it like to be the cynosure of international money markets? It is, the Swiss will tell you, increasingly uncomfortable, if not miserable."

17. For a discussion of dual exchange rate systems, see Fleming (1971), Swoboda (1974), and Sheen (1974).

18. What determines the level of the free rate in the long run? The present model is not equipped to answer that question because the adaptive expectations mechanism implies that in the long run the forward rate is equal to the spot rate. In the absence of a difference between spot and forward rates, interest rates will be equated at any level of the free rate. The free rate has no effect on the real system and therefore, in the present model, is indeterminate in the long run.

19. There is a growing body of partial equilibrium models exhibiting instability in the foreign exchange market because of a failure to link that sector with the asset markets. See, for example, Allen and Miller (1974) and Britton (1970). Minford (1974) in a very interesting formulation shows that instability can be attributed to a failure to consider the monetary effects of exchange rate changes.

References

Allen, W., and Miller, M. 1974. The Stability of the Floating Exchange Rate. Unpublished manuscript. Bank of England.

Argy, V., and Porter, M. 1972. The Forward Exchange Market and the Effects of Domestic and External Disturbances under Alternative Exchange Rate Systems. *IMF Staff Papers* 19, No. 3.

Black, S. 1973. *International Money Markets and Flexible Exchange Rates*. Princeton Studies in International Finance, No. 32. Princeton University.

Black, S. 1975. Exchange Rate Policies for Less Developed Countries in a World of Floating Rates. Unpublished manuscript. Vanderbilt University.

Britton, A. J. C. 1970. The Dynamic Stability of the Foreign Exchange Market. *Economic Journal* 80, 91–96.

Collery, A. 1971. *International Adjustment, Open Economies and the Quantity Theory of Money*. Princeton Studies in International Finance, No. 28. Princeton University.

Corden, M. 1971. *The Theory of Protection*. Clarendon Press, Oxford.

Dornbusch, R. 1974a. Capital Mobility, Flexible Exchange Rates and Macroeconomic Equilibrium. Forthcoming in *Recent Developments in International Monetary Economics* (E. Claassen and P. Salin, eds.). North-Holland, 1976.

Dornbusch, R. 1974b. Tariffs and Nontraded Goods. *Journal of International Economics* 4, 177–185.

Dornbusch, R. 1975. A Portfolio Balance Model of the Open Economy. *Journal of Monetary Economics* 1, 3–19.

Fleming, J. M. 1962. Domestic Financial Policies under Fixed and Floating Exchange Rates. *IMF Staff Papers* 9, 369–379.

Fleming, J. M. 1971. *Essays in International Economics*. Allen and Unwin.

Frenkel, J., and Levich, R. 1975. Transactions Costs and the Efficiency of International Capital Markets. Unpublished manuscript. University of Chicago.

Johnson, H. G. 1975. World Inflation and the International Monetary System. Unpublished manuscript. University of Chicago.

Laursen, S. 1955. The Market for Foreign Exchange. *Economia Internazionale* 8, 762–783.

Magee, S. 1974. U.S. Import Prices in the Currency Contract Period. *Brookings Papers on Economic Activity* 1, 117–164.

Minford, P. 1974. Structural and Monetary Theories of the Balance of Payments. Unpublished manuscript. University of Manchester.

Mundell, R. A. 1964. Exchange Rate Margins and Economic Policy. In Murphy, C. (ed.), *Money in the International Order*. Southern Methodist University Press.

Mundell, R. A 1968. *International Economics*. Macmillan.

Mussa, M. 1976. A Monetary Approach to Balance of Payments Analysis. *Journal of Money, Credit and Banking* (3), 333–351.

Niehans, J. 1975. Some Doubts about the Efficacy of Monetary Policy under Flexible Exchange Rates. *Journal of International Economics* 5, 275–281.

Polak, J. J. 1964. European Exchange Depreciation in the Early Twenties. *Econometrica* 12, 151–162.

Robinson, J. 1936. Banking Policy and the Exchanges. *Review of Economic Studies* 3, 226–229.

Swoboda, A. K. 1974. The Dual Exchange Rate System and Monetary Independence. In Aliber, R. Z. (ed.), *National Monetary Policies and the International Financial System*. University of Chicago Press.

Sheen, J. 1974. Dual Exchange Rates and the Asset Markets. Unpublished manuscript. International Monetary Project. London School of Economics.

Wonnacott, P. 1972. The Floating Canadian Dollar. American Enterprise Institute, Foreign Affairs Study 5.

9   Special Exchange Rates for Capital Account Transactions

The starting point for any discussion of special asset transaction exchange rates is the high mobility of capital. Assets markets are linked internationally in terms of risk and expectations-adjusted returns, and that linkage is potentiallv tight and rapid. That implies severe restrictions on the scope of government strategy. Policies must be such as to give asset holders the world rate of return, or they will seek to purchase assets abroad with one of three results: under a fixed rate, the stock of reserves will be depleted; under a flexible rate, the exchange rate will be depressed to a level where home returns are again in line with those abroad; or because of the threat of these responses, policies will be aligned with the requirements of asset markets rather than with governmental objectives and priorities.

This chapter examines the experience of various Latin American countries with the use of dual and multiple exchange rate systems to delink these markets, and it develops models to explain the macroeconomic outcomes of such systems. These models analyze the impact of dual rates on the balance of trade, foreign reserves and asset holdings, inflation, the government budget, and the supply of and demand for traded versus nontraded goods. The article also looks at overvaluation and the effects of expected depreciation on interest rates and investment. While the relative benefits of these systems for asset holders and wage earners are apparent at many points in the analysis, this is not an essay in applied welfare economics, and empirical investigation would be required to determine the distributional effects of specific uses of the various types and levels of controls.

Section 9.1 briefly describes the ties between domestic and world markets, the rationale for initiation of exchange controls, and the forms such controls may take. Section 9.2 looks briefly at the extent of exchange rate

Originally published in *The World Bank Economic Review*, vol. 1 (1986), pp. 1–33.

differentials which occurred in Mexico and Venezuela in the early 1980s and develops various models of dual market systems. The implications of multiple exchange rates and the development of illegal markets for foreign exchange transactions are examined in section 9.3.

9.1 Linkages between Markets: Rationale and Methods for Severing the Ties

The problem of asset market integration can be understood by looking at three linkages between an economy and the rest of the world. These are the linkages between interest rates, the interaction of prices, and the impact of real exchange rates on employment. These relationships are shown as

$$i = i^* + \frac{\dot{e}}{e} + R(\ ), \tag{1}$$

$$P = f(eP^*), \tag{2}$$

$$N = N\left(\frac{eP^*}{P}\right), \tag{3}$$

where i and i^* are home and foreign interest rates, $\dot{e}/e$ is the expected rate of depreciation of the exchange rate expressed in domestic currency, and R is the risk premium, P and P^* are home and foreign prices, and N is employment.

Equation (1) states that home interest rates are equal to those abroad, adjusted for anticipated depreciation and the risk premium that emerges from political and exchange rate risk. This equation can be viewed as the constraint on financial policies: in integrated asset markets, the home interest rate must be set high enough or savings will be transferred to foreign assets and the currency will come under attack. Equation (2) points out that domestic prices will be affected by the exchange rate: a rapid depreciation of the exchange rate would cause an increase in home inflation. Equation (3) emphasizes that a change in the (real) exchange rate will influence employment. In the long run, real depreciation is likely to raise employment. But in the short run the adjustment process may make the effects run the other way.

These three linkages then mean that asset markets are internationally integrated and that this integration places restraints on policy, or that lack of attention to these constraints has negative implications for inflation and for employment. Moreover, because the reactions are strong and rapid, the issues are of foremost importance. They cannot be disregarded, because reserves are often in short supply and depreciation of the exchange rate can be politically difficult; however, running the world to the tune of assets markets may be undesirable. Hence the interest in institutional arrangements that delink assets markets and free policies to be directed to a government's true priorities.

There are any number of examples of countries where exchange rate movements or capital flows became an inconvenience or more for policy-makers. For example, in the United States in 1980–85, the dollar appreciation, for safe haven reasons or because of the U.S. monetary-fiscal mix, led to overvaluation and an unprecedented shock to manufacturing. Very soon there was talk of renewing the import surcharge that had been adopted to cope with the overvaluation of the early 1970s, and even a renewal of interest equalization taxes came into discussion.

But, of course, the shock can also run the other way when capital flight leads to a fall of the exchange rate and, as a result, an inflation burst. The best example would be the onset of the German hyperinflation in the 1920s. The "balance of payments school" at that time saw the confidence-induced collapse of the exchange rate as the source of domestic inflation, which in turn led to budget deficits; these deficits reinforced the escalating rate of price increases. For a while, the government managed to stabilize the exchange rate, and prices remained stable. Then a loss in confidence (related to the reparations problem) ensued, and in a few weeks the exchange rate increased sevenfold. The exchange rate depreciation raised import prices, wages, and the budget deficit, which opened all mechanisms for uncontrolled price rises and hyperinflation.

The importance of the capital market integration issue has also been high-lighted in the aftermath of the debt problem. Much of the accumulation of Latin American external debt reflects the financing of capital flight (see World Bank 1985). This is strikingly the case for Argentina, Mexico, and Venezuela, where the amounts are extraordinarily large. Once again, the issue arises whether alternative capital market arrangements would have been an effective means to stop capital flight and tax evasion.

There are several ways in which asset markets can be delinked. The first is to decide on the scope for capital controls. One possibility is to maintain the international integration of capital markets (given by equation 1) by keeping interest rates at levels equivalent to international rates, but to delink domestic assets markets, at least partially, from the home economy. The means would be a special, separate exchange rate for financial transactions. Free capital mobility at a fixed or flexible special rate, separate from commercial transactions, would be a way of separating equation (1) from equations (2) and (3). Having more than one exchange rate might make it easier to live with the effects of capital market integration on the exchange rate and the economy.

An alternative is to opt against international integration of asset markets by instituting formal capital control. This may take the form of a prohibition of foreign asset holding by residents. The difficulty is to make that prohibition stick: black markets will emerge, or capital flows will take place implicitly through underinvoicing of exports or overinvoicing of imports in current account transactions. In response, the government may be tempted to quasi-legalize (this is a peculiarly Latin notion) parallel markets for foreign exchange or create domestic equivalents in the form of a dollar-denominated government-issued security or dollar deposits. The effectiveness of capital controls determines here how successfully a government can split markets and isolate the home economy.

A two-way classification helps distinguish the possibilities. First, the rate for asset market transactions may be managed (fixed as a special case) or freely determined. Second, access to the exchange market for capital account transactions may be restricted or completely open. Institutional arrangements fall somewhere within these possible ranges. For example, Mexico in 1983−84 had a heavily managed asset transaction rate with unrestricted access to that market, while Venezuela in the same period also had unrestricted access but considerably less intervention in the rate. Brazil completely restricts access to the official market where the rate is managed. Even Brazil's black market has a somewhat managed rate and an implicit restriction of access by corporations. The remainder of this article examines some of these systems to see what particular problems they solve and what problems they create.

9.2 Dual Exchange Rates

This section discusses systems in which a significant part of commercial transactions is conducted at a uniform fixed rate, while capital account and selected commercial transactions are conducted at another free or managed rate. The fact that the foreign exchange market is opened to capital account transactions establishes an immediate linkage between financial markets (and expectations therein) and the exchange rate or the level of intervention. By separating financial transactions from commercial transactions, the authorities attempt to maintain the advantages of a managed, stable exchange rate for commercial transactions that is not upset by volatility in international capital flows.

Dual rates are typically established by countries that feel they cannot or do not wish to prohibit capital account transactions altogether. In circumstances where the macroeconomy is highly unstable, capital flows will be very volatile and potentially massive. If foreign exchange reserves are limited, a country has essentially two choices. It can set a uniform rate that is so undervalued that there can only be an expectation of appreciation and hence no threat of capital flight. Or alternatively, the rates can be split so that the capital account rate can depreciate to whatever level is required to make the public willing to hold the existing stock of domestic assets.

Each alternative has serious drawbacks: the overdepreciation of a uniform rate represents a shock to real wages and inflation. It poses the question why real wages should be cut merely to stabilize the expectations of wealth holders. But the free rate on the capital account also raises questions. Will it distort allocation, as some commercial transactions slip into the free market? Will it be stable in the absence of intervention? Will there ultimately be exchange rate unification?

Figure 9.1 makes some of these issues more concrete by showing the

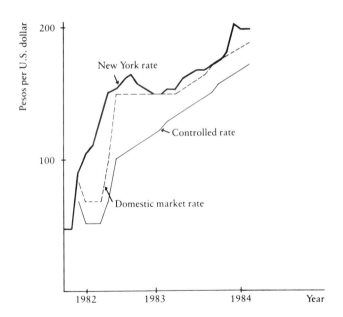

Figure 9.1
Mexican exchange rates. (The New York rate is the cable transfer quote rate. The domestic market rate applies to capital accounts, tourism, and other transactions not covered by the controlled rate. The controlled rate applies to essential imports, most exports, and debt service. Sources: Banco de Mexico and U.S. Federal Reserve Bank, *Federal Reserve Bulletin.*)

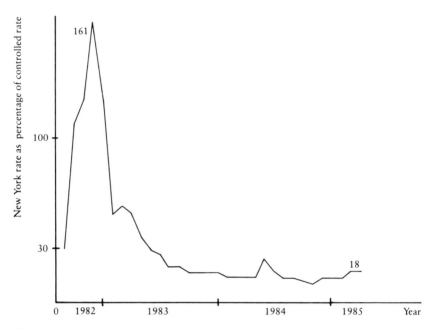

Figure 9.2
The Mexican free market premium on exchange rates. (Sources: Banco de Mexico and U.S. Federal Reserve Bank, *Federal Reserve Bulletin*.)

three different Mexican exchange rates in effect from 1982 to 1984. Figure 9.2 shows the premium of the New York rate over the controlled rate in Mexico. The huge differential up to January 1983 corresponds to the early experimentation with exchange controls of various kinds. Since then, the levels and differentials have been established in a manner such that the Central Bank increasingly has come into a position of managing the two rates, and subsequently the differential has been moderate.

Venezuela's case, by contrast, did not show a settling down (figure 9.3). Following a long tradition of fixed exchange rates, in March 1983 the government abandoned pegging the rate except for essential imports. Specifically, capital movements were to be conducted in a free foreign exchange market. The premium of the capital over the fixed rate reached a level, using monthly averages, of more than 260 percent (figure 9.4). The volatility of the free rate and the extent of discrepancies between free and controlled rates posed important issues for resource allocation and macro-economic policy.

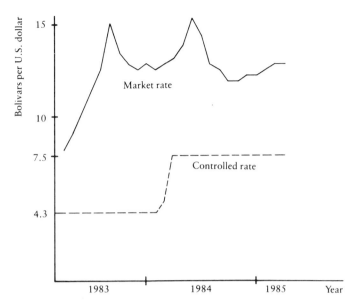

Figure 9.3
Exchange rates in Venezuela. (The market rate applies to capital transactions and all trade except essential imports. The controlled rate applies to essential imports only. Sources: International Monetary Fund, *International Financial Statistics*, and U.S. Federal Reserve Bank, *Federal Reserve Bulletin*.)

A Model of the Dual Market

This section presents a sequence of models of dual markets that build up progressively the key linkages between asset markets and the macro-economy. It starts with a model that assumes full employment, a constant commercial exchange rate, purchasing power parity, rational expectations, and only two assets: domestic money and foreign nominal interest-earning assets.[1]

In the asset market, because domestic currency earns no return, the desired ratio of money to foreign assets, M/eK, depends on the rate of return on foreign assets. This rate of return is the sum of the asset's interest rate plus the additional domestic currency value of the foreign exchange earned as the domestic currency depreciates. This expected rate of depreciation is written $\dot{e}/e$, where e represents the unregulated capital account exchange rate, K the stock of foreign assets, and eK their value in home currency. The desired ratio of money to foreign assets is determined as

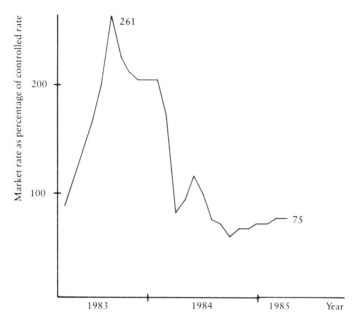

Figure 9.4
The Venezuelan free market premium on exchange rates. (Sources: International Monetary Fund, *International Financial Statistics*, and U.S. Federal Reserve Bank, *Federal Reserve Bulletin.*)

$$\frac{M}{eK} = L\left(i^* + \frac{\dot{e}}{e}\right), \quad L' < 0, \tag{4}$$

or, inverting the equation,

$$\frac{\dot{e}}{e} = h\left(\frac{M}{eK}\right) - i^*, \quad h(\ ) = L^{-1}, h' < 0. \tag{4a}$$

We focus here on domestic events rather than on the effects on the home economy of foreign interest earnings. But the simplification is one of convenience; it does not fundamentally alter the analysis.[2] Since we are not focusing on foreign asset accumulation, we assume that $i^* = 0$. Hence the value of K remains constant over time except for government intervention, and $\dot{e}/e$ simply equals $h(M/eK)$.

In this model, private savings is composed of both a stock adjustment and a flow component: $S = v(w - m - k) + \lambda m + (\lambda - \dot{e}/e)k$. The first component is some proportion, v, of the excess of targeted real asset holdings, w, over actual real asset holdings, $(M + eK)/x$, where x denotes the exchange rate for commercial transactions. The second portion is an adjustment made for anticipated capital losses (or gains) on real balances and foreign assets, $[\lambda m + (\lambda - \dot{e}/e)k]$, with λ being the rate of depreciation of the commercial rate, $\dot{x}/x$. Capital losses are effectively inflation taxes, which reduce the value of nominal money stocks and thus increase the nominal savings needed to meet the real savings target. The impact of an increase in inflation over capital account depreciation $(\lambda > \dot{e}/e)$ will similarly raise nominal savings, while a net depreciation will increase the domestic currency value of foreign assets and thereby reduce the desired rate of savings. Thus, in a steady state, the stock of actual savings may be on target, but individuals will continue to save to compensate for the reduction in real value of savings stocks caused by inflation.

By assuming that taxes and investment are zero, the traditional national income accounts can be revised so that the trade balance, B, will equal private savings, S, less real government spending, G, which is financed by domestic credit creation. If P denotes domestic prices and P^* foreign prices, given purchasing power parity (PPP), $P = x \cdot P^*$. Setting $P^* = 1$ gives $P = x$, which can be applied here without loss of generality. These assumptions, and the composition of private savings described earlier, are the basis of the following expression for the real trade balance:

$$B = S - G = v(w - m - k) + \lambda m + \left(\frac{\lambda - \dot{e}}{e}\right)k - G, \tag{5}$$

where

$$m \equiv \frac{M}{x},$$

$$k \equiv \frac{eK}{x}.$$

The rate of increase in real domestic currency balances, $\dot{M}/x$, is determined by real government spending, G, plus the real trade surplus, B. Thus the change in the real money stock can be written as

$$\dot{m} = v(w - m - k) + \left[\lambda - h\left(\frac{m}{k}\right)\right]k. \tag{6}$$

The other dynamic equation of the model describes the evolution of the real capital account rate, $q \equiv e/x$ (given PPP, deflated here by x). Equivalently, the premium of the capital account rate over the commercial rate is written as

$$\frac{\dot{q}}{q} = \frac{\dot{e}}{e} - \frac{\dot{x}}{x} = h\left(\frac{m}{k}\right) - \lambda. \tag{7}$$

Figure 9.5 shows the schedules along which, respectively, real balances are constant ($\dot{m} = 0$) and the real capital account rate is constant. The schedule for a constant capital account rate ($\dot{q} = 0$) is positive because the premium of the capital to commercial account rates must increase to induce people to increase their real money balances, m. An increase in the premium *now* will preclude expectations of further near-future devaluations. Thus investors will not expect an increase in the value of foreign assets in the near future and will be content to hold the larger money balances. The $\dot{m} = 0$ schedule is drawn with a negative slope, although this need not be the case. The arrows indicate the dynamics and, as is conventional in perfect foresight models of this structure, there is a unique stable trajectory, *JJ*. From any initial stock of real balances, say m_0, the economy converges to the long-run equilibrium at E along the path *JJ*.[3]

The model is closed by specification of the rate of depreciation of the commercial rate. It is assumed that the commercial exchange rate depreciates at a rate, λ, that is sufficient, in the steady state, to generate the inflation tax revenue with which to finance the given level of real government spending.

Given any initial real money stock such as m_0, there is a unique equilibrium on *JJ* and hence a specific value of foreign assets, $q_0 K_0$. With a given value K_0, there is a unique capital account rate at which the asset markets clear. Over time, the system evolves to the steady state equilibrium at E. If real money balances initially are low as at m_0 the path is characterized by rising real money balances and a rising real value of foreign assets or an increasing premium of the capital account rate relative to the commercial rate, e/x. Thus if assets are initially low, savings will be high and there will be trade surpluses that cause the real money stock to rise as the central bank intervenes to sustain the commercial rate. At the same time, the real value of foreign assets is rising because of capital gains.

In the steady state, trade is balanced and the real money stock is constant ($\dot{m} = 0$). The premium of the capital account rate is constant ($\dot{q} = 0$), as the rate depreciates at the same pace as the commercial rate. The seignorage supported by depreciation finances real government spending. The equilibrium dynamics in figure 9.5 are shown for a given rate of depreciation of the commercial rate, λ. It is interesting now to ask how an increase in the rate of depreciation will affect the premium.

It is readily shown that with money demand inelastic with respect to the rate of inflation, an increase in government spending requires an increase in

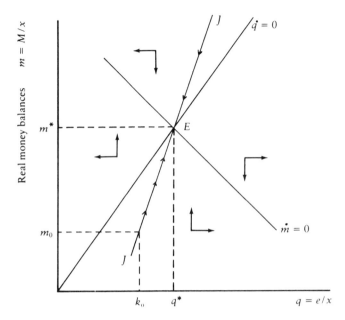

Figure 9.5
Asset market adjustment with dual exchange rates. ($k_0 = eK_0/x$ = home currency value of foreign assets for a given m_0. JJ = stable asset market adjustment path for a given rate of depreciation of the commercial account exchange rate, λ.)

the rate of depreciation to yield the required increase in the inflation tax revenue. Increased rates of depreciation of the commercial exchange rate will immediately bring about a depreciation of the level of the capital account rate or an increase in the premium. Even in the steady state, the premium will increase.

In the steady state, the capital and commercial rates depreciate at the same rate. An increase in the rate of depreciation of the capital account rate shifts asset holders from money to foreign assets. Given the fixed supply of foreign assets, K, only an increase in the premium can bring about the rebalancing of portfolios. The increase in the premium caused by an increased rate of crawl of the commercial rate was demonstrated by Lizondo (1984).

Expectations

Having sketched the effect of a *current* increase in the rate of government spending, the impact of a shift in expectations is now examined. Starting in

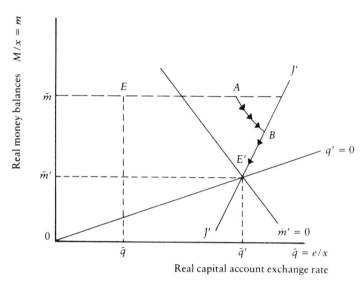

Figure 9.6
Adjustment to an anticipated increase in government spending. (E = initial equilibrium, A = instantaneous depreciation of capital account rate in response to anticipated commercial rate devaluation, B = value of m and q when new commercial rate is implemented, E' = new equilibrium with depreciated commercial rate, $J'J'$ = adjustment path under new commercial rate.)

the steady state, the public anticipates that the government will increase real spending, deficit finance, and depreciation at some known future date. What is the path of adjustment to this disturbance? This is an interesting question if one wants to explain the large fluctuations in the data for the dual market premium.

Figure 9.6 shows the initial equilibrium at point E. As shown in the appendix, an increased steady state rate of depreciation shifts the schedules. The $\dot{q} = 0$ rotates clockwise, and the $\dot{m} = 0$ schedule shifts out and to the right. Only a larger real premium will stabilize relative depreciation rates ($\dot{q} = 0$) for any given value of the money stock.

Now consider the adjustment process. At the moment the expectation of higher future government spending develops, there is an immediate portfolio shift from money to foreign assets, which leads to a jump in the premium from point E to a point like A. The extent of this instantaneous depreciation depends on (among other things) how proximate in time the shift in monetary policy is. If it were almost immediate, the jump would be virtually all the distance to $J'J'$. At point A, despite expectations of a new rate, the dynamics are still governed by the initial monetary policy and

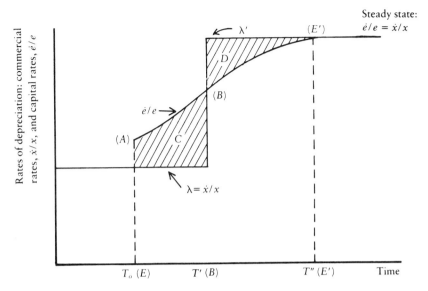

Figure 9.7
Expectation and implementation of commercial account rate depreciation: an increased rate of crawl. (Letters in parentheses refer to points in figure 9.6. $C > D$: increased premium in T_0 to T' is greater than the excess of the commercial over the capital rates in T' to T''; T_0 = initial expectations of depreciation of commercial rate, λ, at time T'; T' = point of actual government devaluation of commercial rate.)

thus, with the high level of the premium, the value of foreign assets is high relative to real balances. This can only be an equilibrium if the rate of depreciation of the capital account rate has risen and hence is now higher than that of the commercial rate. Accordingly, the system moves in the direction of point B with the capital rate increasing and real balances declining. In the perfect foresight model, the economy arrives at B precisely at the time when the more rapid rate of depreciation of the commercial rate is implemented officially. From there on, the movement is along $J'J'$, with some decline in the premium. The new steady state is at point E' with an increased steady state premium $\bar{q}'$.

Note that the rate of depreciation of the capital account rate can be determined from the conditions of monetary equilibrium as shown in equation 4a: $[\dot{e}/e = h(M/ek), h' < 0]$. With a declining ratio of real balances to external assets along the path ABE', the rate of depreciation of the capital account rate must be rising throughout, although the increase is less than that of the commercial rate after the new rate is implemented at point B. Figure 9.7 shows the path of the rate of depreciation of the capital account rate over time. The times T_0 and T' correspond to the initial shift in expectations and the implementation of the new policy (point B). Up to time T_0, we have equal rates of depreciation: $\dot{e}/e = \lambda$. Then, at the time expectations shift, there is a jump in the premium and in the rate of depreciation of the capital account rate, $\dot{e}/e$. Since the rate of depreciation of the commercial rate is still unchanged, the premium is further appreciating until time T'. Now the commercial rate depreciates at the higher rate λ' in excess of the capital account rate, which implies some real appreciation. Over time, the two rates converge to depreciate at the same pace. The increased level of the premium up to the time of the commercial account devaluation, shown by area C in figure 9.7, is larger than the amount by which the commercial account rate depreciation exceeds that of the capital account rate after the devaluation, shown here in area D.

It is interesting to comment also on the trade balance in the adjustment process. As long as monetary policy is unchanged, following the shift in expectations, there is a trade deficit. The deficit arises because the increase in the premium raises wealth relative to target and the real capital gains lead to dissaving. Furthermore, with declining real money balances, seignorage starts falling short of the initial level of spending, and the trade deficit thus further deteriorates. The expectation of a shift in policy will therefore lead to trade deficits and potential difficulties in sustaining the path of depreciation.

Increased real government spending and deficits financed by money creation have been considered here. The increase in spending can be viewed as either spending on goods and services or as transfers abroad by the government, such as government debt service. In this broader interpretation, the exercise is of interest because it suggests that any disturbance that leads to an increased deficit will provoke an increase in the premium. Moreover, since real government spending in excess of real tax collection is being examined, one can also think of the exercise as a loss of real government revenues caused by reduced taxes or a loss of external resources. From this perspective, for an oil-exporting nation the expectation of a decline in real oil prices, for example, would increase the state enterprise and government budget deficits, imply deficit finance, and hence force a depreciation of the capital account rate. This interpretation is suggestive of the case of Mexico in 1985.

Consider now the effect of intervention. Assume the central bank sells foreign assets or foreign exchange in exchange for domestic money. The impact of such an intervention can be decomposed into two separate effects. The private sector now holds increased foreign assets at each level of the premium. With unchanged real balances, the premium would im-

mediately decline to move the economy back to portfolio balance at point
E in figure 9.5. But real money balances in private hands have declined as
part of the open market operation, just as they would have in the case of a
devaluation.

The decline in real balances takes the economy to the southwest of point
E, on JJ, in figure 9.5. Accordingly, the premium declines proportionately
more than the increase in foreign assets. Intervention in the capital account
market thus is effective in depressing the premium. Interestingly, it also
gives rise to a trade surplus via the wealth effects of the decline in the
premium.

Extensions of the Model

The basic model has served to show the linkage between financial policies
and the premium in the dual market. But the analysis needs extension if
some macroeconomic complications coming from dual markets are to be
seen. So far, the dual rate exerts effects only on the value of wealth and
hence on income and spending. But in fact the more important channels
operate presumably via relative prices and domestic interest rates. These,
too, are linked to the free rate, and the important point to recognize is that
financial disturbances have macroeconomic effects via the free exchange
rate. Furthermore these effects often occur as a result of expectations.

We now consider the case where some goods—nonessential imports
and nontraditional exports—are traded along with capital account transactions in the free market. Essential imports, say food and materials, and
traditional exports are traded at a (generally overvalued) fixed rate. Since
part of the goods now is traded at the free rate, the aggregate price level
is influenced by both the commercial and the free rates. Moreover the
premium of the free rate now sets the relative price of those goods entering
via the free market. Instability of asset demands, policies, and expectations
now introduces instability in the price level and in relative prices.

Moreover, if the dual rate regime is chosen to defend the foreign
exchange reserves, this result may not in fact be achieved. Financial disturbances that lead to an increase in the premium draw production resources
into the premium market while inducing consumers to substitute toward
the controlled market. A rise in the premium associated with a "flight from
domestic money" will still lead to reserve depletion, except that it now
takes place via the enlarged trade deficit at the regulated rate rather than
via actual capital flows.

It is important to recognize that now the free market no longer involves finding the price at which an existing stock of foreign assets, K, is held. The market now can generate an accumulation or decumulation of foreign assets via current flows. Specifically, we look at the possibility of trade being diverted from the official market to the free market. The central bank faces larger trade deficits and loses reserves, while in the free market, a trade surplus leads to accumulation of foreign assets. One can think of the implications of shifting transactions to the free market as legalizing the capital flight involved in the underinvoicing of exports or in the import smuggling financed by underinvoiced exports.

To demonstrate these results, most of the previous model's structure is maintained. The specification of asset markets remains unchanged. But now the markets for the two classes of goods need to be separated, while the assumption of given world prices and PPP at the relevant exchange rate for each good is maintained. Let the given foreign prices of all goods be unity, so that e and x denote the prices of goods that trade in the home country at the official and free rate, respectively. The aggregate price level, P, is now an expenditure-weighted function of these two prices:[4]

$$P = P(e, x). \tag{8}$$

In the previous equations, P now replaces x as the deflator for assets.

To simplify matters, depreciation of the regulated rate is dispensed with, so that $\lambda = 0$. Because the free market now involves not only stocks but also flows, the trade balances for the official and the free market need to be specified separately. Let B and V now denote trade balances at international prices of the regulated and free markets, respectively:

$$B = B\left(\alpha, q, a, \frac{\dot{e}}{e}, G\right),$$
$$V = V\left(\alpha, q, a, \frac{\dot{e}}{e}\right), \tag{9}$$

where α denotes the fraction of goods traded at the fixed exchange rate and a is actual wealth.

An increase in the free market rate relative to the fixed official rate will deteriorate the official trade balance, B, and improve V, the trade balance in the free market. The reason is that consumers will substitute toward the now relatively cheaper imported goods traded at the official rate while producers will move resources out of production for the official market and into activities that benefit from the free rate. This substitution is one of the most important features of a dual rate regime once commercial transactions are included in the free market.

Formally, the model is now more complex because the real money stock, the stock of foreign assets, and the premium each must be tracked; hence, a simple phase diagram can no longer help. But one can still get a lot of answers by just looking at comparative steady states, since in long-run equilibrium, actual wealth, a, equals planned real wealth, w, and the depreciation of the unregulated exchange rate is zero: $\dot{e}/e = 0$. Thus, as shown in the appendix, the steady state is defined by the following equations:

$$\bar{V}(\alpha, q, w, 0) = 0, \tag{10}$$

$$a \equiv m + K = w, \tag{11}$$

$$\frac{m}{eK/P} = L(0). \tag{12}$$

In equations (10) and (11), assets are now deflated by the new expenditure-weighted price level, P, rather than the regulated commercial rate, x. The price level, reflecting the free and official exchange rates, respectively, is given the simple form, $P = e^{1-\alpha}x^{\alpha}$. Substituting equation (11) into (12) now yields the relation between the stock of foreign assets and the premium:

$$m + \frac{Ke}{P} = w,$$

$$m + \frac{Ke}{e^{1-\alpha}x^{\alpha}} = w, \tag{11'}$$

$$m + \frac{Ke^{\alpha}}{x^{\alpha}} = w,$$

or

$$w = m + Kq^{\alpha}, \tag{11a}$$

$$\frac{m}{eK/e^{1-\alpha}x^{\alpha}} = L(0), \tag{12'}$$

$$\frac{m}{e^{\alpha}K/x^{\alpha}} = L(0),$$

or

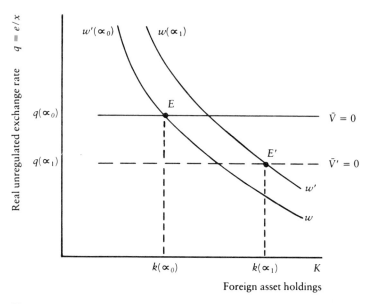

Figure 9.8
Trade diverted to the free market. [Given unchanged real money balances ($\dot{m} = 0$), $w =$ planned real asset holdings, $\bar{V} =$ trade balance of the unregulated market, $\alpha =$ the share of goods traded at the fixed exchange rate.]

$$m = L(0)q^{\alpha}K. \tag{12a}$$

Substituting (12a) into (11a) gives:[5]

$$w = [L(0)q^{\alpha}K] + Kq^{\alpha}$$
$$w = K[L(0) + 1]q^{\alpha} \tag{13}$$

Hence, for a given target level of wealth, in figure 9.8 the downward-sloping schedule ww captures both portfolio preferences and saving behavior. Trade balance in the free market, equation (10), is also shown as a horizontal schedule. The steady state equilibrium for a given w and α is at point E.

Consider now the following policy measure. The government moves some export activity that previously was conducted at the official rate into the free market. The effect of a shift of goods to the free market implies a reduction in the parameter α and a shift of the ww schedule given by:

$$\frac{dK}{d\alpha} = -\frac{\alpha K}{q}.$$

Figure 9.8 shows the effect as a downward shift of the $\bar{V} = 0$ curve. The increased export surplus of the free market raises the stock of foreign assets, K, and must be compensated by a reduced premium so that the schedule for balance in the free market, $\bar{V} = 0$, drops to the position indicated by the dashed lines. (To obtain a downward shift, it must be assumed that

$$\frac{\partial \bar{V}}{\partial q} > 0,$$

so that substitution effects dominate the potentially opposing effect of increased savings undertaken to offset a decline in real wealth caused by the drop in the premium.) Across steady states, the premium declines, and the stock of foreign assets rises.

From equations (11) and (12), it can be shown that across steady states, real money balances are constant:

$$m = \sigma w, \quad \sigma \equiv \frac{\bar{m}}{\bar{w}} = \frac{L(0)}{1 + L(0)}, \tag{14}$$

where σ is the steady state ratio of money to wealth in the absence of inflation.

Consider next the effect on the cumulative balance of payments of a change in reserves and the nominal money stock. Since real money balances are unchanged across steady states, it is enough to look at the behavior of the price level to know how nominal money changes. The initial shift of some goods to the free market, starting from a situation where all goods are traded at the commercial rate, gives unambiguous results. Since some goods are now shifted from the lower commercial rate to the higher free rate (i.e., $q > 1$), the price level must rise. Unchanged real balances in combination with a higher price level then unambiguously imply a cumulative trade surplus, as more exports now sell in world markets at the depreciated exchange rate and import purchases decline in response to the higher domestic currency price. The decline in the premium also decreases wealth and thus spending, which further improves the reserves balance.

But when some goods are already traded at the free rate, a shift of yet further goods to the free market need no longer involve favorable effects on reserves. Now two offsetting effects are at work. The shift of new goods to the free market by itself again raises price levels. But the decline in the premium now lowers the prices of all goods already traded at the free rate and through that channel lowers the price level. If this latter effect is sufficiently important, the price level will fall; hence reserves must decline in the adjustment process.

Consider next a porfolio disturbance, specifically a shift out of money reflected in a decline in the steady state ratio of money to wealth, σ (equation 14). This is, of course, the kind of event against which countries seek to protect themselves with a dual rate. As real money balances fall, if the premium remains unchanged or even declines, there *must* be a cumulative trade deficit at the official rate. The mechanism is the following: The portfolio shift drives up immediately the premium in the free market. As a result there are two effects on the official trade balance. First, the higher premium diverts resources directly to the production of goods traded in the free market and shifts demand toward the goods traded at the official rate. Second, the rise in the premium raises wealth, which increases spending and thereby also increases the official deficit.

Figure 9.9 shows the adjustment starting from an initial equilibrium at E. The portfolio shift leads to a rightward movement of ww, and hence E' is the new equilibrium. If the adjustment process is asymptotic, then there will be a path TT along which the economy will travel, starting with an

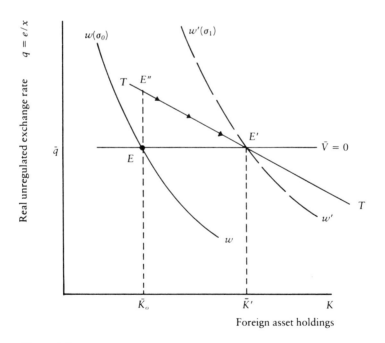

Figure 9.9
A shift out of money: the adjustment process. (E = initial equilibrium, E'' = instantaneous increase in unregulated exchange rate, σ = steady state ratio of money to wealth.)

immediate sharp rise of the premium from E to E''. Subsequently, as foreign assets are being accumulated and money balances reduced, portfolio proportions of M and K come more nearly into line with preferences. The process continues until the full adjustment in portfolios has been achieved by changes in nominal money and external assets.

The unambigous effect is that a porfolio shift is fully absorbed by a loss in reserves, even though this occurs via the regulated market rather than as capital flight. This conclusion is important because it shows that dual rates can break the speed of capital flight but may not be able to stop an equivalent reserve loss occurring via the impact of the premium on the trade deficit.

9.3 Triple and Multiple Rates

The Venezuelan case in which the free market premium reached more than 260 percent of the commercial rate was mentioned earlier. Such a discrepancy is of course a very large distortion. This overvalued rate for some essential imports holds down their prices and thus maintains the real value of wages. But in doing so, it heavily taxes producers of goods traded at the regulated rate. The resulting tendency toward a deficit in the regulated market brings about reserve depletion and thus expectations of devaluation. The expectation then further raises the premium and reinforces the reserve losses.

A typical response to the dilemma is to maintain the regulated rate for essential imports but to shift some exports toward a third market in which the rate is also fixed but at a higher level. In Venezuela, such a multiple system took the form shown in table 9.1.

The change in the exchange rate structure involved a real depreciation with respect to debt service, services, and imports. The relative prices of these goods and services increased as they were shifted from the lowest rate to an intermediate level involving a 25 percent depreciation. What would one expect to be the impact on the free market premium over the basic rate, e/x? The model developed here can still be used, except that it now has another parameter, $\beta \equiv x'/x$, the ratio of the intermediate rate to the basic rate. The ww schedule would remain unchanged. But there will be an effect on the free market trade balance.

$$\bar{V}(\alpha, \beta, w, q) = 0. \tag{10a}$$

The question is whether splitting the basic rate will increase or reduce the trade surplus of the free market. There are two extreme scenarios that

Table 9.1
The Venezuelan multiple exchange rate system

Date	Exchange rate (Bolivars per U.S. dollars)	Transaction category
February 1983	4.3	Petroleum exports, debt service, and basic food
	6.0	Most imports
	Unregulated	All other transactions
February 1984	4.3	Basic food
	6.0	Petroleum exports
	7.50	Services, most imports, and debt service
	Unregulated	Nontraditional exports, nonessential imports, and capital account transactions

can be envisaged. In the first, resources are primarily transferred from the free market into production in the sector with the new higher official exchange rate, while higher prices in that sector transfer consumer demand into the free market. In this case increased demand and reduced supply create a deficit in the free market, $\bar{V}(\bullet)$ declines at each level of q, and the $\bar{V}(\bullet)$ schedule in figure 9.8 shifts upward. In addition, with unchanged real money balances, across steady states the third rate would create a cumulative trade surplus at the official rate. Conversely, at the other extreme, the shift primarily worsens the official trade balance while improving the free market surplus, and the premium declines. The price level $P(e, x, x')$ now could fall (depending on the relative weights of the different markets in total domestic trade), and there might be a cumulative loss of reserves, as can be observed from the equation for real balances written here in terms of nominal money and prices:

$$M = P(e, x, x')\sigma w. \tag{14a}$$

The ambiguity of the effect of the policy move on reserves is, of course, critical. It suggests that an obvious move to increase efficiency—removing some items from a severely undervalued exchange rate—may in fact produce exactly the wrong results for reserves. Moreover there is no presumption that shifting an activity from one rate to another will in fact improve welfare, as is obvious from the second-best nature of the exercise. This point is important because it means that increasing the number of rates by shifting activities from the lowest or basic rate toward the more "realistic" free rate does not necessarily reduce distortions in the economy. It may well increase the misallocation (see Harberger 1959).

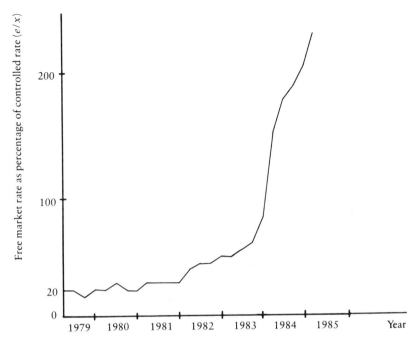

Figure 9.10
The premium of the Dominican Republic's exchange rates. (Source: International Monetary Fund, *International Financial Statistics Yearbook.*)

The Unification Problem

Figure 9.10 shows the premium of the free rate over the official exchange rate for the Dominican Republic. The official rate is constitutionally fixed at 1 peso per U.S. dollar. An increasing number of transactions are conducted at this rate, and as is apparent, the free rate has progressively moved away from the official rate. The Dominican Republic now faces a problem common in Europe after World War I: Should the official exchange rate be restored as a uniform rate, which would require deflation such as the United Kingdom undertook in moving back in 1925 to the prewar parity? Or should a new uniform rate be set that takes into account the level of the free rate, as Poincaré did in 1926 in France?

It is clear that the present system is not viable because it involves huge distortions. In response to the distortions, an increasing number of transactions are shifted to the parallel rate so that the average exchange rate is depreciating over time. Table 9.2 shows the effects of this reallocation on

Table 9.2
Average exchange rates for the Dominican Republic
(pesos per U.S. dollar)

Rate	1982	1983	1984[a]
Effective: imports	1.19	1.31	2.18
Effective: exports	1.0	1.15	1.77
Official	1.0	1.0	1.0
Parallel	1.46	1.61	2.75

Source: World Bank data.
a. Estimate.

the effective exchange rate (weighting the trade categories by their appropriate exchange rate).

Much the same problem, though in perhaps less clear-cut terms, arises for a country in which the free rate and the basic rate are so far apart that the resource allocation costs outweigh any macroeconomic benefits.[6] When the dual rate has gone far out of line, the unification of rates becomes an important macroeconomic issue. The expectations about the manner in which unification will be achieved will affect both the premium (and hence the trade deficit) and also interest rates and activity. If the expectation is one of devaluation of the official rate, as must ordinarily be the case, the free market premium will already reflect that expectation and be correspondingly higher, which thereby worsens the trade deficit. Interest rates will reflect the expectation of depreciation of the free rate and thus will rise in the period ahead of the expected depreciation. Therefore, if the devaluation is delayed, real interest rates for activities tied to the official rate increase, and that of course leads to a decline in investment activity. Bankruptcy problems arise as debt service comes to absorb declining real earnings of the sector that is atrophied by the overvalued official rate.

It is obvious then that a dual rate at a level far from the official rate must be a very transitory policy if it is to be effective. Attempts at unification cannot be avoided, and the real wage problem ultimately cannot be solved by implicit trade taxes and subsidies that affect all markets, especially forward-looking financial markets. A more sensible model is the Mexican solution, in which the dual market is used as a strictly transitory shock absorber. Figure 9.2 shows the premium in the free Mexican market relative to the controlled rate. The divergence was kept small, although financial disturbances were allowed to affect the premium. But fundamental macroeconomic changes were reflected in the official rate; the premium stayed on average well below 20 percent.

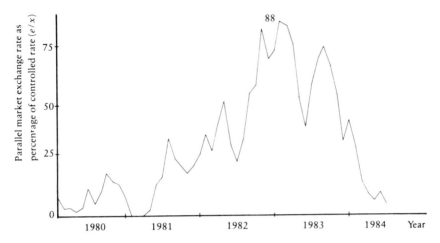

Figure 9.11
The parallel market exchange rate premium in Brazil. (Source: Pechman 1984.)

Black Markets

This analysis has focused on cases in which the government sanctions an official free market for all nonpreferential transactions. In some cases the reaction to the high premium is to exclude certain transactions altogether, in particular capital account transactions, from access to foreign exchange. As a consequence a black market will immediately spring up and function in a manner identical to the dual market already discussed.

Figure 9.11 shows the premium in the Brazilian "black" or parallel market in the past few years. It shows the same erratic pattern as the Venezuelan dual rate; this pattern reflects expectations about major shifts in politics and financial and official exchange rate policy.

The market brings together all unauthorized foreign exchange transactions: import smuggling and coffee export smuggling undertaken to avoid quotas and/or export taxes, unofficial military export revenue, tourism, and capital account transactions. In Dornbusch and others (1983), it is shown that the market is well-behaved: seasonal factors, interest rates, the official real exchange rate, and anticipation of major devaluations ("maxis") explain the behavior of the premium.[7]

Figure 9.12 shows the premium in Argentina in the period since Martínez de Hoz. Except for brief periods of unified exchange markets, there has always been a premium. Politics and real interest rates are the main determinants (see Dornbusch and Moura Silva [forthcoming]). The Argentinian

Figure 9.12
The parallel exchange rate market premium in Argentina. (Source: Organization Techint.)

example shows how politics can cause a free exchange rate to vary far from PPP. An example is the pre-election period in late 1983: the premium rose to more than 100 percent (in daily data) prior to the election and immediately fell by 40 percentage points on the day after the Alfonsín election. The size and movements of the black-market premium affect resource allocation and inflation and thus pose problems for macroeconomic policy.

The traditional view of black markets is to see them as an offshoot of the restriction of commercial transactions. But there is sufficient evidence to support the view that they are closely tied to financial markets. At any point in time there is a given stock of foreign assets in the hands of domestic residents. Given expected returns on domestic assets, there will be a level of the premium that will establish stock equilibrium. The level of the premium in turn influences the flows into and out of the pool of foreign assets in the hands of the public. These considerations are particularly obvious in the case of Argentina. In July 1982, for example, the government chose to solve the problem of the domestic overindebtedness of firms and of the government by freezing nominal interest rates below the rate of inflation. There was an immediate shift of portfolio holders out of domestic assets into black-market dollars. Within a day, the premium shot up to above 100 percent. The high level of the premium in turn encouraged underinvoicing of exports, which deprived the government of foreign exchange and of revenue from export taxes and thereby worsened the financial difficulties of the public sector.

Brazil, similarly, has had periods when the black market showed a large premium, for example, at the outset of the debt crisis in late 1982. The level of the premium was so high that a peculiarly inefficient arbitrage occurred. The government allocated foreign exchange for tourists—$1,000 for every man, woman, or child. Given a premium of nearly 100 percent, mothers with ten babies (who fly free of charge) were able to plunder the central bank by flying to and from Miami to exchange dollars for pesos at the international exchange rate. Lines for passports (required to obtain foreign exchange) were for once even longer than those for food. The large premium may have cost the government as much as one billion U.S. dollars in reserves.

Because the black market is integrated with forward-looking asset markets, it is clear that expectations about future political or economic events will be reflected in the premium even before they materialize. Thus the chance of a Peronist victory pushed up the premium prior to Alfonsín's election. Similarly, anticipated exchange rate action can be seen in the premium. The anticipation of a maxi-devaluation of the official rate, for example, would lead to an immediate rise of the premium in the black market. The increased premium in turn would worsen the financial conditions of the government, not only by posting a visible sign of no confidence but also by drawing resources away from the official asset markets.

An interesting fact, in this context, was the decline of the Brazilian premium in 1984–85 despite large deficits and deteriorating financial conditions. Part of the reason is, of course, the extremely high real interest rate. The rate in Brazil was above 40 percent in real terms and thus more than competitive with any capital gains expected in the black market. But a further element depressing the premium may well have been the fact that the government has ceased purchasing domestic gold, which therefore flowed through the black market. The resulting increased flow of black-market dollars kept a lid on the premium and worked to stabilize expectations.

9.4 Conclusions

This study of special exchange rate systems for capital account transactions points out two problematic characteristics of international financial markets for government policy. These are, first, the range of ways that successful policy implementation is precluded in an economy which is fully open to the influence of international asset markets and, second, the macro-economic repercussions of controlled exchange rate systems which can undermine the long-run effectiveness of such schemes.

In these dual exchange rate systems, capital account transactions are conducted at a free rate, while commercial trade is maintained at an over-valued exchange rate. The models of dual exchange rate systems developed here examine the outcome when a government uses credit creation and thus commercial account depreciation to fund government spending. This strategy increases capital account depreciation and thus the premium of capital over commercial account rates. When the devaluation is foreseen by asset holders, as is common, that expectation and the subsequent capital account depreciation will create a trade deficit. The increase in the premium raises wealth relative to target levels and leads to dissaving and a movement out of money balances, which fuels the trade deficit. It is clear that this form of inflationary finance is not sustainable in the long run and that it will create distortions in other macroeconomic conditions which may, by a government's own assessment, offset the benefit from the initial spending increase.

The distortionary effects of the dual rate system are substantially offset, however, if the central bank intervenes to protect the value of the currency (through sale of foreign assets). The premium declines in response to increased foreign asset holdings, and the lower premium reduces the real value of foreign assets and thus wealth. Savings will increase, which will result in decreased spending and imports and an improved trade balance. Because of declining real money balances, however, seignorage again is not sufficient to fund increased government spending.

More severe macroeconomic distortions may be introduced when some commercial transactions are transferred to the free market or when relatively large parallel markets emerge. In this case the free or parallel market rate directly influences domestic prices. Consumers will substitute toward the now relatively cheaper imported goods traded at the official rate, while producers will move resources out of production for the official market and into activities that benefit from the free rate. These movements will increase supply in the free market, while higher demand and a decline in supply in the fixed rate market will create a trade deficit. The central bank faces larger trade deficits and loses reserves, while in the free market a trade surplus leads to accumulation of foreign assets.

In this situation there are counteracting influences, and the impacts on the price level and savings (and thus on the deficit) are not clear. The effect of *multiple* exchange rates on the trade balances in the various rate markets is similarly indeterminate. The impact on official reserves will depend on the rates of substitution between the new "midrange" market and the prior fixed and free markets. A partial policy move away from a severely over-valued exchange rate, as a second-best exercise, may actually increase misallocation.

It might be argued that the government is helping workers by sustaining real wages via a low official exchange rate financed by external borrowing. But the deficit is increased by the rising premium: the free market runs a surplus that is privately accumulated, while the government borrows abroad to finance "its" deficit. Those who trade at the free rate, particularly asset holders who can move relatively easily between domestic and international markets, may ultimately be the net beneficiaries of the scheme, not labor.

All these outcomes suggest that the dual rate will be most effective if it is maintained in a range close to the free rate. In this way the system can buffer the economy from abrupt financial disturbances, but the rate must be allowed to shift in response to fundamental macroeconomic changes.

9.5 Appendix: The Dual Exchange Rate Model

The dual exchange rate model assumes a single good, purchasing power parity at the commercial rate, x, and two assets: domestic money and a foreign security (or foreign money). Throughout, λ denotes the rate of depreciation of the official rate and u the depreciation rate in the free market.

The portfolio balance is given by:

$$\frac{M}{eK} = L\left(\frac{\dot{e}}{e} + i^*\right), \quad L' < 0, \tag{A1}$$

or, solving for $\dot{e}/e$:

$$\frac{\dot{e}}{e} = h\left(\frac{M}{eK}\right) - i^*, \quad h' < 0, \tag{A1a}$$

where e is the capital account rate, M is domestic money, K is the stock of foreign nominal assets, and i^* is the foreign interest rate, which is assumed to be zero.

Wealth is defined as the sum of real balances and foreign assets:

$$a = m + k. \tag{A2}$$

It is assumed that investment and taxes are zero. A given level of real government spending, G, is financed by domestic credit creation. The growth in the real money stock is determined by the rate of depreciation of the commercial rate, government spending, and the trade surplus, B:

$$\frac{d(M/x)}{dt} = (G + B) - \left(\frac{M}{x}\right)\left(\frac{\dot{x}}{x}\right). \tag{A3}$$

The trade surplus is determined by the discrepancy between savings and real government spending. Real savings depends on the gap between target wealth, w, and actual wealth, a, and on anticipated capital gains:

$$S = v(w - a) - \left(\frac{eK}{x}\right)\left(\frac{\dot{e}}{e} - \frac{\dot{x}}{x}\right) + \left(\frac{M}{x}\right)\left(\frac{\dot{x}}{x}\right). \tag{A4}$$

Accordingly, savings has a stock adjustment component and a component arising from the capital gains realized from external assets and the inflation losses incurred on real balances.

Noting that the trade surplus is the excess of savings over government spending,

$$B = S - G \tag{A5}$$

and hence

$$\frac{d(M/x)}{dt} = S - \left(\frac{M}{x}\right)\left(\frac{\dot{x}}{x}\right)$$
$$= v(w - a) + \left[\lambda - h\left(\frac{M}{eK}\right) + i^*\right]k, \tag{A3a}$$

where $\lambda = \dot{x}/x$ is the given rate of depreciation of the commercial rate that satisfies the condition of steady state deficit finance:

$$\lambda L(\lambda)\overline{k} = G. \tag{A6}$$

It is assumed that there is a unique λ to solve equation (A6) (see Bruno and Fischer 1985).

The system can be studied in terms of the two differential equations governing the evolution of the real value of assets:

$$\dot{m} = v(w - m - k) + \left[\lambda - h\left(\frac{m}{k}\right)\right]k, \tag{A7}$$

$$\dot{q} = q\left[h\left(\frac{m}{k}\right) - \lambda\right]. \tag{A8}$$

These two schedules and the corresponding dynamics are shown in the phase diagram in figure 9.5, where it is assumed that $\dot{m} = 0$ is negatively sloped.

For any initial value of the real money stock, m_0, adjustment takes place along the stable trajectory JJ to the steady state at E. In the adjustment process a trade surplus is accompanied by a real depreciation of the capital account rate.

Once commercial transactions enter the free market, the system of equations becomes

$$\frac{\dot{m}}{m} = \frac{v(w - a) - h(m/k)(1 - \alpha)k}{m} - \alpha h\left(\frac{m}{k}\right),\tag{A9}$$

$$\frac{\dot{K}}{K} = \frac{V(q, a, \lambda)}{K} - (1 - \alpha)h\left(\frac{m}{k}\right),\tag{A10}$$

$$\frac{\dot{q}}{q} = h\left(\frac{m}{k}\right),\tag{A11}$$

where it is assumed that $\dot{x}/x = 0$ and where α is the share of free market goods in the deflator:

$$P = P(e, x).\tag{A12}$$

In the steady state, $h(m/k) = 0$. Thus the steady state system simplifies to:

$$\bar{V}[q, qK[1 + L(0)], 0] = 0,\tag{A13}$$

$$m = L(0)qK,\tag{A14}$$

$$w = K[1 + L(0)]\rho, \quad \rho \equiv q^{\alpha},\tag{A15}$$

where the last two equations imply that:

$$m = \sigma w,$$

$$\sigma = \frac{L(0)}{1 + L(0)}.\tag{A16}$$

This system is used in the text for comparative statics.

Notes

1. For more detailed discussion and derivations, see the appendix.

2. Alternative models have been presented (de Macedo 1983; Lizondo 1984; Flood 1978) in which external asset accumulation plays a significant part.

3. For a comprehensive explanation of the dynamics of phase diagrams, see Sheffrin (1983).

4. The premium and the relative price of goods trading in the free market continue to be denoted by q, where $q = e/x$.

5. When all goods trade at the commercial rate, x, equation 13 reduces to $w = qK[1 + L(0)]$.

6. This may be Venezuela's situation but is probably not Mexico's.

7. In fact, even the bid-ask spreads in the black market can be well explained in terms of the theory of dealership (see Dornbusch and Pechman 1985). Interest

rates and the variability of the premium that proxies the extent of news explain the size of the spread.

References

Aizenman, J. 1983. "Adjustment to Monetary Policy and Devaluation under Two-Tier and Fixed Exchange Rate Regimes." National Bureau of Economic Research Working Paper 1107.

Barratieri, V., and G. Ragazzi. 1971. "Dual Exchange Rates for Capital and Current Transactions: A Theoretical Examination." Banca Nazionale del Lavoro *Quarterly Review*, December.

Bernstein, E. 1950. "Some Economic Aspects of Multiple Exchange Rates." *IMF Staff Papers*, September.

Bruno, M., and S. Fischer. 1985. "Expectations and the High Inflation Trap." Massachusetts Institute of Technology. Processed.

Cumby, R. 1984. "Monetary Policy under Dual Exchange Rates." National Bureau of Economic Research Working Paper 1424.

Decaluwe, B., and A. Steinherr. 1976. "A Portfolio Balance Model for a Two-Tier Exchange Market." *Economica*, May.

Decaluwe, B., and A. Steinherr. 1977. "The Two Tier Exchange Market In Belgium." *Kredit und Kapital Beihefte*, Heft 3.

de Macedo, J. 1983. "Exchange Rate Behavior under Currency Inconvertibility." *Journal of International Economics*, September.

de Vries, M. 1965. "Multiple Exchange Rates: Expectations and Experiences." *IMF Staff Papers*, July.

Dickie, P., and D. Noursi. 1975. "Dual Exchange Markets: The Case of the Syrian Arab Republic." *IMF Staff Papers*, July.

Dornbusch, R. 1976. "The Theory of Flexible Exchange Rate Regimes and Macroeconomic Policy." *Scandinavian Journal of Economics*.

Dornbusch, R., and S. Fischer. 1980. "Exchange Rate and the Current Account." *American Economic Review*, December.

Dornbusch, R., and A. Moura Silva. "Dollar Debts and Interest Rates in Brazil." In *Revista Brasileira de Economia* (forthcoming).

Dornbusch, R., and C. Pechman. 1985. "The Bid-Ask Spread in the Black Market for Dollars in Brazil." *Journal of Money, Credit, and Banking*, November.

Dornbusch, R., et al. 1980. "Inflation Stabilization and Capital Mobility." National Bureau of Economic Research Working Paper 555.

Dornbusch, R., et al. 1983. "The Black Market for Dollars in Brazil." *Quarterly Journal of Economics*, February.

Dornbusch, R., et al. 1984. "Argentina since Martínez de Hoz." National Bureau of Economic Research Working Paper 1466.

Fischer, S. 1982. "Seignorage and the Case for a National Money." *Journal of Political Economy*, April.

Fleming, M. 1971. *Essays in International Economics*. London: Allen and Unwin.

Fleming, M. 1974. "Dual Exchange Markets and Other Remedies for Disruptive Capital Flows." *IMF Staff Papers*, vol. 21.

Flood, R. 1978. "Exchange Rate Expectations in Dual Exchange Markets." *Journal of International Economics*, February.

Flood, R. 1979. "Capital Mobility and the Choice of Exchange Rate System." *International Economic Review*, June.

Flood, R., and N. Peregrim Marion. 1982. "The Transmission of Disturbances under Alternative Exchange Rate Regimes with Optimal Indexing." *Quarterly Journal of Economics*, February.

Gupta, S. 1980. "An Application of the Monetary Approach to Black Market Exchange Rates." *Weltwirtschaftliches Archiv* 2.

Harberger, G. 1959. "Using Resources at Hand More Efficiently." *American Economic Review*, May.

Isze, A., and G. Ortiz. 1984. "Political Risk, Asset Substitution, and Exchange Rate Dynamics: The Mexican Financial Crisis of 1982." El Colegio de Mexico and Banco de Mexico, August. Unpublished manuscript.

Kaminsky, G. 1984. "The Black Market and Its Effects on Welfare and on the Current Account." Central Bank of Argentina, March. Processed.

Kanesa-Thasan, S. 1966. "Multiple Exchange Rates: The Indonesian Experience." *IMF Staff Papers*, July.

Khan, M., and L. Ramierz-Roja. 1984. "Currency Substitution and Government Revenue from Inflation." International Monetary Fund, September. Unpublished manuscript.

Kiguel, M. 1984. "Relative Price Dynamics under Dual Exchange Rate Markets, Rational Expectations, and Currency Substitution." Unpublished manuscript. University of Maryland.

Lanyi, A. 1975. "Separate Exchange Markets for Capital and Current Transactions." *IMF Staff Papers*, November.

Lizondo, J. 1984. "Exchange Rate Differentials and Balance of Payments Under Dual Exchange Markets." Washington, D.C.: International Monetary Fund.

Macedo, J. 1982. "Exchange Rate Behavior with Currency Inconvertibility." *Journal of International Economics*, February.

Marquez, J. 1984. "Currency Substitution, Duality, and Exchange Rate Indeterminacy: An Empirical Analysis of the Venezuelan Experience." Federal Reserve Board, *International Finance Discussion Papers* 242.

Mathieson, D. 1979. "Financial Reform and Capital Flows in a Developing Economy" *IMF Staff Papers*, September.

McKinnon, R. 1982. "The Order of Economic Liberalization: Lessons from Chile and Argentina." *Carnegie Rochester Conference Series* 17.

McKinnon, R., and D. Mathieson. 1981. "How to Manage a Repressed Economy." *Essays in International Finance* 145, December.

Obstfeld, M. 1984. "Capital Controls, the Dual Exchange Rate, and Devaluation." National Bureau of Economic Research Working Paper 1324.

Olgun, H. (1984), "An Analysis of the Black Market Exchange Rate in a Developing Country: The Case of Turkey." *Weltwirtschaftliches Archiv* 2.

Ortiz, G. 1983a. "Currency Substitution in Mexico." *Journal of Money, Credit, and Banking*, May.

Ortiz, G. 1983b. "Dollarization in Mexico: Causes and Consequences." In P. Aspe Armella and others (eds.), *Financial Policies and the World Capital Market*. Chicago: University of Chicago Press.

Pechman, C. 1984. *O Dolar Paralelo No Brasil*. Rio de Janeiro: Paz e Terra.

Peregrim Marion, N. 1981. "Insulation Properties of a Two-Tier Exchange Market in a Portfolio Balance Model." *Economica*, February.

Sheffrin, Steven. 1983. *Rational Expectations*. Cambridge: Cambridge University Press.

Sheik, M. 1976. "Black Market for Foreign Exchange, Capital Flows, and Smuggling." *Journal of Development Economics* 1.

Swoboda, A. 1974. "The Dual Exchange Rate System and Monetary Independence." In R. Z. Aliber, ed., *National Monetary Policies and the International System*. Chicago: University of Chicago Press.

Williamson, J. (ed.). 1981. *Exchange Rate Rules: The Theory, Performance, and Prospects of the Crawling Peg*. New York: St. Martin's.

World Bank. 1985. "The Outflow of Capital." *Research News* 6, no. 1.

10   The Black Market for Dollars in Brazil

(with Daniel Valente
Dantas, Clarice Pechman,
Roberto de Rezende
Rocha, and
Demetrio Simões)

This chapter develops a model of the black market for dollars in Brazil. Although some of the institutional features are special to Brazil (smuggling, Argentinian tourists, etc.), the general approach applies to any market for foreign exchange. The central feature of our model is the emphasis on the interaction of stock and flow conditions in the black market in determining both the premium on foreign exchange and the rate of change of the stock of black dollars. The general approach is familiar from the literature on exchange rate determination oriented along asset market and current account lines (Kouri 1976; Dornbusch 1976, 1980; Rodriguez 1980; Dornbusch and Fischer 1980), and the literature on dual exchange rates, especially in Flood (1976). The general approach we adopt has already been used to analyze the pricing of inconvertible currencies in Braga de Macedo (1981), although that paper treats the black market more nearly in the fashion of a dual exchange rate regime, giving emphasis in particular to the general equilibrium interaction between the black market and the macroeconomy. Our study, quite on the contrary, assumes that the black market is altogether a sideshow with no effect on interest rates or the course of the official exchange rate. That assumption certainly is warranted for the case of Brazil where the black market, though having an estimated daily turnover of $10 million, is entirely negligible with respect to financial markets.

Figure 10.1 shows monthly observations for the premium in the black market—the percentage excess of the black-market price of dollars over the official exchange rate. The market takes the form of trade in currency, but there is also the possibility of cable transfers and acquisition of deposits.[1] The market is illegal in that the dealers are not allowed to trade in foreign exchange and that the participants are not allowed to hold foreign exchange. The black market is not clandestine, however. Indeed, it is called

Originally published in *Quarterly Journal of Economics* (February 1983), pp. 25–40.

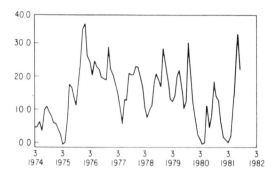

Figure 10.1
The premium (monthly data). (Source: Dealers' notes.)

the "parallel market," suggesting an intermediate position of legality in that it is illegal but also conspicuously public and, it would appear, officially tolerated. The figures reveal substantial volatility in the premium, an average premium of about 15 percent, but also periods where the premium declines to zero.

Most recently, in early 1981, the premium actually turned negative under the impact of a very tight monetary policy. This episode is interesting in that it reveals the risk aspect of participation in the markets. When the premium becomes negative, market participants are paying in excess of the official rate in selling dollars for cruzeiros. This negative premium is essentially a "laundering charge" paid by people who have no right to possess the dollars that they are offering for sale. Only when the government announced that banks were allowed to buy dollars from anyone without the need for identification did the premium return to zero.[2]

In discussing the determinants of the black-market premium, we shall first develop a model of the portfolio balance considerations that govern the holding of stocks of black dollars and of the rate of net additions to the existing stock. The following section discusses several comparative static applications to show the working of the model. Two special applications are then developed: an anticipated future devaluation and the role of seasonal factors in the market. The chapter concludes by showing empirical results that support the model and in particular the idea of a systematic seasonal factor.

10.1 The Model

The black market is treated in a partial-equilibrium fashion, taking as given the prevailing interest rates in Brazil and abroad, the official exchange rate, and the cruzeiro value of nondollar assets. There is a stock demand for dollars that are held as part of a diversified portfolio. Demand for dollars depends positively on their relative yield and on wealth. Equilibrium in the market requires that demand equal the existing supply:

$$EB = \theta(i^* + d - i)(C + EB), \quad \theta' > 0. \tag{1}$$

In (1) B denotes the existing stock of dollars, and E the cruzeiro price of dollars in the black market. EB thus represents the supply of black dollars. Demand is proportional to wealth $C + EB$, where C denotes the value of cruzeiro assets. Demand depends positively on the relative yield $i^* + d - i$, where i^* and i are the nominal interest rates on dollars and cruzeiros and d is the rate of depreciation of the cruzeiro in the black market.

It is convenient to restate the asset market equilibrium condition in terms of the ratio of black dollars to wealth and in terms of the black-market premium. For this purpose, we define the premium (actually one plus the premium) as $x = E/\bar{E}$, where $\bar{E}$ is the official exchange rate. Using the definition in (1) and dividing by wealth, we obtain

$$\frac{xB}{xB + \bar{C}} = \theta(i^* + d - i), \quad x \equiv \frac{E}{\bar{E}}, \tag{2}$$

where $\bar{C} \equiv C/\bar{E}$ (the dollar value of cruzeiro assets valued at the official exchange rate) is taken as exogenous.

The rate of depreciation of the official exchange rate is taken as given and is denoted by $\bar{d}$. The rate of change of the premium $\dot{x}/x$ is then equal to the difference between the rates of depreciation of black dollars and of the official rate:

$$\frac{\dot{x}}{e} \equiv d - \bar{d}. \tag{3}$$

Substituting from (3) into the stock market equilibrium condition and inverting the equation yields a relationship between three variables we are concerned with, the stock of black dollars, the premium, and its rate of change:

$$\frac{\dot{x}}{x} = G\left(\frac{xB}{\bar{C}}\right) - (i^* + \bar{d} - i), \quad G' > 0. \tag{4}$$

Equilibrium in the stock market, from (4), requires that an increase in the relative supply of black dollars $(xB/\bar{C})$ be accompanied by an increase in the relative yield. The rise in the relative yield can come from a higher official, depreciation-adjusted differential $i^* + \bar{d} - i$, or from a rising black-

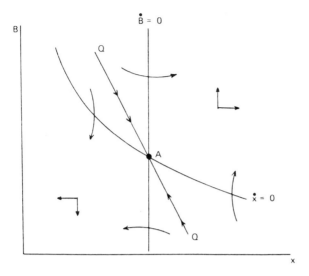

Figure 10.2

market premium $\dot{x} > 0$. Conversely, a rise in the official differential will create an excess demand that needs to be offset by a rise in supply through a higher level of the premium or through an offsetting decline in demand due to a falling premium.

In figure 10.2 we show the schedule $\dot{x} = 0$ along which the premium is constant. The schedule is drawn for a given depreciation-adjusted interest differential $i^* + \bar{d} - i$, and for a given value of $\bar{C}$. From (4) it is apparent that the schedule is a rectangular hyperbola. Points above and to the right of the schedule imply that the relative supply of black dollars is larger than what the public is willing to hold at going nominal interest differentials, and accordingly, $\dot{x}/x$ is required to be positive and conversely below the schedule.

The flow market for black dollars arises from a variety of sources. Coffee export smugglers remit their foreign exchange earnings through the black market, while manufactures-import smugglers acquire foreign exchange in the black market. Argentinian tourists are an important source of dollar inflows, whereas Brazilian tourists, who are limited to a $1,000 allowance of official foreign exchange, give rise to outflows. For a given commercial policy we describe the current account of the black market or the *net* rate of addition to the stock of black dollars as a function of the premium and of the official *real* exchange rate $\bar{e}$:

$$\dot{B} = F(x, \bar{e}), \quad F_x > 0, \quad F_{\bar{e}} > 0. \tag{5}$$

A rise in the premium will raise the net rate of inflow as it reduces the import smuggling and Brazilian tourism abroad, while increasing the use of the black market by export smugglers and Argentinian tourists to Brazil. A real depreciation of the official exchange rate, similarly, gives rise to increased net inflows, since it reduces the relative cost of Brazilian goods (manufactures or hotels) and thus reduces depletion of the black market by smugglers and tourists.

In figure 10.2 we show the schedule $\dot{B} = 0$, which represents a balanced current account for the black market. The schedule is drawn for a given official real exchange rate and a given commercial policy and foreign exchange allowance. Points to the right imply a premium so high as to make for a surplus in the black market and thus a growing stock, while points to the left imply a declining stock. The arrows in figure 10.2 indicate that there is a unique trajectory QQ along which the market would converge to a steady state at point A. We assume conditions of perfect foresight *and* that the market indeed picks this stable trajectory, although there is nothing in the model that would lead to this outcome.[3] Under this assumption, then, starting from an initial stock of black dollars below the steady state implies a relatively high and falling premium that gives rise to a current account surplus and hence a rising stock. As the stock rises over time, holders are compensated by reduced rates of depreciation of the black rate relative to the official rate.

10.2 The Effects of Real and Financial Changes on the Black Market

The model developed in the preceding section implies that the premium on black dollars at any point in time depends on the existing stock as well as on the nominal interest differential (adjusted for official depreciation), the stock of cruzeiro assets, commercial policy and the official real exchange rate. In this section we look at the impact and long-run effects of changes in these determinants.

Consider first a tightening of Brazilian monetary policy as reflected in a reduction in the depreciation-adjusted yield differential $i^* + \bar{d} + i$. Such a change increases the attractiveness of cruzeiro assets relative to black dollars and thus leads to a shift on the demand side out of dollars. To restore stock equilibrium with an unchanging premium, the relative supply of black dollars has to fall. This is shown in figure 10.3 by a shift of the stock equilibrium schedule to $\dot{x}' = 0$. From an initial equilibrium at A, the rise in Brazilian interest rates thus leads to an immediate fall in the premium

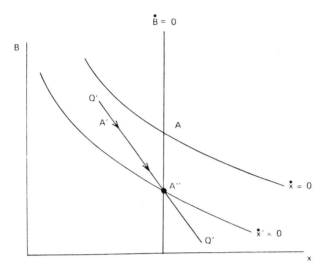

Figure 10.3

to point A'. This adjustment is the impact effect of the portfolio shift. Over time the lower premium gives rise to a depletion of the stock of black dollars until the market converges to point A''. Here the premium is restored to its initial level, but of course the relative supply of dollar assets is reduced. The example makes the point that changes in financial markets have an immediate impact on the level of the premium and that the black market shares the volatility that we experience in other financial markets.

Changes in the conditions governing the flow market are represented by shifts in the $\dot{B} = 0$ schedule. Real depreciation of the official rate, for example, leads to increased net inflows into the market and thus shifts the $\dot{B} = 0$ schedule to the left; an increase in coffee export taxes leads to increased export smuggling and increased remittances through the black market, again shifting $\dot{B} = 0$ to the left. A tightening of import controls or a reduction of tourist allowances, by contrast, would increase the flow demand for black dollars and thus lead to a rightward shift as a higher premium is required to offset the increased drain. It is apparent from the analysis in figure 10.3 that any such change will lead to an immediate jump in the premium as the market adjusts to the new information. Subsequently, the premium and the stock of black dollars evolve to their new long-run equilibrium.

These effects are shown in figure 10.4 for the case of a real depreciation. The impact effect is to reduce the premium as the market jumps from A to

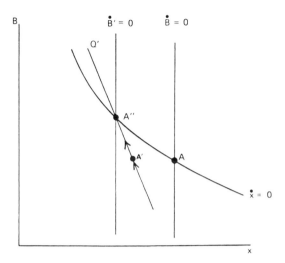

Figure 10.4

A'. But at A' there is now a current account surplus in the black market that leads to a gradual buildup of stocks. At point A' the decline in the premium has reduced the relative supply of black dollars $xB/\bar{C}$. Black dollars are depreciating (at a declining rate), while the stock of dollars is rising. Flow market disturbances, just as the stock market disturbance analyzed above, have an immediate effect on the premium as the market reevaluates the long-run value of black dollars. Given the stock of dollars B, the change in the valuation creates a portfolio disequilibrium that has to be offset by a changing level of the premium.

10.3 The Anticipation of a Future Maxi-Devaluation

In this section we study the adjustment process in the black market to the current anticipation of a *future* depreciation of the level of the exchange rate.[4] To single out the speculative aspects, we focus on a purely nominal depreciation of the official rate that is anticipated to occur at a point T, in the future, becoming known presently. The effects of the anticipation are developed in figure 10.5

The initial equilibrium is a point A with the black market in steady state. The anticipation of a future maxi leads all speculators to recognize that in the long run the economy will return to an unchanged premium and that hence the maxi-devaluation of the official rate must also be reflected in a depreciation of the black rate. The recognition of that depreciation or of the

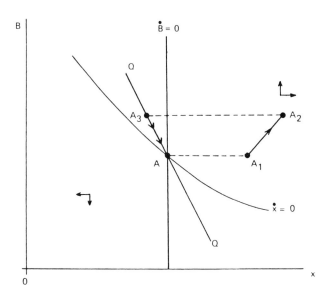

Figure 10.5

potential capital gain on dollars leads to an *immediate* shift in demand toward dollars and, given the available stock, to an immediate jump in the premium from A to A_1.

As yet, the official rate is unchanged as is the nominal yield differential adjusted for the rate of official depreciation $i^* + \bar{d} - i$. Accordingly, both the $\dot{B} = 0$ and $\dot{x} = 0$ remain in their positions. It follows that the dynamics at point A' are governed by these schedules and that there will be a rising premium combined with a growing stock of black dollars. This is the movement from A_1 to A_2. The very day the maxi-devaluation does occur the premium declines from A_2 to A_3. This decline is due *entirely* to the official depreciation, there is no movement at all in the black rate, since all jumps here were anticipated in the initial jump of the black rate and the subsequent cumulative rise in the premium.

The transitory accumulation of black dollars induced by the high level of the premium in the period preceding the actual devaluation now has to be worked off. This occurs along the path $Q'Q'$ on which the reduced premium encourages depletion of the black dollar pool.

The path of the premium in the adjustment process is shown in a separate fashion in figure 10.6 as it behaves over time. The diagram is suggestive of what in fact happened in August–December 1979.

The advent of a new finance minister in Brazil led to the expectation of a

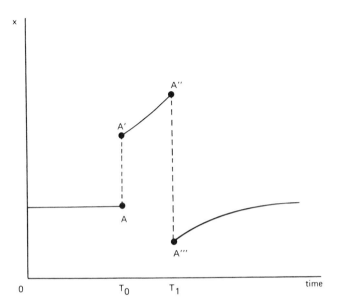

Figure 10.6

maxi-devaluation, which indeed materialized in December 1979. The anticipation led to a sharp increase in the premium that was sustained until the day of the actual depreciation, at which time the premium collapsed.

10.4 Seasonal Factors

An important aspect of the Brazilian black market is the seasonal pattern of net inflows due to tourism, especially on the part of Argentinian visitors to Brazil. The tourist season is the early period of the year from before Christmas to after Carnival and another minor period in July. In these months there is a seasonally high rate of inflow into the black market that gives rise to a seasonal accumulation of dollars and a seasonal decline in the premium. Because this seasonal factor is perfectly anticipated, it gives rise not to jumps in the premium but rather to a gradual movement as shown in figure 10.7.

There is no attempt here to model the exact details of the seasonal pattern. We appeal rather to the general shape of the adjustment path as it has to emerge from the assumption of perfect foresight. First, we note that the fact of a seasonal influences the current account but not the equilibrium in the market for asset stocks. Accordingly, the $\dot{x} = 0$ schedule remains unaffected and continues to govern the evolution of the premium as in-

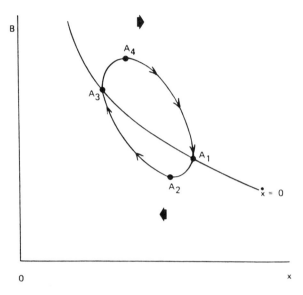

Figure 10.7

dicated by the arrows. We also note that the seasonal pattern has "always" been known, implying that it is fully anticipated.[5] Therefore the evolution of the premium in response to the seasonal will be smooth rather than a jump that occurs only in the case of "news." The difficulty in explaining the seasonal in the premium is that it has no natural starting point. Still, suppose that point A_1 shows the peak sometime before the tourist season. At A_1 the premium is constant, having risen to that level along with falling stocks of dollars. Now at A_1 portfolio holders recognize the oncoming tourist season and the prospective accumulation of black dollars. In response the premium starts declining and thereby, as the market moves clockwise from A_1, induces a decumulation of dollars before the tourist season gets underway. After a minimum level of dollar stocks is reached, the tourists start arriving and replenish the stock of dollars. The premium keeps declining throughout, although at a falling rate until a minimum is reached at A_3. At A_3 dollar stocks are still rising, but now the premium is also increasing.

From equation (4) and figure 10.7 it is apparent that there is also a seasonal pattern in the rate of change of the premium. In periods where the relative supply of black dollars $xB/\overline{C}$ is high *and* rising, the rate of increase of the premium must accelerate; conversely when the relative supply is low and falling, the premium is declining at an increasing rate.[6] These facts

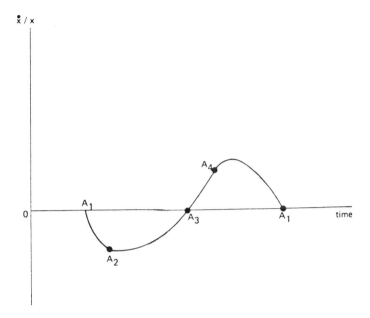

Figure 10.8

allow us to place the turning points of the rate of change of the premium in terms of figure 10.7 as shown in figure 10.8. Starting from the seasonal peak at A_1, the premium is falling, and so is the stock of dollars. Therefore, before the tourist season and into the season, the rate of decline of the premium is increasing. Point A_2 is in the season itself with the seasonally large inflow of tourist dollars offsetting the depletion induced by the seasonally low premium. From A_2 to A_3 the stock of dollars is growing, and so is the relative supply of dollars $xB/\overline{C}$ as we move back toward the $\dot{x} = 0$ schedule. Accordingly, the rate of decline of the premium falls toward zero. After A_4 there is a turning point, still in the tourist season. Here the seasonally low premium induces a large depletion that is barely offset by the seasonally high tourist inflows and the rate of increase in the premium reaches its maximum. Thereafter the relative supply of dollar assets is declining, and so is the rate of increase of the premium.

Although both points A_2 and A_4 lie in the tourist season, their relative position depends on the particular pattern of tourist inflows. Point A_2 precedes the peak, whereas point A_4 follows the peak, as is clear from the fact that depletion is higher the lower is the premium. The two points may be very close in time if the tourist flows are sharply concentrated, but they are quite distant if tourist flows are rather flatly distributed.

10.5 Empirical Results

Table 10.1 shows some empirical evidence on the determinants of the black-market premium. The table reports regressions of the premium, using bimonthly averages for the period May–June 1974 to March–April 1981, on seasonal dummies, the real exchange rate ($\bar{e}$), and the official, depreciation-adjusted interest differential ($i^* + \bar{d} - i$). These variables explain an important part of the variation in the premium.

Equation (1) in table 10.1 shows the regression of the premium on a constant, the real exchange rate, and the depreciation-adjusted interest differential. The constant term shows a premium of nearly 30 percent. Both the real exchange rate and the interest differential have the expected sign and are significant. A real depreciation or increase in $\bar{e}$ leads to a decline in the premium. An increase in U.S. interest rates relative to those in Brazil, adjusted for official depreciation, leads to an increase in the premium. The equation explains a substantial part of the variation in the premium, although a correction for serial correlation is required.

The role of seasonal factors is explored in equation (2). Seasonal factors were introduced by running a regression of the premium on a constant, the real exchange rate, and the interest differential as well as six bimonthly dummies. The sum of coefficients for the seasonal dummies was constrained to be zero. In table 10.1 we report the estimated seasonal components of the premium for the various months. Thus the coefficient of J/F, for example, yields the amount by which the premium in January/February exceeds the annual average. We note that the introduction of the seasonal dummies raises the explanatory power, while leaving the estimated coefficients for the real exchange rate and the interest differential unaffected.

The seasonal dummies invite two comments. First, as a group they have significant explanatory power. An F-test reveals that as a group they are significant at the 1 percent level. Second, the dummies show the expected pattern over the year. The seasonal peaks in November–December at which time it is 5 percent above the annual average. It declines from there until March/April when the premium falls to 5.7 percentage points below the annual average, rising from there again to the November–December peak. The seasonal dummy thus has the shape shown in figure 10.8.

The most interesting aspect of equation (2) is the size of the seasonal variation in the premium. For example, from November to December, when the premium is 5 precentage points above the annual average, it falls to the average by January/February. There is thus a 5 percentage point decline occurring over a period of only two months. This represents a substantial

Table 10.1
The black-market premium, 1974–1981

Constant	$\bar{e}$	$i^* + \bar{d} - i$	J/F	M/A	M/J	J/A	S/O	N/D	R^2	Rho	DW	SSR
(1) 29.4	−0.09	12.7	—	—	—	—	—	—	0.59	0.52	1.8	1,128.6
(7.6)	(−3.9)	(2.0)										
(2) 29.0	−0.09	11.2	0.01	−5.7	−2.5	0.06	3.1	5.0	0.74	0.58	2.2	693.4
(7.8)	(−4.1)	(1.9)	(0.01)	(−4.1)	(−1.8)	(0.05)	(2.2)	(3.5)				

Note: The left-hand variable is the percentage premium. The t-statistics are shown in parentheses. The number of observations is 43.

seasonal variation, since it yields an annualized rate of return from seasonal smoothing of 34 percent. In other months the seasonal changes in the premium are somewhat smaller, but they are surprising in their magnitude. The size of the seasonal variations suggests an important risk perceived by speculators that makes cruzeiros and black dollars substantially imperfect substitutes.

10.6 Concluding Remarks

This chapter has developed a model of the black market for dollars in Brazil. The model emphasizes the interaction of portfolio decisions, depending on the relative returns to holding black dollars versus domestic assets, and the flow market for black dollars in which smugglers and tourists mingle. The central role of the portfolio decisions, in conjunction with the assumption of rational expectations or perfect foresight, implies that changes in financial markets or in the flow market induce an immediate jump in the premium and a subsequent adjustment path for both the premium and the stock of dollars. The model explains how an expectation of future official devaluation leads to an immediate depreciation in the black market and a subsequent decline in the premium when the expected official depreciation actually occurs. The model also lends itself to an examination of seasonal patterns. These arise in the flow markets, but they have an effect on the premium because domestic assets and black dollars are not perfect substitutes. Accordingly, a seasonally high stock of dollars leads to a seasonally low level of the premium.

There are a number of directions in which the model can be extended. The most immediate extensions are to an explicit model of the stochastic process of the official and black-market exchange rate and to implied portfolio diversification formulation of the stock demand. Another point is an analytical, exact formulation of the seasonal pattern that is discussed here only in its general shape. Although both extensions are of interest in technical respects, they may not yield much insight beyond what is already shown here. The more interesting extension is to account further for the very sizable seasonal movements in the premium that suggest a substantial lack of substitutability.

Notes

We received helpful comments from Olivier Blanchard, Carl van Duyne, Stanley Fischer, Paul Krugman, Julio Rotemberg, Jeffrey Sachs, and Mario Simonsen. Financial support was provided by a grant from the National Science Foundation.

1. The stock of U.S. currency (bills and coins) outstanding at the end of 1980 was $116.4 billion. With a U.S. population of 222.8 million, this amounts to per capita holdings of $522.4. This entirely unreasonable figure has been traditionally explained by holdings of organized crime and the liberal professions for purposes of tax evasion. Even casual observation suggests that holdings, legal or otherwise, in the rest of the world are likely to be an important part of this missing money.

2. The case of a persistent discount on dollars in the black market is familiar from the case of Colombia where the black market serves to channel the proceeds from illegal narcotics exports.

3. This is a common difficulty associated with a saddle-point equilibrium in perfect foresight models. See Fischer (1979) and Blanchard (1979) for a further discussion.

4. The analysis of currently anticipated future disturbances is familiar in the exchange rate literature from Black (1972), Wilson (1979), Rogoff (1979), and Fischer (1979). The analysis here most closely follows Dornbusch and Fischer (1980).

5. See Fischer (1979) for a discussion of fully anticipated disturbances in their impact under perfect foresight.

6. To place the maximum and minimum of $\dot{x}/x$, we note that they occur at points of tangency between a rectangular hyperbola and the trajectory in figure 10.7 of x and B. These rectangular hyperbolae define the maximum and minimum levels of the relative supply of dollars xB. By the Viner-Wong theorem, these points of tangency must lie to the left of point A_2 and to the right of point A_4.

References

Black, S. 1972. "The Use of Rational Expectations in Models of Speculation." *Review of Economics and Statistics* 54 (May): 161–166.

Blanchard, O. 1979. "Backward and Forward Solutions for Economies with Rational Expectations." *American Economic Review* 69 (May): 114–118.

Braga de Macedo, J. 1981. "Exchange Rate Behavior under Currency Inconvertibility." Unpublished manuscript. Revised. Princeton University.

Dornbusch, R. 1976. "Capital Mobility, Flexible Exchange Rates and Macroeconomic Equilibrium." In E. Claassen and P. Salin, eds., *Recent Issues in International Monetary Economics*. Amsterdam: North-Holland.

Dornbusch, R. 1980. *Open Economy Macroeconomics*. New York: Basic Books.

Dornbusch, R., and S. Fischer. 1980. "Exchange Rates and the Current Account," *American Economic Review* 70 (December): 960–971.

Fischer, S. 1979. "Anticipations and the Non-neutrality of Money," *Journal of Political Economy* 87 (April): 225–252.

Flood, R. 1978. "Exchange Rate Expectations in Dual Exchange Markets," *Journal of International Economics* 8 (February): 65–67.

Kouri, P. 1976. "The Exchange Rate and the Balance of Payments in the Shortrun and in the Longrun." *Scandinavian Journal of Economics* 78: 280–304.

Rodriguez, C. 1980. "The Role of Trade Flows in Exchange Rate Determination: A Rational Expectations Approach." *Journal of Political Economy* 88 (December): 1148–1158.

Rogoff, K. 1979. "Essays on Expectations and Exchange Rate Dynamics." Ph.D. thesis. MIT.

Wilson, C. 1979. "Anticipated Disturbances and Exchange Rate Dynamics." *Journal of Political Economy* 87 (June): 639–647.

11

PPP Exchange Rate Rules and Macroeconomic Stability

Taylor (1979) developed a macroeconomic model of long-term overlapping wage contracts where, under rational expectations, disturbances have persistent effects on output and prices because relative and absolute wages exhibit short-term stickiness. This stickiness arises because labor, in setting the money wage, is not only concerned with employment but also with the relative wage position compared to ongoing and anticipated future contracts. This tendency for relative wage fixity is reinforced if the government pursues an accommodating monetary policy that dispenses with the need for wage-price discipline. In Dornbusch (1980, 1981) the Taylor model was extended to a small open economy to demonstrate that PPP-(purchasing power parity) oriented exchange rate rules operate in the same direction as accommodating monetary policy. They stabilize output at the cost of increased instability of prices.[1]

This chapter takes up once more the question of exchange rate rules in the context of the Taylor model. We show here that the exchange rate rule affects the output price level stability trade-off through two separate channels. On one hand, a PPP-oriented exchange rate rule tends to maintain the real exchange rate constant, thereby stabilizing demand. The other channel, introduced here, considers the effect of exchange rate rules through the supply side on the price level. The exchange rate affects costs and prices through the domestic currency cost of imported intermediate goods. To the extent that wage disturbances that tend to raise prices are accompanied by exchange depreciation, because of a PPP rule, the impact of wage movements on prices is amplified. Thus the second channel suggests that exchange rate policy can dampen or amplify the impact of wage disturbances on prices and output.

Originally published in *Journal of Political Economy*, vol. 90, no. 1 (February 1982), pp. 158–165. © 1982 by The University of Chicago. All rights reserved.

This second channel, operating through the cost side of the economy, introduces the possibility that increased exchange rate accommodation lowers rather than raises the persistence of disturbances, while raising the impact of unanticipated wage disturbances on prices and output. These results are of interest in view of the widely shared belief that a PPP-oriented exchange rate policy is good policy advice for small countries. We now pursue these issues in the context of the extended Taylor model.

11.1 The Model

The model is stated in terms of the deviations of output and prices from their given trend. All variables are expressed in logs. The level of real output, y, is demand determined, with demand depending on the real money supply, $m - p$, and on the real exchange rate, $e - p$:

$$y = a(m - p) + b(e - p), \quad a, b > 0. \tag{1}$$

A rise in the real money stock raises demand as does a real depreciation of the currency, that is, a rise in $e - p$. A real depreciation raises aggregate demand, given the elasticity condition which is assumed to be satisfied with b positive, because it shifts demand from foreign goods to home output.[2]

Monetary and exchange rate policies are specified by rules which the authorities follow in setting nominal money and the nominal exchange rate:

$$m = \alpha p, \quad e = \beta p, \quad 0 \le \alpha, \beta \le 1. \tag{2}$$

The coefficients α and β measure the extent to which monetary and exchange rate policies are accommodating. Unit values imply that output is maintained constant because real money and the real exchange rate are held constant. Values of α and β that are less than unity imply less than full accommodation, so that a rise in prices lowers real balances and appreciates the real exchange rate, thereby inducing a fall in demand and output. The extent to which a rise in prices leads to a contraction in demand and output is summarized by the parameter θ:[3]

$$y = -\theta p, \quad \theta \equiv a(1 - \alpha) + b(1 - \beta). \tag{3}$$

We now turn to the wage–price process. Prices are determined by wage costs and the costs of imported intermediate goods. The domestic price of intermediate goods is given by the exchange rate:

$$p = \left(\frac{\phi}{2}\right)(x + x_{-1}) + (1 - \phi)e. \tag{4}$$

The price equation reflects the assumption that there are at any time two overlapping or concurrent wage contracts in force. They stipulate, respectively, x as the current wage in the first year of the contract and x_{-1} as the current wage on a two-year contract entered into last year. Current economy-wide wage costs are taken as the average of the two contracts. The terms ϕ and $1 - \phi$ represent the cost shares of labor and intermediate goods, respectively. In combination with the exchange rate rule in (2), we can write the price equation as

$$p = k(x + x_{-1}), \quad k \equiv \frac{\phi/2}{1 - \beta(1 - \phi)}. \tag{5}$$

It is apparent from (5) that a more accommodating exchange rate policy—a value of β more nearly equal to unity—tends to raise the impact of wage disturbances on prices. Conversely, maintaining a constant nominal exchange rate in the face of wage disturbances tends to dampen their impact on the level of prices but raises the impact on the real exchange rate. The extent to which the exchange rate can serve a stabilizing role on the supply side depends on the share of intermediate goods in costs, $1 - \phi$.

We complete the model by looking at wage formation. The current wage is set by reference to ongoing and anticipated future contracts but depends also on expected employment during the currency of the contract:

$$x = \psi x_{-1} + (1 - \psi)\tilde{x}_{+1} + \gamma[\psi\tilde{y} + (1 - \psi)\tilde{y}_{+1}] + u, \quad \psi, 1 - \psi, \gamma \geqslant 0, \tag{6}$$

where a tilde denotes an expectation and u is a white noise error term.

In equation (6) the coefficient ψ measures the extent to which wage setting is, respectively, forward- and backward-looking. The coefficient γ measures the cyclical responsiveness of *relative* wages. A large value of γ implies that high employment exerts a large effect on current wages, relative to past and anticipated future wages.

Applying rational expectations, by using (3) and (5) to generate the expectations, and collecting terms yields:

$$c\tilde{x} = \psi\tilde{x}_{-1} + (1 - \psi)\tilde{x}_{+1}, \quad c \equiv \frac{1 + \theta\gamma k}{1 - \theta\gamma k}. \tag{6'}$$

with a solution, assumed stable:[4]

$$x = \rho x_{-1} + u, \quad \rho \equiv \frac{c - [c^2 - 4\psi(1 - \psi)]^{0.5}}{2(1 - \psi)}. \tag{7}$$

Using (7) in (5) yields the equation for the price level,

$$p = \rho p_{-1} + k(u + u_{-1}), \tag{8}$$

and for output,

$$y = -\theta p = \rho y_{-1} - \theta k(u + u_{-1}). \tag{9}$$

We now turn to a discussion of the effects of exchange rate indexation on the stability of output and prices. We note briefly the results in Taylor (1979) and Dornbusch (1980, 1981). In these models the term k was equal to $k = 0.5$. Therefore it is clear from the definitions of c and ρ in (6') and (7) that increased monetary or exchange rate accommodation reduces θ and hence raises the inertia or persistence of wages and prices as measured by ρ. With more accommodating policies, output is more stable. That stability of output is taken into account in wage settlements and is reflected in a more protracted phasing out of disturbances. From here we proceed to the effect of increased exchange rate indexation in the extended model that allows for exchange rate effects on both the supply side and the demand side, as reflected in a value of $k = (\phi/2)/[1 - \beta(1 - \phi)]$.

11.2 The Effects of Exchange Rate Indexing

In this section we investigate the implications of an increase in exchange rate indexation—a rise in β—when the exchange rate plays a role in determining aggregate demand but also exerts direct cost effects. Given the definitions of k, c, and ρ, we observe that a rise in β affects the extent of persistence as follows:

$$\frac{\partial \rho}{\partial \beta} = \delta[b\phi - a(1 - \alpha)(1 - \phi)], \quad \delta > 0, \tag{10}$$

where δ is a function of the parameters. Equation (10) implies that increased exchange rate accommodation may raise or lower the persistence of disturbances depending on the relative size of the two channels through which the exchange rate operates.

Suppose the elasticity of demand with respect to the real exchange rate is large and that the share of labor costs is large. Under these conditions the term in brackets in (10) is likely to be positive, and we have the conventional result, in the spirit of Taylor's analysis, that increased accommodation increases output stability but raises persistence. The other case, by no means unlikely, arises when the exchange rate exerts a substantial effect on the cost side and when aggregate demand is relatively unresponsive to the real exchange rate. Unless monetary accommodation is sufficiently high, we then have a case where higher exchange rate indexation will reduce persistence.

This latter case arises when the gain in stability of output achieved by real exchange rate stability is more than offset by the indexation effect on the cost side that tends to reduce demand unless money is fully accommodating. This interpretation becomes apparent when we look at the effect of a wage disturbance on output, $dy/dx = -\theta k$, and ask how that effect varies with the extent of exchange rate accommodation:

$$\frac{\partial(dy/dx)}{\partial \beta} = \frac{k}{1 - \beta(1 - \phi)}[b - (1 - \phi)(b + a)(1 - \alpha)]. \tag{11}$$

Labor, in setting wages, takes into account the output effects of wage settlements. If higher exchange rate indexation implies a larger adverse effect of high wage settlements on output, then relative wages will be more flexible and persistence will be reduced. It is interesting to note that (10) and (11) show the interdependence of monetary and exchange rate accommodation, once the exchange rate operates also through the supply side. The increased cost indexation, following from a higher β, implies a larger adverse effect on real balances and hence on output the smaller the extent of monetary accommodation. Conversely, if monetary accommodation is relatively complete, the increased cost effects of a high β do not have important effects on demand and persistence.

The analysis suggests that monetary and exchange rate policies can, in certain cases, be coordinated both to reduce the impact of price disturbances on output and at the same time reduce the persistence or inertia in wages. If the expression $\phi b - (1 - \phi)a$ is negative, then it is apparent from (10) that increasing indexation can be accompanied by some increase in monetary accommodation and still not enhance persistence.

11.3 Indexation and the Variability of Output

An important difference between the Taylor model and our analysis lies in the consequence of exchange rate indexation for the impact of unanticipated disturbances. This is apparent in (8) and (9), where the unanti-

Table 11.1
Exchange rate indexation, and the variability of output and prices

β	0	0.25	0.5	0.75	1
Case 1					
σ_y^2	0.47	0.5	0.55	0.63	0.75
σ_p^2	0.21	0.27	0.35	0.50	0.75
Case 2					
σ_y^2	0.47	0.43	0.38	0.32	0.24
σ_p^2	0.21	0.27	0.38	0.57	0.96

Note:—$\phi = \gamma = \psi = \alpha = 0.5$, $\sigma_u^2 = 1$. Case 1: $a = 2$, $b = 0.5$. Case 2: $a = b = 1$.

cipated wage movements ($u + u_{-1}$) are multiplied by k, which now is not a constant but rather a function of β.[5] From (9), in conjunction with (11), it will be noted that a policy that reduces persistence will also raise the impact of unanticipated disturbances on output. It therefore appears that we cannot discuss the policy trade-off merely in terms of persistence and the coefficient θ but rather should look at the asymptotic variances of output and prices. With prices and output in this model following an ARMA(1,1) (first-order autoregressive moving average) process the variances are

$$\sigma_p^2 = \frac{2}{1-\rho} k^2 \sigma_u^2, \quad \sigma_y^2 = \theta^2 \sigma_p^2. \tag{12}$$

The numerical example in table 11.1 illustrates how the variances behave as a function of the extent of exchange rate indexation. The two cases reported correspond to different signs for the expression in (10) and (11). The table reveals that, independently of the sign, an increase in exchange rate indexation *always* raises the variability of prices. As regards the variability of output there are two possibilities. With the cost channel of exchange rates dominating, the variability of output is increased by a move toward more full indexation. Conversely, if the aggregate demand role of the real exchange rate dominates, more accommodation implies a more stable behavior of output.

We noted earlier the interdependence of monetary and exchange rate policies in determining the effectiveness of increased exchange rate indexation. Equation (11) suggests that, with the possibility of an adverse effect of exchange rate accommodation on output stability, it becomes

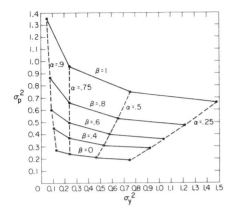

Figure 11.1

important to recognize that these effects can be dampened or averted by a commensurate increase in the extent of monetary accommodation. Of course, this stabilizing role of monetary policy comes at the cost of increased instability of prices.

Figure 11.1 looks once more at case 1 of table 11.1, this time considering the trade-off between output and price level variability arising from different combinations of monetary accommodation and exchange rate indexation. The solid lines correspond to iso-β schedules, and the dashed lines are iso-α lines, thus holding constant monetary accommodation.

The figure reveals that increased monetary accommodation (a movement up and to the left along an iso-β line) always reduces output variability but raises price level variability. Moreover a given change in monetary accommodation has larger absolute impact on the variances, the larger the extent of exchange rate indexation. A rise in exchange rate indexation, by contrast, may raise or lower output variability depending on the degree of monetary accommodation. It must, however, always raise price variability.

11.4 Concluding Remarks

Purchasing-power-parity-oriented exchange rate policies have been widely adopted among developing countries as a way of isolating the foreign trade sector from the vagaries of the macroeconomy. By and large such policies have been accepted as sensible, implicitly placing a high cost on the variability of real exchange rates. Such policy advice is questioned here by drawing attention to the macroeconomic costs of higher exchange rate indexation: increased instability of prices and potentially increased instability of output. The analysis also draws attention to the fact that higher monetary accommodation stabilizes output not only directly but also by offsetting or dampening the adverse effects of exchange rate indexation working through the cost side of the economy.

The analysis then suggests that the search for optimal stabilization policies should not take the target of a constant real exchange rate as given, but rather should consider the problem in a broader context that evaluates the relative costs of real instability, price level instability, and target instability.

Notes

Financial support was provided by a grant from the National Science Foundation.

1. For a multicountry model, see Taylor (1980).

2. Foreign prices are assumed given, and any repercussion effects from abroad are neglected.

3. If the domestic consumer price index, rather than the price of domestic goods, appears as the real balance deflator, equation (1) would read:

$$y = a[m - \lambda p - (1 - \lambda)e] + b(e - p); \tag{1'}$$

hence the coefficient θ in (3) becomes $\theta' = -a(1 - \alpha) - b(1 - \beta) + a(1 - \lambda)(\alpha - \beta)$, where λ is the share of domestic goods in the real balance deflator.

4. To arrive at (6'), we take the expectation across (6), noting that $E(u) = 0$ and $x = \tilde{x}$, $x_{-1} = \tilde{x}_{-1}$. To proceed from (6') to (7), we define the difference operator $x = \rho x_{-1}$, and, substituting in (6'), obtain a quadratic equation in $\rho: c\rho \tilde{x}_{-1} = \psi \tilde{x}_{-1} + (1 - \psi)\rho^2 \tilde{x}_{-1}$. Solving for ρ yields the expression (7).

5. The term u_{-1} is a wage disturbance unanticipated when the contract x_{-1} was set. It represents an unanticipated component of the price level as of period $t - 1$.

References

Dornbusch, Rudiger. 1980. *Open Economy Macroeconomics* New York: Basic.

Dornbusch, Rudiger. 1981. "Exchange Rate Rules and Macroeconomic Stability." In *Exchange Rate Rules: The Theory, Preformance and Prospects of the Crawling Peg*, edited by John Williamson. London: Macmillan.

Taylor, John B. 1979. "Staggered Wage Setting in a Macro Model." *A.E.R. Papers and Proc.* 69 (May): 108–113.

Taylor, John B. 1980. "Macroeconomic Trade-offs in an International Economy with Rational Expectations." Unpublished manuscript, mimeographed, Princeton University.

12   Exchange Rate
Economics: 1986

In the past fifteen years key exchange rates have moved in larger and more persistent ways than advocates of flexible rates in the late 1960s would have left anyone free to imagine. Certainly there was no expectation of constancy for nominal exchange rates. But real exchange rate movements of 30 or 40 percent were certainly not suggested as a realistic possibility. Moreover, where these large movements did occur, they did not obviously appear to be connected with fundamentals, and hence seemed difficult to explain in terms of the exchange rate theories at hand. The persistence of rate movements was as surprising as the rapid unwinding of apparent misalignments when they did ultimately happen. Research on exchange rate economics has grown tired searching for risk premia determinants or for new macroeconomic models. With a shift of interest toward the microeconomic effects of exchange rate movements, research is now turning in a fresh direction. It is therefore a good time to take stock of what is known of exchange rate economics, what has been learnt since the early 1970s and where more research needs to be done.

The past fifteen years provide a natural dividing line between the Keynesian and monetary approaches of the 1960s, and the more recent analysis that takes into account exchange rate expectations and portfolio issues. These took off in the early 1970s as well as the brand-new approaches that concentrate on (partial equilibrium) microeconomics. To review these ideas, the chapter starts with a brief look at the U.S. experience with flexible exchange rates. From there we proceed to use the Mundell-Fleming model as a comprehensive framework of analysis. The following section draws attention to persistent effects of policy disturbances. The next three topics deal with the link between exchange rates and prices, the political economy

Originally published in *Economic Journal*, vol. 97 (March 1987), pp. 1–18. Some new material added in this edition.

of exchange rate movements, and the question of policies toward excess
capital mobility.

12.1 The U.S. Experience with Floating Rates

The most striking result of the flexible rate experience is the recognition
that the "law of one price" is a poor description of the facts. Figure 12.1
shows the real exchange rate of the U.S. dollar over the past ten years. In
the transition from fixed rates to floating in the early 1970s (not shown),
the dollar depreciated by nearly 40 percent. An index of competitiveness in
manufacturing (using the IMF series shown in figure 12.1) stood at 153 in
1968–70 and fell to 112 by 1973–75 which is also about the average for
the period 1975–86. Over the next ten years the dollar depreciated sharply

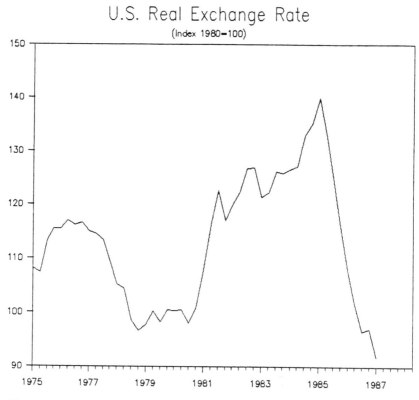

Figure 12.1
U.S. real exchange rate

until 1980. Then appreciation ensued, raising the dollar well above the level of the 1970s. Since 1985 the dollar has been on a slide, taking it back by late 1986 to the average of the 1970s.

The recognition that real exchange rate changes have taken place on a massive scale, and that they have major and potentially persistent macroeconomic effects, points to several important directions for research:

1. Why do exchange rates move so much and so persistently?

2. Does the fact that real exchange rates remain misaligned so persistently imply that they must therefore ultimately overshoot to remedy the accumulated consequences of over- or undervaluation?

3. Does a review of available theories and evidence suggest that exchange rate movements are based on irrational speculation rather than fundamentals?

4. What are linkages between movements in the exchange rate and changes in relative prices?

5. Do the large and persistent movements lead to the inevitable conclusion that exchange rate management offers a chance for better macroeconomic performance? If so, what is the externality, and thus what is the appropriate policy instrument, exchange-rate-oriented monetary policy or a reduced scope for capital movements?

We are certainly not at a point to answer these questions in a satisfactory manner. But it is worthwhile seeing where the literature has gone and what suggestions are available. We start by asking whether the standard models of exchange rate determination can give a satisfactory account of rate movements in the past decade.

Why Do Exchange Rates Move?

There are two standard models of exchange rate determination. One focuses on an expectations-augmented, open economy IS–LM model in the tradition of Meade, Fleming, and Mundell. The other highlights the role of portfolio diversification and relative asset supplies. In choosing between these models, an important question is to decide how relevant portfolio diversification effects are as part of an explanation for exchange rate movements. In other words, are monetary and fiscal policy most of the story, or do relative supplies of debts and other claims also play an important role?

The Extended Mundell-Fleming Models

The textbook model today is an open economy IS–LM model with perfect capital mobility, sluggish price adjustment, rapid asset market or interest rate adjustment, and rational expectations in asset markets.

A streamlined version is written in loglinear form and takes output as given. Complications stemming from output adjustments can easily be introduced but do not actually change the basic dynamics. In the same way we do not explicitly focus on wage–price interaction:[1]

$$m - p = hi, \tag{1}$$

$$i = i^* + \dot{e}, \tag{2}$$

$$\dot{p} = \eta[\xi(e - p) + g + \delta(i - \dot{p})]. \tag{3}$$

Here m and p are the nominal money stock and prices, i and e are the nominal interest rate and the exchange rate, respectively, and g is a variable representing fiscal policy. All variables other than interest rates are in logs.

Equation (1) represents monetary equilibrium or the LM schedule. Equation (2) states that with an adjustment for anticipated depreciation, assets are perfect substitutes. Perfect foresight is imposed by equating actual and anticipated depreciation. Equation (3) specifies that price adjustment is linked to the excess demand for goods which in turn depends on the real exchange rate, fiscal policy, and the real interest rate.

This model exhibits the familiar overshooting property: a one-time monetary expansion leads to an immediate depreciation of the exchange rate. The exchange rate overshoots its new long-run level—which is proportional to the increase in money. In the transition period following the initial overshooting the exchange rate appreciates while prices are rising. The process continues until the initial real equilibrium is reestablished.

The overshooting model can also be stated in terms of relationships between the real interest differential, the current actual real exchange rate and the long-run equilibrium exchange rate. Suppose that the real exchange rate adjusts gradually to its longrun level $\bar{q}$:

$$\dot{q} = \Omega(\bar{q} - q). \tag{4}$$

The coefficient Ω measures the speed of adjustment of the real exchange rate and hence depends, under rational expectations, on all the structural parameters. From (2), using the definition of the real exchange and the real interest rates, we can write the rate of change of the real exchange rate as

$$\dot{q} = r - r^*. \tag{5}$$

Combining (4) and (5) yields the key relation:

$$q = \bar{q} - \beta(r - r^*), \quad \beta = \frac{1}{\Omega} \tag{6}$$

The model thus predicts that when real interest rates are high relative to the rest of the world, the real exchange rate is high and depreciating.

Wilson (1979) has shown that this model also lends itself to the investigation of currently anticipated future disturbances or of transitory disturbances. This exercise highlights the flexibility of asset prices which move ahead of the realization of disturbances. Exchange rates move immediately, driven entirely by anticipations, and bring about alterations of prices and interest rates before any monetary or fiscal changes are actually implemented.

The strong feature of the model is the contrast between instantly flexible assets prices which are set in a forward-looking manner, and the sluggish adjustment of prices. The linkage of the domestic asset market to foreign rates of interest produces exchange rate dynamics which yield the required rate of return on home assets. Any "news" will make the exchange rate jump instantly to that level such that the expected capital gains or losses precisely offset the nominal interest differential. In this sense, the structure is extraordinarily rigid, just as was the original Mundell-Fleming model.

Of course, there is room for some flexibility: output adjustment can be brought into the model, import prices can appear in the real money balances' deflator, or a J-curve can be introduced to allow a more gradual response of demand to the real exchange rate. But these are niceties that do not add much to the basic flavor of the results.

An Alternative Money Supply Process

A once and for all change in the money stock, with sticky prices in goods markets and perfect foresight in asset markets, leads to an overshooting of exchange rates. Lyons (1987) has rightly pointed out that the "once and for all" model is not very interesting as a policy experiment. In a much richer model of a stochastic money supply process and rational expectations, he shows that innovations in money growth, because they are extrapolated into cumulative increases in money, lead to sizable short-run movements in exchange rates in response to even small changes in money.

This is a promising direction for modeling exchange rate responses, putting the emphasis on the extrapolation of current events. A simple example can explain what is involved. Suppose that innovations in money are serially correlated, and suppose that inflation only adjusts gradually. A positive innovation in money is extrapolated into a cumulative accumulation of money relative to the trend growth. This implies that in the long run the exchange rate will have moved to a higher path as will the price level. Because inflation is not fully flexible in the short run, the real money stock is seen as growing, and hence nominal interest rates will be declining for some time before inflation builds up to erode the growth in nominal balances. Ultimately, the system returns to the initial rate of inflation, money growth, and depreciation.

Figure 12.2 shows the exchange rate path in response to this experiment. Initially, up to time T_0 the economy moves along the solid line. At T_0 the innovation occurs and is extrapolated. The public recognizes that asymptotically the economy will converge to the higher exchange rate path, reflecting the cumulative increase in money relative to trend shown by the dashed line. But there will be an immediate depreciation of the exchange rate from A to A'. The overshooting reflects the fact that forward-looking asset holders anticipate the cumulative depreciation and will only hold domestic assets, in the face of reduced interest rates, if the exchange rate is appreciating. Along the new exchange rate path the rate of appreciation, following the initial jump, will accelerate for some time as nominal interest

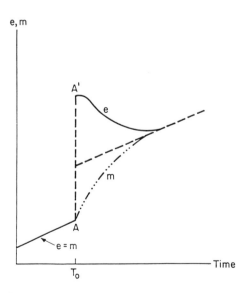

Figure 12.2

rates initially decline. The basic point of the Lyons analysis is that the forward-looking expectations about the evolution of money, extrapolating the serial correlation of disturbances, must find their way immediately into the spot exchange rate. The analysis has obvious extensions to fiscal policy and other determinants of the exchange rate.

Fiscal Policy

A major insight comes from a different application: fiscal policy. A fiscal expansion in this model brings about currency appreciation. Fiscal expansion creates an excess demand for goods, leading to an expansion in output or prices and hence, with a given nominal money stock, to upward pressure on the interest rate. Incipient capital inflows bring about an exchange rate appreciation and full crowding out. This is, of course, exactly the property captured by the Mundell-Fleming model. Fiscal policy works in the way they described even when price adjustments and expectations are introduced.

An interesting extension is to consider a transitory fiscal expansion. This corresponds, for example, to the U.S. experience of the 1980s. Suppose that fiscal policy follows an adjustment process such as

$$\dot{g} = -\beta(g - \bar{g}), \tag{7}$$

where $\bar{g}$ is the long-run level of government spending. According to (7), a fiscal expansion is being phased out over time at the rate β.

Now suppose that at time T_0 a fiscal expansion to level g_0 takes place and that from there on fiscal policy will follow the rule of (7). It is possible to solve for the path of the real exchange rate to establish the following results: There will be an immediate real appreciation. Then, under the impact of excess demand, prices will keep rising so that further real appreciation occurs. Over time, the exchange rate overvaluation builds up even as the fiscal policy is being wound down. A recession develops that now forces deflation and hence, gradually, a return to the initial level of the real exchange rate.

If a future transitory fiscal expansion is anticipated or is gradually phased in, the adjustment process is somewhat more complicated. The adjustment path is shown in figure 12.3. Upon the news of the fiscal program there will be an initial nominal and real appreciation shown as a jump from A to B. Then the overvaluation exerts a deflationary pressure. As prices decline and real balances rise, the nominal interest rate falls. To match the lower

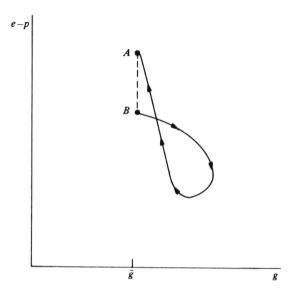

Figure 12.3
The real exchange rate effects of a transitory fiscal expansion

interest rate, the exchange rate will be appreciating. That process continues until the fiscal expansion actually gets underway, and leads to excess demand and inflation. Only when real balances and hence interest rates have been pushed up beyond their initial level, does the corrective depreciation start. The depreciation then continues, along with the phasing out of the fiscal expansion, until the initial equilibrium is restored.

Fiscal policy thus appears in addition to monetary policy as an important driving force for the exchange rate. Sustained shifts in government spending or taxes will bring persistent movements of the real exchange rate. Feldstein (1986) and Hutchinson and Throop (1985) have documented that shifts in the full employment budget, along with real interest rates, can in fact explain the large shifts in real exchange rates that have occurred. Interestingly the empirical tests hold up not only for the very recent experience in the United States. They work equally well when applied to multilateral exchange rates for the entire floating rate period.

Fiscal policy, including the expectations of correction associated with Gramm-Rudman, provides one interpretation of the dollar movements in the 1980s. The alternative is to argue the case of at least partial irrationality as has been done by Frankel (1985a), Frankel and Froot (1986) and Krugman (1986).

12.2 Persistence Effects

Three features of the extended Mundell-Fleming model account for its strong and unambiguous predictions. First, there is the absence of any effects, dynamic or otherwise, associated with the current account. Second, that home and foreign assets are perfect substitutes. Third, that there are only two classes of assets, money and bonds, and no real assets. We consider now what alternative models might look like and what they imply for exchange rate economics.

Current Account Effects

A period of fiscal expansion leading to appreciation will also involve cumulative current account imbalances. The case of the United States stands out, as now more than 2 percent of GNP is borrowed from the rest of the world in financing the persistent deficit, adding in each year to come to a seemingly ever growing external indebtedness. Sometime in 1985 the United States passed from net creditor to net debtor status.

The accumulated net external indebtedness will, of course, show up in the current account in the form of reduced income from net foreign assets. The reduction in net external assets means that following a period of deficits, the current account cannot be balanced simply by returning to the initial real exchange rate. Now there will be a deficit stemming from the increased debt service. Therefore, to restore current account balance, an overdepreciation is required.

The current account can be represented in the following manner. Let d be the net external assets and i^* the rate of return on net foreign assets. The term $\dot{d}$ denotes the current account surplus or accumulation of net foreign assets:

$$\dot{d} = f(e - p, g) + i^*d. \tag{8}$$

The real exchange rate that yields current account balance will therefore depend on the rate of return on assets and on the cumulated history of fiscal policy and other shocks to the current account. A transitory fiscal binge requires a subsequent permanent real depreciation to yield the improvement in the noninterest current account that is necessary to service the debt.

Such a permanent response to transitory deficits is clearly not part of the standard model. The question is whether it represents a realistic, quantitatively important effect. This is the case addressed in trade theory under the heading of the "transfer problem." It depends in large part on the impact on demand for domestic goods of an international redistribution of wealth and spending, and on the production response to changes in relative prices.

The discussion of the transfer problem is not complete without a consideration of how the budget will be balanced. The fiscal expansion gives rise to a budget deficit which is financed by issuing debt. The debt in turn will have to be serviced at some point by increased taxes. The question then is whether the taxation yields an equal current account improvement at constant relative prices. If so, then there is no need for terms of trade adjustments. At the going levels of output, disposable income and absorption by domestic residents decline but part of reduced spending falls on domestic goods rather than imports. To achieve the transfer *at full employment* ordinarily requires a real depreciation. The real depreciation will shift demand toward domestic goods.

This discussion of fiscal policy effects on real exchange rates clearly provides scope for an application of the Barro-Ricardo equivalence ideas to the open economy. A particularly complete rendition is offered in Frenkel and Razin (1986).

Portfolio Effects

A separate persistence effect can arise via the impact of a fiscal and current account imbalance on the relative supply of assets. Suppose that, contrary to (2), assets are not perfect substitutes, so that there is a risk premium,[2]

$$i = i^* \dot{e} + \alpha(b - b^* - e), \tag{2a}$$

where b and b^* are the supplies of domestic and foreign debt in national currencies.[3]

If current account imbalances are financed by an increase in the relative supply of domestic debt, then the cumulative imbalance would require an increase in the relative yield on domestic securities or a change in the relative valuation via exchange rate changes. A depreciation would be a means of correcting an increase in the relative supply of domestic securities by reducing their value in foreign currency, thus restoring portfolio balance at an unchanged yield differential. Other things equal, we would therefore expect a period of debt accumulation to have a permanent effect on exchange rates, so as to bring interest differentials in line with the changed relative supply of assets.

The responsiveness of exchange rates to relative asset supplies has been addressed in a number of important papers by Frenkel.[4] He concludes that relative asset supplies in fact do not provide a satisfactory account of relative yields, at least in the context of a capital asset pricing model. The impact of relative asset supplies is practically negligible. That is an uncomfortable conclusion for a whole strand of research which places major emphasis on the imperfect substitutability of assets as a major feature of open economy macroeconomics.

Work by Sachs and Wyplosz (1984), Dornbusch and Fischer (1980), and Giovannini (1983) raises the following problem: if as a result of debt accumulation, via the transfer problem or via risk premia, an ultimate depreciation is required, why should we expect an initial appreciation? Is it not likely that for certain parameters and paths of subsequent budget correction there should be an immediate path of sustained real depreciation. It turns out that all the parameters in the model—trade elasticities, wealth elasticities, risk premium responses, etc.—matter for this question. Even in very highly simplified models no firm conclusions emerge about the path of the exchange rate.

Real Assets

The standard model remains oversimplified even when long-term issues of current account balancing and a risk premium are taken into account. The simplification lies in the omission of real capital from portfolios, and in disregarding the effect over time of investment on the capital stock and thus the supply side of the economy.

Concurrently with the imbalance in the current account and the resulting shift in net foreign assets, capital accumulation takes place. Portfolio adjustments in response to the changing relative asset supplies bring about changes in the value of real assets and in relative yields. The flow of investment and the changes in the value of real capital potentially dominate the effects of current account imbalances. A good week on the stock market produces a change in wealth that is several times the magnitude of an entire year's deficit in the current account. Although it is true that the current account is important because persistent imbalances cumulate, exactly the same argument must be made for investment.

Work by Gavin (1986) shows that the inclusion of the stock market in the standard model offers important additional channels for exchange rate dynamics. Unfortunately, the inclusion of the stock market removes at the same time the simplicity of the standard model. Now virtually anything is possible. And that result is arrived at by looking only at the portfolio implications of a money–debt–capital model and the ensuing yield and wealth effects, without even taking into account the accumulation of physical capital. Among the sources of ambiguity are two different effects: an expansion in demand will bring about both an increase in output and an increase in interest rates. The net effect on the valuation of the stock market is therefore uncertain. Thus wealth may rise or fall, and this is important in judging the induced effects on money demand and spending. The second important consideration is the relative substitutability of money and debt, and debt and capital. This is relevant for the extent of yield changes and hence for the direction and magnitude of exchange rate changes.

The money–debt–capital model is also important in highlighting that current accounts are not necessarily financed by sales of domestic bonds or foreign bonds. There need not be any link between cumulative current account imbalances and yield differentials between home and foreign nominal bonds. There would be a significant distinction, for example, between fiscal deficits and investment deficits. The difference is also relevant from the point of view of the transfer problem. Deficits that arise as a result of increased investment have different implications than deficits that have their source in fiscal imbalances.

Hysteresis Effects

A final channel for persistence effects is introduced by an industrial organization approach to the consequences of extended rate misalignments. When an industry is exposed to foreign competition and entry by a persistent overvaluation, it may close down and perhaps even re-open in the low wage country. Firms already producing in the low wage country may make the necessary investment to enter the market where home firms are handicapped by overvalued labor. A period of overvaluation or undervaluation thus changes the industrial landscape in a relatively permanent fashion. These considerations are at the center of a new literature that seeks to interpret the U.S. experience following the five-year overvaluation.[5] The upshot of the literature is, of course, that overvaluation leads ultimately to the need for overdepreciation to remedy the accumulation of adverse trade effects.

Overvaluation, for example, due to monetary contraction or fiscal expansion, brings in foreign firms and displaces domestic firms. When the overvaluation is ultimately undone, the foreign firms are still there and the domestic firms may exist no longer. Worse yet, they now may even be producing abroad. A period of sustained undervaluation is required to bring forth the required investment. The possibility of entry, and the choice of labor market from which to supply a particular market, thus opens an important dynamic theory of adjustment to the exchange rate. Expectations about the persistence of changes in relative labor costs become important for the determination of relative prices. Now pricing between firms not only involves current strategic interaction, which we will consider shortly, but also the impact of pricing strategies on entry, location, and investment.

There is some offset to these considerations from the side of factor prices. To the extent that an industry has a captive factor supply, we would expect that wages come down with the exchange rate, thus maintaining a firm in existence. Conversely, in expanding countries, wages might rise and thus offset some of the gain in profitability arising from depreciation.

12.3 Exchange Rates and Pricing

The monetary approach to the balance of payments used purchasing power parity (PPP) as an essential ingredient in explanations of exchange rate determination. Today PPP is certainly no longer a cornerstone for modeling. Attention has shifted to modeling changes in equilibrium relative prices. The simple Keynesian model assumes that wages and prices in the national currencies are given, so that exchange rate movements change relative prices one for one. A newer approach recognizes the sluggishness of wages but builds on a theory of equilibrium price determination along industrial organization lines.[6]

Relative Prices

An interesting setting for exchange rate–wage–price relationships is a world of imperfect competition. Here firms are price-setters. They may or may not interact strategically, but they certainly face the problem of how their pricing decision should react to a change in the exchange rate. Consider the simple case of an oligopoly.[7]

The typical setting would be the following. We look at the home market when n home firms and n^* foreign firms compete. The profits of the typical home and foreign firms, with constant unit labor costs in their respective currencies given by w and w^*, are

$$\pi = (p_i - w)D_i(p_i, p_j),\tag{9}$$

$$\pi^* = (p_j - ew^*)D_j(p_i, p_j).\tag{10}$$

These profits are maximized, subject to the strategic assumptions about the determinants of the demand facing each firm and responses of other firms in the market. It is clear that there is no general solution to the problem. The impact of an exchange rate change on equilibrium prices will depend on a number of factors. Specifically, these include:

1. Whether goods are perfect substitutes or differentiated products.
2. The market organization—oligopoly, imperfect competition, etc.
3. The relative number of domestic and foreign firms.
4. The functional form of the market demand curve.

Even though there is no presumption about the effects of exchange rates on the changes in equilibrium prices, it is immediately clear that there is an important link between open economy macroeconomics and industrial organization. There is no presumption that an exchange rate movement affects all markets equally. Some markets may involve a homogeneous good and, for example, a duopoly. Other markets may involve differentiated products and Chamberlinian competition. Yet other markets may be close to perfect competition. But whichever is the case, once the exchange rate changes, given wages, there will be an adjustment in the equilibrium price.

Of course, this pricing issue, depending on market organization, may be repeated at different levels from import to retail. The same pricing issue arises on the export side.

Figure 12.4 shows as an example the dollar transactions prices for imports and exports of scientific instruments. Up to 1985 import prices decline and then, accompanying the depreciation, they rise in dollar terms. Export prices rise throughout as if they were based on domestic costs alone.

For the case of differentiated products, an appreciation tends to bring about a rise in the relative price of domestic goods. Imported variants decline in price both absolutely and relatively. For homogeneous products the industry price declines, with the decline being larger the less monopolized the market and the larger the relative number of foreign firms.

An interesting, and perhaps surprising, result appears here: currency appreciation, in certain cases, may lead to a more than proportionate decline in market price. This result occurs because the favorable cost-shock for foreign firms makes expansion overly profitable and overcomes the tendency to preserve profits by restricting output. But these results are very specific to market structure and functional form. In public finance, as

IMPORT AND EXPORT PRICES

(INDEX 1979:4 = 100)

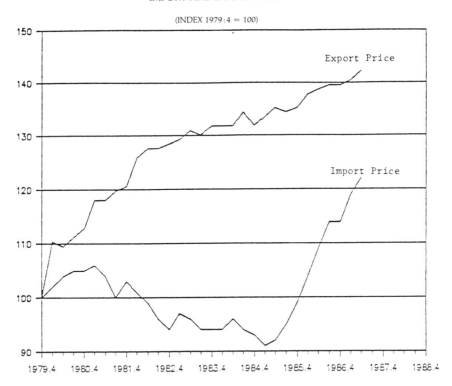

Figure 12.4
Import and export prices

Seade (1983) has shown, a similar result occurs: a tax on an oligopolistic industry may raise profits.

To show how specific the results are to the details of the market, consider a simple duopoly market with a domestic and a foreign firm. Let the inverse market demand function be

$$P = P(Q), \quad P'(Q) < 0, \quad Q \equiv q + q^*, \tag{11}$$

where Q denotes total quantity demanded and q and q^* are the supplies by the home and foreign firms. Let the elasticity of the slope of the inverse demand function be denoted by σ:

$$\sigma = -\left(\frac{P''}{P'}\right)Q, \tag{12}$$

which may be zero, as in the linear case, positive or negative.

Suppose that each of the two firms assumes that the other maintains a given level of output. The equilibrium then is the Cournot-Nash solution for industry output and price. The elasticities of output, and of the industry price in response to an exchange rate change, are

$$\hat{Q} = \left[\frac{(ew^*/P)(P/P'Q)}{3 - \sigma}\right]\hat{e}, \quad \hat{P} = \left(\frac{ew^*/P}{3 - \sigma}\right)\hat{e},$$

where a ^ denotes a percentage change.

Consider now three cases. First, with a linear market demand function the term $\sigma = 0$. Accordingly, the pass-through of depreciation to the prices is one-third of the marginal cost–price ratio for the foreign country. Because we are in a situation of oligopoly the marginal cost–price ratio is less than unity. The elasticity of industry price with respect to the exchange rate is thus definitely a fraction and much less than a half.

Next we look at a constant semielasticity demand curve, $Q = A\exp(-\alpha P)$. For this case the elasticity $\sigma = 1$, and the price elasticity is already increased to a half of the marginal cost–price ratio. Going further to a constant elasticity demand curve $Q = AP^{-a}$ yields a value of $\sigma = 1 + 1/a$. Let $a = 1$ so that spending on the good is constant. In that case the elasticity of price is equal to the marginal cost–price ratio.

The examples show that the impact of exchange rate movements on prices is far from straightforward. Market structure, conjectural variations, and functional form all come into play. Even though this application of industrial organization ideas to the effects of exchange rate movements does not emerge with firm results, it is quite apparent that it offers a major avenue for theoretical research and for applied studies. Exchange rate changes affect home and foreign firms differentially, to an extent which varies between industries. Focusing on the adjustment to major exchange rate movements may therefore help identify market structures and thus enrich industrial organization research.

Commodity Prices

One of the more interesting price effects of real exchange rate movements between major industrial countries occurs in the area of commodities. It is readily established that a real dollar exchange rate depreciation (in terms of value added deflators for manufactured goods) will lead to a rise in the dollar price of commodities, and a rise in their real price to U.S. users. Conversely, abroad the real price declines as does the absolute price in foreign currencies.

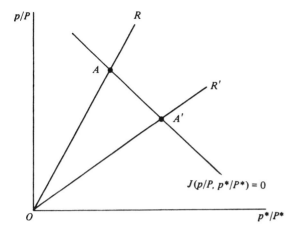

Figure 12.5
Real exchange rate movements and the real prices of commodities

This result can be seen by looking at the commodity market equilibrium condition where J is the excess demand for any particular commodity, say cotton:

$$J\left(\frac{p}{P}, \frac{p^*}{P^*}, \ldots\right) = 0, \tag{13}$$

where p and p^* are the national currency commodity prices and P and P^* are the deflators. Excess demand is a declining function of the real prices in the two regions. In figure 12.5 the market equilibrium schedule is shown as downward sloping. Points above and to the right correspond to an excess supply. Let $\phi = P/eP^*$ be the real exchange in terms of manufacturing deflators rate, which is shown as the ray OR through the origin. Using the law of one price for commodities, $p = ep^*$, and the definition of the real exchange rate in (13) we obtain

$$J\left(\frac{p}{P}, \phi, \ldots\right) = 0, \tag{14}$$

or

$$\frac{p}{P} = h(\phi, \ldots), \quad h' < 0. \tag{14a}$$

A real appreciation of the dollar corresponds to a rise in ϕ rotating downward the OR ray. The model predicts a decline in real commodity prices in the United States as a result of dollar appreciation. Equation (14a) shows that a real appreciation of the dollar will lead to a decline in the real price of commodities to U.S. users, and a real price increase abroad. Given the U.S. deflator, P, the nominal commodity price quoted in dollars will decline. In this perspective the large dollar appreciation of 1980–85 helps explain the sharp decline of dollar commodity prices in world trade. In fact, the dollar appreciation and world cyclical movements are not enough to explain fully the decline in these prices.

Exchange Rates and Inflation

The impact of exchange rates on inflation is well established for any Banana Republic and, indeed, for any industrial country. The experience of the 1980s makes it clear that it even applies to the United States. There are several channels through which exchange rates affect inflation. The least controversial effect of exchange rates on inflation concerns the prices of homogeneous commodities traded in world markets.

Changes in commodity prices influence directly the rate of inflation for food and hence influence wages. They also affect industrial materials costs in manufacturing. But exchange rates influence inflation also via several other channels. Their influence is important because they are rapid and quite pervasive.

One channel working in addition to commodity prices involves the prices of traded goods and the prices of those goods directly competing with traded goods. The industrial organization analysis considered earlier applies to determine the magnitude and speed of response for prices. The less monopolistic a market, and the lower entry costs, the more pervasive the price effects.

There are also inflation effects via wages. These can arise because wages respond to the competitive pressure of an appreciation or depreciation in affected industries. They also come about as wages respond to changes in the cost of living.

Adding together these various channels yields a pervasive pattern of cost and price effects that are directly or indirectly associated with exchange rate movements. It is interesting to note that in the United States the magnitude of these effects is still under discussion. Estimates of the impact of a 10 percent dollar appreciation on the price level, range between one and two percentage points. The reason it is so difficult to establish the size of the impact is apparent. There have been only three recent episodes involving a major change in inflation. Each coincided with an oil price change, a large change in unemployment, and a major change in the dollar. As a result it is nearly impossible to extract a precise estimate for the size of each of these three elements in the inflation process.[8]

12.4 The Political Economy of Overvaluation

The literature on political business cycles has drawn attention to the systematic pursuit of macroeconomic goals on a timetable dictated by political elections. The exchange rate fits very well into that scheme. It does so via its effects on output and inflation, but also as a highly visible indicator of confidence in policy.

The political business cycle implication of exchange rate movements is strongly enhanced by the relative timing of output and inflation results. A real appreciation quickly raises real wages in terms of tradables and quickly reduces inflation. The impact on activity is much more gradual. The implication of these timing relationships is that a policy of real appreciation, conducted at the right time, can make an administration look particularly successful at controlling inflation, while at the same time delivering increases in real disposable income.

Díaz-Alejandro (1966) was the first to draw attention to the fact that devaluation in the short-term may reduce activity, in addition to having inflationary effects. Only in the long term do output and employment expand. The reason is that in the short run a devaluation cuts real wages in terms of tradables, thereby reducing purchasing power and the demand for home goods. These income effects dominate in the short run. The neoclassical substitution effects take time to build up. The short-time effects are sufficiently powerful to be highly relevant for political decision making.

The reverse side of this coin is overvaluation. In the short term it involves less inflation and an increase in real income, and hence it wins popularity contests. Only over time, as substitution effects become important and output declines due to the loss of competitiveness, do the costs emerge. No wonder that overvaluation is a very popular policy. It created broad short-term political support in Chile for Pinochet, in Argentina for the policies of Martinez de Hoz, for the Thatcher government in the United Kingdom, and in the United States for Reaganomics.

Whether the policy mix was deliberate or not, there is little doubt that for a while the real appreciation was celebrated as a mark of achievement rather than being seen as a highly destructive misalignment. Only as the deindustrialization effects became visible, and politically alarming did the policymakers back track and start viewing overvaluation with concern. In the meantime it had bought a strong disinflation.

In the U.S. case the oil price decline of 1986 came just in time to offset the cut in real income and the inflationary impact implied by dollar depreciation. The timing of appreciation and depreciation thus looked like a masterpiece of political economy. The only cloud remains the very serious blow to industry, the effects of which do appear to persist even after an already significant depreciation. Of course, in addition, there is the cost of servicing the accumulated debt.

These episodes of overvaluation raise the interesting issue of why an electorate would favor exchange rate misalignment. Given the welfare costs associated with uneven tax structures over time, and the costs resulting from de- and reindustrialization, one would expect voters to favor steady policies rather than large fluctuations in the real exchange rate and the standard of living. Yet the evidence runs counter to this observation, overvaluation being one of the best tricks in the bag.

There is an international dimension to the issue of inflation stabilization via overvaluation. Under flexible exchange rates, a tightening of monetary policy exerts immediate disinflationary effects via currency appreciation. When used by a large country, such a policy amounts to exporting inflation. Investigation of policy coordination and of the game-thoretic implications of these effects has been an important part of international economics research.[9]

A recent study by Edison and Tryon (1986) makes an important point in this connection. The authors find that in simulations with the Federal Reserve MCM model an asymmetry is apparent. For the United States (the large country) foreign repercussions and the particulars of foreign policy responses are relatively unimportant in their impact on inflation and growth. For foreign countries, by contrast, the details of U.S. policy have a major impact. This asymmetry should be expected to influence the nature of Europe's policy responses to U.S. actions.

12.5 Excess Capital Mobility and Policy Responses

In this concluding section we consider policy issues that follow from the fact that macroeconomic disturbances exert significant *excess* effects on real exchange rates, trade flows, and on the standard of living. There are broadly two approaches: one is to accept the fact of international capital mobility and use monetary policy coordination to avoid exchange rate effects of disturbances; the other is to interfere with capital flows in order to pursue macroeconomic objectives more freely.

Target Zones and Exchange-Rate-Oriented Monetary Policy

A strong case for some form of managed exchange rates is returning in the aftermath of the extreme exchange rate fluctuations. In particular, among those arguing for more fixed exchange rates are Williamson (1983) and McKinnon (1984).

The McKinnon position for a fixed exchange rate has at its center the assumption that international portfolio shifts are behind exchange rate movements. In an initial version of this argument shifts between M_1 in one country and another were the source of disturbance. Monetary authorities, being committed to *national* monetary targets, would not accommodate these money demand shifts, and exchange rate volatility was seen as the inevitable consequence. More recent versions of the hypothesis recognize that international portfolio shifts are more likely to take the form of shifts in the demand for interest bearing assets denominated in different currencies. But the recommendation remains to fix exchange rates, using exchange-rate-oriented monetary policy to hold rates and accommodate money demand shifts. In other words *unsterilized* intervention is to be used.

This policy recommendation prescribes exactly the wrong kind of intervention. To offset the exchange rate impact of shifts in the demand for bonds, the currency denomination of the world bond portfolio should be allowed to change. That means *sterilized* intervention is the correct answer. In response to exchange rate appreciation the authorities should intervene, leaving money supplies unchanged but increasing the supply of home bonds and reducing the supply of foreign currency bonds. That, of course, is sterilized intervention. The case for sterilized intervention is well established, and has been a basic principle of asset market management ever since Poole's authoritative analysis of the choice between interest rate and monetary targets. The remaining problem, of course, is to determine whether it is portfolio shifts or shifts in fundamentals that are moving rates.

The case for fixing exchange rates whatever the source of disturbance is advanced by those favoring target zones. Their position is that exchange rates do not necessarily reflect fundamentals but rather irrationality, band wagons, and eccentricity. The large movements in exchange rates interfere with macroeconomic stability, but they can and should be avoided by a firm commitment to exchange rate targets. On the surface it is difficult to see any difficulty with this prescription, but on further inspection two serious difficulties emerge. First, it is certainly not an established fact that exchange rates move irrationally and without links to fundamentals. Or, if they do move in this way, it is not clear that they do so more than stock prices or long-term bond prices. Why single out one price for fixing if it may mean that the other prices have to move even further away from their fundamental equilibrium levels?

The second objection concerns a lack of instruments. Governments are unlikely to agree on coordinating their fiscal policies. But if real exchange rates are to remain fixed in the face of uncoordinated fiscal policy changes, then monetary accommodation is required. In the context of the dollar appreciation of 1980–85, for example, that would have meant a more aggressively expansionary monetary policy in the United States and hence no disinflation. It is questionable whether the objective of fixed rates is sufficiently important to warrant bad monetary policy.[10]

Policies toward Excess Capital Mobility

But there is an alternative, extreme answer to international exchange rate instability which is more attractive. The stickiness of wages relative to exchange rates creates a macroeconomic externality which possibly justifies closing or restricting some markets. Tobin (1982) has made the case for throwing more sand into the international financial system, so as to reduce the overwhelming influence of capital flows over productive activity and trade. The proposal, known as the "Tobin tax," involves a uniform tax on all foreign exchange transactions, to be levied in all countries of the world. The consequence of the tax is to make short-term hot money roundtrips unprofitable. Under this system capital flows would therefore be more nearly geared to considerations of the long-term profitability of investment rather than the overnight speculation which now dominates.

It might be argued that it is too late for stopping the flow of international capital, that throwing sand in the wheels is no longer sufficient. But why stop there and not use rocks? An operational way of doing this is to combine the stability of inflation and real activity that comes from fixed rates with a dual exchange rate system for capital account transactions. If capital markets are irrational and primarily speculative it might be as well to detach them altogether from an influence on real activity. Rather than use scarce macropolicy tools to adapt the real sector to the idiosyncrasy of financial markets, a separate exchange rate would detach the capital account and deprive it from distorting influences on trade and inflation.[11]

Notes

This chapter was originally presented at a meeting on exchange rates of the Royal Economic Society. I am indebted to Charles Goodhart, Stanley Fischer, Simon Johnson, and the conference participants for their helpful comments and suggestions. Financial support was provided by a grant from the National Science Foundation.

1. See Dornbusch (1976, 1983). Some of the extensions are considered in Dornbusch (1986).

2. The formula for the risk premium here omits wealth terms. It also focuses on debt rather than all nominal outside assets. For a more complete treatment, see Dornbusch (1982).

3. In a model with a risk premium there is a serious difficulty in linking goods and assets markets. There is certainly no excuse for using the interest rate on bonds in home currency as *the* domestic interest rate used as a determinant of domestic spending. The *ad hoc* model becomes a liability. The correct treatment, drawing on an optimization model would use the marginal cost of capital which is based on the marginal financing pattern which in turn is derived by solving the firm's and household's complete intertemporal optimization problem.

4. See especially Frankel (1985b, 1986) and Frankel and Froot (1986).

5. See especially Baldwin (1986), Krugman (1985), and Baldwin and Krugman (1986).

6. See Dornbusch (1987), Krugman (1986), Feinberg (1986), Mann (1986), and Flood (1986).

7. This analysis draws on Dixit (1986) and Seade (1983).

8. See Dornbusch and Fischer (1984), Sachs (1985), and Woo (1984) on the exchange rate effects on U.S. inflation.

9. See Cooper (1969), Hamada (1985), Buiter and Marston (1985), and Oudiz and Sachs (1984).

10. For a further discussion see Fischer (1986).

11. For a discussion of a dual rate system and extensive references to the literature see Dornbusch (1986c).

References

Baldwin, R. 1986. "Hysteresis in trade." Unpublished manuscript. Massachusetts Institute of Technology, April

Baldwin, R., and Krugman, P. 1986. "Persistent trade effects of large exchange rate shocks." Unpublished manuscript. Massachusetts Institute of Technology, July.

Buiter, W., and Marston, R. (eds.). 1985. *International Economic Policy Coordination*. Cambridge University Press.

Cooper, R. 1969. "Macroeconomic policy adjustment in interdependent economies." *Quarterly Journal of Economics*, February.

Díaz-Alejandro, C. 1966. *Exchange Rate Devaluation in a Semi-Industrialized Country: The Experience of Argentina 1955–1961*. Cambridge, Mass.: MIT Press.

Dixit, A. 1986. "Comparative statics for oligopoly." *International Economic Review* 27, pp. 107–122.

Dornbusch, R. 1976. "Expectations and exchange rate dynamics." *Journal of Political Economy*, December.

Dornbusch, R. 1982. "Exchange risk and the macroeconomics of exchange rate determination." In *International Financial Management* (ed. R. Hawkins *et al.*). Greenwich, Conn.: JAI Press.

Dornbusch, R. 1983. "Flexible exchange rates and interdependence." *IMF Staff Papers*, March, reprinted in *Dollars, Debts and Deficits*. Cambridge, Mass.: MIT Press, 1986.

Dornbusch, R. 1986a. "Inflation, exchange rates and stabilization." *Princeton Essays in International Finance*, no. 165, October.

Dornbusch, R. 1986b. "Flexible exchange rates and excess capital mobility." *Brookings Papers on Economic Activity*, no. 1.

Dornbusch, R. 1986c. "The open economy implications of monetary and fiscal policy." In *The Business Cycle* (ed. R, Gordon). University of Chicago Press.

Dornbusch, R. 1986d. "Special exchange rates for capital account transactions." *The World Bank Economic Review*, vol. 1, no. 1.

Dornbusch, R. 1987a. "Exchange rates and prices." *American Economic Review*, May.

Dornbusch, R. 1987b. "Purchasing power parity." NBER Working Paper No. 1591. In *The New Palgrave's Dictionary of Economics*, Macmillan (in press).

Dornbusch, R. and Fischer, S. 1980. "Exchange rates and the current account." *American Economic Review*, December

Edison, H., and Tryon, R. 1986. "An empirical analysis of policy coordination in the United States, Japan and Europe." Board of Governors of the Federal Reserve, International Finance Discussion Papers, no. 286, July.

Feinberg, R. M. 1986. "The interaction of foreign exchange and market power effects on German domestic prices." *Journal of Industrial Economics*, no. 1, September.

Feldstein, M. 1986. "The budget deficit and the dollar." *NBER Macroeconomics Annual*.

Fischer, S. 1986. "Symposium on exchange rates, trade and capital flows: comments." *Brookings Papers on Economic Activity*, no. 1.

Flood, E. 1986. "An empirical analysis of the effects of exchange rate changes on goods prices." Unpublished manuscript. Stanford University.

Frankel, J. 1982. "In search of the exchange risk premium: a six-currency test assuming mean-variance optimization." *Journal of International Money and Finance*, no. 1.

Frankel, J. 1985a. "The dazzling dollar." *Brookings Papers on Economic Activity*, no. 1.

Frankel, J. 1985b. "Portfolio crowding-out empirically estimated." *Quarterly Journal of Economics*. Supplement.

Frankel, J. 1986. "The implications of mean-variance optimization for four questions in international finance." *Journal of International Money and Finance*, Supplement, March.

Frankel, J., and Froot, K. 1986. "The dollar as an irrational speculative bubble." *The Marcus Wallenberg Papers on International Finance*, no. 1.

Frenkel, J., and Razin, A. 1986. "The international transmission and effects of fiscal policy." *American Economic Review*, May.

Gavin, M. 1986. "The stock market and exchange rate dynamics." Board of Governors of the Federal Reserve. International Finance Discussion Papers, no. 278.

Giovannini, Alberto. (1983). *Three Essays on Exchange Rates*. Unpublished dissertation. Massachusetts Institute of Technology.

Giovannini, Alberto. 1985. "Exchange rates and traded goods prices." Unpublished manuscript. Columbia University.

Hamada, K. 1985. *The Political Economy of International Monetary Interdependence*. Cambridge, Mass.: MIT Press.

Hutchinson, M., and Throop, A. 1985. "The U.S. budget deficit and the real value of the dollar." Federal Reserve Bank of San Francisco. *Economic Review*, no. 4, Autumn.

Krugman, P. 1985. "Is the strong dollar sustainable?" In *The U.S. Dollar—Recent Developments*. Federal Reserve Bank of Kansas.

Krugman, P. 1986. "Pricing to market when the exchange rate changes." *NBER Working Paper*, no. 1926, May.

Lyons, R. 1987. "Exchange Rates and money supply expectations." Unpublished manuscript. Massachusetts Institute of Technology.

Mann, C. 1986. "Prices, profit margins and exchange rates." *Federal Reserve Bulletin*, June.

McKinnon, R. 1984. *An International Standard for Monetary Stabilization*, Institute for International Economics.

Oudiz, G., and Sachs, J. 1984. "Macroeconomic policy coordination among the industrial economies." *Brookings Papers on Economic Activity*, no. 1.

Sachs, J. 1985. "The dollar and the policy mix: 1985." *Brookings Papers on Economic Activity*, no. 1.

Sachs, J., and Wyplosz, C. 1984. "Real exchange rate effects of fiscal policy." *NBER Working Paper*, no. 1255.

Seade, J. 1983. "Prices, profits and taxes in oligopoly." Working Paper, University of Warwick.

Tobin, J. 1982. "A proposal for international monetary reform." In *Essays in Economics: Theory and Policy*. Cambridge, Mass.: MIT Press.

Williamson, J. 1983. *The Exchange Rate System*. Institute for International Economics.

Wilson, C. 1979. "Exchange rate dynamics and anticipated disturbances." *Journal of Political Economy*, December.

Woo, W. T. 1984. "Exchange rates and prices of nonfood, nonfuel products." *Brookings Papers on Economic Activity*, no. 2.

III

Equilibrium Real Exchange Rates

The essays that appear in this part of the book have in common the determination of equilibrium relative prices—the terms of trade in a Ricardian continuum of goods world, the real interest rate in intertemporal trade models, or the real exchange rate in a model of home goods and traded goods.

Purchasing power parity is the focus of a survey article which introduces this part. Most of the time purchasing power parity (or PPP) does not hold in any interesting sense. Certainly the notion that the equilibrium exchange rate is such that a dollar should buy the same basket of goods in the United States and in Japan would only hold in an extraordinary world. What is really interesting about PPP is the systematic directions in which the literature has documented divergences from PPP. These may be short-lived, as in the models of macroeconomic overshooting, or they may be permanent, as documented in the important work of Irving Kravis and his associates. Even though there are almost annual attempts to demonstrate the revival of PPP, the striking fact of the available empirical evidence is how large and how persistent the divergences can be. Gustav Cassel was impressed with the correlation between inflation and depreciation, but more impressive in my judgment is the fact of 50 or 75 percent changes in real exchange rates.

Ricardian trade and payments theory are discussed in the following article. The model is a sturdy framework for all of classical open economy macroeconomics: questions of the price specie flow mechanism or of purchasing power parity emerge naturally in this framework. But it is also interesting to study real trade questions and the interaction between real and monetary phenomena. The ability to treat a wide range of topics within a single, simple analytical framework makes this model my preferred teaching tool of open economy macroeconomics.

The following two essays deal with the relative price of home goods in terms of traded goods. In one case the focus of analysis is a tariff that changes domestic relative prices. In the other case the model is used to study intertemporal issues where the rate of change of the real price of home goods becomes a component of the consumption-based real interest rate. Both models are interesting in that they show that even in a "small" country, there remains an important role for relative prices in allocating resources between home and traded goods and between current and future consumption.

This part of the book concludes with an essay on international lending in a two-country model with long-term debt. The model highlights the role of debt operations as intertemporal transfers and the question of optimal restrictions on capital market integration is raised.

Much of research in open economy macroeconomics today is intertemporal and optimizing. The work by Lars Svensson and Assaf Razin initially gave impetus to this new and fruitful approach. The two essays on intertemporal trade that conclude this part of the book fall within that tradition. Rather than assuming the behavioral equations, as is done in many of the rest of my essays, here everything is derived from microeconomic foundations. Once the exercise is done, interesting results are obtained, but one is hard pressed to find that the difference from old-fashioned assuming rather than deriving is as fundamental as is often made out.

13

Purchasing Power Parity

Purchasing power parity (PPP) is a theory of exchange rate determination. It asserts (in the most common form) that the exchange rate change between two currencies over any period of time is determined by the change in the two countries' relative price levels. Because the theory singles out price level changes as the overriding determinant of exchange rate movements it has also been called the "inflation theory of exchange rates."

The PPP theory of exchange rates has somewhat the same status in the history of economic thought and in economic policy as the quantity theory (QT) of money: by different authors, and at different points in time, it has been considered an identity, a truism, an empirical regularity, or a grossly misleading simplification. The theory remains controversial, as does the QT, because strict versions are demonstrably wrong, whereas soft versions deprive it of any useful content. In between there is room for theory and empirical evidence to specify the circumstances under which, and the extent to which, PPP provides a useful though not exact description of exchange rate behavior.

The analogy with the QT holds particularly in the effects of monetary disturbances. The QT fails to hold exactly when disturbances are primarily monetary—for instance, in the course of hyperinflations—because changes in the expected rate of inflation generate systematic movements in velocity that break the one-to-one link between money and prices. In the same way monetary disturbances cause exchange rate movements that at least temporarily deviate from PPP, implying changes in the exchange-rate-adjusted relative price levels or "real" exchange rates. It is true that when the economy, following a major monetary disturbance, has settled down again, the cumulative changes in money, prices, and the exchange

Forthcoming in *The New Palgrave: A Dictionary of Economics* (New York: Stockton Press, 1988).

rate will tend to be the same or at least close. In that sense PPP holds. The same is decidedly not true, however, in the course of the disturbance.

And in the long run, just as changes in real income or financial innovation bring about trend changes in velocity that destroy the one-to-one relationship between the money supply and prices, there are also trend deviations from PPP: productivity growth differentials between countries, for example, lead to trend changes in real exchange rates.

13.1 Statement of the Theory

Let p_i and p_i^* represent the price of the ith commodity at home and abroad, stated in home and foreign currency, respectively, and e the exchange rate. The exchange rate is quoted in the American manner as the number of units of domestic currency per unit of foreign money. Further let P and P^* be the price level at home and abroad quoted in the respective currencies.

The strong or absolute version of PPP relies on the "law of one price" in an integrated, competitive market. Abstracting from all and any frictions the price of a given good will be the same in all locations when quoted in the same currency, say dollars: $p_i = e p_i^*$. Consider now a domestic price index $P = f(p_1, \ldots, p_i, \ldots, p_n)$ and a foreign price index $P^* = g(p_1^*, \ldots, p_i^*, \ldots, p_n^*)$. If the prices of each good, in dollars, are equalized across countries, and if the same goods enter each country's market basket with the same weights [i.e., the homogeneous-of-degree-one $g(\cdot)$ and $f(\cdot)$ functions are the same], then absolute PPP prevails. The law of one price in this special case extends not only to individual goods but also to aggregate price levels. Spatial arbitrage then takes the form of the *strong* or *absolute* version of PPP:

$$e = \frac{P}{P^*} = \frac{\$ \text{ price of a standard market basket of foods}}{\pounds \text{ price of the same standard basket}}, \tag{1}$$

where the right-hand side is the common multiple of the price of each good in one currency and in the other. Specifically if $p_i/p_i^* = k$ for all i, we then have $e = P/P^* = k$. Note now the implication of absolute PPP. Whatever the monetary or real disturbances in the economy, because of instantaneous, costless arbitrage, the prices of a common market basket of goods in the two countries, measured in a common currency will be the same or $P/eP^* = 1$ at all times.

There can be no objection to (1) as a theoretical statement. Objections arise, however, when it is interpreted as an empirical proposition. In fact, the (spot) prices of a given commodity will not necessarily be equal in different locations at a given time. Transport costs and other obstacles to trade, in particular tariffs and quotas, do exist and hence the location of delivery does matter. Therefore we would not expect the price even of an ounce of gold of a specified fineness always to be the same in New York and in Calcutta. The fact that prices of the perfectly homogeneous commodity are not equalized across space at every point in time does not suggest market failure; it may simply reflect the inability to shift commodities costlessly and instantaneously from one location to the other. Information costs and impediments to trade stand in way of strictest spatial equalization of price. But these impediments to trade do not preclude that common currency prices of any given good in different locations should be closely related and, indeed, arbitraged. They just will not be literally equalized. Impediments to trade and imperfection of competition, of course, also make it possible that spatial price differentiation can occur thus further limiting strong PPP.

The *weak* or *relative* version of PPP therefore restates the theory in terms of changes in relative price levels and the exchange rate: $e = \theta P/P^*$, where θ is a constant reflecting the given obstacles to trade. Given these obstacles, an increase in the home price level relative to that abroad implies an equiproportionate depreciation of the home currency:

$$\hat{e} = \hat{P} - \hat{P}^*, \tag{2}$$

where a ^ denotes a percentage change.

Equation (2) is the statement of PPP as it was applied by the Swedish economist Gustav Cassel to an analysis of exchange rate changes during World War I:

> The general inflation which has taken place during the war has lowered this purchasing power in all countries, though in a different degree, and the rates of exchange should accordingly be expected to deviate from their old parities in proportion to the inflation of each country. At every moment the real parity is represented by this quotient between the purchasing power of the money in the one country and the other. I propose to call this parity *"purchasing power parity."* As long as anything like free movement of merchandise and a somewhat comprehensive trade between the two countries takes place, the actual rate of exchange cannot deviate very much from this purchasing power parity. (Cassel 1918, p. 413)

Absolute PPP in (1) was stated in terms of the relative prices in different currencies and locations of a *given* and common basket of identical goods. Going from there to relative PPP as in (2) may merely be a way of circumventing the qualifications arising from transport costs or obstacles to trade. But often more is involved because the shift, in practice, leads to a use of PPP in terms of particular price indexes such as CPIs, WPIs, or GDP deflators. Once that is done, we go beyond the law of one price because the shares of various goods in the different national indexes may not be the same and the goods that enter the respective indexes may not be strictly identical as is clearly the case for nontraded goods.

Once shares in the indexes are no longer equal and commodities are not strictly identical, the appeal to the law of one price can no longer serve as support for PPP. Now PPP can only hold, even in the weak form, if the conditions of the homogeneity postulate of monetary theory are justified. The homogeneity postulate asserts that a purely monetary disturbance, leaving unchanged all equilibrium relative prices, will lead to an equiproportionate change in money and all prices, including the price of foreign exchange. In this very special experiment PPP holds even if the law of one price does not apply. The constancy of real variables under the assumption of a purely monetary disturbance (i.e., an unanticipated, nonrecurrent increase in money) ensures that once the economy has adjusted, the exchange depreciation matches the inflation of any individual price or the price of any market basket so that (2) applies. To appreciate the difference of this experiment from absolute PPP, note that under these conditions (2) could even be stated in terms of indexes on nontraded goods prices.

PPP theory as a theory of equilibrium must be supplemented by an adjustment mechanism. In the case of identical commodities the theory is simply that of spatial arbitrage. But when the goods are not strictly identical, more is required. A high degree of substitution in world trade is generally assumed to be the mechanism through which exchange-rate-adjusted prices are kept in line internationally. A further point concerns causation. In much of the literature, especially in the writing of Cassel, exchange rates adjust to prices. But there is an important alternative tradition that singles out exchange rate depreciation as an independent source of inflation.

Criticism of PPP focuses on systematic ways in which relative price changes destroy the strict validity of PPP. Keynes (1923, p. 80), although strongly supporting the idea of PPP as a broad guide, recognized these possible departures from purely monetary disturbances:

> If on the other hand these assumptions are not fulfilled and changes are taking place in the "equation of exchange," as economists call it, between the services and products of one country and those of another, either on account of movements of capital, or reparation payments, or changes in the relative efficiency of labor, or changes in the urgency of the world's demand for that country's special products,

or the like, then the equilibrium point between purchasing power parity and the rate of exchange may be modified permanently.

This limitation of PPP led Samuelson (1964, p. 153) to argue:

Unless very sophisticated, indeed, PPP is a misleading, pretentious doctrine, promising what is rare in economics, detailed numerical prediction.

13.2 History

Versions of the PPP theory have been traced to the Salamanca school in sixteenth-century Spain and to the writings of Gerrard de Malynes appearing in 1601 in England. The Swedish, French, and English bullionists in the second part of the eighteenth century and in the early nineteenth century present further statements of PPP. Particularly noteworthy is the Bullion Report in England (1810, p. ccxxii):

Whether this $13\frac{1}{2}$ per cent, which stands against this country by the present exchange on Lisbon, is a real difference of exchange, occasioned by the course of trade and by the remittances to Portugal on account of government, or a nominal and apparent exchange occasioned by something in the state of our currency, or is partly real and partly nominal, may perhaps be determined by what your committee have yet to state.

During the nineteenth century classical economists, including in particular Ricardo, Mill, Goschen, and Marshall, endorsed and developed more or less qualified PPP views. This history is reviewed and discussed in Viner (1937), Schumpeter (1954), Holmes (1967), and Officer (1984).

Even though PPP theory was well established by the time of World War I, the forceful use and development of the theory by Cassel have made him the outstanding protagonist of the theory. He turned the theory into a paradigm with all the necessary trappings: an alleged challenge to gold standard orthodoxy, a catchy name, a formula, and the claim of empirical support for the new view.

Cassel's first contributions on the subject were published in 1916 in the *Economic Journal*. He argues the inflation theory of exchange rates and proceeds to a demonstration using price level and exchange rate data for the belligerent countries, the United States and Sweden. Keynes as the editor appends a footnote drawing attention to the contribution and noting his surprise that war disturbances notwithstanding, PPP should hold. A further challenge was the implication of PPP that the pre-war par with gold might not be reestablished, or more guardedly, might require a powerful deflation in a country like Britain.

Cassel never abandoned an uncompromising PPP view of exchange rates even though he already in 1918 started recognizing the possibility that exchange rates might transitorily diverge from PPP. A decade later in Cassel (1928a, p. 16) a clear statement of his final position is made:

> The fact that the rate of exchange corresponding to Purchasing Power Parity possesses such a remarkable stability is a sufficient reason for regarding Purchasing Power Parity as the fundamental factor determining the rate of exchange and for classifying all other factors that may influence the rate and perhaps make it deviate from the Purchasing Power Parity as factors of secondary importance, most suitably grouped under the head of "disturbances."

He identified three groups of disturbances: actual and expected inflation or deflation, new hindrances to international trade, and shifts in international movements of capital. Even though these disturbances are recognized, their quantitative effect on deviations from PPP is invariably seen as "confined within rather narrow limits" (Cassel 1928a, pp. 28–29). In insisting on the proposition that deviations from PPP are limited and transitory, Cassel neglected paying close attention to the determinants of purchasing power *dis*parities. Even though he recognized that inflation first leads to undervaluation, and stabilization leads later to an overvaluation (Cassel 1928b, p.26) never took these ideas further. His emphasis was on PPP. But he points out with some merit (Cassel 1928b) that without some quantifiable concept of PPP, a sensible discussion of over- or undervaluation can hardly begin.

Keynes (1923, 1971, chap. 3) takes up PPP, crediting Ricardo with the invention and Cassel with the name. Keynes recognized PPP as an important empirical possibility. Giving it all the right qualifications, he still endorses it for all practical purposes:

> This theory does not provide a simple or ready-made measure of the "true" value of the exchanges. When it is restricted to foreign-trade goods, it is little better than a truism. When it is not so restricted, the conception of purchasing power parity becomes much more interesting, but is no longer an accurate forecaster of the course of the foreign exchanges. Thus defined "purchasing power parity" deserves attention, even though it is not always an accurate forecaster of the foreign exchanges. The practical importance of our qualifications must not be exaggerated. (Keynes 1923, pp. 77–78)

Cassel received support for PPP from the monetary disturbances of the 1913 to 1928 period. Extensive PPP studies were conducted for the U.S. government (see Young 1925) and for the League of Nations. PPP emerged in the discussion of the resumption of the pre-war gold par in Britain in 1925, and Jacques Rueff used wage-based PPP to calculate an appropiate par for France's stabilization under Poincaré in 1926–28. Yet, though it became a regular tool of applied macroeconomics, there was also plenty of controversy. Viner (1933) challenged the doctrinal view that classical economists had a concept of PPP, arguing that without the notion of a price level PPP could not be conceived. In fact, Viner had little patience with PPP. The opposition is easily recognied today: Viner and other critics always reacted to the overstated claim that PPP must hold as a matter of fact or of theory, pointing out that only a purely monetary disturbance provided the theoretical or practical experiment in which PPP would apply. For them PPP as a theory was simply misstated, and as a practical proposition overstated.

A new wave of interest in PPP emerged at the end of World War II when once again exchange rates had to be set following the wartime suspension of trade and convertibility (see Metzler et al 1947). Renewed interest in PPP followed in the late 1950s and early 1960s. Yeager (1958) and Haberler (1961) emphasized the practical usefulness of PPP and highlighted the role of high price elasticities in international trade as the factor supporting PPP. High elasticities in world trade would ensure that real disturbances have only small effects on relative prices, thus establishing more nearly the conditions under which exchange rate movements reflect differences in monetary experiences. Hendrik Houthakker (1962) drew attention to dollar overvaluation, using absolute PPP calculations based on consumer price comparisons. Samuelson, in 1964, formalized much of the PPP discussion: while endorsing the Houthakker thesis of dollar overvaluation, he doubted that a proper test was given by the fact that one could buy cheaper abroad than in the United States a given market basket of goods.

In the late 1930s Sir Roy Harrod had drawn attention to the fact that divergent international productivity levels could, via their effect on wages and home goods prices, lead to permanent deviations from Cassel's absolute version of PPP. This idea was already developed by Ricardo and has become central to work on international real income comparisons. Balassa (1964) and Samuelson (1964) elaborated similar ideas to argue that there are systematic trend deviations from PPP. This "productivity bias" to PPP is discussed in more detail later.

PPP had yet another intellectual upturn with the move to flexible exchange rates in the early 1970s. The then fashionable "monetary approach to the balance of payments" developed by Robert Mundell (1968, 1971), Harry Johnson and their students readily adapted to become a PPP-based monetary approach to the exchange rate (see Frenkel and Johnson 1975, 1978; Mussa 1979). The exchange rate under strict PPP conditions was interpreted as a monetary phenomenon. The absolute version of PPP in (1) combined with the QT for each country ($MV = PY$ and $M^*V^* = P^*Y^*$) yielded the key equation determining exchange rates by relative money supplies, velocities, and real incomes:

$$e = \left(\frac{M}{M^*}\right)\left(\frac{V}{V^*}\right)\left(\frac{Y^*}{Y}\right). \tag{3}$$

Empirical research on the 1920s and on the very early data of the 1970s initially seemed to lend support to PPP and the monetary approach.

But large movements in real exchange rates of the 1970s led to the currently dominant PPP skepticism. The new direction following the Mundell-Fleming model of the 1960s emphasized fluctuations in real exchange rates or the terms of trade (import relative to export prices) arising from the discrepancies between flexible, forward-looking asset markets, and asset prices and short-run sticky prices and wages. Work on exchange rate dynamics (Dornbusch 1976) developed these ideas about transitory deviations from PPP in a rational expectations context.

Concern with PPP continued to be very active in the late 1970s and the early 1980s. The real exchange rates of the main currencies underwent large, persistent fluctuations with important effects on trade flows and resource allocation. At the same time currency experiments in Latin America involved dramatic real appreciations with ruinous consequences for several countries. Sometimes in history there was bafflement as to how, all things considered, PPP could work so closely. This time, however, the surprise was on the other side: How can real exchange rates get that far out of line? We now review in more detail the theory of and evidence on deviations from PPP.

13.3 Purchasing Power Disparities

Qualifications to PPP take one of two forms: Departures from PPP can be "structural" in the sense that they arise systematically in response to new and lasting changes in equilibrium relative prices, or they occur in a "transitory" fashion as a result of disturbances to which the economy adjusts with differential speeds in goods and assets markets. These qualifications imply that even the weak or relative form of PPP cannot be expected to hold closely.

These disparities arise primarily for the following reasons: First, the terms of trade may change as a consequence of changes in trade patterns. Second, economic growth systematically affects the relative price of home and traded goods. Third, monetary and exchange rate changes bring about transitory deviations in real price ratios and in PPP as a consequence of imperfectly flexible wages and prices.

Structural Departures

The literature is replete with qualifications to PPP singling out particular real disturbances that change equilibrium relative prices. Thus it has been recognized since Ricardo that real prices of home goods are high "in countries where manufactures flourish." It also has been argued that the "price level is high in borrowing countries." The Ricardo-Harrod-Balassa theory provides a framework for these ideas.

Consider a Ricardian model where the law of one price applies to traded goods and where there is also a home good. With perfect competition and constant returns prices are given by unit labor costs. We define as R the relative consumer price levels of two countries measured in a common currency:

$$R = \frac{P}{eP^*}. \tag{4}$$

With identical homothetic tastes and the law of one price the international component of price indexes is the same in both countries and hence cancels out in (4). The relative price level is then determined by the relative prices of home goods in the two countries, measured in a common currency. Let h and h^* be the levels of productivity in traded goods (at the competitive margin) relative to home goods in each country. It is readily shown (see Dornbusch, Fischer, and Samuelson 1977) that the relative price level then reduces to

$$R = R\left(\frac{h}{h^*}\right), \quad R' > 0. \tag{4a}$$

A uniform rise in traded goods productivity at home would bring about a rise in the relative price level of the home country or a real appreciation. The mechanism is the following: with the law of one price applying to traded goods, increased productivity in the traded goods sector increases wages in that industry and hence raises economywide wages. But without accompanying productivity gains in the home goods sector, costs and prices there must rise and hence the growing country's relative price level increases as shown by (4a).

In (4a) the national productivity relatives h and h^* are measured in the traded goods sector at the competitive margin. Shifts in technology, tastes, commercial policies, or labor force growth will all change the equilibrium competitive margin and hence will change the real exchange rate.

Thus real factors, as the literature since Ricardo has recognized, will introduce systematic departures from PPP. For example, a shift in world demand toward the home country's goods would raise the relative wage and reduce the range of goods produced by the home country. The rise in the relative wage, given productivity, raises the relative price level of the home country. Likewise an increase in spending relative to income (i.e., borrowing or a current account deficit) will lead to a rise in the relative price level of the spending country.

A variant of the Ricardian productivity differential model as an explanation for the relatively low price of nontradables in poor countries has been advanced by Lipsey and Kravis (1983) and Bhagwati (1984). They rely on differences in factor endowments and factor rewards rather than differences in production functions. In the poor labor-abundant country, the labor-using nontraded services can be produced at a relatively low cost compared to the rich, capital-abundant country. Whichever is the model, this effect, as we will discuss later, has found ample support in empirical research on international real income and price comparisons.

Transitory Deviations

There is no difficulty in accepting that prices of close substitutes, or even identical goods, could diverge across space at any point in time. This would be the case because, in the shortest time period, transportation and information costs make arbitrage difficult or even impossible. These difficulties would explain that PPP holds up to a constant and white noise error (see Aizenman 1984). But in fact we have to explain relatively *persistent* and often *large* deviations from PPP. These can arise from divergent speeds of adjustment of the exchange rate compared with wages and prices. Particularly when flexible exchange rates behave like asset prices while wages are determined by long-term contracts, there is room for relative prices to show relatively persistent deviations from PPP.

Okun (1981) made the distinction between "auction goods" and "customer goods." The former are in the nature of homogeneous commodities traded in spot markets on organized exchanges, the latter are differentiated and marketed in established customer relations. The former typically have flexible and highly arbitraged prices, the latter are priced on the basis of normal unit costs, and their prices tend to be sticky. This characterization is implicit in the Mundell-Fleming model of international capital mobility under flexible exchange rates, which has been the standard frame of reference for the discussion of open economy macroeconomics since the 1960s. This model assumes that prices in each country are fixed and hence exchange rate changes move the terms of trade one for one, thus bringing about permanent changes in real exchange rates. But even when prices are only sticky in the short run, there will still be relatively persistent deviations from PPP, although in the long run money is fully neutral.

Theoretical approaches to support the relative stickiness of prices can rely on the presence of long-term labor contracts combined with oligopolistic pricing in goods markets. A model of imperfect competition is essential because the less-than-perfect degree of substitution is a key ingredient in PPP deviations. Less than perfect substitution means that we are not dealing with the law of one price and arbitrage but with firms' decisions to set relative prices. A suggestive framework is the Dixit-Stiglitz (1977) model of product diversification with imperfect competition. Given constant returns and labor as the only factor, each firm will set prices as a fixed and common markup over wages. In the world market for the products of a particular industry the relative price of domestic and foreign variants of the product is determined by relative unit labor costs measured in a common currency:

$$\frac{p}{ep^*} = \frac{w}{ew^*} , \tag{5}$$

where w and w^* denote unit labor costs at home and abroad in the respective currencies. Given sluggish wages, for contract reasons or otherwise, exchange rate movements will be one for one reflected in changes in the real exchange rate.

The assumption that firms base their pricing entirely on home cost, as it appears in this model, leaves no room for the alternative of spatial price differentiation. There is yet no definitive or even large body of literature that develops industrial organization aspects of pricing under flexible and volatile exchange rates.

Empirical Evidence

There is little doubt that the prices of primary commodities traded on major organized exchanges in different locations are fully arbitraged when literally all adjustments for contracts (maturity, delivery terms and location, etc.) are made. But all available evidence suggests that PPP in the strong or weak version does not apply in the same fashion to manufactured goods. The lack of a close conformity with PPP is as much true for individual commodity prices as it is for aggregate price indexes. Moreover this absence of a very tight PPP relation appears particularly true during major monetary dislocations.

Studies of high inflation episodes always appear to offer support for PPP in that they show close *cumulative* movements of internal prices and the exchange rate. But even here the evidence is deceptive as becomes clear when one looks at relative prices that do show large variations. Indeed, particularly during high inflation, the differing frequencies of adjustments of wages, prices, and the exchange rate introduce considerable variability in relative prices that only disappears in the most intense stages of hyper-inflation where all pricing comes to be based on the exchange rate.

Kravis and Lipsey (1978) and Isard (1977) have shown tests of the law of one price at the level of narrowly defined manufactured goods. The studies established for the same good (or highly substitutable goods) quite definitely persistent price discrepancies between domestic and export prices, between domestic and import prices, and between export prices to different markets. The evidence on the slack in the law of one price at the level of individual commodities is sufficiently strong for Isard (1977, p. 941) to conclude:

> The denial of the law of one price in this context—at the most diaggregated product level for which price data can be readily matched—provides a strong presumption that it is impossible to assemble available data into aggregate price indexes which can be expected to obey the law of one price (except, perhaps, when product coverage is restricted to primary commodities).

Empirical studies on time series PPP relationships for aggregate price indexes in the past twenty years also show evidence of persistent deviations. Once relative prices are not strictly constant, PPP will perform differently depending on the particular price index chosen for comparison. Commonly the choice is among CPIs, WPIs, and GDP deflators. WPIs are often ruled out on the argument that conceptually they are poorly defined, being neither producer nor consumer price indexes. The preference is most often given to GDP deflators that have a clear methodological definition. Figure 13.1 shows relative GDP deflators expressed in a common currency in the 1972 to 1983 period for Germany and for Japan, each relative to the United States. The figure clearly brings out that relative GDP deflators expressed in a common currency are far from constant, thus refuting the weak version of PPP.

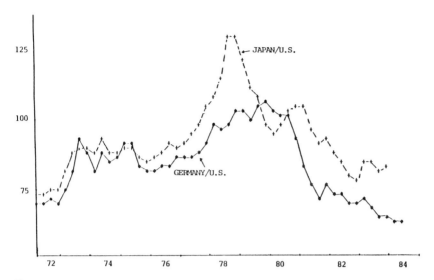

Figure 13.1
Relative GDP deflators in a common currency (index 1980 = 100)

As a measure of the departure from PPP, table 13.1 shows the correlation of annual rates of change of various price indexes for the period 1971 to 1983. In each case the bilateral comparison is conducted on exchange-rate-adjusted price indexes so that inflation rates are measured in a common currency. The table reports correlation coefficients for the CPI, GDP deflator, the GDP deflator for manufacturing, and export prices of nonelectrical machinery. The latter example is shown as a particular case of a relatively disaggregated traded good. The weak form of the PPP hypothesis would predict that the correlation coefficients are approximately unity. In fact, as is apparent, the values are far off unity and in many cases even negative.

Table 13.2 presents correlations of the quarterly rates of inflation of GDP deflators (in U.S. dollars) of a wider group of countries for the flexible rate period 1971 to 1983. The table shows once more correlations far off Cassel's hypothetical value of one. Interestingly, even for the more integrated European countries the correlation is low, though much larger than correlations involving the United States.

The very strong deviations from PPP can likewise be found in looking at relative prices. Table 13.3 shows the variability of relative GDP deflators, measured in a common currency and using the United States as the numeraire country. The data for these relative price variability measures are

Table 13.1
Correlation of inflation rates expressed in U.S. dollars, 1971–1983 (annual data)

	United States–Germany	United States–Japan	Germany–Japan
GDP deflators	−0.16	−0.22	0.64
Consumer prices	0.28	0.36	0.60
Export prices of machinery	−0.24	−0.10	0.58
Deflator for manufactures	−0.10	−0.13	0.61

Table 13.2
Correlations of inflation rates expressed in U.S. dollars, 1971–1983 (GDP deflators, quarterly data)

	United States	Japan	United Kingdom	France	Germany
Japan	0.07	1			
United Kingdom	0.32	0.32	1		
France	0.25	0.50	0.55	1	
Germany	0.04	0.49	0.50	0.79	1
Italy	0.24	0.40	0.63	0.76	0.68

quarterly and correspond to the fixed and flexible rate periods. The table shows a large increase in variability in the shift to flexible exchange rates.

The evidence on deviations from PPP leaves little doubt that they have been large and persistent. To pin down the major sources of these movements, however, is significantly more difficult. Among the chief explanations are capital flows induced by internationally divergent monetary-fiscal mixes interacting with sluggish wages and prices. Thus it would appear that a country that shifts in the direction of tight money and easy fiscal policy, for example, will experience real appreciation.

Besides these dominant macro shocks there is of course a host of other factors. Jacob Frenkel (1981a, 1981b, pp. 694–695) has noted in this context:

The experience during the 1970s illustrates the extent to which real shocks (oil embargo, supply shocks, commodity booms and shortages, shifts in the demand for money, differential productivity growth) result in systematic deviations from PPP ... It should be noted, however, that to some extent the overall poor performance of the purchasing power parities doctrine is specific to the 1970s. During the floating rate period of the 1920s, the doctrine seems to have been much more reliable.

Although PPP failed altogether in the 1970s, it is now apparent that even the evidence from the 1920s is far from supportive as Krugman (1978) and Bernholz (1982) have shown.

The lack of solid empirical evidence in support of PPP extends to the assumption that divergent price developments "cause" exchange depreciation. From the study of experiences of high inflation it is clear that in some instances capital flight and exchange depreciation precipitated increases in inflation. In fact, Nurkse (1944) makes much of the point that expectations acting via capital flight on the exchange rate, not actual money and prices, often initiate inflationary episodes.

Table 13.3
Coefficient of variation of relative GDP deflators (quarterly data, deflators measured in common currency)

	Germany–United States	Japan–United States	United Kingdom–United States
1960–72	9.0	9.3	5.5
1973: III–83	14.0	13.4	17.7

We conclude with a reference to evidence on structural PPP deviations. The evidence here establishes quite firmly that over time real exchange rates, rather than showing constancy or a tendency to fluctuate around a constant level, in fact exhibit a distinct trend. Productivity levels or real incomes influence systematically the relative prices of traded and non-traded goods within a country and hence international relative price levels across countries and across time.

In the context of an international income comparison project Kravis and associates have constructed indexes of relative national price levels using an absolute price comparison approach. Drawing on a detailed sample of prices, they construct matched sets of the price of individual commodity groups in a particular country relative to a reference country. For commodity i the price relative p_i/p_i^*, where the p's are measured in the respective countries' currencies with an asterisk denoting the reference country. Using an arithmetic average with weights a_i given by final expenditure shares, a PPP index is defined:

$$PPP \equiv \sum a_i \left(\frac{p_i}{p_i^*} \right). \tag{6}$$

The expenditure shares a_i used in the weighting may be those of either one of the countries or some other appropriate weighting scheme. With the help of this PPP index the (Kravis) real price level of a country (relative to the reference country) is defined as the PPP index in (6) divided by the actual exchange rate:

$$Kravis\ real\ price\ level \equiv \frac{PPP}{e}. \tag{7}$$

This real price level definition represents a measure of the deviation from the law of one price at the aggregate level.

Kravis and Lipsey (1983, p. 21) report the results of a cross-sectional study of thirty-four countries where the 1975 real price level as defined in (7) of the sample of countries (relative to the United States) is explained by the country's real income compared to the United States. The evidence shows that the higher is a country's relative income, the higher is its relative price level. Work by Hsieh (1982) using a time series approach further supports the extensive evidence on divergent productivity trends as a source of structural PPP deviations. It must be noted, though, that the evidence on structural deviations continues to be challenged by Officer (1984).

13.4 Implications of Purchasing Power Disparities

The fact that exchange rate movements often or even predominantly do not conform to tight PPP patterns poses important issues for macroeconomic measurement, linkages, and policy. We review here several implications.

Real Income Comparisons

With strict PPP based on the law of one price, the purchasing power of a given income in one country and currency can be compared with the purchasing power of the income of any other country by simply measuring incomes in a common currency. If one income is twenty times larger than the other, measured in the same currency at actual exchange rates, then its command over goods and services is twenty times larger. But the fact that PPP does not hold leads to systematic biases in the comparisons. Specifically, as the work of Kravis and associates (1978, 1982, 1983) has shown, the real income of poor countries is severely underestimated when actual exchange rates are used to make the comparison. The low relative price of nontradables in poor countries (due to the productivity differential discussed earlier) yields for poor countries true purchasing power of income significantly above what exchange-rate-converted income suggests.

Table 13.4 reports on the magnitude of biases in a sample of thirty-four countries separated into six income groups with the United States as the numeraire country. Note that the biases are particularly large for countries whose incomes are only a small fraction of the U.S. level so that productivity differential effects play a maximal role. The poorer a country, the lower the *real* price level. An interesting point is that these real price level differences apply to both commodities and services. One reason they also apply to goods is that these always have a local retail component, which on account of labor costs (though perhaps not transport), will tend to be low in poor countries.

The ratio of dollar income to real income for each group (column 2 divided by column 1) represents the extent to which exchange rate conversions understate real income. For low income countries actual real income is two to three times what exchange-rate-converted incomes suggest. These structural deviations from PPP of course would be invariant under a purely monetary disturbance so that the weak form of PPP would still apply.

Table 13.4
Kravis-Heston-Summers international real income comparisons (index: U.S. = 100)

Group	(1) Real income (mean per capita)	(2) Dollar income (mean per capita)	(3) Real price of commodities	(4) Services	(5) GDP
1	9.0	3.7	57.2	20.7	40.6
2	23.1	12.1	65.1	34.1	51.7
3	37.3	24.2	83.1	41.2	64.7
4	52.4	38.7	94.0	46.3	73.5
5	76.0	82.3	119.0	94.6	107.5
United States	100.0	100.0	100.0	100.0	100.0

Source: Kravis, Heston, and Summers (1982).

Interest Rate Linkages and PPP

Under perfect international mobility of capital and risk-neutral speculation, there is a linkage between nominal interest rates and the anticipated rate of depreciation, which is given by the open economy Fisher equation:

$$i = i^* + x, \tag{8}$$

where i and i^* are the nominal interest rates at home and abroad and x is the anticipated rate of depreciation of the home currency. Adding and subtracting anticipated inflation rates on both sides yields an equation in terms of inflation-adjusted or real interest rates:

$$r^* = r + \frac{\dot{R}}{R}. \tag{8a}$$

Real interest parity, according to (8a), prevails when the real interest differential equals the expected rate of real appreciation, $\dot{R}/R$. From the real interest parity condition it is apparent that under exact PPP, the real exchange rate is constant. In the absence of restrictions on capital flows, real interest rates must therefore be strictly equalized across countries.

The real interest parity equation has two interesting implications. A first one is the linkages between the level of real exchange rates and monetary policy. Suppose that in a medium-term macroeconomic context, following a disturbance, the actual real exchange rate adjusts only gradually to the trend level R' according to the process: $\dot{R}/R = (1/a)(R'-R)$. Here $1/a$ is the speed of adjustment, which depends among other things on the extent to which wages and prices are sticky. Combining this process with (8a) yields an equation for the equilibrium real exchange rate:

$$R = R' + a(r - r^*). \tag{9}$$

The result shown here is that when real interest rates at home exceed those abroad, the real exchange rate will be appreciated relative to its trend value. A tightening of monetary policy, by raising real interest rates, would thus bring about a (transitory) real appreciation. Equation (9) emerges from the dynamic Mundell-Fleming model and is often thought to explain real exchange rate movements and their tendency to return only gradually to their long-run value.

A second way to look at (8a) draws on the fact that the traded–nontraded goods distinction has implications for real exchange rates. Suppose the law of one price holds for traded goods and that shares in the two countries' price indexes are the same. Then, as argued before, the real exchange rate is equal to the relative price of nontraded goods (in a common currency) in the two countries. Structural disturbances such as differential productivity growth or changes in aggregate demand will now have a systematic impact on relative nontraded goods prices and hence on real interest rate differentials. Specifically the country with the higher growth rate of productivity has a rising relative price of home goods and thus has a lower real rate of interest. As another example, a country where aggregate demand is transitorily high has a home goods price that is high but falling. Accordingly, the real interest rate is high relative to that abroad. Deviations from PPP, trend or short run, thus introduce an equilibrium international interest rate differential.

PPP deviations affect interest differentials another way. In (8) we assumed risk neutrality. But once risk-averse speculators are admitted, the possibility that exchange rate movements could deviate from a strict PPP pattern introduces portfolio risk associated with the currency composition of the portfolio. PPP deviations are thus a basic motive for international portfolio diversification. A risk premium will appear, and among the determinants of this premium is the variability of the real exchange rate. The risk premium will be an increasing function of real exchange rate uncertainty (see the survey in Branson and Henderson 1984).

Finance-theory-oriented literature has posed the important question of whether deviations from PPP imply economic inefficiency (see Roll 1979). Inefficiency means that a rational speculator, using available information, could make excess profits by borrowing in one country, and buying and holding a commodity basket representing the foreign country's CPI. If the rate of real depreciation predictably exceeds the real rate of interest in a country, there exists the possibility that markets are inefficient. For example, an investment in foreign goods would yield a real rate of return in terms of domestic goods equal to $-\dot{R}/R$. An investment in home financial assets yields an expected real return r. Let the random differential between these two investments be $K \equiv r + \dot{R}/R$. Finance theory predicts that in an information-rational market $K_t = E(K_t|I_{t-1}) + u_t$, where u_t is a white noise error uncorrelated with any information I_{t-1} available at time $t-1$. Hence a regression of K_t on variables known at time $t-1$ will not yield a statistically significant coefficient or serial correlation in the errors. The evidence does not lend unambiguous support to this efficiency hypothesis, possible explanations being risk premia and the obvious difficulty of storing the CPI (see Cumby and Obstfeld 1984).

Exchange Rate Policy

In Cassel's view even small deviations from PPP would bring about large changes in trade flows and hence a rapid discipline to move prices back into line internationally. But the reversion toward PPP has often not been quick, and deviations from PPP have taken more nearly the pattern of persistent swings in a country's external competitiveness. The changes in competitiveness in turn have implied large swings in external balances, in output and in employment in the traded goods sector. Changes in exchange rates that deviate from PPP at the same time influence the path of a country's inflation: real depreciation increases inflation, and real appreciation dampens inflation. These effects of purchasing power disparities make the exchange rate an important issue in macroeconomic policy.

Countries with high inflation cannot afford a fixed exchange rate since the loss in external competiveness would soon lead to excessive and growing external deficits and large unemployment. If freely fluctuating rates are deemed too unstable, the policy answer is often a crawling peg. In a crawling peg regime the rate of depreciation follows a PPP path such that over time the real exchange rate remains constant (see Williamson 1965, 1982). Such a policy is an important advance over a system of occasional devaluations (too little, too late), but it is not without risks for two reasons. First, freezing the real exchange rate may be a bad policy when disturbances in fact call for a path of, say, real depreciation. Second, there is a trade-off between stability of the real exchange rate and price stability. A policy of fully accommodating any and all price or cost disturbances by an offsetting depreciation may in fact remove price stability altogether (see Dornbusch 1982).

Purchasing-power-parity issues enter exchange rate policy also when a country seeks to gain macroeconomic advantages by a deliberate policy of driving the exchange rate away from PPP. A real depreciation serves to gain competitiveness and shift employment toward the depreciating country. In the 1930s this was called a "beggar-thy-neighbor" policy, and in post World War II Europe it became "export-led growth." A policy of appreciation, by contrast, serves to reduce inflationary pressure as the rate of increase of traded goods prices is pushed below the prevailing rate of inflation. These macroeconomic effects of purchasing power disparities are not difficult to bring about: easy money, in the short and medium term, serves to depreciate the exchange rate and thus create employment. This policy is more effective and more lasting, the more sticky the wages and the smaller the connection between wages, prices, and the exchange rate.

By contrast, in an economy that is strongly indexed—and in particular, with exchange rate influences on indexation—an attempt at creating employment via easy money would be frustrated as exchange depreciation precipitates offsetting wage and price inflation.

Deviations from PPP have also been used as a disinflation policy (see Fischer 1984). Deliberate fixing of the exchange rate, or preannounced rates of depreciation, below the prevailing rate of inflation has been adopted in various countries to break inflation. The experience has been almost uniformly disappointing, and worse. The resulting overvaluation very often has led to excessive external deficits, borrowing and capital flight, and ultimately only moderate success at disinflation. The cases of Chile and Argentina in the late 1970s were particularly extreme. Exchange rate policies led to extreme overvaluation. But these economies had been opened to unrestricted trade or free capital flows. The public therefore could speculate against the overvalued currency by massive imports or capital flight, while the governments financed the resulting deficits by external borrowing. In the end the scheme collapsed, leaving the private sector with foreign goods or foreign assets and the governments with huge foreign debts.

Purchasing power disparities are relevant for the exchange rate choice between flexible and fixed or managed rates. In a world where exchange rate movements conform strictly to PPP and monetary policy governs prices, there is no issue. Flexible rates then allow a country to chose its preferred rate of inflation. But once disparities are possible—as a result of both structural trends and perhaps short-term capital movements—the fixed versus flexible rate choice becomes more difficult. Flexible rates are preferable because there is no risk that the government pegs a rate that no longer corresponds to equilibrium. But flexible rates suffer the handicap that disequilibrating capital flows can drive the real exchange rate away from the level warranted by the fundamentals of the goods market. In particular, if exchange rates respond more to asset markets than to price levels, persistent real appreciation or depreciation become a possibility. Figure 13.1 is suggestive of such disequilibrium movements. When these do occur, there is invariably a call for PPP-based foreign exchange market intervention to bring rates back to "fundamentals." Explicit target zones have been proposed as a means of maintaining the advantages of flexible rates within limits to maintain approximate PPP (see Williamson 1983).

Flexible rates are also a concern because disequilibrating capital flows can provoke large changes in the rate of inflation. A loss of confidence, whether warranted or not, induces a capital outflow and a real exchange depreciation. If domestic financial policies are linked via the budget or indexation to the exchange rate, the real depreciation can initiate a sharp increase in inflation. Much of the discussion of the merits of flexible rates has concentrated on the question of whether speculative capital flows "cause" the inflation or whether they merely respond to an inflationary situation, bringing exchange depreciation in line with prevailing inflation. The Graham-Nurkse-Robinson view asserts, contrary to Milton Friedman, that destabilizing capital flows are the central element in the outbreak of major inflation experiences. Exchange stabilization, similarly, is seen as an essential step in stopping a runaway inflation and initiating a stabilization program.

Purchasing power parity is also relevant in the context of devaluation of a fixed rate. In the monetary approach to the balance of payments, a firm tenet is the proposition that a devaluation cannot exert a lasting effect on relative prices or the balance of trade. Exchange depreciation raises the prices of all traded goods in the same proportion, and any effect then must be limited to a temporary depression of home goods prices due to reduced absorption. As money responds to the external surplus, real absorption rises and the initial real equilibrium is restored. This approach has the disturbing implication that devaluation does not appear to be an effective means of coping with trade or employment problems. In practice, a devaluation will work well when it is designed to speed up the adjustment from an initial disequilibrium in a situation where wages and prices are less than fully flexible downward. But a devaluation is likely to be ineffective if it is accompanied by a monetary expansion and wage increases, thus eliminating any real effects.

13.5 Concluding Remark

Purchasing power parity remains an essential element of open economy macroeconomics for two reasons. First, it is a bench-mark by which to judge the level of an exchange rate. Cassel argued that without PPP, there would be no meaningful way of discussing over- or undervaluation. That recognition has found a very concrete expression in the real exchange rate series now routinely calculated and reported by governments, international organizations, and financial institutions. These series show exchange-rate-adjusted price relatives for a country relative to its trading partners. The series are constructed on the basis of GDP deflators, unit labor costs, manufacturing prices, and wholesale prices for all major industrialized countries and increasingly for developing countries too. They are used to judge changes in a country's external competitiveness, thus implicitly assuming, as Cassel did, that movements in *equilibrium* relative prices are negligible. Changes in real exchange rates then (and only then) unambiguously translate into changes in competitiveness from which to expect changes in trade flows and net exports.

There is no question that these data provide a useful bench-mark for policy discussion. But the objections remain the same as those that have been brought over the past seventy years. For example, from 1978 to 1984 the U.S. dollar appreciated on a trade-weighted basis in real terms by 25 percent, using GDP deflators in manufacturing as the basis of comparison. How much of this real appreciation represents a movement away from fundamentals? The base year, 1978, may have represented an excessive undervaluation. Furthermore macro and micro structural changes may have increased the equilibrium relative price of U.S. goods. With the present state of knowledge it is difficult to judge whether the overvaluation is 10 or 20 percent and hence to decide whether there is a major market failure calling for intervention.

The second use of PPP is to serve as a prediction model for exchange rates. Under perfectly flexible wages and prices a monetary expansion would lead to equiproportionate increases in wages, prices, and the exchange rate, leaving all real variables unchanged. This combination of the QT and PPP is an important insight in guiding policy. Expansionary monetary policy can only be effective if wages and prices are less than fully flexible and will be more effective the more flexible the exchange rate. The essential channel is the real depreciation of the exchange rate that serves to create employment, at least for a while. Similarly, exchange depreciation can only be effective if money wages and prices are unresponsive. Policy can be effective only if PPP fails to hold. Macroeconomic theory goes increasingly in the direction of information, contracting, and pricing models to explore what is the basis of PPP failure and to determine the resulting extent and persistence of policy effects.

Note

I am indebted to Susan Collins, Stanley Fischer, Jeffrey Frankel, Dale Henderson, Irving Kravis, Paul Samuelson, and John Williamson for suggestions and comments.

References

Aizenman, J. 1984. "Testing Deviations from Purchasing Power Parity (PPP)." NBER Working Paper No. 1475.

Balassa, B. 1964. "The Purchasing Power Parity Doctrine: A Reappraisal." *Journal of Political Economy*, December.

Bernholz, P. 1982. *Flexible Exchange Rates in Historical Perspective*. Princeton Studies in International Finance. No. 49. Princeton University Press.

Bhagwati, J. 1984. "Why Services Are Cheaper in Poor Countries." *Economic Journal*, June.

Branson, W., and Henderson, D. 1984. "The Specification and Influence of Asset Markets." In P. Kenen and R. Jones (eds.), *Handbook of International Economics* Vol. 2. North-Holland.

Cassel, G. 1916. "The Present Situation of the Foreign Exchanges." *Economic Journal*, March.

Cassel, G. 1918. "Abnormal Deviations in International Exchanges." *Economic Journal*, December.

Cassel, G. 1922. *Money and Foreign Exchange After 1914*. Macmillan, 1930.

Cassel, G. 1928a. *Foreign Investments*. Lectures of the Harris Foundation. University of Chicago Press.

Cassel, G. 1928b. *Post-war Monetary Stabilization*. Columbia University Press.

Cumby, R., and Obstfeld, M. 1984. "International Interest Rate and Price Level Linkages under Flexible Rates: A Review of Recent Evidence." In J. Bilson and R. Marston (eds.), *Exchange Rate Theory and Practice*. University of Chicago Press.

Dixit, A., and Stiglitz, J. 1977. "Monopolistic Competition and Optimum Product Diversity." *American Economic Review*, June.

Dornbusch, R. 1976. "Expectations and Exchange Rate Dynamics." *Journal of Political Economy*, December.

Dornbusch, R. 1982. "PPP Exchange Rate Rules and Macroeconomic Stability," *Journal of Political Economy*, February.

Dornbusch, R., Fischer, S., and Samuelson, P. 1977. "Comparative Advantage, Trade and Payments in a Ricardian Model with a Continuum of Goods." *American Economic Review*, December.

Fischer, S. 1984, "Real Balances, the Exchange Rate and Indexation: Real Variables in Disinflation." NBER Working Paper No. 1497.

Frenkel, J. A. 1981. "Flexible Exchange Rates, Prices and the Role of News: Lessons from the 1970s." *Journal of Political Economy*, August.

Frenkel, J. A., and Johnson, H. G. (eds.). 1975. *The Monetary Approach to the Balance of Payments*. Allen & Unwin.

Frenkel, J., and Johnson, H. G. (eds.). 1978. *The Economics of Flexible Exchange Rates*. Addison Wesley.

Great Britain. 1810. *Report from the Select Committee on the High Price of Gold Bullion.* House of Commons.

Haberler, G. 1961. "A Survey of International Trade Theory." Special Papers in International Economics. Princeton University.

Harrod, R. 1939. *International Economics.* University of Chicago Press, 1957.

Holmes, J. 1967. "The Purchasing Power Parity Theory: In Defense of Gustav Cassel as a Modern Theorist." *Journal of Political Economy,* October.

Houthakker, H. 1962. "Exchange Rate Adjustment." In *Factors Affecting the United States Balance of Payments.* 87th Congress. U.S. Government Printing Office.

Hsieh, D. 1982. "The Determinants of the Real Exchange Rate." *Journal of International Economics,* May.

Isard, P. 1977. "How Far Can We Push the Law of One Price." *American Economic Review,* December.

Katseli, L. 1984. "Real Exchange Rates." In J. Bilson and R. Marston (eds.), *Exchange Rate Theory and Practice.* University of Chicago Press.

Kravis, I., and Lipsey, R. 1983. *Toward an Explanation of National Price Levels.* Princeton Studies in International Finance. No. 52. Princeton University Press.

Kravis, I., and Lipsey, R. 1978. "Price Behavior in the Light of Balance of Payments Theories." *Journal of International Economics,* May.

Karvis, I., Heston, A., and Summes, R. 1978. "Real GDP Per Capita for more than One Hundred Countries," *Economic Journal,* June.

Kravis, I. 1982. *World Product and Income: International Comparisons of Real Gross Product,* Johns Hopkins University Press.

Krugman, P. 1978. "Purchasing Power Parity and Exchange Rates." *Journal of International Economics,* August.

Keynes, J. M. 1923. *A Tract on Monetary Reform.* Macmillan and St. Martin's Press for the Royal Economic Society, 1971.

League of Nations International Currency Experience. 1978. *Lessons of the Interwar Period.* Arno Press.

Metzler, L. A. et al. 1947. *International Monetary Policies.* Board of Governors of the Federal Reserve, Postwar Economic Studies. No. 7, September.

Mundell, R. A. 1968. *International Economics.* Macmillan.

Mundell, R. A. 1971. *Monetary Theory.* Goodyear.

Mussa, M. 1979. "Empirical Regularities in the Behavior of Exchange Rates and Theories of the Foreign Exchange Market." In K. Brunner and A. Meltzer (eds.),

Policies for Employment, Prices, and Exchange Rates. Carnegie Rochester Conference Series. Vol. 11. North-Holland.

Officer, L. 1984. *Purchasing Power Parity and Exchange Rates.* JAI Press.

Okun, A. 1981. *Prices and Quantities.* Brookings.

Roll, R. 1979. "Violations of Purchasing Power Parity and Their Implications for Efficient International Commodity Markets." In M. Sarnat and G. Szego (eds.), *International Finance and Trade.* Ballinger.

Samuelson, P. A. 1964. "Theoretical Notes on Trade Problems." *Review of Economics and Statistics*, May.

Samuelson, P. A. 1974. "Analytical Notes on International Real Income Comparisons." *Economic Journal*, September.

Samuelson, P. A. 1984. "Second Thoughts on Analytical Income Comparisons." *Economic Journal*, June.

Viner, J. 1955. *Studies in the Theory of International Trade.* Allen & Unwin.

Williamson, J. 1965. *The Crawling Peg.* Essays in International Finance. No. 50. Princeton University Press.

Williamson, J. 1983. *The Exchange Rate System.* Institute for International Economics. MIT Press.

Williamson, J. (ed.). 1982. *The Crawling Peg: Past Performance and Future Prospects.* Macmillan.

Yeager, L. 1958. "A Rehabilitation of Purchasing Power Parity." *Journal of Political Economy*, December.

Young, J. P. 1925. *European Currency and Finance.* Commission of Gold and Silver Enquiry. United States Senate. Serial 9. Reprinted by Gareland, 1983.

14

Comparative Advantage, Trade, and Payments in a Ricardian Model with a Continuum of Goods

(with S. Fischer and
P. A. Samuelson)

This chapter discusses Ricardian trade and payments theory in the case of a continuum of goods. The analysis thus extends the development of many-commodity, two-country comparative advantage analysis as presented, for example, in Gottfried Haberler (1937), Frank Graham (1923), Paul Samuelson (1964), and Frank W. Taussig (1927). The literature is historically reviewed by John Chipman (1965). Perhaps surprisingly, the continuum assumption simplifies the analysis neatly in comparison with the discrete many-commodity case. The distinguishing feature of the Ricardian approach emphasized in this chapter is the determination of the competitive margin in production between imported and exported goods. The analysis advances the existing literature by formally showing precisely how tariffs and transport costs establish a range of commodities that are not traded, and how the price-specie flow mechanism does or does not give rise to movements in relative cost and price levels.

The formal *real* model is introduced in section 14.1. Its equilibrium determines the *relative* wage and price structure and the efficient international specialization pattern. Section 14.2 considers standard comparative static questions of growth, demand shifts, technological change, and transfers. Extensions of the model to nontraded goods, tariffs, and transport costs are then studied in section 14.3. Monetary considerations are introduced in section 14.4, which examines the price-specie mechanism under stable parities, floating exchange rate regimes, and also questions of unemployment under sticky money wages.

Originally published in *American Economic Review*, Vol. 67, no. 5 (December 1977), pp. 823–839.

14.1 The Real Model

In this section we develop the basic real model and determine the equilibrium relative wage and price structure along with the efficient geographic pattern of specialization. Assumptions about technology are specified first. Then we deal with demand. Last, we construct the equilibrium and explore some of its properties. Throughout this section we assume zero transport costs and no other impediments to trade.

Technology and Efficient Geographic Specialization

The many-commodity Ricardian model assumes constant unit labor requirements $(a_1, \ldots, a_n)$ and $(a_1^*, \ldots, a_n^*)$ for the n commodities that can be produced in the home and foreign countries, respectively. The commodities are conveniently indexed so that relative unit labor requirements are ranked in order of diminishing home country comparative advantage,

$$\frac{a_1^*}{a_1} > \cdots > \cdots > \frac{a_i^*}{a_i} > \cdots > \frac{a_n^*}{a_n},$$

where an asterisk denotes the foreign country.

In working with a continuum of goods, we similarly index commodities on an interval, say $[0, 1]$, in accordance with diminishing home country comparative advantage. A commodity z is associated with each point on the interval, and for each commodity there are unit labor requirements in the two countries, $a(z)$ and $a^*(z)$, with relative unit labor requirement given by

$$A(z) \equiv \frac{a^*(z)}{a(z)}, \quad A'(z) < 0. \tag{1}$$

The relative unit labor requirement function in (1) is by strong assumption continuous, and by construction (ranking or indexing of goods), decreasing in z. The function $A(z)$ is shown in figure 14.1 as the downward sloping schedule.

Consider now the range of commodities produced domestically and those produced abroad, as well as the relative price structure associated with given wages. For that purpose we define as w and w^* the domestic and foreign wages measured in any (common!) unit. The home country will efficiently produce all those commodities for which domestic unit labor costs are less than or equal to foreign unit labor costs. Accordingly, any commodity z will be produced at home if

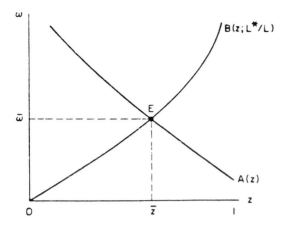

Figure 14.1

$$a(z)w \le a^*(z)w^*. \tag{2}$$

Thus

$$\omega \le A(z), \tag{2'}$$

where (3) defines the parameter ω, fundamental to Ricardian analysis,

$$\omega \equiv \frac{w}{w^*}. \tag{3}$$

This is the ratio of our real wage to theirs (our "double-factoral terms of trade"). It follows that for a given relative wage ω the home country will efficiently produce the range of commodities

$$0 \le z \le \tilde{z}(\omega), \tag{4}$$

where taking (2') with equality defines the borderline commodity z, for which

$$\tilde{z} = A^{-1}(\omega), \tag{5}$$

$A^{-1}(\ )$ being the inverse function of $A(\ )$. By the same argument the foreign country will specialize in the production of commodities in the range

$$\tilde{z}(\omega) \le z \le 1. \tag{4'}$$

The minimum cost condition determines the structure of relative prices. The relative price of a commodity z in terms of any other commodity z', when both goods are produced in the home country, is equal to the ratio of home unit labor costs:

$$\frac{P(z)}{P(z')} = \frac{wa(z)}{wa(z')} = \frac{a(z)}{a(z')}, \quad z \leq \tilde{z}, \quad z' \leq \tilde{z}. \tag{6}$$

The relative price of home produced z in terms of a commodity z'' produced abroad is by contrast

$$\frac{P(z)}{P(z'')} = \frac{wa(z)}{w^*a^*(z'')} = \frac{\omega a(z)}{a^*(z'')}, \quad z < \tilde{z} < z''. \tag{7}$$

In summarizing the supply part of the model, we note that any specified relative real wage is associated with an efficient geographic specialization pattern characterized by the borderline commodity $\tilde{z}(\omega)$ as well as by a relative price structure. (The pattern is "efficient" in the sense that the world is out on, and not inside, its production-possibility frontier.)

Demand

On the demand side, the simplest Mill-Ricardo analysis imposes a strong homothetic structure in the form of J. S. Mill or Cobb-Douglas demand functions that associate with each ith commodity a *constant expenditure share*, b_i. It further assumes *identical* tastes for the two countries or *uniform* homothetic demand.

By analogy with the many-commodity case, which involves budget shares

$$b_i = \frac{P_i C_i}{Y}, \quad b_i = b_i^*,$$

$$\sum_1^n b_i = 1,$$

we prescribe for the continuum case a given $b(z)$ profile:

$$b(z) = \frac{P(z)C(z)}{Y} > 0,$$

$$b(z) = b^*(z), \tag{8}$$

$$\int_0^1 b(z)dz = 1,$$

where Y denotes total income, C demand for and P the price of commodity z.

Next we define the fraction of income spent (anywhere) on those goods in which the home country has a comparative advantage:

$$\vartheta(\tilde{z}) \equiv \int_0^{\tilde{z}} b(z)dz > 0,$$

$$\vartheta'(\tilde{z}) = b(\tilde{z}) > 0,$$

$$(9)$$

where again $(0, \tilde{z})$ denotes the range of commodities for which the home country enjoys a comparative advantage. With a fraction ϑ of each country's income, and therefore of world income, spent on home-produced goods, it follows that the fraction of income spent on foreign-produced commodities is

$$1 - \vartheta(\tilde{z}) \equiv \int_{\tilde{z}}^1 b(z)dz, \quad 0 \le \vartheta(z) \le 1. \tag{9'}$$

Equilibrium Relative Wages and Specialization

To derive the equilibrium relative wage and price structure and the associated pattern of efficient geographic specialization, we turn next to the condition of market equilibrium. Consider the home country's labor market, or equivalently the market for domestically produced commodities. With $\tilde{z}$ denoting the *hypothetical* dividing line between domestic- and foreign-produced commodities, equilibrium in the market for home-produced goods requires that domestic labor income wL equals world spending on domestically produced goods:

$$wL = \vartheta(\tilde{z})(wL + w^*L^*). \tag{10}$$

Equation (10) associates with each $\tilde{z}$ a value of the relative wage w/w^* such that market equilibrium obtains. This schedule is drawn in figure 14.1 as the upward sloping locus and is obtained from (10) by rewriting the equation in the form

$$\omega = \frac{\vartheta(\tilde{z})}{1 - \vartheta(\tilde{z})} \left(\frac{L^*}{L}\right) = B\left(\tilde{z}; \frac{L^*}{L}\right), \tag{10'}$$

where it is apparent from (9) that the schedule starts at zero and approaches infinity as $\tilde{z}$ approaches unity.

To interpret the $B(\ )$ schedule, we note that it is entirely a representation of the demand side, and in that respect it shows that if the range of domestically produced goods were increased at constant relative wages, demand for domestic labor (goods) would increase as the dividing line is shifted—at the same time that demand for foreign labor (goods) would decline.[1] A rise in the domestic relative wage would then be required to equate the demand for domestic labor to the existing supply.

An alternative interpretation of the $B(\ )$ schedule as the locus of trade balance equilibria uses the fact that (10) can be written in the balance-of-trade form:

$$[1 - \vartheta(\tilde{z})]wL = \vartheta(\tilde{z})w^*L^*. \qquad (10'')$$

This states that equilibrium in the trade balance means imports are equal in value to exports. On this interpretation, the $B(\ )$ schedule is upward sloping because an increase in the range of commodities hypothetically produced at home at constant relative wages lowers our imports and raises our exports. The resulting trade imbalance would have to be corrected by an increase in our relative wage that would raise our import demand for goods and reduce our exports, and thus restore balance.

The next step is to combine the demand side of the economy with the condition of efficient specialization as represented in equation (5), which specifies the competitive margin as a function of the relative wage. Substituting (5) in (10') yields as a solution the unique relative wage $\bar{\omega}$, at which the world is efficiently specialized, is in balanced trade, and is at full employment with all markets clearing:

$$\bar{\omega} = A(\bar{z}) = B\left(\bar{z}; \frac{L^*}{L}\right). \qquad (11)$$

The equilibrium relative wage defined in (11) is represented in figure 14.1 at the intersection of the $A(\ )$ and $B(\ )$ schedules.[2] Commodity $\bar{z}$ denotes the equilibrium borderline of comparative advantage between commodities produced and exported by the home country $(0 \leq z \leq \bar{z})$, and those commodities produced and exported by the foreign country $(\bar{z} \leq z \leq 1)$.

Among the characteristics of the equilibrium we note that the equilibrium relative wages and specialization pattern are determined by technology, tastes, and relative size (as measured by the relative labor force).[3] The relative price structure associated with the equilibrium at point E is defined by equations (6) and (7) once (11) has defined the relative wage $\bar{\omega}$ and the equilibrium specialization pattern $\bar{z}(\bar{\omega})$.

The equilibrium levels of production, $Q(z)$ and $Q^*(z)$, and employment in each industry, $L(z)$ and $L^*(z)$, can be recovered from the demand structure and unit labor requirements once the comparative advantage pattern has been determined.

We note that with identical homothetic tastes across countries and no distortions, the relative wage $\bar{\omega}$ is a measure of the well-being of the representative person-laborer at home relative to the well-being of the representative foreign laborer.

14.2 Comparative Statics

The unique real equilibrium in figure 14.1 is determined jointly by tastes, technology, and relative size, L^*/L. We can now exploit figure 14.1 to examine simple comparative static questions.

Relative Size

Consider first the effect of an increase in the relative size of the rest of the world. An increase in L^*/L by (10) shifts the $B(\ )$ trade balance equilibrium schedule upward in proportion to the change in relative size and must, therefore, raise the equilibrium relative wage at home and reduce the range of commodities produced domestically. It is apparent from figure 14.2 that the domestic relative wage increases *proportionally less* than the decline in domestic relative size.

The rise in equilibrium relative wages due to a change in relative size can be thought of in the following manner. At the initial equilibrium, the

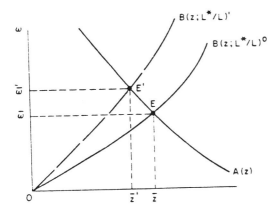

Figure 14.2

increase in the foreign relative labor force would create an excess supply of labor abroad and an excess demand for labor at home—or, correspondingly, a trade surplus for the home country. The resulting increase in domestic relative wages serves to eliminate the trade surplus while at the same time raising relative unit labor costs at home. The increase in domestic relative unit labor costs in turn implies a loss of comparative advantage in marginal industries and thus a needed reduction in the range of commodities produced domestically.

The welfare implications of the change in relative size take the form of an unambiguous improvement in the home country's real income and (under Cobb-Douglas demand) a reduction in real income per head abroad. We observe too that from the definition of the home country's share in world income and (10), we have

$$\frac{wL}{wL + w^*L^*} = \vartheta(\bar{z}).$$
(12)

It is apparent, as noted earlier, that a reduction in domestic relative size in raising the domestic relative wage (thereby reducing the range of commodities produced domestically) must under our Cobb-Douglas demand assumptions lower the home country's share in total world income and spending—even though our per capita income rises.

Technical Progress

To begin with, we are concerned with the effects of uniform technical progress. By equation (1), a uniform proportional reduction in foreign unit labor requirements implies a reduction in $a^*(z)$ and therefore a proportional downward shift of the $A(z)$ schedule in figure 14.1. At the initial relative wage $\bar{\omega}$, the loss of our comparative advantage due to a reduction in foreign unit labor costs will imply a loss of some industries in the home country and a corresponding trade deficit. The resulting induced decline in the equilibrium relative wage serves to restore trade balance equilibrium, and to offset in part our decline in comparative advantage.

The net effect is therefore a reduction in domestic relative wages, which must fall proportionally short of the decline in relative unit labor requirements abroad. The home country's terms of trade therefore improve as can be noted by using (7) for any two commodities z and z'', respectively, produced at home and abroad:

$$\hat{P}(z) - \hat{P}(z'') = \hat{\omega} - \hat{a}^*(z'') > 0,$$
(13)

where a ^ denotes a proportional change. Domestic real income increases, as does foreign real income.[4] The range of goods produced domestically declines since domestic labor, in efficiency units, is now relatively more scarce.

An alternative form of technical progress that can be studied is the international transfer of the least cost technology. Such transfers reduce the discrepancies in relative unit labor requirements—by lowering them for each z in the relatively less efficient country—and therefore flatten the $A(z)$ schedule in figure 14.1. It can be shown that such harmonization of technology must benefit the innovating low-wage country, and that it may reduce real income in the high-wage country whose technology comes to be adopted. In fact, the high-wage country must lose if harmonization is complete so that relative unit labor requirements now become identical across countries and all our consumer's surplus from international trade vanishes.[5]

Demand Shifts

The case with a continuum of commodities requires a careful definition of a demand shift. For our purposes it is sufficient to ask: What is the effect of a shift from high z commodities toward low z commodities? It is apparent from figure 14.2 that such a shift will cause the trade balance equilibrium schedule $B(\ )$ to shift up and to the left. It follows that the equilibrium domestic relative wage will rise while the range of commodities produced by the home country declines. Domestic labor is allocated to a narrower range of commodities that are consumed with higher density, whereas foreign labor is spread more thinly across a larger range of goods.

Welfare changes cannot be identified in this instance because tastes themselves have changed. It is true that domestic relative income rises along with the relative wage. Further we note that since $\bar{\omega}$ rises, the relative well-being of home labor to foreign labor (reckoned at the new tastes) is greater than was our laborers' relative well-being (reckoned at the old tastes).

Unilateral Transfers

Suppose foreigners make a continual unilateral transfer to us. With uniform homothetic tastes and no impediments to trade, neither curve is shifted by the transfer since we spend the transfer *exactly* as foreigners would have spent it but for the transfer. The new equilibrium involves a recurring trade deficit for us, equal to the transfer, but there is no change in the terms of trade. As Bertil Ohlin argued against John Maynard Keynes, here is a case where full equilibration takes place solely as a result of the spending transfers. When we introduce nontraded goods later, Ohlin's presumption will be found to require detailed qualifications, as it also would if tastes differed geographically.

14.3 Extensions of the Real Model

Extensions of the real model taken up in this section concern nontraded goods, tariffs, and transport costs. The purpose of this section is twofold. First we establish how the exogenous introduction of nontraded goods qualifies the preceding analysis. Next we turn to a particular specification of tariffs and transport costs to establish an equilibrium range of endogenously determined nontraded goods as part of the equilibrium solution of the model. Transfers are then shown to affect the equilibrium relative price structure and the range of goods traded.

Nontraded Goods

To introduce nontraded goods into the analysis, we assume that a fraction k of income is everywhere spent on internationally traded goods, and a fraction $(1 - k)$ is spent in each country on nontraded commodities. With $b(z)$ continuing to denote expenditure densities for traded goods, we have accordingly

$$k \equiv \int_0^1 b(z)dz < 1, \tag{14}$$

where z denotes traded goods.[6] As before the fraction of income spent on domestically exportable commodities is $\vartheta(z)$, except that ϑ now reaches a maximum value of $\vartheta(1) = k$.

Equation (1) remains valid for traded goods, but the trade balance equilibrium condition in $(10'')$ must now be modified to

$$[1 - \vartheta(\bar{z}) - (1 - k)]wL = \vartheta(\bar{z})w^*L^*, \tag{15}$$

since domestic spending on imports is equal to income less spending on *all* domestically produced goods, including nontraded commodities. Equation (15) can be rewritten as

$$\omega = \frac{\vartheta(\bar{z})}{k - \vartheta(\bar{z})}\left(\frac{L^*}{L}\right),$$ (15')

where k is a constant and therefore independent of the relative wage structure.

We note that (15') together with (5) determines the equilibrium relative wage and efficient geographic specialization $(\bar{\omega}, \bar{z})$. Further it is apparent that (15') has exactly the same properties as (10') and that accordingly a construction of equilibrium like that in figure 14.1 remains appropriate. The equilibrium relative wage again depends on relative size, technology, and demand conditions. In this case demand conditions explicitly include the fraction of income spent on traded goods:

$$\bar{\omega} = \frac{\vartheta(\bar{z})}{k - \vartheta(\bar{z})}\left(\frac{L^*}{L}\right) = A(\bar{z}).$$ (11')

This nicely generalizes our previous equilibrium of (11) to handle exogenously given nontraded goods.[7]

Two applications of the extended model highlight the special aspects newly introduced by nontraded goods. First consider a shift in demand (in each country) toward *nontraded* goods. To determine the effects on the equilibrium relative wage, we have to establish whether this shift is at the expense of high or low z commodities. In the former case the home country's relative wage increases, whereas in the latter case it declines. If the shift in demand in each country is uniform so that $b(z)$ is reduced in the same proportion for all z in both countries, then the relative wage remains unchanged.

Consider next a transfer received by the home country in the amount T measured in terms of foreign labor. As is well known, and already shown, with identical homothetic tastes and *no* nontraded goods, a transfer leaves the terms of trade unaffected. In the present case, however, the condition for balanced trade, inclusive of transfers, becomes

$$T = (k - \vartheta)[\omega L + T] - \vartheta[L^* - T]$$ (16)

or, in equilibrium,

$$\bar{\omega} = \frac{1 - k}{k - \vartheta(\bar{z})}\left(\frac{T}{L}\right) + \frac{\vartheta(\bar{z})}{k - \vartheta(\bar{z})}\left(\frac{L^*}{L}\right).$$ (16')

It is apparent from (16') that a transfer receipt by the home country causes the trade balance equilibrium schedule in figure 14.1 to shift upward at each level of z. Accordingly, the equilibrium domestic relative wage increases and the range of commodities produced domestically is reduced. The first step in achieving this result is that at the initial relative wage only a fraction of the transfer is spent on imports in the home country, while foreign demand for domestic goods similarly declines only by a fraction of their reduced income. The resulting surplus for the home country has to be eliminated by, second, an increase in the domestic relative wage and a corresponding improvement in the home country's terms of trade.[8]

The analysis of nontraded goods therefore confirms in a Ricardian model the "orthodox" presumption with respect to the terms of trade effects of transfers.[9]

Transport Costs: Endogenous Equilibrium for Nontraded Goods

The notion that transport costs give rise to a range of commodities that are nontraded is established in the literature and is particularly well stated by Haberler (1937). In contrast with the previous section we shall now endogenously determine the range of nontraded commodities as part of the equilibrium. We assume, following the "iceberg" model of Samuelson (1954), that transport costs take the form of "shrinkage" in transit so that a fraction $g(z)$ of commodity z shipped actually arrives. We further impose the assumption that $g = g(z)$ is identical for all commodities and the same for shipments in either direction.

The home country will produce commodities for which domestic unit labor cost falls short of foreign unit labor costs adjusted for shrinkage, and we modify (2′) accordingly:

$$wa(z) \leq \left(\frac{1}{g}\right) w^* a^*(z), \tag{17}$$

or

$$\omega \leq \frac{A(z)}{g}.$$

Similarly the foreign country produces commodities for which foreign unit labor cost falls short of adjusted unit labor costs of delivered imports:

$$w^* a^*(z) \leq \left(\frac{1}{g}\right) wa(z), \tag{18}$$

or

$$A(z)g \leq \omega.$$

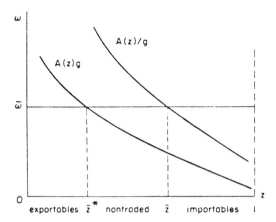

Figure 14.3

In figure 14.3 we show the adjusted relative unit labor requirement schedules $A(z)/g$ and $A(z)g$. It is apparent from (17) and (18) that for any given
relative wage the home country produces and exports commodities to the
left of the $A(z)g$ schedule, both countries produce as nontraded goods
commodities in the intermediate range, and the foreign country produces
and exports commodities in the range to the right of $A(z)/g$.

To determine the equilibrium relative wage, we turn to the trade balance equilibrium condition in (19)—together with (20) and (21)—which is
modified to take account of the endogenous range of nontraded goods:

$$(1 - \lambda)wL = (1 - \lambda^*)w^*L^*. \tag{19}$$

The variable λ is the fraction of home country income spent on our
domestically (or home) produced goods—exportables and nontraded—
and λ^* is the share of foreigners' income spent on goods they produce.
Both λ and λ^* are endogenously determined because the range of goods
produced in each country depends on the relative wages:

$$\lambda(g\omega) \equiv \int_0^{\bar{z}} b(z)dz, \quad \lambda'(g\omega) < 0,$$

$$\lambda^*\left(\frac{\omega}{g}\right) \equiv \int_{\bar{z}}^1 b(z)dz, \quad \lambda^{*\prime}\left(\frac{\omega}{g}\right) > 0. \tag{20}$$

The dependence of $\lambda(\ )$ and $\lambda^*(\ )$ on the variables specified in (20) and the
respective derivatives follow from (21) below.

The limits of integration $\bar{z}$ and $\bar{z}^*$ are derived from the conditions for efficient production in (17) and (18) by imposing equalities and so defining the borderline commodities. Thus in figure 14.3, $\bar{z}$ is the borderline between domestic nontraded goods and imports for the home country, and $\bar{z}^*$ denotes the borderline betwen foreign nontraded goods and the home country's exports:

$$\bar{z}^* = A^{-1}\left(\frac{\omega}{g}\right), \quad \frac{d\bar{z}^*}{d(\omega/g)} < 0,$$

$$\bar{z} = A^{-1}(g\omega), \quad \frac{d\bar{z}}{d(g\omega)} < 0. \tag{21}$$

Of course, equilibrium $\bar{z}$ and $\bar{z}^*$ are yet to be determined by the interaction of technology and demand conditions.

From (21) an increase in the relative wage reduces the range of commodities domestically produced and therefore raises the fraction of income spent on imports. Abroad the converse holds. An increase in the domestic relative wage increases the range of goods produced abroad and therefore reduces the fraction of income spent on imports. It follows that we can solve

$$\bar{\omega} = \frac{1 - \lambda^*(\bar{\omega}/g)}{1 - \lambda(g\bar{\omega})}\left(\frac{L^*}{L}\right)$$

$$\equiv \varphi(\bar{\omega}; \frac{L^*}{L}, g), \quad \frac{\partial\varphi}{\partial\bar{\omega}} < 0, \tag{19'}$$

for the unique equilibrium relative wage as a function of relative size and transport costs:

$$\bar{\omega} = \bar{\omega}\left(\frac{L^*}{L}, g\right). \tag{22}$$

Because (19')'s right-hand side declines as $\bar{\omega}$ rises, a rise in L^*/L must still raise $\bar{\omega}$; a rise in g can shift $\bar{\omega}$ in either direction, depending on the $B(z)$ and $A(z)$ profiles.

The equilibrium relative wage in (22), taken in conjunction with (21), determines the equilibrium geographic production pattern, $\bar{z}$ and $\bar{z}^*$. Since the range of nontraded goods $\bar{z}^* \leq z \leq \bar{z}$ depends in this formulation on the equilibrium relative wage, it is obvious that shifts in given parameters will shift the range of nontraded commodities. Thus a transfer that raises the equilibrium relative wage at home causes previously exported commodities to become nontraded, and previously nontraded commodities to become importables.

Tariffs

We consider next the case of zero transport cost but where each country levies a uniform tariff on imports at respective rates t and t^*, with proceeds rebated in lump-sum form. This case, too, leads to cost barriers to importing, and to a range of commodities that are not traded, with the boundaries defined by

$$\bar{z} = A^{-1}\left(\frac{\omega}{1 + t}\right) \tag{23}$$

and

$$\bar{z}^* = A^{-1}(\omega(1 + t^*)).$$

From (23) it is apparent that the presence of tariffs in either or both countries must give rise to nontraded goods because in this case $\bar{z} \neq \bar{z}^*$.

The trade balance equilibrium condition at international prices becomes, in place of (19),

$$(1 - \lambda)\frac{Y}{1 + t} = (1 - \lambda^*)\frac{Y^*}{1 + t^*}, \tag{24}$$

where Y and Y^* denote incomes inclusive of lump-sum tariff rebates. Using the fact that rebates are equal to the tariff rate times the fraction of income spent on imports, we arrive at the trade balance equilibrium condition in the form:[10]

$$\omega = \left(\frac{1 - \lambda^*}{1 - \lambda}\right)\left(\frac{1 + t\lambda}{1 + t^*\lambda^*}\right)\left(\frac{L^*}{L}\right), \tag{25}$$

where λ and λ^* are functions of (ω, t, t^*). The implicit relations (25) can be solved for the equilibrium relative wage as a function of relative size and the tariff structure:

$$\bar{\omega} = \bar{\omega}\left(\frac{L^*}{L}, t, t^*\right). \tag{26}$$

From (26) and (23) it is apparent now that the range of nontraded goods will be a function of both tariff rates. It is readily shown that an increase in the tariff improves the imposing country's relative wage and terms of trade. Furthermore, as is well known, when all countries but one are free traders, then one country can always improve its own welfare by imposing a tariff that is not too large.

A further question suggested by (26) concerns the effect of a uniform increase in world tariffs. Starting from zero, a small uniform increase in tariffs raises the relative wage of the country whose commodities command the larger share in world spending. This result occurs for two reasons. First, at the initial relative wage a larger share of spending out of tariff rebates falls on the goods of the country commanding a larger share in world demand. Second, the tariff induces new nontraded goods and therefore increases net demand for the borderline commodity of the country whose residents have the larger income, or equivalently, the larger share in world income.

If countries are of equal size as measured by the share in world income, such a uniform tariff increase has zero effect on relative wages, but of course reduces well-being in both places. Multilateral tariff increases, in this case, unnecessarily create some nontraded goods, and artificially raise the relative price of importables in terms of domestically produced commodities in each country exactly in proportion to the tariff.

14.4 Money, Wages, and Exchange Rates

In this section we extend the discussion of the Ricardian model to deal with monetary aspects of trade. Specifically we shall be interested in the determination of exchange rates in a flexible rate system, in the process of adjustment to trade imbalance under fixed rates, and in the role of wage stickiness. The purpose of the extension is to integrate real and monetary aspects of trade.

Flexible Exchange Rates

The barter analysis of the preceding sections is readily extended to a world of flexible exchange rates and flexible money wages. Assume a given nominal quantity of money in each country, M and M^*, respectively. Further, in accordance with the classical Quantity Theory, assume constant expenditure velocities V and V^*.[11] A flexible exchange rate, and our stipulating the absence of nonmonetary international asset flows, will ensure trade balance equilibrium and therefore the equality of income and spending in each country. The nominal money supplies and velocities determine nominal income in each country:

$$WL = MV \quad \text{and} \quad W^*L^* = M^*V^* \tag{27}$$

where W and W^* (now in capital letters) denote domestic and foreign money wages in terms of the respective currencies. Further, defining the exchange rate e as the domestic currency price of foreign exchange, the foreign wage measured in terms of domestic currency is eW^*, and the relative wage therefore is $\omega \equiv W/eW^*$.

From the determination of the equilibrium real wage ratio $\bar{\omega}$ by our earlier "real" relations, we can now find an expression for the equilibrium exchange rates:

$$\bar{e} = \left(\frac{1}{\bar{\omega}}\right)\left(\frac{\overline{W}}{\overline{W}^*}\right) = \left(\frac{1}{\bar{\omega}}\right)\left(\frac{MV}{M^*V^*}\right)\left(\frac{L^*}{L}\right), \tag{28}$$

where $(27')$ defines equilibrium money wages:

$$\overline{W} = \frac{MV}{L} \tag{27'}$$

and

$$\overline{W}^* = \frac{M^*V^*}{L^*}.$$

In this simple structure and with wage flexibility, we can keep separate the determinants of all equilibrium real variables from all monetary considerations. Monetary changes or velocity changes in one country will be reflected in equiproportionate changes in prices in that country and in the exchange rate in the fashion of the neutral-money Quantity Theory. However, a real disturbance, as (28) shows, definitely does have repercussions on the nominal exchange rate as well as on the real equilibrium.

Using the results of section 14.2, we see that an increase in the foreign relative labor force causes, under flexible exchange rates and given $\overline{M}$ and $\overline{M}^*$, a depreciation in the home country's exchange rate as does uniform technical progress abroad. A shift in real demand toward foreign goods likewise leads to a depreciation of the exchange rate as well as to a reduction in real $\bar{\omega}$. A rise in foreign tariffs will also cause our currency to depreciate. Each of these real shifts is assumed to take place while (M, M^*) are unchanged and on the simplifying proviso that real income changes leave V and V^* unchanged.

Fixed Exchange Rates

In the fixed exchange rates case we assume currencies are fully convertible at a parity pegged by the monetary authorities. In the absence of capital flows and sterilization policy, a trade imbalance is reflected in monetary flows. In the simplest metal money model, the world money supply is redistributed toward the surplus country at precisely the rate of the trade surplus. We assume that the world money supply is given and equal to $\bar{G}$, measured in terms of domestic currency. The rate of increase of the domestic quantity of money is therefore equal to the reduction in foreign money, valued at the fixed exchange rate $\bar{e}$:

$$\dot{M} = -\bar{e}\dot{M}^*, \tag{29}$$

where $\dot{M} \equiv dM/dt$.

For a fixed rate world we have to determine in addition to the real variables, $\bar{\omega}$ and $\bar{z}$, the levels of money wages, W and W^*, as well as the equilibrium balance of payments associated with each short-run equilibrium. In the long run the balance of payments will be zero as money ends up redistributed internationally to the point where income equals spending in each country. In the short run an initial misallocation of money balances implies a discrepancy between income and spending and an associated trade imbalance. To characterize the preferred rate of adjustment of cash balances in the simplest and most manageable way, we assume that spending by each country is proportional to money holdings.[12] On the further simplifying assumption that velocities are equal in each country, $V = V^*$,[13] world spending is equal to

$$VM + eV^*M^* \equiv V\bar{G}. \tag{30}$$

For the tastes and technology specified in section 14.1, world spending on domestically produced goods is given by

$$V\bar{G} \int_0^{\bar{z}} b(z)dz \equiv \vartheta(\omega)V\bar{G},$$
$$\bar{z} = A^{-1}(\omega). \tag{31}$$

In equilibrium, world spending on our goods must equal the value of our full-employment income WL:

$$WL = \vartheta(\omega)V\bar{G}. \tag{32}$$

Equilibrium requires, too, that world spending on foreign goods equals the value of foreign full-employment income:

$$\bar{e}W^*L^* = [1 - \vartheta(\omega)]V\bar{G}. \tag{33}$$

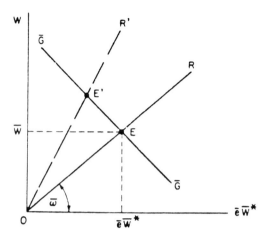

Figure 14.4

Equations (32) and (33) express what would seem to be the *joint* determination of real and monetary variables. But, in fact, we could have taken the shortcut of recognizing that the real equilibrium is precisely that of the barter analysis developed in section 14.1. Dividing (32) by (33) and substituting from (11) for the equilibrium relative wage $\bar{\omega}$, we can employ equations (32) and (33) to determine money wage levels.

The equilibrium determined by equations (32) and (33) can be analyzed in terms of figure 14.4. The figure emphasizes the separation of real and monetary aspects of the equilibrium under our assumptions of traded goods only, and no distribution effects. From the ratio of (32) and (33) we obtain the equilibrium relative wage $\bar{\omega}$ as a function of tastes and technology solely from the barter model. This equilibrium relative wage is plotted as the ray OR in figure 14.4.

The equality of world income and spending

$$WL + \bar{e}W^*L^* = V\bar{G} \qquad (30')$$

is shown as the downward sloping straight line $\bar{G}\bar{G}$, which is drawn for given velocity, world quantity of money, and labor forces. Point E is the equilibrium where relative prices and the level of wages and prices are such that all markets clear. At a level of wages and prices higher than point E, there would be a world excess supply of goods, and conversely at points below E.

Figure 14.4 immediately shows some comparative static results. Thus a doubling of both countries' labor forces, from the analysis of the barter model, will leave the relative wage unaffected but will double world output. Given unchanged nominal spending $V\overline{G}$, wages and prices will have to halve. This would be shown by a parallel shift of the $\overline{G}\overline{G}$ schedule halfway toward the origin. A shift in demand toward the home country's output by contrast would rotate the OR ray to a position like OR' since it raises our relative wage. The ensuing monetary adjustment is then an increase in our money wage and money income and a decline in foreign wages, prices, and incomes (point E').

The real and nominal equilibrium at point E in figure 14.4 is independent of the short- and long-run distribution of the world quantity of money. The independence of the real equilibrium derives from the uniform homothetic tastes. The independence of the nominal equilibrium is implied by identical velocities. What does, however, depend on the short-run distribution of world money is the transition period's balance of payments. As in the absorption approach of Sidney Alexander (1952), we know this: when goods markets clear, the trade surplus or balance of payments $\dot{M}$ of the home country is equal to the excess of income over spending, or

$$\dot{M} = \overline{W}L - VM. \tag{34}$$

With the nominal wage independent of the distribution of world money, equation (34) therefore implies that the trade balance monotonically converges to equilibrium at a rate proportional to the discrepancy from long-run equilibrium:[14]

$$\dot{M} = V(\overline{M} - M); \quad \overline{M} = \vartheta(\overline{\omega})\overline{G}. \tag{34'}$$

The assumptions of this section were designed to render inoperative most of the traditional mechanisms discussed as part of the adjustment process: changes in the terms of trade, in home and/or foreign price levels, in relative prices of traded and nontraded goods (there being none of the latter), in double factoral terms of trade, and any discrepancies in the price of the same commodity between countries. The features of the adjustment process of this section rely on (1) identical, constant expenditure velocities, (2) uniform-homothetic demand, and (3) the absence of trade impediments. If velocities were constant but differed between countries, the absolute *levels* of money wages and prices, though not *relative* wages or prices, would depend on the world distribution of money. Relaxation of the uniform-homothetic taste assumption would make equilibrium relative prices a function of the distributions of spending. Finally, the presence of nontraded goods would, together with Ricardo's technology, provide valid justification for some of the behavior of relative prices and price levels frequently asserted in the literature; this behavior is studied in more detail in the next section.

The Price-Specie Flow Mechanism under More General Conditions

We now discuss the adjustment process to monetary disequilibrium and enquire into the price effects associated with a redistribution of the world money supply when there are nontraded goods. Common versions of the Hume price-specie flow mechanism usually involve the argument that in the adjustment process, prices decline along with the money stock in the deficit country, while both rise in the surplus country. There is usually, too, an implication that the deficit country's terms of trade will necessarily worsen in the adjustment process and indeed have to do so if the adjustment is to be successful.

The preceding discussion demonstrated that the redistribution of money associated with monetary imbalance need have no effects on real variables (production, terms of trade, etc.) or on nominal variables other than the money stock and spending. Although this is clearly a very special case, it does serve as a bench-mark since it establishes that the monetary adjustment process would be effective even in a one-commodity world.

To approach the traditional view of the adjustment process more clearly and to provide formal support for that view, we consider an extension to the monetary realm of our previous model involving nontraded goods. We return to the assumption that a fraction $(1 - k)$ of spending in each country falls on nontraded goods, and accordingly equations (32) and (33) become

$$WL = \vartheta(\omega)V\overline{G} + (1 - k)\gamma V\overline{G}, \quad \gamma \equiv \frac{M}{\overline{G}}, \tag{32'}$$

$$\overline{e}W^*L^* = [k - \vartheta(\omega)]V\overline{G} + (1 - \gamma)(1 - k)V\overline{G}. \tag{33'}$$

These hold both in final equilibrium and in transient equilibrium where specie is flowing. Equations (32') and (33') imply that the equilibrium relative wage does depend on the distribution of the world money supply. Solving these equations for the equilibrium relative wage we have

$$\overline{\omega} = \overline{\omega}(\gamma), \quad \frac{\partial \overline{\omega}}{\partial \gamma} > 0. \tag{35}$$

An increase in the home country's initial share in the world money supply γ raises our relative wage.

Using this extended framework, we can draw on the analysis of the transfer problem in section 14.2 to examine the adjustment that follows an initial distribution of world money between the two countries that differs from the long-run equilibrium distribution.

Suppose our M is initially excessive, say from a gold discovery here. Assume also that the gold discovery occurred when the world was in long-run equilibrium with the previous world money stock. As a result of our excess M, we spend more than our earnings, incurring a balance-of-payments deficit equal to the rate at which our M is flowing out. In effect, the foreign economy is making us a real transfer to offset our deficit. As seen earlier, we, the deficit country, are devoting some of our excess spending to nontraded goods, shifting some of our resources to their production at the expense of our previous exports. We not only export fewer types of goods, but also import more types, and import more of each ($\bar{\omega}$ rises and $\bar{z}$ falls).

During the transition, while the real transfer corresponding to our deficit is taking place, our terms of trade are more favorable than in the long-run state. The new gold raises both their W^* and our W, but in addition, our W is up relative to their W^*. Therefore the price level of goods we continue to produce is up relative to the price level of goods they continue to produce. This is true both for our nontraded goods and for our exportables. The prices of goods we produce rise relative to the prices of goods they produce in proportion to the change in relative wages.

Thus the price levels in the two countries have been changed differentially by the specie flow and implied real transfer. But that does not mean that any traded good ever sells for different prices in two places. In fact, the divergence in weighted average (consumer) price levels is due to nontraded goods. The price level will rise in the gold-discovering country relative to the other country the greater is the share of nontraded goods in expenditure, $1 - k$. It is a bit meaningless to say, "What accomplished the adjustment is the relative movements of price levels for nontraded goods in the two countries," since we have seen that the adjustment can and will be made even when there are no such nontraded goods. It is meaningful to say, "The fact that people want to direct some of their expenditure to nontraded goods makes it necessary for resources to shift in and out of them as a result of a real transfer, and such resource shifts take place only because the terms of trade (double-factoral and for traded goods) do shift in the indicated way."

The adjustment process to a monetary disturbance is stable in the sense that the system converges to a long-run equilibrium distribution of money with balanced trade. To appreciate that point, we supplement equations

(32′) and (33′) with (34) which continues to describe the monetary adjustment process. We note, however, that now W and W^* are endogenous variables whose levels in the short run do depend on the distribution of the world money supply. A redistribution of money toward the home country would raise our spending and demand for goods, and reduce foreign spending and demand. As before, spending changes for traded goods offset each other precisely so that the net effect is an increase in demand for nontraded goods at home and a decline abroad. As a consequence our wages will rise and foreign wages decline. Therefore, starting from full equilibrium, a redistribution of money toward the home country will create a deficit equal to

$$\frac{d\dot{M}}{dM} = -V(1 - \delta), \quad 0 \leqslant \delta < 1, \tag{36}$$

where δ is the elasticity of our nominal wages with respect to the quantity of money and is less than unity.[15] Equation (36) implies that the price-specie flow mechanism is stable.

It is interesting to observe in this context that the presence of nontraded goods in fact *slows down* the adjustment process by comparison with a world of only traded goods (contrary to J. Laurence Laughlin's turn of the century worries). As we saw before, with all goods freely tradable, wages are independent of the distribution of money, and accordingly $\delta = 0$. Further we observe that the speed of adjustment depends on the relative size of countries. Thus the more equal countries are in terms of size, the slower tends to be the adjustment process.

In concluding this section, we note that nontraded goods (and/or localized demand) are essential to the correctness of traditional insistence that the adjustment process necessarily entails absolute and relative price, wage, and income movements. They are, of course, in no way essential to the existence of a stable adjustment process, nor is there at any time a need for a discrepancy of prices of the same commodity across countries in either case.[16]

A final remark concerns the adjustment to real disturbances such as demand shifts or technical progress. It is certainly true that whether the exchange rate is fixed or flexible, real adjustment will have to take place and cannot be avoided by choice of an exchange rate regime. So long as wages and prices are flexible, it is quite false to think that fixed parities "put the whole economy through the wringer of adjustment," whereas in floating rate regimes "only the export and import industries have to make the real adjustment." It is true, however, that once we depart from flexible

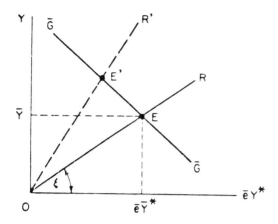

Figure 14.5

wages and prices there may well be a preference for one exchange rate regime over another. The next section is devoted to that question.

Sticky Money Wages

The last question we address in this section concerns the implications of sticky money wages. For a given world money supply, *downward* stickiness of money wages implies the possibility of unemployment. We assume upward flexibility in wages, once full employment is attained.

We start with a fixed exchange rate, $\bar{e}$. The relation between wages and the world quantity of money is brought out in figure 14.5. Denote employment levels in each country, as opposed to the labor force, by the new symbols $\bar{L}$ and $\bar{L}^*$, respectively; denote nominal incomes by Y and Y^*. The equality of world income and spending is again shown by the $\bar{G}\bar{G}$ schedule, the equation of which now is

$$V\bar{G} = Y + \bar{e}Y^* \equiv \overline{W}\bar{L} + \bar{e}\overline{W}^*\bar{L}^*, \tag{37}$$

where $\overline{W}$ and $\overline{W}^*$ are the fixed money wages set at too high sticky levels. The schedule is drawn for given money wages, a given world quantity of money, and a pegged parity for $\bar{e}$. The ray OR now is predetermined by the given sticky relative wage $\bar{\omega} = \overline{W}/\bar{e}\overline{W}^*$. From equations (32) and (33) the ratio of money incomes $Y/\bar{e}Y^*$ is just a function of the relative wage now given exogenously by rigid money wages and the exchange rate:

$$\frac{Y}{\bar{e}Y^*} = \frac{\vartheta(\omega)}{1 - \vartheta(\omega)} \equiv \zeta\left(\frac{\overline{W}}{\bar{e}\overline{W}^*}\right), \quad \zeta'(\omega) < 0. \tag{38}$$

Point E is the nominal equilibrium where, by assumption, the world quantity of money is insufficient relative to wage rates to ensure full employment. Although that equilibrium is one with unemployed labor, it is efficient in other respects. Specifically, geographic specialization follows comparative advantage as laid out above, but now labor employed adjusts to sticky wage patterns of specialization.

Employment levels $\bar{L}$ and $\bar{L}^*$ now are determined by (39)

$$\bar{L} = \frac{\bar{Y}}{\bar{W}}, \quad \bar{L}^* = \frac{\bar{e}\,\bar{Y}^*}{\bar{W}^*}, \tag{39}$$

where $\bar{Y}$ and $\bar{Y}^*$ are the equilibrium levels of nominal income determined by equations (37) and (38) or by point E in figure 14.5.

Consider now the impact of a foreign increase in money wages. The effect of the implied reduction in our relative wages and the resulting increase in our relative income are shown in figure 14.5 by the rotation from OR to OR'.

The new equilibrium is at E' where our money income and employment have risen while income and employment decline abroad. Thus an increase in the foreign wage rate, by moving the terms of trade against us, shifts comparative advantage and employment toward the home country. The extent to which the home country benefits from the adverse terms of trade shift in terms of employment will depend on both the substitutability in demand and the elasticity of the $A(z)$ schedule in figure 14.1. We observe, too, that the move from E to E' will bring about a transitory balance-of-payments surplus. Given the initial distribution of money and hence of spending, the foreign decline in income and the increase at home implies that we will spend less than our income and therefore have a trade surplus. This surplus persists until money is redistributed to match the new levels of income at E'.

Next we move to flexible exchange rates. Under flexible rates an increase in the foreign money wage $\bar{W}^*$, given money supplies in each country, will similarly have real repercussion effects on relative prices and employment at home. Now employment in each country is determined by money supplies and prevailing wages:

$$\bar{L} = \frac{V\bar{M}}{\bar{W}}, \quad \bar{L}^* = \frac{V\bar{M}^*}{\bar{W}}. \tag{39'}$$

Given the employment levels thus determined, we know from the analysis of the earlier barter model that there is a unique relative wage at which the trade balance achieves equilibrium. The higher is $\bar{M}^*/\bar{W}^*$, the higher will be employment abroad—and therefore the higher will be our relative wage $\bar{\omega}$. It is thus apparent that an increase in the foreign money wage, $\overline{W}^*$, will reduce employment abroad. Employment declines only in proportion to the increase in wages and thus declines by less than it would under fixed exchange rates when specie is lost abroad.

We saw in the barter model that a reduction in effective foreign labor causes a decline in our relative wage, but that the decline in our relative wage falls proportionately short of the foreign reduction in labor. Now, at the initial exchange rate, the increase in foreign wages reduces our relative wage and their employment in the same proportion. The decline in our relative wage is therefore excessive. Domestic goods are underpriced and the exchange rate appreciates to *partly* offset the gain in cost competitiveness. The net effect is therefore a decline in our relative wage and an appreciation of our exchange rate (a decline in e) that falls short of the foreign increase in wages. Since our terms of trade unambiguously deteriorate without any compensating gain in employment, it must be true that welfare declines at home. Abroad, the loss in employment is offset by a gain in the terms of trade, but there too the net effect is a loss in welfare under our strong Mill-Ricardo assumption.

The adjustment to money wage disturbances under fixed and flexible rates differs in several respects. Under fixed rates employment effects are transmitted, while under flexible rates they are bottled up in the country initiating the disturbance. Under fixed rates the terms of trade move one for one with money wage, while under flexible rates exchange rate movements partly offset increases in the foreign money wage rate.

The difference between fixed and flexible rates in relation to the adjustment process is further brought out by an example of a real disturbance. Consider a shift in world demand toward our goods. Under fixed rates the resulting increase in our relative income will, from (38), move us in figure 14.5 from E to E'. Employment rises at home and falls abroad. Demand shifts are fully reflected in employment changes. Under flexible rates, by contrast, with given wages and money, a demand shift has no impact on employment—as we observe from (39). At the initial exchange rate the demand shift would give rise to an excess demand for our goods and to an excess supply abroad. Domestic income and employment would tend to rise while falling abroad. The resulting trade surplus causes our exchange rate to appreciate until the initial employment levels and therefore trade balance equilibrium are restored. The demand shift is fully absorbed by a change in the terms of trade and a shift in competitive advantage that restores demand for foreign goods and labor.

Real and nominal equilibria are thus seen to be uniquely definable in our continuum model with constant-velocity spending determinants. The difference between sticky and flexible wage rates under fixed exchange rates is understandable as the difference between (a) having the crucial relative wage $\bar{\omega}$ be imposed in the sticky wage case with employment having then to adjust; or (b) having the full employment be imposed and $\bar{\omega}$ having to adjust. Under floating exchange rates, sticky nominal wages impose employment levels in each country and the crucial relative wage $\bar{\omega}$ then adjusts to those employment levels.

14.5 Appendix: Historical Remark

Figure 14.1 seems to be new. G. A. Elliot (1950) gives a somewhat different diagram, one that makes explicit the meaning of Marshall's 1879 "bales" (which, by the way, happen to work only in the two-country constant labor costs case). In terms of the present notations, Elliott plots for the U.S. offer curve the following successive points traced out for all ω on the range $[0, \infty]$: on the vertical axis is plotted our total real imports valued in foreign labor units ("our demand for bales of their labor," so to speak), namely,

$$\int_{\bar{z}}^{1} \left[\frac{P^*(z)}{w^*} \right] C(z)dz = \int_{\bar{z}}^{1} a^*(z)C(z)dz, \tag{A1}$$

and on the horizontal axis, our total real exports valued in home labor units ("our supply of bales of labor to them"), namely,

$$\int_{0}^{\bar{z}} \left[\frac{P(z)}{w} \right] [Q(z) - C(z)]dz = L - \int_{0}^{\bar{z}} a(z)C(z)dz. \tag{A2}$$

It is to be understood that $\bar{z}$ is a function of ω, namely the inverse function $A^{-1}(\omega)$, and also that $C(z)$ are the amounts demanded as a function of our real income L and of the $P(z)/W$ function defined for each, namely $\min [\omega a(z), a^*(z)]$. Because we have a continuum of goods, we avoid Elliott's branches of the offer curve that are segments of various rays through the origin. The reader will discern by symmetry considerations how the foreign offer curve is plotted in the same (L, L^*) quadrant, by varying ω to generate the respective coordinates

$$\left[\int_{0}^{\bar{z}} a(z)C^*(z)dz, \quad L^* - \int_{\bar{z}}^{1} a^*(z)C^*(z)dz \right]. \tag{A3}$$

Our model forces the Elliott-Marshall diagram to generate a *unique* solution under uniform-homothetic demand. Unlike our figure 14.1, the Elliott diagram can handle the general case of nonhomothetic demands in the two countries; but then, as is well known, multiple solutions are possible, some locally stable and some unstable. The price one pays for this generality is that, as Edgeworth observed, the Marshallian curves are the end products of much implicit theorizing, with much that is interesting having taken place offstage.

Notes

Helpful comments from Ronald W. Jones are gratefully acknowledged. Financial support was provided by a Ford Foundation grant to Dornbusch, NSF GS-41428 to Fischer, and NSF 75-04053 to Samuelson.

1. Throughout this chapter we refer to "domestic" goods as commodities produced in the home country rather than to commodities that are nontraded. The latter we call "nontraded" goods.

2. See the appendix for the relation of the diagram to previous analyses.

3. The construction of the $B( )$ schedule relies heavily on the Cobb-Douglas demand structure. If, instead, demand functions were identical across countries and homothetic, an analogous schedule could be constructed. In the general homothetic case, however, a set of relative prices is required at each z to calculate the equivalent of the $B( )$ schedule; the relative prices are those that apply on the $A(\bar{z})$ schedule for that value of z. In this case the independence of the $A( )$ and $B( )$ schedules is obviously lost. In the general homothetic case there is still a unique intersection of the $A( )$ and $B( )$ schedules. For more general nonhomothetic demand structures, it is known that an equilibrium exists; but even in the case of two Ricardian goods there may be *no* unique equilibrium even though there will almost always be a finite number of equilibria. See Gerard Debreu and Stephen Smale. Extensions of our analysis with respect to the demand structure and the number of countries are developed in unpublished work by Charles Wilson.

4. The purchasing power of foreign labor income in terms of domestically produced goods is $w^*L^*/wa(z) = L^*/a(z)\bar{\omega}$ and in terms of foreign goods $L^*/a^*(z)$. The fact that foreigners' real income per head rises is guaranteed by our Cobb-Douglas demand assumption. In the general homothetic case, a balanced reduction in $a^*(z)$ can be immiserizing abroad if the real wage falls strongly in terms of all previously imported goods; however, the balanced drop in $a^*(z)$ in the general homothetic case *always* increases our real wage.

5. Complete equilization of unit labor requirements implies that the $A( )$ schedule is horizontal at the level $\omega = A(z) = 1$. In this case geographic specialization becomes indeterminate and inessential.

6. We can think of the range of nontraded goods as another $[0, 1]$ interval with commodities denoted by x and expenditure fractions on those goods given by $c(x)$. With these definitions we have $\int_0^1 c(x)dx \equiv 1 - k$, a positive fraction.

7. Diagrams much like figures 14.1 and 14.2 again apply: the descending $A(z)$ schedule is as before; and now the new rising schedule looks much as before. As before, a rise in L^*/L and a balanced drop in $a^*(z)$ will raise $\bar{\omega}$ and lower $\bar{z}$.

8. At constant relative wages the current account worsens by $[(1 - k - \vartheta) + \vartheta]dT = (1 - k)dT$ which is less than the transfer, since it is equal to the fraction of income spent on nontraded goods.

9. The pre-Ohlin orthodox view of Keynes, Taussig, Jacob Viner, and other writers is discussed in Viner (1937) and Samuelson (1952, 1954). A recent treatment with nontraded goods is Ronald Jones (1975).

10. Tariff rebates in the home country are equal to $R = (1 - \lambda) Yt/(1 + t)$. With $Y \equiv WL + R$ we therefore have $Y = WL(1 + t)/(1 + \lambda t)$ as an expression for income inclusive of transfers. From equations (20) and (23) we have $\lambda = \lambda[\omega/(1 + t)]$ and $\lambda^* = \lambda^*(\omega(1 + t^*)]$, having substituted the tariff instead of transport costs as the obstacle to trade.

11. This is a strong assumption since it makes spending independent of income and nonliquid assets even in the short run.

12. The assumption that spending is proportional to cash balances is only one of a number of possible specifications. Conditions for this expenditure function to be optimal are derived in Dornbusch and Michael Mussa. In general, expenditure will depend on both income and cash balances.

13. In the long-run equilibrium, higher V than V^* leaves us with a smaller share of the world money stock than foreigners, but with nominal and real income *shares* in the two countries the same as when $V = V^*$.

14. Suppose $V > V^*$ and our share of the world money supply is initially larger than our equilibrium share. Then, as we lose M, total world nominal income and nominal GNP falls. Always our share of nominal world GNP stays the same under the strong demand assumptions. Total world real output never changes during the transition; only regional consumption shares change. Therefore *both* countries' nominal price and wage levels fall in the transition, but such balanced changes have no real effects on either the transient or the final real equilibrium.

15. The value of δ can be calculated from equations (32') and (33') to be

$$\delta \equiv (1 - k) \frac{\gamma(1 - \gamma)}{\gamma(1 - \gamma) + \vartheta \varepsilon},$$

where ε is the elasticity of the share of our traded goods in world spending, $\varepsilon \equiv -\vartheta'\omega/\vartheta > 0$. The elasticity δ is evaluated at the long-run equilibrium where $\gamma \equiv \vartheta/k$. If $A'(z)$ falls slowly, ε will be large.

16. The continuum Ricardian technology is special in that there can be no range of goods both imported and produced at home. Therefore the cross elasticity of supply between nontraded goods and exports must be greater than the zero cross elasticity between nontraded goods and imports. Consequently, a transfer must shift the terms of trade (for goods and factors) in the stated orthodox way, favorably for the receiver.

References

Alexander, S. 1952. "The Effects of a Devaluation on the Trade Balance." *Int. Monet. Fund Staff Pap.* 2 (April): 263–278.

Chipman, J. S. 1965. "A Survey of International Trade. Part I: The Classical Theory." *Econometrica* 33 (July): 477–519.

Debreu, G. 1970. "Economies with a Finite Set of Equilibria." *Econometrica* 38 (May): 387–392.

Dornbusch, R., and Mussa, M. 1975. "Consumption, Real Balances and the Hoarding Function." *Int. Econ. Rev.* 16 (June): 415–421.

Elliott, G. A. 1950. "The Theory of International Values." *J. Polit. Econ.*, 58 (February): 16–29.

Graham, F. 1923. "The Theory of International Balances Re-examined." *Quart. J. Econ.* 38 (November): 54–86.

Haberler, Gottfried. 1937. *The Theory of International Trade*. London.

Jones, R. W. 1975. "Presumption and the Transfer Problem." *J. Int. Econ.*, 5 (August): 263–274.

Laughlin, James Laurence. 1903. *Principles of Money*. New York.

Mill, John S. 1848. *Principles of Political Economy*. London.

Ricardo, David. 1817. *On the Principles of Political Economy and Taxation*. Edited by Sraffa, P. London, 1951.

Samuelson, P. A. 1952. "The Transfer Problem and Transport Costs: The Terms of Trade When Impediments Are Absent." *Econ. J.* 62 (June): 278–304. Reprinted in Joseph Stiglitz, ed., *Collected Scientific Papers of Paul A. Samuelson*. Vol. 2. Cambridge, Mass., ch. 74.

Samuelson, P. A. 1954. "The Transfer Problem and the Transport Costs. Part II: Analysis of Effects of Trade Impediments." *Econ. J.* 64 (June): 264–289. Reprinted in Joseph Stiglitz, ed., *Collected Scientific Papers of Paul A. Samuelson*. Vol. 2. Cambridge, Mass., ch. 75.

Samuelson, P. A. 1964. "Theoretical Notes on Trade Problems." *Rev. Econ. Statist.* 46 (May): 145–154. Reprinted in Joseph Stiglitz, ed., *Collected Scientific Papers of Paul A. Samuelson*. Vol. 2. Cambridge, Mass., ch. 65.

Smale, S. 1966. "Structurally Stable Systems Are Not Dense." *Amer. J. Math.* 88: 491–496.

Taussig, Frank W. 1927. *International Trade*. New York.

Viner, Jacob. 1937. *Studies in the Theory of International Trade*. New York.

Wilson, C. 1977. "On the General Structure of Ricardian Models with a Continuum of Goods: Applications to Growth, Tariff Theory and Technical Change." Unpublished paper. Univ. Wisconsin-Madison.

15   Tariffs and Nontraded Goods

This chapter discusses the effects of tariffs in a small country that consumes and produces three commodities: exportables, importables and nontraded goods. That subject has been previously studied in two altogether different ways. A general equilibrium approach in a well specified two-country model has been developed by McDougall (1970). An alternative treatment with a strong flavor of partial equilibrium analysis underlies or is implicit in a large body of applied work and policy discussions.[1] The latter approach is typically developed in terms of independent markets for imports and exports with an emphasis on nominal prices, the exchange rate and the trade balance and a de-emphasis on the role of nontraded goods.

The purpose of this chapter is to reinterpret the latter approach as a special case of the general equilibrium model and to demonstrate that the analysis may be conveniently developed in the formal context of the pure theory of trade by reference to relative prices, the budget constraint and the conditions of equilibrium in the nontraded goods market. Such an analysis is useful because it highlights the crucial role of nontraded goods in the analysis and points out the implicit assumptions and theoretical basis that underlie the particular measures of the protective effects of tariffs, their welfare cost and the social cost of foreign exchange that have been developed in this model.

15.1 The Model

The home country consumes and produces both exportables and importables as well as a nontraded good. The country is small so that the relative price of traded goods in the world market is taken as given. Income is assumed to equal expenditure, the tariff proceeds are redistributed via

Originally published in *Journal of International Economics* vol. 7 (May 1974), pp. 177–185.

lump-sum subsidies, and initial distortions are absent. The relative prices of both traded goods in terms of home goods are flexible so as to allow the nontraded goods market to clear.

The formal model may be reduced to the equilibrium condition in the home goods market. The excess demand for nontraded goods, N, is a function of the relative prices of importables and exportables in terms of home goods, P_m and P_e respectively, and real income measured in terms of home goods, I. In equilibrium the excess demand for nontraded goods will be zero:

$$N(P_m, P_e, I) = 0. \tag{1}$$

The domestic relative price of importables in terms of exportables, P_m/P_e, is determined by the given world terms of trade, P^*, and the tariff wedge, $T = (1 + t)$:

$$\frac{P_m}{P_e} = P^* T. \tag{2}$$

To verify that equilibrium in the nontraded goods market implies trade balance equilibrium we consider the budget constraint which states that income equals expenditure or, equivalently, that the value of output plus the tariff proceeds equals expenditure and which may be written in the following manner:

$$P_e(E - P^* M) - N = 0, \tag{3}$$

where M and E denote imports and exports.[2] In this form the budget constraint states that the trade balance surplus, measured in terms of home goods, is identically equal to the excess demand for home goods. It follows that we may study the equilibrium properties of the model in terms of either the equilibrium trade balance or equilibrium in the home goods market.

15.2 The Effects of a Traiff

The effects of a tariff are derived by differentiating the market equilibrium condition in equation (1) and noting that the redistribution of tariff proceeds implies that the imposition of a (small) tariff yields zero net income effects.[3] Define the compensated excess demand elasticities of home goods with respect to the relative prices of importables and exportables as θ_m and θ_e, respectively.[4] Using these elasticities and denoting a proportional change in a variable by a $\hat{}$, we have

$$\theta_m \hat{P}_m + \theta_e \hat{P}_e = 0. \tag{4}$$

Since terms of trade are given, the change in the domestic relative price of importables in terms of exportables is identically equal to the tariff:

$$\hat{P}_m - \hat{P}_e = \hat{T}. \tag{5}$$

Substituting this result in equation (4), we can solve for the change in the equilibrium relative prices of traded goods in terms of nontraded goods:

$$\hat{P}_e = -\frac{\theta_m}{\theta_m + \theta_e} \hat{T}, \tag{6}$$

and

$$\hat{P}_m = \left[1 - \frac{\theta_m}{\theta_m + \theta_e}\right]\hat{T} = \frac{\theta_e}{\theta_m + \theta_e} \hat{T}. \tag{7}$$

The effects of a tariff as shown in equations (6) and (7) will depend on the substitution or complementarity relationship between home goods and the two traded goods. Consider first the case where the home good substitutes with each of the traded goods so that both the cross price elasticities of excess demand θ_m and θ_e are positive.[5] In that case the relative price of importables will increase in terms of home goods while the equilibrium relative price of exportables declines in terms of nontraded goods. Furthermore these price changes are less than proportionate to the tariff.

An interpretation of these results is offered in figure 15.1. The schedule $N = 0$ shows the relative prices of exportables and importables in terms of home goods such that the nontraded goods market clears. The schedule is a blowup of the neighborhood of the free trade equilibrium and is constructed by varying the tariff rate and redistributing the tariff proceeds so that along the schedule real income is constant. Accordingly the schedule is negatively sloped since it only reflects substitution effects. The free trade equilibrium is at point A where the ray OR, the slope of which measures the relative price of traded goods, intersects the $N = 0$ schedule. At the free trade equilibrium the relative prices of traded goods in terms of home goods are P_m^0 and P_e^0 and associated with these prices, and indeed all points along $N = 0$, we have trade balance equilibrium.

The imposition of a tariff raises the domestic relative price of importables in terms of exportables by the amount of the tariff and accordingly rotates the ray OR to OR'. The new equilibrium will be at point D with relative prices of importables and exportables in terms of home goods P_m'

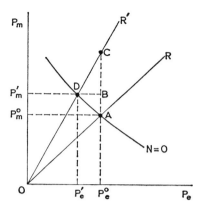

Figure 15.1

and P'_e, respectively. We note that the increase in the relative price of importables in terms of home goods, BA/AP_e^0, falls short of the tariff, CA/AP_e^0, and similarly for the decline in the relative price of exportables.

Figure 15.1 is useful in interpreting the reference to exchange rate adjustments attendant upon a tariff that have been made in the literature.[6] For that purpose we decompose the move from A to D into two steps. At the initial relative price of exportables in terms of home goods, P_e^0, the imposition of a tariff raise the price of importables in terms of both exportables and home goods by the amount of the tariff so that the economy would find itself at point C. At that point, however, there is an excess demand for nontraded goods and a matching trade balance surplus. To attain the equilibrium at point D, home goods would have to appreciate in terms of *both* traded goods or, equivalently, the prices of both traded goods would have to fall equiproportionately in terms of home goods. It is the latter adjustment from point C to D that has been identified with an exchange rate appreciation, an identification that derives from the (implicit) assumption that the nominal prices of home goods are fixed so that the adjustment in relative prices has to be brought about by a decline in the nominal prices of traded goods.[7] It is in this sense that the change in the equilibrium (relative) price of importables has been interpreted as the tariff, CA/AP_e^0, less the "exchange rate appreciation," CB/AP_e^0.

Consider next the effects of tariffs in the presence of complementarity. We note that the term $(\theta_m + \theta_e)$ in equations (6) and (7) is positive since it is the negative of the own price elasticity of excess demand for home goods. It follows that if home goods and importables are complements, $\theta_m < 0$, the tariff causes the prices of both traded goods to appreciate in terms of home goods. This is so since at a constant price of exportables the tariff creates an excess supply of home goods and thus requires an increase in the price of both traded goods in terms of home goods to eliminate the excess supply. Conversely, if exportables and home goods are complements, $\theta_e < 0$, the prices of both traded goods decline in terms of home goods.[8]

15.3 A Special Case

A special case of the model developed so far has been widely employed in policy discussions and empirical work concerned with the resource allocation and welfare effects of a tariff. That specialization assumes that the cross price elasticity between traded goods is zero and thus implies not only that home goods and both traded goods are substitutes but also that θ_m and θ_e can be identified with the compensated elasticity of demand for imports (defined positive) and the elasticity of supply of exports respectively. This special case furthermore assumes that real income is not an argument in the demand for imports or supply of exports so that by implication the marginal propensity to spend on home goods is unity.

With these assumptions we may write the demand for imports and supply of exports as follows:

$$M = M(P_m), \quad E = E(P_e). \tag{8}$$

Using the budget constraint in equation (3), we may rewrite the equilibrium condition in equation (1) in terms of the trade balance equilibrium condition

$$P^* M(P_m) = E(P_e), \tag{9}$$

and close the model by the relationship between prices in equation (2), that is $P_m = P^* P_e T$.

The particular assumptions of this model allow for simple measures of the protective effect of a tariff, its welfare cost and the "social cost of foreign exchange." These measures can be interpreted in terms of figure 15.2. There we show the supply of exports, E, and the demand for imports measured in terms of exports at international prices, $P^* M$. The demand for imports is drawn as a function of the relative price of exportables. This is possible because by equation (2) we can write $P_m = P^* P_e T$ so that for a given tariff the demand for imports can be shown as a function of P_e. Initial free trade equilibrium obtains at point A where the trade balance is in equilibrium, $P^* M = E$, and hence by equation (3) equilibrium obtains in the home goods market.

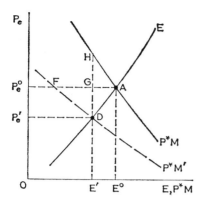

Figure 15.2

The imposition of a tariff shifts the demand for imports downward to P^*M' in the proportion of the tariff. At the initial relative price of exportables, P_e^0, the demand for imports declines to point F, and accordingly there is a trade balance surplus equal to AF and an excess demand for home goods equal to AF times P_e^0. The excess demand for home goods causes their relative price to increase in terms of both traded goods until the economy reaches point D where full equilibrium again obtains.

An indication of the direction and magnitude of resource movements is the change in the equilibrium relative prices. The increase in the equilibrium relative price of imports in terms of home goods measures the protection granted to that industry. As is seen from figure 15.2, the price increase, HG/GE', falls short of the tariff, HD/DE', due to the depreciation of traded goods in terms of home goods. This discrepancy between the tariff rate and the appropriate measure of protection has led in the literature to the concept of a "net protective rate."[9] That rate is defined as the tariff less the change in the equilibrium "exchange rate." It follows from the preceding discussion that it is properly identified with the increase in the equilibrium relative price of imports in terms of home goods and thus for a small tariff is measured by equation (7).

Consider now the welfare cost of a discrete tariff. To develop a formal expression, we assume a social utility function $U = U(C_n, C_m, C_e)$, and substituting for consumption in terms of production and trade, we have $U = U(Q_n, Q_m + M, Q_e - E)$. Next we differentiate that utility function and divide by the marginal utility of nontraded goods to obtain the change in utility measured in terms of home goods denoted by dV:[10]

$$dV \equiv \frac{dU}{\partial U/\partial C_n} = P_m dM - P_e dE. \tag{10}$$

The expression for the welfare change in equation (10) can be related to the tariff by use of equation (9). Differentiating that equation yields $dE = P^*DM$ which after substitution in equation (10) and use of equation (2) gives the following expression for the marginal welfare change:

$$dV = \left(\frac{t}{T}\right) P_m dM = tP_e P^* dM. \tag{11}$$

The welfare cost of a discrete tariff is given by the integral of equation (11) and on the special assumptions of this model can be identified with the familiar "triangle" measure HDA in figure 15.2. For that identification to be correct, we do require both assumptions of this model, zero cross price effects between traded goods and zero marginal propensities to spend on traded goods. Together, these assumptions ensure that we deal with compensated import demand and export supply schedules that will not shift in response to cross price effects or the income effects of a discrete tariff.[11]

Closely related to the welfare cost of a tariff is the concept of the "social cost of foreign exchange" or more appropriately the shadow price of external resources.[12] To determine that shadow price, we assume that the home country receives external resources, say aid, so that we can rewrite the trade balance equilibrium condition in equation (9) as

$$P^*M(P_m) = E(P_e) + A, \tag{12}$$

where A denotes aid receipts measured in terms of exportables. Differentiating that equilibrium condition and substituting in equation (10) yields an expression for the shadow price as the welfare gain per unit of aid, both measured in terms of home goods:

$$\frac{dV}{P_e dA} = 1 + tP^* \frac{dM}{dA}. \tag{13}$$

We note from equation (13) that the shadow price will differ from unity by a factor that will depend on the given tariff and the change in imports induced by aid. The latter term can be derived by differentiating the trade balance equilibrium condition in equation (12) holding constant the tariff and hence the domestic relative price of traded goods. Performing that operation and using the definition of the elasticity of demand for imports, we obtain $P^* dM/dA = \theta_m/(\theta_m + \theta_e)$, and hence the expression for the shadow price becomes:

$$\frac{dV}{P_e\,dA} = 1 + t\frac{\theta_m}{\theta_m + \theta_e}.\tag{14}$$

The second term in equation (14) constitutes the rationale for shadow pricing and has a straightforward interpretation. Under a tariff imports are socially overpriced and welfare will increase if the public can be induced to expand imports over the existing distortion.[13] Aid receipts will produce such an expansion in imports since they raise expenditure on nontraded goods raising their relative price and hence by the substitution effect increasing imports.[14] The increase in imports per unit of aid, given by the ratio $\theta_m/(\theta_m + \theta_e)$, multiplied by the distortion in the form of the tariff accordingly measures the excess benefit of aid.[15]

Notes

I am indebted to J. Chipman, M. Corden, S. Engerman, R. Jones and M. Mussa for their helpful comments. I wish in particular to acknowledge the many suggestions I have received from J. Bhagwati.

1. See, in particular, Corden (1971, ch. 5) who studies the small country case and Balassa (1971a, b) and Basevi (1968) who consider the case of variable terms of trade.

2. Denoting production and consumption of the ith commodity by Q_i and C_i, respectively, we can write income, inclusive of tariff proceeds, as $I \equiv Q_n + P_m Q_m + P_e Q_e + (t/T)P_m M$ and expenditure as $C_n + P_m C_m + P_e C_e$. Imposing the equality of income and expenditure and using the definitions of M, E, and N as well as equation (2), we arrive at the budget constraint as shown in equation (3).

3. Denoting the marginal propensity to spend on home goods by $\gamma \equiv \partial C_n/\partial I$, we can write the effect on demand of income changes and of the income effects implicit in price changes, as $\gamma(dI - C_m dP_m - C_e dP_e)$. Noting that $dI = Q_m dP_m + Q_e dP_e + P_m M dt$, and substituting that expression, we have the net income effect on demand for home goods as $\gamma(\hat{P}_e + \hat{T} - \hat{P}_m)P_m M = 0$.

4. The compensated excess demand elasticities for nontraded goods are defined as follows: $\theta_m \equiv (\partial N/\partial P_m)(P_m/P_m M)$ and $\theta_e \equiv (\partial N/\partial P_e)(P_e/P_e E)$ and may be positive or negative depending on the substitution or complementarity relationship on the demand and supply side. Treating traded goods as a composite commodity, we note that $\theta_m + \theta_e$ is the excess demand elasticity with respect to the relative price of traded goods and must be positive since traded goods as a group and home goods must be substitutes.

5. We note that since we restrict only the sign of the *excess* demand elasticities, this does not require that home goods and traded goods are substitutes both on the demand and supply side. We further note that the assumption that home goods substitute with both traded goods does not restrict the relationship between

traded goods. They may be substitutes, complements or unrelated. The latter case is explored in detail in section 15.3.

6. See, for example, Balassa (1971a, pp. 326–328) and (1971b, pp. 310–313), Basevi (1968, pp. 842–849) and Corden (1971, ch. 5).

7. Although the analogy with exchange rate changes may be suggestive, it should be emphasized that the requisite adjustment is one of relative prices and that, in this model, it is altogether immaterial whether such an adjustment comes via a change in the nominal prices of home goods at constant traded goods prices or via a change in the nominal prices of traded goods at constant nominal prices of home goods. Indeed, there is nothing in this model that will determine nominal prices or an exchange rate and the frequently encountered assumption that in the "background" monetary and fiscal policy maintain the nominal price of home goods is an unsatisfactory way of concealing what is essentially a nonmonetary economy. For a discussion of tariffs in a properly specified monetary economy, see Mussa (1973).

8. For the case of complementarity, the home goods market equilibrium schedule is positively sloped. It will intersect the OR ray from below for the case where importables and home goods are complements and intersect it from above when home goods and exports are complements.

9. See Corden (1971, ch. 5) and Balassa (1971a, b).

10. In arriving at equation (10) we have used the fact that from consumer maximization the ratios of marginal utilities are equated to the domestic price ratios and that producer maximization implies that the change in the value of output at domestic prices is zero, $dQ_n + P_m dQ_m + P_e dQ_e = 0$.

11. The very restrictive assumptions underlying the triangle measure have not been sufficiently emphasized in actual applications. See, for example, Basevi (1968). This issue is nontrivial since at the level of aggregation that is considered there is no reason to expect that the assumptions should be a good approximation of the real world.

12. For a survey article on the social cost of foreign exchange, see Bacha and Taylor (1971). Section 3 of that paper deals with the measure that is developed here.

13. This line of argument is obviously familiar from the literature on distortions; for a review, see in particular Bhagwati (1971).

14. The argument can readily be interpreted in terms of figure 15.2. Aid receipts are added to the supply of exports and accordingly shift that schedule to the right. At the initial equilibrium price there is trade balance surplus and matching excess demand for nontraded goods. To restore equilibrium, the relative price of traded goods in terms of home goods has to decline thereby increasing imports and decreasing exports.

15. The measure in equation (14) requires zero marginal propensities to spend on traded goods; it does not require, however, zero cross price elasticities. This is so because we maintain constant the relative price of traded goods.

References

Bacha, E., and Taylor, L. 1971. Foreign exchange shadow prices: A critical review of current theories. *Quarterly Journal of Economics* 85, no. 2, 197–224.

Bhagwati, J. 1971. The generalized theory of distortions and welfare. In J. Bhagwati et al., *Trade, Balance of Payments and Growth*. North-Holland, Amsterdam, 69–90.

Balassa, B. 1971a. *The Structure of Protection in Developing Countries*. Johns Hopkins Press, Baltimore.

Balassa, B. 1971b. Effective protection in developing countries. In J. Bhagwati et al., *Trade, Balance of Payments and Growth*. North-Holland, Amsterdam, 300–323.

Basevi, G. 1968. The restrictive effect of the US tariff and its welfare value. *American Economic Review* 58, no. 4, 840–852.

Corden, M. 1971. *The Theory of Protection*. Clarendon Press.

McDougall, I. A. 1970. Non-traded commodities and the pure theory of international trade. In A. McDougall and R. H. Snape, eds., *Studies in International Economics*. North-Holland, Amsterdam, 157–192.

Mussa, M. 1973. Tariffs and the balance of payments: A monetary approach. Unpublished manuscript. University of Rochester.

16

Real Interest Rates, Home Goods, and Optimal External Borrowing

This chapter investigates optimal external borrowing in a small open economy that faces a given world rate of interest and experiences supply disturbances. The main point of the chapter is to study the interaction of alternative disturbances—present versus future, transitory versus permanent—and the equilibrium real interest rate in setting the path of consumption and the external indebtedness. This question of optimal consumption choices in an open economy, intertemporal setting is receiving renewed attention, for example, in Obstfeld (1981), Sachs (1981), and Svensson and Razin (1983).

In choosing a small country setting, the present study focuses on a simpler model, but it brings in an interesting issue related in earlier work by Bruno (1976) and by Martin and Selowsky (1981). It is argued that in a small country with a nontraded goods sector the relevant real interest rate is not the given world interest rate but the real interest rate stated in terms of the domestic consumption basket. Differences between the world real interest rate and the home real interest rate arise to the extent that the *relative* price of home goods is changing over time. Specifically, if the relative price of home goods is rising, the home real interest rate is lower than the world rate of interest. Conversely, if the relative price of home goods is falling, the home real interest rate exceeds the world rate. To the extent that disturbances affect the relative price structure over time, they also affect the home real interest rate and therefore the optimal path of consumption and borrowing.

Originally published in *Journal of Political Economy*, vol. 91, no. 1 (February 1983), pp. 141–153.

16.1 The Consumer

We assume a small country producing traded and nontraded goods with a fixed labor force that is mobile between sectors and given supplies of specific factors in traded and home goods sectors, respectively. The world rate of interest is fixed in terms of traded goods and equals r^*. The home country can borrow and lend at r^* unlimited amounts, respecting, of course, the intertemporal budget constraint.

The respresentative household solves an intertemporal maximization problem, choosing a path of consumption and debt that maximizes discounted lifetime utility:

$$V = \sum_0^\infty D^t U_t(c_T, c_N), \quad D \equiv \frac{1}{1+\delta}, \tag{1}$$

subject to

$$\sum_0^\infty (c_N p_t + c_T - y_t) R^{-t} + b_0 = 0, \quad R \equiv (1 + r^*) \tag{2}$$

and the transversality condition

$$\lim_{t \to \infty} b_t R^{-t} = 0. \tag{3}$$

Equation (1) is the discounted value of utility of the infinitely lived household with D the discount factor and $U(\ )$ the stationary utility function. Consumption of traded and nontraded goods are the arguments in the utility function and are denoted c_T and c_N, respectively, with the time subscript omitted. Equation (2) is the lifetime budget constraint that sets the present value of consumption in excess of income discounted at the world interest rate plus initial debt, b_0, equal to zero. In the budget constraint y_t denotes the value of current output measured in traded goods and p_t is the relative price of home goods in terms of traded goods. Equation (3) is the transversality condition that ensures that debt cannot grow boundlessly through borrowing that finances debt service indefinitely.

In what follows we assume a specific functional form of the utility function:

$$U_t = \frac{1}{1-\Theta} c_t^{1-\Theta}, \quad c = c_T^a c_N^{1-a}, \quad \Theta > 0, 1 > a > 0. \tag{4}$$

The utility function shows "constant relative risk aversion" with the parameter $\Theta \equiv -U''c/U'$ a measure of the concavity of the utility function and $1/\Theta$ the intertemporal elasticity of substitution. The term c is an index of consumption and has a Cobb-Douglas functional form.

It is shown in the appendix that consumer maximization leads to an optimal consumption profile that depends on the ratio of the consumption-based home real rate of interest relative to the rate of time preference:

$$\frac{c_t}{c_{t+1}} = \xi_t^{-1/\Theta}. \tag{5}$$

The term ξ in (5) is the ratio of the home real interest rate to the rate of time preference and is defined as

$$\xi_t \equiv \frac{(1 + r^*)(p_t/p_{t+1})^{1-a}}{1 + \delta} \equiv k(p_t/p_{t+1})^{1-a}, \quad k \equiv \frac{1 + r^*}{1 + \xi} \equiv DR. \tag{5a}$$

We note that in (5a) the home relative price structure over time appears as a component of the real interest rate relevant to consumption choices. The lower the future compared to the current *relative* price of home goods, the higher the *home* real interest rate for any given world interest rate r^* fixed in terms of traded goods.

The time profile of optimal consumption has two determinants. One is the relation between the world rate of interest and the home discount rate, the term $k \equiv DR$. We assume that the discount rate equals the world interest rate so that $k = 1$. The other determinant of the optimal consumption time profile is the relative price structure over time, p_t/p_{t+1}. It is apparent from (5a) that when relative prices remain constant the ratio is unity and hence the consumption profile is flat.

The parameter Θ represents the concavity of the utility function and measures the ease of intertemporal consumption substitution. If the $U(\ )$ function is near linear, substitutability is perfect and $1/\Theta$ tends to infinity. Conversely, if consumption shows very little intertemporal substitutability, consumption remains an entirely flat profile and consumers smooth completely, whatever the pattern of real interest rates. The schedule cc in figure 16.1 represents equation (5). It is vertical for the case where $1/\Theta$ tends to zero because of a lack of substitutability, and it is flat for the case where $1/\Theta$ tends to infinity.

16.2 The Home Goods Market

The demand for home goods can be expressed in terms of the relative price and the level of consumption as shown in the appendix:

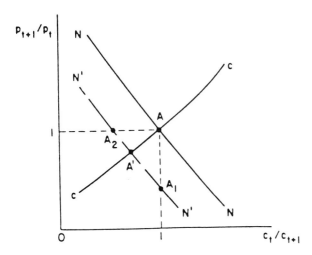

Figure 16.1

$$c_{N,t} = \lambda^a c_t p_t^{-a}, \quad \lambda \equiv \frac{1-a}{a}. \tag{6}$$

Home goods demand is proportional to consumption, the factor of proportionality depending positively on the relative price of traded goods.

On the supply side, home goods output is assumed to be a function of the relative price, a shift parameter q_t, and the supply elasticity e:

$$y_{N,t} = q_t p_t^e. \tag{7}$$

Equilibrium in the home goods market then yields a relation between consumption and the relative price:

$$p_t = (q_t / \lambda c_t)^{-1/(a+e)} \tag{8}$$

and

$$\frac{p_{t+1}}{p_t} = \left[\left(\frac{q_{t+1}}{q_t} \right) \left(\frac{c_t}{c_{t+1}} \right) \right]^{-1/(a+e)}. \tag{9}$$

Equation (9) is shown, for $(q_{t+1}/q_t) = 1$, as the NN schedule in figure 16.1. The schedule is negatively sloped since a high current relative to future consumption level implies a high current relative to future demand for home goods, which thus requires a high current relative price of home goods. The elasticity of the relative price with respect to the consumption profile is given by $-1/(a + e)$ and thus is smaller the higher the supply elasticity and the larger the share of traded goods in consumption.

From (9) we note that the equilibrium relative price is affected by the position of the supply curve. A higher current supply lowers the current real price of home goods and appears in figure 16.1 as a rightward shift of *NN*.

16.3 Stationary Equilibrium

With output stationary and the home discount rate equal to the world interest rate, point *A* in figure 16.1 represents the stationary equilibrium. Consumers choose a flat profile of consumption since there is no incentive to tilt consumption toward the present or the future because of differences between home interest rates and those prevailing in the world. The flat level of consumption $\bar{c}$ will be chosen so as to satisfy (2), (3), and (8).

Figure 16.1 shows as the schedule *cc* the optimal consumption profile between adjacent periods as a function of the intertemporal relative price structure given by (5) and (5a). Current consumption rises relative to future consumption as the relative price of home goods rises over time. The elasticity of substitution with respect to the intertemporal relative price structure is $(1 - a)/\Theta$, which reflects both the coefficient of concavity and the share of home goods in the consumption basket. The explanation for the positively sloped *cc* schedule and for the elasticity $(1 - a)/\Theta$ is the following: the household substitutes in response to changes in the real interest rate. Increased real interest rates lead the consumer to raise future relative to current consumption. Now suppose the relative price of home goods is expected to fall. Then a unit of traded goods borrowed today has relatively little purchasing power in terms of the consumption basket today but costs a lot in terms of the consumption basket upon repayment of the loan next period. Since the loan adds less to consumption today than it costs to repay tomorrow, it is clear that with falling relative prices of home goods the real interest rate in terms of our consumption basket exceeds the world real rate. Conversely, if the relative price of home goods were rising the home real interest rate would be less than the world rate. Changing relative prices induce consumers to choose a profile of consumption that is tilted toward the present or the future.

Two factors determine the extent to which changing relative prices of home goods affect the consumption profile. One is the share of home goods in consumption, $1 - a$, the other is the coefficient of concavity. If the home goods share is negligible, the home real interest rate is practically equal to the given world rate. Variations in relative prices over time are only important if the share of home goods in consumption is significant. The larger the share the flatter the cc schedule, because now even a small change in the relative price structure over time involves a relatively large change in the home real interest rate. The other determinant, as already mentioned, is the intertemporal elasticity of substitution $1/\Theta$, which governs the extent to which the consumer adjusts the consumption profile in response to the real interest rate.

In the stationary equilibrium, spending will fall short of or exceed income in every period depending on the initial debt position. With an initial indebtedness the country would run an indefinite trade surplus, spending falling short of output, thus transferring the debt service. We consider next how this equilibrium is affected by transitory or permanent disturbances in output.

16.4 An Output Increase

Suppose that households currently learn about a permanent increase in home goods output starting next period. Thus $q_{t+1} = q'$ starting next period. We want to investigate the effect of the output increase on the profile of consumption, relative prices, and borrowing.[1] In figure 16.1 we show that the rise in future home goods output leads to a shift of the NN schedule to $N'N'$. At each level of relative consumption the future relative price of home goods will fall compared to that prevailing today. The new equilibrium is at point A'. Thus a future rise in output reduces current consumption relative to the future because the output increase raises the home real rate of interest.

The equilibrium relative price structure and the equilibrium consumption profile can be derived by equating (5) and (9) to yield

$$\frac{q_{t+1}}{p_t} = \left(\frac{q_{t+1}}{q_t}\right)^{-\Theta\beta} k^\beta, \quad \beta \equiv \frac{1}{\Theta(a+e) + (1-a)} \tag{10}$$

and

$$\frac{c_t}{c_{t+1}} = \left(\frac{q_{t+1}}{q_t}\right)^{-(1-a)\beta} k^{-(a+e)\beta}. \tag{11}$$

Consider now the extent to which the consumption profile is moved by a change in future output. Two reference points are A_1 and A_2 corresponding, respectively, to the cases of zero and infinite intertemporal substitution elasticities. Consider first the case where there is no substitutability in consumption and where, accordingly, the consumption profile remains entirely flat although at a higher level. In this case the expectation of higher future income immediately raises current consumption and therefore the consumption of home goods. The current relative price of home goods rises, though the future relative price of home goods must fall, if one takes into account the effect of increased home goods supply. Unambiguously p_{t+1}/p_t, as shown in figure 16.1 at point A_1, must decline. In this case a future rise in home goods output raises the home real interest rate in response to the current consumption of anticipated future incomes. The current account *must* deteriorate since present consumption of traded goods rises both in response to consumption smoothing and in response to the higher present relative price of home goods. Traded goods supply declines as resources are shifted toward the home goods market. The resulting trade deficit supports the intertemporal consumption smoothing with the current deficit being financed by a future permanent flow of saving.

The case of perfect intertemporal substitution is particularly interesting since here it can be shown that the trade balance must improve. With perfect substitutability there is no concern for intertemporal smoothing of consumption, and we can start from a bench-mark of no change in current consumption and therefore continued balanced trade and an unchanged present relative price of home goods. Starting next period the increased supply of home goods leads to a decline in their relative price. The relative price of home goods, from this hypothetical position, is seen as falling over time, and thus the home real interest rate has risen relative to the rate of discount. With the profile of consumption perfectly responsive to interest rate movements, consumers reduce current consumption in favor of the future. The reduction in current demand and the rise in future demand in turn lead to lower home goods demand today and to increased home goods demand in the future, thus dampening the change in p_{t+1}/p_t up to the point where relative prices are equalized across time.

We have thus established that with perfect substitution current consumption must fall in the face of higher future home goods output.[2] It remains for us to establish that the trade balance must go into surplus. This is the case because the reduction in consumption directly reduces traded goods demand, whereas the higher relative price of traded goods leads to decreased demand and increased production of traded goods. Thus with perfect intertemporal substitution future increases in home goods must improve today's trade balance. The result stands in sharp contrast with the case where consumption smoothing dominates.

In general, the trade balance effects will therefore depend on two opposing tendencies: preference for consumption smoothing will give rise to an
increase in the home real interest rate, and this in turn will cause some
reduction in current relative to future income or some tendency for future
consumption to rise more and current consumption to rise less than permanent income. Whether current consumption rises or falls depends in the
general case on all the parameters (a, e, Θ). It is shown in the appendix that
with a zero supply elasticity, the borderline case is that of logarithmic
utility, $\Theta = 1$, for current consumption and the trade balance to be unchanged. With home goods supply price elastic a trade deficit will already
arise with a value of Θ somewhat less than unity.

A further disturbance is a current, transitory rise in home goods output.
In this event there is a rightward shift in NN, and the current period
equilibrium involves a rise in present relative to future consumption induced by the fall in the home equilibrium real interest rate. With zero
substitutability, the consumption profile remains flat and rises uniformly,
though by less than the increase in current income. Therefore a present
trade surplus develops, financing a long-run trade deficit.

When intertemporal substitution is perfect, we encounter the other limiting case. Here current income growth (in the home goods sector) leads to a
trade deficit. We explain this result with the help of figure 16.2. We will
show that to equalize relative prices across periods, we require an increase

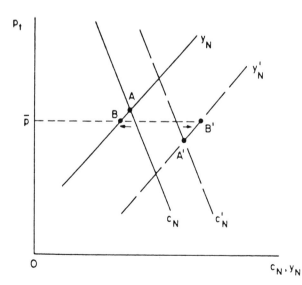

Figure 16.2

in current consumption that is proportionately larger than the rise in income, thus giving rise to a deficit. The schedules c_N and y_N show the initial, predisturbance demand and supply schedules in the home goods market. Equilibrium obtains at point A with balanced trade. Now current home goods supply rises to y_N', with future supply remaining unchanged at y_N. Suppose hypothetically that current consumption and, hence, home goods demand rise in proportion to the increase in income, shifting the current demand schedule to c_N'. We note two points. First, the demand schedule shifts proportionately less than the supply schedule because aggregate income rises only by the share of home goods times home goods supply growth. Second, if demand increases in proportion to income, the current equilibrium at point A' would be one of trade balance and hence A would continue to represent the future equilibrium once supply falls back.

In fact the combination A and A' cannot be an equilibrium if substitution is perfect. This equilibrium implies a rising relative price of home goods and therefore a home real interest rate that has fallen and will induce substitution toward the present and away from the future. That substitution in turn raises current home goods demand and the relative price while lowering future demand and relative price. The process of substitution must continue until the real interest rate again equals the discount rate, that is, until relative prices are equalized over time. Such an equilibrium is shown at points B and B', where future demand has declined and present demand has risen proportionately more than income. Accordingly we have shown that in equilibrium consumption (and home goods demand) must rise more than income or there will be a current trade deficit.

Our analysis has established so far that the presumption in favor of consumption smoothing—surpluses for a country with transitory income gains and deficits in the case of future income gains—must be qualified in the case where nontraded goods are present. Disturbances in the home goods sector will affect the real interest rate and through that channel cause the consumption profile to tilt in a manner that dampens or even offsets the tendency toward consumption smoothing, but the perverse results can arise only when the intertemporal elasticity of substitution, $1/\Theta$, is larger than unity.

16.5 Transitory Changes in the World Interest Rate

So far we have assumed a given world rate of interest r^* and furthermore equality of the world interest rate and the domestic discount rate, $(1 + r^*)/(1 + \delta) = 1$. We now assume that there is a transitory increase in the

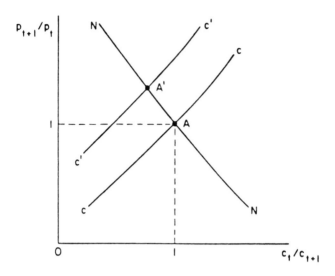

Figure 16.3

world rate of interest in the present period. From (5) a rise in the current world rate of interest tilts the consumption profile toward the future. In figure 16.3 this is shown as the leftward shift of cc to $c'c'$. The rise in the world rate of interest lowers the relative price of home goods today compared to the future.

Consider first the case of zero intertemporal substitution. Starting with a zero initial debt and hence the equality of income and spending along the stationary path, we see that higher interest rates have no effect on the consumption profile, which remains flat at the unchanged level of income. The existence of an initial debt or net foreign assets modifies the result in the following manner. With external net assets the higher interest receipts raise current income and therefore raise the consumption path. Conversely, with initial debt there is a reduction in the consumption profile.

The case of some substitutability, as shown in figure 16.3, leads to a reduction in present relative to future consumption. Starting from zero debt, that implies a reduction in present consumption and a rise in the entire future path of consumption. Thus the home country will run a trade surplus in the high interest period and a trade deficit when interest rates return to their initial levels. The extent of intertemporal substitution can be seen from the expression for the equilibrium relative consumption levels:

$$\frac{c_t}{c_{t+1}} = k^{-(a+e)/[\Theta(a+e)+(1-a)]}. \tag{12}$$

Equation (12) shows the role of the nontraded goods sector. If either the share of traded goods approaches unity or the elasticity of home goods supply tends toward infinity, the elasticity in (12) tends to $-1/\Theta$, which is the result of the small open economy without home goods. The presence of the home goods sector tends to dampen the effect of international interest rate changes on the consumption profile and the trade balance.

The home goods sector dampens the response of the consumption profile to a transitory world interest rate increase because of an offsetting movement in the domestic component of the real interest rate. As current consumption declines relative to future consumption, the relative price of traded goods today rises relative to its future level, thus exerting a dampening effect on the relevant real interest rate and therefore on intertemporal consumption substitution and the trade balance.

16.6 Concluding Remarks

We have studied the role of the nontraded goods sector in influencing the consumption and trade balance response to changes in output or in the world rate of interest. The finding is that the presence of a nontraded goods sector, as already noted by Bruno (1976) and Martin and Selowsky (1981), introduces a discrepancy between the home real rate of interest and that prevailing in the rest of the world. The distinction implies that changes in the time profile of home goods output will affect the profile of consumption and the trade balance. The extent to which this occurs is related to the share of traded goods in consumption, the intertemporal elasticity of substitution, and the elasticity of home goods supply. Transitory changes in the world rate of interest likewise affect the time profile of consumption. This time, the home goods market serves to dampen the movements in the consumption profile as the international and domestic components of the real interest rate move in offsetting directions.

The model lends itself readily to other applications. For example, current tax-financed government spending could be studied to determine the impact on the trade balance. It is obvious from the results we have seen that with imperfect substitution there will be a trade deficit reflecting the consumer's smoothing of the tax burden by international borrowing. But because current consumption does not fall enough to offset fully increased government spending, relative home goods prices will be high and falling. Thus government spending raises the home *real* interest rate and thereby induces consumption shifting that dampens the trade deficit. The extent to which the real interest rate increase leads to crowding out of current consumption depends, once again, on the degree of intertemporal substitution. Other applications include the anticipation of tariff changes as well as the two-country model.

The present model is oversimplified for a complete analysis of trade balance issues. For that purpose it would be interesting to introduce also capital accumulation to study the interaction of saving and investment on relative prices and the balance of trade.

16.7 Appendix

We use equations (1), (2), and (4) to derive the first-order conditions establishing the optimal composition of current consumption between home goods and traded goods as well as the optimal consumption profile. Differentiating (1), using (2), with respect to consumption of current goods yields:

$$\frac{U_t^N}{U_t^T} = p_t, \tag{A1}$$

where U^i is the partial derivative of $U(\ )$ with respect to the ith argument.

Maximizing (1), using (2), with respect to consumption in $t + 1$ and using (A1) leads to

$$\frac{U_t^N}{U_{t+1}^N} = DR\left(\frac{p_t}{p_{t+1}}\right). \tag{A2}$$

Substituting for the derivatives from the specific functional form $U = [1/(1 - \Theta)]c^{1-\Theta}$ with $c = c_T^a c_N^{1-a}$, we derive from (A1):

$$\frac{c_N}{c_T} = \frac{\lambda}{p_t}, \quad \lambda \equiv \frac{1-a}{a}, \quad c_N = \lambda^a c_t p_t^{-a}, \tag{A3}$$

and thus

$$U_t^N = (1 - a)c_t^{-\Theta}\left(\frac{c_T}{c_N}\right)^a = (1 - a)c_t^{-\Theta}\left(\frac{\lambda}{p_t}\right)^{-a}. \tag{A4}$$

Therefore (A2) can be rewritten as

$$DR\left(\frac{p_t}{p_{t+1}}\right) = \left(\frac{c_t}{c_{t+1}}\right)^{-\Theta}\left(\frac{p_t}{p_{t+1}}\right)^a \tag{A5}$$

or, with $\Theta > 0$,

$$\frac{c_t}{c_{t+1}} = k^{-1/\Theta}\left(\frac{p_{t+1}}{p_t}\right)^{(1-a)/\Theta} \equiv \xi_t^{-1/\Theta}, \quad k \equiv DR, \tag{A6}$$

which is the equation of the cc schedule in (5).

We next show the current account for the case of a permanent increase in output, starting in $t + 1$ with a supply of home goods and traded goods inelastic. With home goods markets clearing $y_N = c_N$, $y'_N = c'_N$. Furthermore as of period $t + 1$ the consumption profile will be flat. Traded goods consumption has to satisfy the budget constraint so that

$$c'_T = y'_T - (c_T - y_T)r^*. \tag{A7}$$

Equation (A7) states that from $t + 1$ on consumption equals output of traded goods adjusted for the debt service on the first-period trade deficit. The value of utility V is then equal to

$$V = \frac{(1/\delta)(c'^a_T y'^{1-a}_N)^{1-\Theta} + (c^a_T y^{1-a}_N)^{1-\Theta}}{1 - \Theta}, \tag{A8}$$

which is to be maximized with respect to c_T subject to (A7). Maximization leads to the solution for current consumption of traded goods:

$$c_T = y_T \frac{K + r^* K}{1 + r^* K}, \tag{A9}$$

where

$$K \equiv \left(\frac{y_N}{y'_N}\right)^{[(1-a)(1-\Theta)]/[1-a(1-\Theta)]}.$$

There is accordingly a trade surplus or deficit as $K \lessgtr 1$. It is readily verified that for $\Theta < 1$ there is a trade surplus, trade balance obtains in the logarithmic case of $\Theta = 1$, and a deficit prevails for a larger value of Θ, if one notes that $y_N/y'_N < 1$.

Notes

Financial support was provided by a grant from the National Science Foundation. The chapter owes much of its inspiration to work by Ricardo Martin and Marcelo Selowsky. I wish to acknowledge helpful suggestions from an anonymous referee and from Ian McKenzie, who found a critical error in an earlier draft.

1. A future increase in output in the traded goods sector that leaves home goods supply unchanged will lead to a rise in the level of consumption. There will be current borrowing to finance the higher, flat consumption profile with the debt serviced and paid once income rises. Because the relative price of nontraded goods remains unchanged over time, rising once and for all, there are no interest rate effects on the time profile of consumption.

2. Note that if future output growth was "balanced," occurring in the same proportions in home and traded goods industries, the trade balance would remain in balance with current consumption equal to current income. Therefore our results rely critically on *unbalanced* growth in the home goods sector (see McKenzie 1982).

References

Bruno, Michael. 1976. "The Two-Sector Open Economy and the Real Exchange Rate." *A.E.R.* 66 (September): 566–577.

Martin, Ricardo, and Selowsky, Marcelo. 1981. "Energy Prices, Substitution, and Optimal Borrowing in the Short Run: An Analysis of Adjustment in Oil Importing Developing Countries." Unpublished manuscript, World Bank, February.

McKenzie, Ian M. 1982. "Optimal Consumption-Saving Behavior, Real Exchange Rates and Capital Movements." Unpublished manuscript, Massachusetts Inst. Tech.

Obstfeld, Maurice. 1981. "Aggregate Spending and the Terms of Trade: Is There a Laursen-Metzler Effect?" Working Paper no. 682. Nat. Bur. Econ. Res., June.

Sachs, Jeffrey D. 1981. "The Current Account and Macroeconomic Adjustment in the 1970s." *Brookings Papers Econ. Activity*, no. 1, pp. 201–268.

Svensson, Lars E. O., and Razin, Assaf. 1983. "The Terms of Trade and the Current Account: The Harberger-Laursen-Metzler Effect." *J.P.E.*

17

Intergenerational and International Trade

Intertemporal trade theory, in an optimizing framework, has been studied in influential papers by Gale (1971, 1974) and more recently by Buiter (1981), Fried (1980), Kareken and Wallace (1977), Svensson and Razin (1983), Sachs (1982), and Persson (1983). Although the basic models differ, these studies address common welfare questions relating to international lending. This chapter shares the same objective but also overlaps with a strand of literature that studies the time path of long-term asset prices in a stochastic optimal consumption setting. This literature, in particular Lucas (1978), Grossmann and Shiller (1981), and Leroy and LaCivita (1981), explores the effects of present and anticipated future output disturbances on asset prices and relates asset price movements to the movements in underlying fundamentals. The present study combines the two strands of literature in a deterministic model with international lending, overlapping generations and long-term, real assets.

The intergenerational model turns out to be interesting for open economy issues: opening trade in securities with sufficiently comprehensive compensation will improve welfare. But under more restricted compensation welfare deteriorates in the low interest rate country, even taking into account the possibility of intergenerational transfers. Debt issue must worsen the current account and deteriorate steady state welfare for the issuing country. Current, permanent income growth raises welfare and deteriorates the long-run trade balance. Of particular interest are results regarding future events or transitory disturbances. Here we show that transitory rise in income has the same effect on the current account as a permanent change, although asset prices change more than in the permanent case if the intertemporal elasticity of substitution in consumption is

Originally published in *Journal of International Economics*, vol. 18 (February 1985), pp. 123–139.

less than unity. Sections 17.1 and 17.2 set out the basic intergenerational model of consumption and saving for the closed economy. In section 17.4 the open economy equilibrium is introduced and the model is applied to discuss the benefits from trade in securities and some comparative static results are derived.

17.1 The Model

Households live two periods, working in the first but consuming in both. In the working part of their life they receive an exogenous disposable income, w, which is in part consumed and in part saved to finance second period consumption. At any point there are two generations, with an equal number of households. The only assets in the economy are *real* consols that pay one unit of the single consumption good indefinitely. Specifically there is no productive capital nor storeable output. These consols are issued by the government and serviced by a lump-sum tax on the working generation.

Thus, with a stock of debt outstanding equal to b, disposable income of the young, w, is equal to output less debt services:

$$w \equiv \tilde{w} - b, \tag{1}$$

where $\tilde{w}$ is the output endowment. The young apply their savings to purchasing consols from the old. The old, in the second period of their lives, consume the coupon income and sales proceeds of the consols. The consol price depends on the long-term interest rate, but the saving response of the young is geared to the short-term interest rate. We therefore note the relation between short- (one period) and long-term asset prices:

$$p_t = q_t(1 + p_{t+1}), \tag{2}$$

where p_i is the consol price in period i which equals the present value of the next period coupon plus the resale price. The term q_t is the one period discount factor that depends on the short-term interest rate.

Households maximize a two-period utility function:

$$U = V(c_1) + V(c_2), \quad V' > 0, \ V'' < 0, \ \lim_{c \to 0} V'(c) \to \infty, \tag{3}$$

subject to the budget constraint $c_1 + qc_2 = w$ yielding the first-order condition:

$$qV'(c_1) = V'(c_2). \tag{4}$$

The first-order condition, in conjunction with the budget constraint, gives rise to the consumption and savings functions:

$$c_1 = c_1(q, w), \quad s = s(q, w). \tag{5}$$

17.2 Equilibrium Asset Prices in the Closed Economy

Asset prices are determined by the equilibrium condition in the goods or asset market. Equilibrium obtains when the demand for goods by the two generations is equal to the total supply or, equivalently, when saving by the young equals the value of consols outstanding:[1]

$$s\left(\frac{p_t}{1 + p_{t+1}}, w_t\right) = p_t b_t, \tag{6}$$

where we have substituted from (2) for q_t in terms of present and future long-term asset prices.

We can equivalently state the equilibrium condition in terms of the first-order condition in (4), using (2) and (6), to obtain:

$$p_t V'(w - p_t b) = [1 + p_{t+1}] V'(b_t[1 + p_{t+1}]). \tag{6a}$$

The equilibrium asset price satisfying (6) or (6a) is in general governed by a difference equation. A special case, however, arises for the logarithmic utility function, $V(c) = \ln c$. In this case the equilibrium consol price is equal to[2]

$$p_t = \frac{w_t}{2b_t}. \tag{7}$$

The interesting feature of (7) is that *long-term* asset prices depend only on *current* disposable income and *current* asset stocks outstanding. The future path of income or asset supplies has no effect on consol prices.

The general case is described by equation (6a) and one possibility is shown in figure 17.1. The schedule $J(w, b)$ shows the difference equation in (6a) on the assumption that the elasticity of the marginal utility of consumption, $\theta(c) = -V''(c)c/V'(c)$, is smaller than unity. In that case the relation between p_t and p_{t+1} is positive with an intercept $0 < \bar{p}_t < w/b$. A unique steady state equilibrium will exist at point A since, by assumption, the marginal utility of consumption tends to infinity as consumption tends toward zero so that p_{t+1} must grow indefinitely as p_t approaches w/b.[3]

The case where the elasticity of the marginal utility is larger than unity leads to a negatively sloped $J(\cdot)$ schedule, as shown in figure 17.4 later. We

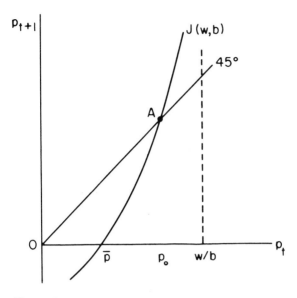

Figure 17.1
The determination of equilibrium asset prices

note that the elasticity of the marginal utility has a ready interpretation in terms of intertemporal substitution. At a zero interest rate consumption is equalized across time. In that case $1/\theta(c)$ measures the intertemporal elasticity of substitution.[4] Thus, the case of nearly constant marginal utility implies a high degree of intertemporal substitution and conversely for a highly concave utility function.

Point A in figure 17.1 is the steady state equilibrium. Consider now the adjustment process. It is apparent from the diagram that the only dynamics possible is an immediate jump to the steady state level of prices p_0. A path starting with a high level of current prices would imply that the value of bonds comes to exceed the wage of the young, implying a path that cannot be sustained. Alternatively, a lower starting price involves ultimately negative prices for the right to future incomes. Accordingly, the only adjustment consistent with perfect foresight is an immediate jump to point A.

In the case of an elasticity of substitution smaller than unity the $J(\cdot)$ schedule is negatively sloped, as in figure 17.4, and two possibilities arise in respect to the dynamics. If the slope at the 45° line is larger than unity in absolute value we have again an immediate jump to the steady state as the only perfect foresight path that does not violate the budget constraint. But in the alternative case adjustment consistent with perfect foresight and the

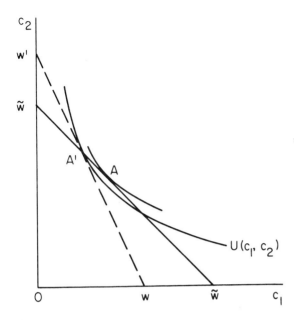

Figure 17.2
Welfare aspects of an economy with consols

equilibrium conditions of the model can be a damped oscillation starting from any initial condition. In the constant elasticity case this possibility arises if the elasticity of saving with respect to the relative price of future goods is positive but small.[5]

Welfare Aspects

In figure 17.2 we show the schedule $\tilde{w}\tilde{w}$ which is the social consumption possibility schedule and is a 45° line. The budget line facing an individual is, however, ww' which differs from $\tilde{w}\tilde{w}$ by the presence of debt service, $\tilde{w}-w$, and positive interest. Equilibrium will be at a point like A. The equilibrium is steady state welfare maximizing. Increased debt, because it raises the equilibrium interest rate, moves the economy to a point on $\tilde{w}\tilde{w}$ to the north-west of A'. It lowers welfare by moving the economy further away from a zero interest rate equilibrium.

The existence of consols (or simply sufficiently long-term bonds) in this model imposes a welfare cost because interest rates cannot be zero. In this respect the model differs from one where government debt takes the form of government issue of one-period debt. It is readily verified that if the government were to issue a stock of debt equal to $\tilde{w}/2$, rolled over every period and thus not requiring debt service, the economy would be in a socially efficient state with zero interest and equal consumption in every period.

The equilibrium at point A' implies lower steady state welfare than point A which would be attainable under an alternative debt scheme. But that does not imply that the equilibrium at A' is Pareto inferior. It is clear that society cannot move from A' to A, raising first-period consumption of the young, without making the older generation, in the transition, worse off.

Another feature of the consols, which sets them apart from money as it has been studied in overlapping generation models in particular by Neil Wallace, is the presence of a coupon. To smooth consumption intertemporally all that is required is *any* kind of government debt, including debt that is a claim to nothing such as a zero-coupon consol. But the fact that the consol does carry a coupon imposes a structure different from monetary models because of the need to raise revenue for debt service.

We conclude by showing the welfare change associated with a change in income or asset prices. From (1), the budget constraint and the first-order conditions the change in lifetime utility, measured in terms of first period consumption, is

$$\frac{dU}{V'(c_1)} = dc_1 + q\,dc_2 = dw - c_2\,dq. \tag{8}$$

Thus a household's welfare is improved by a rise in disposable income and by a decline in the relative price of future goods or rise in the short-term rate of interest. The young are lenders and therefore a decline in the relative price of future goods improves their terms of trade and welfare.

The Effects of Changes in Income

For comparative static questions we look at figure 17.3, where we show the effect of an increase in income. The simplest case is that of a current, unanticipated and permanent increase in income. This is shown by an outward rotation of the schedule $J(w, b)$, to J'.[6] Initial steady state equilibrium was at point A, and the new equilibrium is at A'. The increase in income therefore raises asset prices or lowers interest rates. The interpretation is straightforward: higher income, at unchanged interest rates, raises saving by the young and thus creates an excess demand for debt. To restore equilibrium in the capital market, asset prices must rise. The increase

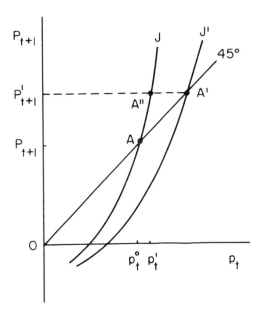

Figure 17.3
The effect of an increase in income

in asset prices or fall in interest rates establishes capital market equilibrium by lowering saving and increasing the value of consols outstanding.

A current, permanent increase in income will raise asset prices independently of the saving response to interest rates. This can be seen from figure 17.4, where we show the case of $\theta(c) > 1$ so that saving declines with increased interest rates. Increased income here also raises asset prices. This is the case because the effect of the decline in interest rates exerts a relatively stronger effect on the value of bonds outstanding than on the supply of saving. The result is possible because the elasticity of saving with respect to the interest rate is less than unity.[7]

We consider next an increase in income expected to occur one period hence. In this case, as already demonstrated, asset prices one period hence will be higher and equal to p'_{t+1} in figures 17.3 and 17.4. But present income and hence current saving are not changed. The present asset prices therefore continue to be determined by the schedule $J(w, b)$. At a future asset price p'_{t+1}, the current equilibrium asset price is thus indicated by point E'' in either of the diagrams.

There is an interesting difference between the two cases. If saving responds positively to the rate of interest (figure 17.3), a future increase in

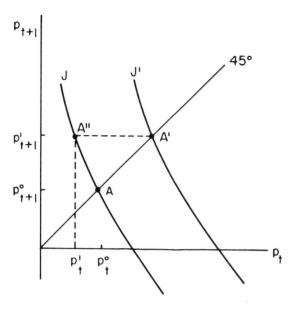

Figure 17.4
An anticipated future income increase

income raises both future and present asset prices. In this case all generations, the old, the current young, and future generations benefit. The old
make capital gains, while the young have the advantage of higher short-
term interest rates, and future generations have the benefit of increased
income. This is possible because high intertemporal substitutability allows
the shifting of consumption of the young to the future when output is
more plentiful. In fact, while the consol price rises in the present period and
thus the long-term interest rate declines, the short-term interest rate rises.
This induces intertemporal substitution, freeing resources so that the old
can share in the future income.[8]

The case where intertemporal substitutability is low, and thus saving
responds negatively to higher interest rates, is shown in figure 17.4. Higher
future income leads to a current fall in consol prices at point A''. With
present consol prices falling, the old lose as a consequence of higher future
incomes, but the current young gain relatively more because the short-term
interest rate rises strongly. The explanation is as follows: At unchanged
present consol prices, higher prices next period represent prospective
capital gains for the young. With income effects dominating substitution
effects, the young respond by reducing saving, preferring to consume
presently part of these capital gains. As a consequence there is an excess

supply of bonds and an excess demand for goods leading to increased short-term rates. It is clear then that the attempt to smooth consumption, when it dominates substitution, accounts for large interest rate and asset price movements. This is, of course, the point noted by Grossman and Shiller (1981).

The response of short- and long-term interest rates today to a future disturbance is further explored in (9). We define the short-term interest rate as $1 + r_t = 1/q_t$ and the long-term rate as $R_t \equiv 1/p_t$. With these definitions, using the goods market equilibrium condition and the definition of q_t, we can show the following:

$$\frac{dr_t - dR_t}{dp_{t+1}} = \left[(1 + q)\frac{1}{1 - \lambda} + 1 \right] p_{t+1},$$

$$\frac{dr_t}{dp_{t+1}} = \left[1 + \frac{1}{1 - \lambda} \right] p_{t+1}, \quad \hat{p}_t = -\frac{\lambda q_t}{1 - \lambda}\hat{p}_{t+1},$$

(9)

where λ is the elasticity of saving with respect to the asset price q_t and is a quantity smaller than unity (see note 6). From (9) an increase in future asset prices or a decline in the future long-term interest rate must raise the present short-term rate and must raise it relative to the present long-term rate. Furthermore the increase in the short- relative to the long-term rate is larger if the saving response to the interest rate is negative and large.

Debts and Deficits

A change in outstanding debt affects both the supply of debt and the value of disposable income. With a marginal propensity to save that is less than one, increased debt creates an excess supply of bonds and, in terms of figures 17.3 or 17.4, leads to a leftward shift of the J-schedule. Thus debt issue lowers steady state asset prices and raises steady state interest rates. Steady state welfare unambiguously declines.

The transition effects of the debt issue depend on the manner in which the debt is introduced. Assume that the government gives the bonds to the current old and that the bonds yield a coupon already in the transition period, financed by taxes on the young. Then the economy moves immediately to the new steady state. If, on the contrary, the bonds were given to the old without a current period coupon, or if they were given to the young, there would be a transition period in which the welfare distribution depends on how the bonds are introduced.

Consider now a simple case of deficit finance: the government transfers an amount T to the present old generation, raising the revenue by issuing consols in the amount $db = T/p$. Starting next period the service of the consols is ensured by increased taxation so that, except during the current period, the budget is balanced. What is the effect of such deficit finance on interest rates? From the analysis of figures 17.3 and 17.4 we have already seen that starting next period the steady state asset price must fall. In the long run the increased supply of debt must generate some crowding out, even though the debt service is fully financed by taxation. In the present period where there is a budget deficit the effect on short- and long-term interest rates is uncertain.

A clear solution prevails if saving responds positively to the interest rate, the case on which we concentrate now. In that event both the current short-and long-term interest rates must increase. As of a given asset price there is an increased supply of bonds outstanding, while demand is reduced because of anticipated capital losses. Equilibrium asset prices must fall to reduce the value of bonds outstanding and to raise saving by reducing expected capital losses. Moreover, it can be easily (though tediously) shown that in this case the long-term rate rises more than the short-term rate. Accordingly, in this case during periods of deficit finance the term structure is positively sloped.

The analysis extends readily to the case of anticipated future deficits due to either transfers or government spending. If saving responds positively to the interest rate the long-term rate will be rising. But the short-term rate will now decline prior to an anticipated deficit.[9]

17.3 The Open Economy

We now assume two countries identical in respect to tastes and population, but with potentially different incomes and debt outstanding. We are interested in determining the equilibrium asset price in the world as well as patterns of lending. Throughout we look at the case of one good and one asset. A $\tilde{}$ denotes stocks outstanding, so that $\tilde{b}^*$ is the existing stock of foreign-issued consols and b the actual holdings by the home country's old.

Equilibrium in the world goods market requires the balance of world income ($\tilde{w} + \tilde{w}^*$) and world consumption by the two generations in each country:

$$\tilde{w} + \tilde{w}^* = c_1 + c_1^* + (\tilde{b} + \tilde{b}^*)(1 + p). \tag{10}$$

An alternative way to write the equation is

$$s(q, w) - p\tilde{b} = p\tilde{b}^* - s^*(q, w^*).$$ (10a)

In this form we focus on the capital market. The excess of home saving over the value of debt outstanding equals net foreign lending.

The determination of equilibrium asset prices in the open economy is the same as that already studied in figure 17.1 for the closed economy. We can directly turn to some questions of comparative statics and welfare.

Opening Trade

The first question concerns the welfare effects of the opening of trade in securities. Suppose the two countries were initially in autarky and that now international lending becomes possible. For concreteness we assume that the home country has the higher ratio of disposable income to debt, $w/\tilde{b} > w^*/\tilde{b}^*$. The autarky asset price in the home country would therefore be higher than that abroad.

On opening of trade in securities asset prices at home would fall, and abroad they would rise. At home the old would experience capital and welfare losses, and abroad they would gain. The rise in interest rates at home would benefit the young, and the fall in interest rates abroad would hurt the young generation there. Thus the opening of trade, through distribution effects, makes some groups worse off. This is a theme familiar from traditional trade theory, also demonstrated in the intertemporal trade literature referred to earlier.

Since the opening of trade benefits the young, but hurts the old, we can ask whether a simple transfer would make the opening of trade possible without deteriorating any group's welfare in general. Consider first a situation where taxes can only be levied on the generation in the transition. To maintain the welfare of the old, their consumption level in the absence of trade, c_2, would have to be maintained. They would accordingly have to be compensated for consol price changes in the amount $-\tilde{b}\,dp$. This transfer reduces the disposable income of the young whose welfare changes by

$$\frac{dU}{V'} = \tilde{b}\,dp - c_2\,dq = q\tilde{b}\,dp,$$ (11)

which is unambiguously negative. The reason for the net welfare deterioration is that the young gain from the terms of trade improvement for only one period while the old suffer a capital loss on a consol.

An alternative is to compensate the old by a transfer from the young *and* from all future generations, who will come to benefit from the higher interest rate. To do this the government would issue consols, the proceeds of which serve to compensate the old, and the service being ensured by increased taxes on the present and future young. The increase in debt is equal to $db = -[\bar{b}/(1 + p)]\,dp$ and this is only a fraction of the capital losses incurred by the old.[10] Using this expression now in (8) we have

$$\frac{dU}{V'} = dw - c_2\,dq = \frac{b\,dp}{1 + p} - \frac{qc_2(1 - q)\,dp}{p} = 0. \tag{11a}$$

The calculation shows that opening to trade with compensation, at the margin, has no impact on welfare. The reason is the following. The gains from trade experienced by the young, $c_2\,dq$, are exactly equal to their share in the losses of the old with whom, in the initial equilibrium, they trade. Hence full compensation for these terms of trade effects leaves welfare exactly unchanged.

But this does not mean that there are no gains from trade once price changes in the transition to the open economy equilibrium can be larger than infinitesimal. Figure 17.5 illustrates the possibility for the logarithmic utility case: $U = \ln c_1 + \ln c_2$. It is readily shown that the free trade price is given by

$$p' = ap + (1 - a)p^*, \quad a \equiv \frac{b}{b + b^*}. \tag{12}$$

The free trade price therefore is the weighted average of the autarky prices p and p^* with weights given by the relative bond supplies. Consumption in the two periods is given by $c_1 = (w + k)/2$ and $c_2 = (w + k)/2q'$, where $k \equiv b(p' - p)/(1 + p')$ is the compensation tax. Using these expressions the value of the utility function is

$$U = -2\ln 2 + 2\ln(w + k) + \ln\left(1 + \frac{1}{p'}\right). \tag{13}$$

This function has a minimum at $p = p'$, a result we already saw in (11a). In figure 17.5 we plot the home and foreign utility functions against the free trade prices. Since the free trade price settles in the range between the autarky prices p and p^*, there will in general be gains from trade for both countries.

We have now shown that when compensation takes the form of an equal tax on the current and each future generation, there will be gains from trade. We can return to the question of whether there can be a gain, for sufficiently large discrepancies between free trade and autarky prices, even

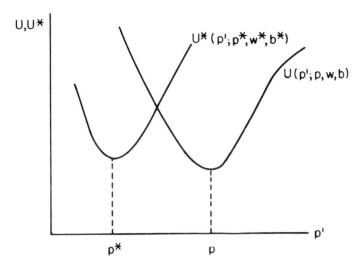

Figure 17.5
The gains from trade

in the case where the full compensation is paid by the current young. Figure 17.6 shows an example for the logarithmic case. It can be shown that in this case the autarky price lies in the range of the utility function where it is positively sloped. In the example shown the autarky price can settle near p^* if the foreign relative bond supply is large.[11] In that case it is possible that the home country is better off, present and future generations, even though the compensation is fully paid by the transition generation. We also note that in the high interest rate country welfare *must* improve independently of the magnitude of price change in the transition to free trade.

Some Comparative Statics

We now study the effects of permanent, current changes in income and in debt on equilibrium interest rates, the current account and welfare. We start with the case of a permanent rise in home income.

From the goods market equilibrium conditions in (10a) we find that a rise in home income raises the equilibrium price of goods or lowers the interest rate, just as it does in the closed economy:

$$\hat{p} = \frac{x}{1 - \lambda(1 - q)} \hat{w}, \quad x \equiv \frac{s}{s + s^*}. \tag{14}$$

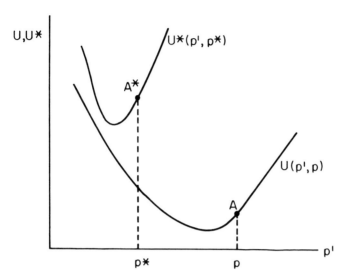

Figure 17.6
Gains from trade with compensation paid by the current generations only

The extent of the decline in interest rates or rise in asset prices depends on the response of saving to the interest rate. Consider next the current account effects.

We define the net rate of capital outflow or the aggregate current account surplus of the home country as K:

$$K = s(q, w) - pb. \tag{15}$$

The current account equals the excess of saving or lending by the young generation over bond sales—the excess of consumption over income from debt for the older generation—by the old. In the steady state the current account will be zero and the trade surplus will equal the net external debt service liability, $\bar{b} - b$. Using (14) and (15) yields

$$\frac{dK}{dw} = \alpha(1 - x), \quad \alpha \equiv \frac{qc_2}{w}. \tag{16}$$

The current account effects thus depend only on the average propensity to consume in the second period and on the relative size of the home country. The larger the home country, the smaller will be the current account effect of income growth. The higher the propensity to save, the larger will be the current account effect.

The current account surplus of the home country is only transitory, leading to an increased home net lending position, and therefore to a steady state deterioration in the home country's trade balance. Here is an interesting result in that higher income induces a steady state deterioration in the trade balance. The trade balance deterioration reflects the fact that the initial current account surplus has increased home debt holdings and with that has raised income relative to the endowment. Since in the new steady state aggregate disposable income is equal to expenditure, expenditure exceeds output and thus there is a trade deficit financed by income from net external assets.

Consider now the welfare effects of higher home income. The higher bond prices imply capital gains and increased welfare for the present old. Abroad steady state welfare declines since the fall in interest rates worsens the terms of trade of the young who are net lenders and whose welfare therefore deteriorates. At home the higher income raises welfare of the young, but this is dampened by the adverse rise in the relative price of future goods. The net effect, however, is a welfare improvement. Accordingly, the possibility of Edgeworth-like damnifying growth does not arise in this model.

The analysis of changes in debt is straightforward. From (10a) we calculate the effect of home debt issue on steady state asset prices as

$$\hat{p} = -\frac{(\alpha + p)}{p(\tilde{b} + \tilde{b}^*)(1 - \lambda(1 - q))} d\tilde{b}. \tag{17}$$

Thus home debt issue must lead to a decline in asset prices or a rise in the equilibrium interest rate. Steady state welfare abroad must rise since lifetime utility, as shown in (8), rises if asset prices decline, the young being net lenders. In the home country, debt issue, just as in the closed economy, exerts offsetting effects through the reduction in disposable income due to higher taxes and the change in interest rates. Just as in the closed economy case, it can be shown that the net effect is a reduction in lifetime utility both for the currently young and in the steady state.

The effect of home debt issue on the long-run trade balance and external indebtedness can be definitely established: home debt issue reduces net external assets, $b - \tilde{b}$, and therefore leads to an improvement in the long-run trade balance. This result is to be expected since abroad real income increases via the rise in interest rates thereby leading, through substitution and income effects, to higher second period consumption. With bond prices falling, $c_2^* = (1 + p)b^*$ implies that foreign bond holdings increase. The long-run trade balance improvement for the home country thus reflects the counterpart of the differential foreign increase in real income and welfare.

We studied, for the closed economy, the case of currently anticipated future income growth. In that case the equilibrium current short-term interest rate rises immediately and falls once the increase in income occurs. Exactly the same result will, of course, arise in the world economy. The only question is whether future income disturbances have effects on today's current account.

It is readily verified that the present current account is unaffected by the future income growth. The reason is the complete symmetry of this one-good, one-asset model, with identical consumers who in the steady state have zero capital flows. To have an impact on the current account, disturbances must affect the two countries' net saving differentially. This is the case of current disturbances but it does not arise for future disturbances, except when preferences differ.

17.4 Concluding Remarks

The intergenerational exchange model sets a minimal framework for addressing intertemporal issues in trade theory. The introduction of long-term debt, and hence the term structure of interest, makes current accounts depend not only on relative present incomes but also on future events. The model is a minimal framework, and for that reason cannot go much further. But it is immediately obvious that extensions to a multiple commodity setting open up interesting questions, as does the possibility of introducing real capital. Another range of questions is concerned with taxation of international lending and with an optimal external debt. These issues are left for further work.

Notes

Financial support was provided by a grant from the National Science Foundation. I wish to acknowledge especially helpful comments from Lars Svensson, Zvi Eckstein, Elphanan Helpman, and Steve Zeldes.

1. Goods market equilibrium requires that output, $\tilde{w}$, be equal to demand: $\tilde{w} = c_1(q, w) + (1 + p)b$ or $w - c_1 \equiv s = pb$.

2.Fischer (1981) has discussed this case in a stochastic setting in interpreting results by Lucas (1978).

3. The slope of the $J(\cdot)$ schedule is

$$\frac{dp_{t+1}}{dp_t} = \frac{V'(c_2) + (1 + p_{t+1})bV''(c_2)}{V'(c_1) - p_t bV''(c_1)}.$$

Noting the definition of the elasticity of marginal utility, we can see that the slope is positive if $\theta(c)$ is less than unity.

4. From the first-order condition we have, by logarithmic differentiation, $d \ln(c_1/c_2) = (1/\theta(c)) d \ln q$, where by assumption the expression is evaluated at $c_1 = c_2 = c$. To fix ideas, we can think of a constant elasticity utility function:

$$V(c) = \frac{1}{1 - \theta} c^{1-\theta}.$$

In this case equation (6a) becomes

$$p_{t+1} = \left[\frac{p_t^{1/\theta}}{w/b - p_t} \right]^{\theta/1-\theta} - 1.$$

5. Using the expression for the slope of the $J(\cdot)$ function, it is readily shown that the condition $(-1) dp_{t+1}/dp_t < 1$ implies $(c_1/w)(1 - 1/\theta) < 1/(1 + q)$. The expression $(c_1/w)(1 - 1/\theta) = \partial \ln s/\partial \ln q$ is the elasticity of saving with respect to the relative price of future goods.

6. The rightward shift of the $J(\cdot)$ schedule from (6a) is given by

$$\frac{dp_t}{dw} = -\frac{p_t V''(c_1)}{V'(c_1) - p_t bV''(c_1)} > 0.$$

7. The elasticity of saving with respect to the short-term asset price q_t is given by

$$\lambda \equiv \frac{\upsilon \ln s}{\partial \ln q} = \frac{\phi[\theta(c_2) - 1]}{\theta(c_1) + \theta(c_2)\phi},$$

where $\phi \equiv c_1/qc_2$. It is readily shown that with an elasticity of the marginal utility $\theta(c_i)$ larger than unity, the elasticity of saving with respect to the asset price must be less than unity. Hence an increase in asset prices creates an excess demand for bonds.

8. The analysis is easily extended to the case where future income growth is transitory or occurs at a more distant point in time. In the latter case the consol price will rise gradually toward the long-run level if saving responds positively to the rate of interest. Otherwise, asset prices show a backward dampened oscillation. See also Fischer (1979).

9. For a derivation and further discussion, see Dantas and Dornbusch (1984).

10. The government taxes the present and future young by an equal amount, db. Taxes on the current young, db, plus the value of the bond transfer, $p\,db$, must equal the capital losses. Hence we have $\bar{b}\,dp = -(1 + p)\,db$ or $db = -\bar{b}\,dp/(1 + p)$.

11. Figure 17.6 is drawn on the assumption $p > p^*$ and $w = w^*$. Disposable income after the opening of trade is $w + (p' - p)b$. The value of utility as a function of p' therefore is $U = 2\ln 2 + 2\ln(w + k) + \ln(1 + 1/p')$, with $k = (p' - p)b$.

References

Buiter, W. 1981. Time preference and international lending and borrowing in an overlapping-generations model. *Journal of Political Economy* 89: 769–797.

Calvo, G. 1978. On the indeterminacy of interest rates and wages with perfect foresight. *Journal of Economic Theory* 19: 321–337.

Dantas, D., and Dornbusch, R. 1984. Anticipated budget deficits and the term structure of interest. Unpublished manuscript. Massachusetts Institute of Technology.

Diamond, P. 1965. National debt in a neoclassical growth model. *American Economic Review* 55: 1126–1150.

Dornbusch, R. 1983. Real interest rates, home goods and optimal external borrowing. *Journal of Political Economy* 91: 141–153.

Fischer, S. 1979. Anticipations and the nonneutrality of money. *Journal of Political Economy* 87: 225–252.

Fischer, S. 1981. A model of asset trade. Unpublished lecture notes. Massachusetts Institute of Technology.

Fried, J. 1980. The intergenerational distribution of the gains from technical change and from international trade. *Canadian Journal of Economics* 13: 65–81.

Gale, D. 1971. General equilibrium with imbalance of trade. *Journal of International Economics* 1: 159–188.

Gale, D. 1974. The trade imbalance story. *Journal of International Economics* 4: 118–137.

Grossman, S., and Shiller, R. 1981. The determinants of the variability of stock prices. *American Economic Review* 71: 222–227.

Kareken, J., and Wallace, N. 1977. Portfolio autarky: A welfare analysis. *Journal of International Economics* 7: 19–44.

LeRoy, S., and LaCivita, C.J. 1981. Risk aversion and the dispersion of asset prices. *Journal of Business* 54: 535–548.

Lucas, R. 1978. Asset prices in an exchange economy. *Econometrica* 46: 1429–1445.

Persson, T. 1983. Deficits and intergenerational welfare in open economies. NBER Working Paper 1083.

Sachs, J. 1982. The current account in the macroeconomics adjustment process. *Scandinavian Journal of Economics* 84: 147–159.

Svensson, L., and Razin, A. 1983. The terms of trade and the current account: The Harberger-Laursen-Metzler effect. *Journal of Political Economy* 91: 97–125.

IV

Inflation and Stabilization

Introduction to Part IV

This final part of the book brings together five essays on inflation and stabilization in the open economy. The first essay on real balances and consumption develops a classical analysis of the link between money and spending: the infinitely lived household which derives utility services from money holdings had been introduced by Miguel Sidrauski in the money and growth literature. In this article money does not compete with real assets, and accordingly no portfolio decision needs to be made. The only short-run decision to be made concerns the rate of consumption, given real balances. The optimal rate of adjustment of real balances follows a simple stock adjustment rule which is often postulated in the monetary approach to the balance of payments. It is interesting to note that the coefficient of adjustment of real balances depends positively on the rate of inflation. The higher the rate of inflation, the more rapid the adjustment to discrepancies between current and long-run consumption.

The model developed in the next essay assumes that the household faces a given price level. But assume the household is the representative consumer in a small country and assume also purchasing power parity. With these simple assumptions the model becomes a useful framework to ask questions about the response of consumption and the trade balance to changes in the level or rate of change of the exchange rate. Guillermo Calvo has developed highly interesting work in this direction.

The question of the government budget and the consequences of a shift from money to debt finance—what has come to be known as the Sargent-Wallace problem—are studied in the following article. The essay was written for a Festschrift in honor of Karl Brunner. Although Brunner's work in the 1960s was in the monetarist camp, it always struck me that his beliefs were more similar to those of Tobin than of monetarism. The essay pays homage to his sophisticated analysis by showing that a shift from money to debt finance may raise inflation and reduce capital intensity—an outcome that simple monetarism would scarcely predict.

The Latin American experience of overvaluation and external borrowing is modeled in an article that was presented as the first Miguel Sidrauski Lecture of the Latin American Econometric Society in Buenos Aires in July 1980. The Sidrauski lecture is sponsored by the Latin American Econometric Society to honor the memory of the Argentine economist Miguel Sidrauski who died in 1968 at the very beginning of an extraordinarily promising career. At the time the lecture was given Argentina was in the midst of a large overvaluation which had resulted from a policy of prefixing the exchange rate designed to bring down inflation. The predictions of the model—current account problems, unemployment, collapse, and an ultimate resumption of inflation—were not widely believed at the time, even though they materialized within a year.

In the aftermath of Tom Sargent's important essay "The End of Four Big Inflations" interest in the monetary economics of hyperinflation has returned on a major scale. The experience of high inflation in Latin America and Israel in the 1980s, of course, reinforced the interest already created by Sargent's important and challenging essay. The article on the German hyperinflation takes issue with Sargent's basic message: inflation comes to a halt when the government credibly changes fiscal policy. By relying on sources of the time, I try to make the case that there was in fact no "credible" change in fiscal policy.

The key to stabilization, I argue, was the fixing of the exchange rate and then, over the succeeding month, the experience of de facto stabilization. In an economy where all prices are based on the dollar, it is not surprising that fixing the exchange rate, and sustaining the rate, is a much more forceful way of stabilizing than the sheer announcement of policies which then may or may not be executed. Of course, there is no lasting stabilization without attention to the fiscal fundamentals of price stability. But, and this is the point, when there is no effective way of establishing fundamental change except by demonstrating it over time, then exchange rate fixing can generate a powerful tool of de facto stabilization.

The concluding essay deals with the recent experience of stabilization in Latin America and Isreal. The essay makes the case for incomes policy as a means of supplementing fiscal correction in the stabilization of inflation. A stabilization that works only on the demand side cannot fail to create a recession and as such is politically unacceptable. Incomes policy alone cannot yield a lasting stabilization. The combination of both offers a realistic possibility of stopping inertial inflation in the three digits and above without the risk of recession. The case for a combination is made by showing that stopping inflation involves a game-theoretic coordination problem which can be resolved by exchange rate, price, and wage controls.

18

Consumption, Real Balances, and the Hoarding Function

(with Michael Mussa)

This chapter discusses the relationship between consumption and real money balances in a model of intertemporal optimization. Patinkin (1965) demonstrated the theoretical importance of the real balance effect in neoclassical monetary theory. Archibald and Lipsey (1958) focussed on the implications of the real balance effect for the question of stability. Douglas (1968), Marty (1964), Motley (1969), and Sidrauski (1967) emphasized the capital-theoretic implications of the real balance effect, viewed as an issue of asset accumulation. The present analysis builds on this capital-theoretic approach and investigates the implications of a model of lifetime utility maximization for the time paths of consumption and money holdings.

Our specific objective is to present a model in which optimal consumption and real money holdings are related to each other through a "hoarding function" which specifies the rate at which the household saves in order to close the gap between actual real money holdings, m, and long-run desired money holdings, m^*. More particularly, we develop the structure required to make optimal hoarding proportional to the gap between m and m^*, with a constant factor of proportionality, v^*, which is equal to consumption velocity.

The consumption function which is implied by this proportional hoarding function will be shown to be

$$c = y + v^*(m - m^*).$$

The household consumes its income, y, plus some fraction, v^*, of the difference between actual current real money holdings and long-run desired money holdings. This form of the consumption function has played an important role in discussions of monetary theory, for instance, in

Originally published in *International Economic Review*, vol. 16, no. 2 (June 1975), pp. 415–421.

Friedman's (1969) analysis of the optimum quantity of money. It has also been used as a component in more general models of macroeconomic behavior in order to provide a direct link between money balances and expenditure. More recently, it has been employed in theoretical analyses of the balance of payments.[1] Our present purpose is to provide a rigorous foundation for this particular form of the consumption function in terms of a model of intertemporal optimization.

18.1 A Model of Intertemporal Allocation

We assume an infinitely lived "household" which receives a constant stream of real income, y, and seeks to maximize its total lifetime utility, U, by choice of optimal time paths of consumption, c, and real money holdings, m. Total lifetime utility is assumed to be given by the present discounted value of the flow of utility, $u(c, m)$, which the household enjoys at each moment of time. The flow of utility is a function of the rate of commodity consumption and the level of real money holdings. m is included as an argument in the flow of utility function in order to represent the "nonpecuniary services" of money. To calculate lifetime utility, the flow of utility is discounted at the "pure rate of time preference, " δ. The flow of utility function, $u(c, m)$, is assumed to be homogeneous of degree one in its two arguments, twice continuously differentiable, increasing as a function of either c or m, and strictly quasi-concave, and it is assumed to satisfy the limit conditions:

$$\lim_{c/m \to \infty} \left(\frac{u_m}{u_c} \right) = \infty,$$

$$\lim_{c/m \to 0} \left(\frac{u_m}{u_c} \right) = 0.$$

Formally, the household's intertemporal allocation problem is to maximize U, given by (1), by choice of the time paths, $c(t)$ and $m(t)$, subject to the budget constraint (2), the nonnegativity conditions (3), and the initial condition (4):

$$U = \int_0^\infty u(c(t), m(t)) e^{-\delta t} \, dt, \tag{1}$$

$$\dot{m}(t) \equiv \frac{dm(t)}{dt} = y - c(t), \tag{2}$$

$$c(t) \geq 0, \, m(t) \geq 0, \quad \text{for all } t \geq 0, \tag{3}$$

$$m(0) = \bar{m}, \tag{4}$$

given.

To find the solution of the household's intertemporal allocation problem, we will employ the Pontryagin technique.[2] Form the Hamiltonian H:

$$H(c; m, \lambda) \equiv [u(c, m) + \lambda(y - c)]e^{-\delta t}. \tag{5}$$

In this Hamiltonian, $\lambda(t)$ is the dual state variable to $m(t)$ and has the interpretation of the "shadow value of real money balances at time t." The optimal time paths of c, m, and λ must satisfy the following conditions:[3]

$$\frac{\partial H}{\partial c} = u_c - \lambda = 0, \tag{6}$$

$$\dot{m} = \frac{\partial H}{\partial(\lambda e^{-\delta t})} = y - c, \tag{7}$$

$$\dot{\lambda} - \lambda\delta = -\frac{\partial H}{\partial m}e^{-\delta t} = -u_m, \tag{8}$$

$$\lim_{t \to \infty} \lambda(t)e^{-\delta t} \geq 0, \tag{9}$$

$$\lim_{t \to \infty} \lambda(t)e^{-\delta t} m(t) = 0. \tag{10}$$

The first of these conditions, (6), imposes the requirement that the Hamiltonian be maximized with respect to the current choice variable, $c(t)$, at every moment of time, given the values of the state variables, m and λ. The next two conditions, (7) and (8), are the transition laws for the state variables. Condition (7) is a repetition of the budget constraint (2). Making use of (6), (8) may be rewritten in the form

$$\frac{\dot{\lambda}}{\lambda} = \delta - \gamma\left(\frac{c}{m}\right), \tag{11}$$

where

$$\gamma\left(\frac{c}{m}\right) \equiv \frac{u_m}{u_c}. \tag{12}$$

The ratio u_m/u_c has the interpretation of the "marginal nonpecuniary rate of return on real money balances" or, alternatively, the "own rate of return on real money balances." This ratio depends only on the ratio of c to m

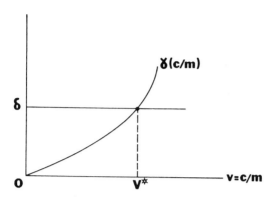

Figure 18.1

because of the assumption that the flow of utility function is homogeneous in c and m. The behavior of the own rate of return on money as a function of c/m is exhibited in figure 18.1. The limit conditions of $u(c, m)$ ensure that u_m/u_c approaches zero as $v = c/m$ approaches zero and approaches infinity as v approaches infinity, while quasi-concavity implies that $\gamma(c/m)$ is everywhere an increasing function of v. From (11), it follows that there will be a unique value of c/m, say $v^* = c^*/m^*$, for which $\dot{\lambda} = 0$. To emphasize that this value of v is a function of δ, we may write

$$v^* = v^*(\delta), \quad v^{*\prime} > 0. \tag{13}$$

$v = c/m$ has the interpretation of "consumption velocity," the ratio of consumption expenditures to real money balances. We will now show that there is a path for c, m, and λ along which $v = v^*(\delta)$ which satisfies the initial condition (4) and all of the conditions of optimality, (6) to (10), and is, therefore, the optimal time path for the household. Given the initial value of m, $\bar{m}$, the condition that $v = v^*$ determines the initial value of c to be

$$c(0) = v^*\bar{m}. \tag{14}$$

This initial value of c together with the initial value of m and the condition (6) determine the initial value of λ to be

$$\lambda(0) = u_c(c(0), \bar{m}). \tag{15}$$

Since (6) and (8) together with the assumption that $v = v^*$ imply $\dot{\lambda} = 0$, it follows that

$$\lambda(t) = \lambda(0), \quad \text{for all } t \geq 0. \tag{16}$$

Given that $c(t)/m(t) = v^*$, (7) becomes

$$\dot{m}(t) = -v^* m(t) + y. \tag{17}$$

Imposing the initial condition $m(0) = \bar{m}$, this differential equation has the solution

$$m(t) = m^* + e^{-v^* t}(m^*), \tag{18}$$

where

$$m^* = \frac{y}{v^*}. \tag{19}$$

Given the assumption that $v = v^*$, it follows that the time path of consumption must be

$$c(t) = v^* m(t). \tag{20}$$

By construction, the time paths of c, m and $\dot{\lambda}$ determined by (14) through (20) satisfy the optimality conditions (6) through (8) and the constraints (2) through (4). Since along this path, $\lambda(t) = \lambda(0) > 0$, it follows that the first "transversality" condition, (9), is satisfied. Substituting from (16) and (18) into the left-hand side of (10), it follows that this second "transversality" condition is also satisfied. Since the paths of c, m, and λ determined by (14) through (20) satisfy all of the conditions of optimality, they must be the optimal paths of these variables.[4]

18.2 The Hoarding Function

The determination of the optimal time paths of c and m may be shown graphically by making use of figure 18.2. The optimal value of velocity, v^*, is determined by the slope of the ray through the origin, OR^*, along which $u_m/u_c = \delta$. The optimal path of c and m lies along this ray. In particular, the starting point for the optimal path is the point along OR^* for which $m = \bar{m}$. In figure 18.2, where it is assumed that $\bar{m}$ is greater than m^*, the starting point for the optimal path is A. At A, consumption is greater than income, y. Hence, by the budget constraint, (2), money balances must be falling. As money balances fall, the optimum point moves down OR^* from A toward B. B is the optimum steady state position for the household. At B, the household is consuming exactly its income, and money balances are equal to their optimum steady state value, $m^* = y/v^*$.

At any moment of time, t, the houshold's position along R^* is determined by the household's current money balances, $m(t)$. The rate at which the household moves along R^* is determined by the rate of change of m.

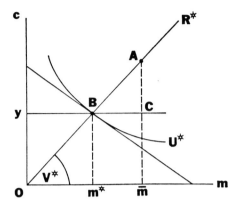

Figure 18.2

From (17) and (19) it follows that the rate of change of m is determined by the hoarding function

$$\dot{m}(t) = v^*(m^* - m(t)).\tag{21}$$

The household accumulates money balances at a rate which is proportional to the difference between its current money holdings and its optimal steady-state holdings, where the factor of proportionality is consumption velocity, v^*.

The behavior of consumption along the optimum path may also be described in terms of the hoarding function. From (2) it follows that

$$c(t) = y + v^*(m(t) - m^*).\tag{22}$$

The household consumes more (less) than its income in proportion to the excess (deficiency) of its current real money holdings over its long-run desired money holdings. In this sense there is a direct real balance effect on consumption.

18.3 Effects of a Change in Income

The level of income, y, is treated as a parameter in the household's intertemporal allocation problem. The effect of a (permanent) change in the level of income is to raise long-run consumption by exactly the change in y so that the long-run marginal propensity to consume is unity.

In the short run, with a given level of real balances m, however, the change in consumption will be zero since consumption is always proportional to real balances and the latter are, instantaneously, unaffected by the change in income. Thus the short-run or instantaneous marginal propensity to consume out of income is zero, while the marginal propensity to hoard is unity. Only as the accumulated hoarding over time affects the level of money balances will the rate of consumption respond to the change in income. This result, that the short-run marginal propensity to consume out of income is equal to zero, depends critically on the assumption that the change in income is permanent and on the result that the marginal propensity to consume out of cash balances is equal to consumption velocity.

18.4 Concluding Remarks

A particular and explicit functional form for the relation between consumption, hoarding, income, and cash balances has been derived in this chapter in the framework of a model of intertemporal optimization. It implies a proportional adjustment of cash balances and a constant consumption velocity. Not surprisingly the restrictions that have to be imposed on the problem to generate a particular functional form—as opposed to proving existence and qualitative properties of an optimal solution—are very stringent, and none of them can be relaxed if the object is to maintain the functional form of the behavioral equations.

There is scope, however, for relaxation of some of the assumptions if the purpose is merely to derive consumption functions with real balances as an argument. In particular, the restriction of linear homogeneity will not be required although some structure will be needed. Similarly, if the purpose is merely to study long-run relationships between variables, we can derive some of the properties developed above from a less restrictive set of assumptions.

A more fundamental departure from the spirit of this model is introduced if there is an alternative asset which bears a rate of return and which the household can trade for stocks of cash balances at a point in time without transactions costs. With such an extension the household would always and instantaneously be in portfolio equilibrium along the optimal path and consumption would either grow, remain constant or fall as the rate of interest exceeded, equalled or fell short of the rate of time preference.[5]

Notes

1. See Dornbusch (1973).

2. For an exposition of this technique, see Arrow (1968).

3. We assume that nonnegativity condition is always satisfied. The assumption that has been made concerning the behavior of u_m/u_c for extreme values of c/m ensures that this is a reasonable restriction.

4. See Arrow (1968, thm. 7). Note that the second-order condition given by Arrow in theorem 7 cannot be used in the present case since the assumption that $u(c, m)$ is linear homogeneous implies that the maximized Hamiltonian is a linear function of m. A procedure similar to that described by Cass (1965) is required in order to prove that the proposed optimum path is a utility maximum rather than a utility minimum.

5. For a discussion of such models and a derivation of explicit functional forms, see Kudoh (1975) and Mussa (1976).

References

Archibald, C., and Lipsey, R. 1958. "Monetary and Value Theory: A Critique of Lange and Patinkin." *Review of Economic Studies* 25 (October), 1–23.

Arrow, K. J. 1968. "Applications of Control Theory to Economic Growth." In *Lectures in Applied Mathematics*. Vol. 12. Providence, R. I.: American Mathematical Society.

Cass, D. 1965. "Optimum Growth in an Aggregative Model of Capital Accumulation." *Review of Economic Studies* 32 (June), 233–240.

Dornbusch, R. 1973. "Devaluation, Money and Nontraded Goods," *American Economic Review* 63 (December), 871–880.

Douglas, A. 1968. "A Theory of Saving and Portfolio Selection." *Review of Economic Studies* 35 (October), 453–464.

Friedman, M. 1969. *The Optimum Quantity of Money and Other Essays*. Chicago: Aldine.

Kudoh, K. 1975. "A Note on a Consumption Function in Monetary Theory." *Journal of Money, Credit and Banking* 7 (February), 117–121.

Marty, A. 1964. "The Real Balance Effect: An Exercise in Capital Theory," *Canadian Journal of Economics and Political Science* 30 (August), 360–367.

Motley, B. 1969. "The Consumer's Demand for Money: A Neoclassical Approach," *Journal of Political Economy* 77 (September/October), 817–826.

Mussa, M. 1976. *A Study in Macroeconomics*. Amsterdam: North-Holland.

Patinkin, D. 1965. *Money, Interest and Prices*. 2nd ed. New York: Harper and Row.

Sidrauski, M. 1967. "Rational Choice Patterns and Growth in a Monetary Economy," *American Economic Review* 62 (May), 534–544.

19   Inflation, Capital, and Deficit Finance

The short-run effects of financial policy on the level and composition of output and its allocation between the government and the private sector are agreed upon to a significant extent. A more novel question concerns the intermediate and long-run consequences of policies that arise from the requirements of financing budgetary imbalance and the implications of financial asset accumulation through the budgetary process for the accumulation of real capital as well as for the rate of inflation. Questions that can be addressed in this context are, for example, whether increased government spending will, in the long run, reduce the capital stock and raise the rate of inflation, or whether a shift toward money finance will raise the capital stock.

The effects of alternative strategies of government finance, and more particularly the effects of debt finance, have been analyzed in the traditional aggregate demand oriented framework of macroeconomics. In this framework, with fixed-price and neo-Keynesian variants, the question is raised whether an increase in government spending, financed at least in part by debt, will prove expansionary. There is the further question whether such a model is stable in the sense that the budget returns to balance with increased real taxes matching the change in government spending and real debt service. Such models go back to Christ (1968), and more recent work includes the contributions in Blinder and Solow (1973) and Stein (1976). A different approach to these questions is offered in the money, growth, and inflation literature. Here the question is asked how the choice of an exogenously fixed growth rate of the nominal quantity of money, and hence of the rate of inflation, affects long-run capital intensity. Ordinarily money creation in these models, reviewed in Dornbusch and Frenkel (1973), takes

Originally published in *Journal of Money Credit and Banking*, part 2 (February 1977), pp. 141–150.

the form of transfers. The analysis lends itself, though, to an extension where government spending, taxes, and deficit finance via money and debt creation are allowed to affect the rate of inflation and the long-run capital intensity. This approach is developed in Brunner and Meltzer (1975), Burmeister and Phelps (1971), Foley and Sidrauski (1971), Mundell (1971), and Stein (1976). This chapter follows the same line of analysis and develops a model where both inflation and capital intensity are endogenous and are determined by fiscal variables and the financing policy with respect to the budget.

19.1 The Model

To formalize the long-run relation between inflation, capital intensity, and the budget we assume a standard neoclassical monetary model.[1] Output is produced according to a linear homogeneous production function and the labor force is fixed. Therefore output net of depreciation y is simply a function of the capital stock, as is the yield on capital r:

$$y = y(k), \quad y_k \equiv r(k). \tag{1}$$

We will be concerned exclusively with the steady state, and for this reason aggregate demand consists of consumption spending and government spending. By the definition of the steady state, net investment spending is zero. Steady-state goods market equilibrium or equivalently the condition of zero net investment, requires that net supply equal aggregate demand:

$$y(k) = c(w) + g, \tag{2}$$

where c, w, and g denote respectively consumption, real wealth, and government spending. Consumption is a function of wealth only. The omission of an interest rate from the consumption function can be interpreted as a cancelling of the income and substitution effects of a change in the rate of interest.

Real wealth is defined as the sum of real balances m, real debt holdings b, and real capital:[2]

$$w \equiv m + b + k. \tag{3}$$

Portfolio choices are described by the demand for real money balances. Debt and capital are assumed perfect substitutes. The fraction of wealth held in the form of money is a function of the nominal rate of interest i. Money, as is conventionally assumed, does not bear interest. Accordingly an increase in the rate of interest lowers the fraction of wealth the public wishes to hold in the form of money. The condition of monetary equilibrium is the balance between money demand and money supply:

$$m = \sigma(i)w. \tag{4}$$

In (4) i is the nominal rate of interest, $i = r + \pi$, where π is the rate of inflation. The model is closed by the government budget constraint. It is assumed that a fraction v of the budget is financed by debt creation and a fraction $1-v$ by the issue of money. The assumption of a proportional tax on real income—rather than progressive taxation of nominal income—ensures the possibility of steady-state inflation. Thus in the steady state, nominal debt and money grow at the same rate, namely, the rate of inflation. Accordingly, we can write

$$\pi m = (1 - v)\theta, \quad \pi b = v\theta, \tag{5}$$

where θ is the real budget deficit. From (5) it follows that in the steady state, money and debt stand in a relation that is determined by the financing parameter v:

$$b = \frac{mv}{1 - v}. \tag{6}$$

The real budget deficit finally is given by

$$\theta \equiv g - t(y + ib) + ib, \tag{7}$$

where t is the tax rate on income from production and debt and where ib is the real flow of debt service.

Equations (1) though (7) complete the steady-state model. The system can be used to determine the long-run equilibrium capital stock and the rate of inflation. Furthermore questions can be asked concerning the comparative static results of changes in parameters. In particular, we are interested in the response of inflation and capital intensity to the exogenous variables, namely, the tax rate, government spending, and the financing composition of the budget.

Consider first the determination of long-run equilibrium capital and inflation. For that purpose we substitute from (6) and (3) in (4) to express real balances and real wealth as functions of the capital stock

$$m = x(k, v, \pi)k; \quad w = \left[1 + \left(\frac{x}{1 - v}\right)\right]k; \quad b = \left(\frac{vx}{1 - v}\right)k, \tag{8}$$

where

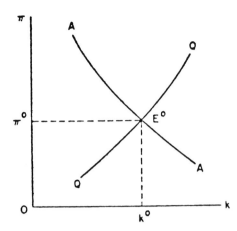

Figure 19.1
Equilibrium inflation and capital stock

$$x \equiv \frac{\sigma(1 - v)}{1 - v - \sigma} = x(k, v, \pi) > 0; \quad x_k > 0, x_\pi < 0, x_v > 0, \tag{9}$$

is the equilibrium ratio of money to capital. An increase in the capital stock lowers the real rate of interest and therefore raises the fraction of wealth held in the form of money so that x_k is unambiguously positive. An increase in v, the fraction of the budget financed by debt, will increase by (8) the ratio of wealth to capital and therefore raise real balances relative to the capital stock.

Substituting the equation for equilibrium wealth in (8) into the consumption function in (2) yields an equation for goods market equilibrium in terms of the two endogenous variables, inflation and capital, for given fiscal parameters. In figure 19.1 we show the locus QQ along which the goods and asset markets are in equilibrium in the sense that (8) and (2) hold. The QQ schedule is positively sloped on the assumption that an increase in inflation reduces consumption and therefore creates an excess supply:[3]

$$c_k > 0, \quad \alpha \equiv y_k - c_k < 0, \quad c_\pi < 0. \tag{10}$$

The interpretation of the QQ schedule is as follows: An increase in the capital stock directly raises net supply. Consumption spending is raised by an increase in capital in two ways. First, the increase in capital directly raises wealth. Second, the increase in capital lowers the real interest rate and therefore, by (9), raises the ratio of money to capital and thus further increases wealth. An increase in inflation, by lowering the ratio of money to capital and thus lowering wealth at each capital stock, reduces consumption. To maintain balance between net supply and aggregate demand, given that we assume $\alpha < 0$, a higher capital stock has to be associated with a higher rate of inflation.

Consider next the relation between the capital stock and inflation that is implied by the requirement of budget financing in (5). Substituting from (8) and (7) in (5), we obtain the following relation:

$$\pi x(k, v, \pi)k = (1 - v)\left[g - ty + \frac{ivxk(1 - t)}{1 - v}\right], \tag{5'}$$

or

$$A(k, \pi; v, t, g) \equiv \pi x k - (1 - v)\left[g - ty + \frac{ivxk(1 - t)}{1 - v}\right] = 0, \tag{5''}$$

which is shown in figure 19.1 as the negatively sloped schedule AA. This schedule combines portfolio balance and budget financing. The schedule is negatively sloped because an increase in the capital stock is assumed to raise the tax base and tax collection and therefore to give rise to a reduction in the inflation rate necessary to finance the reduced budget deficit. Formally the schedule is drawn on the assumption that[4]

$$A_k > 0, \quad A_\pi > 0. \tag{11}$$

Initial long-run equilibrium obtains at point E^0 where goods and asset markets clear and where the budget is financed by money and debt creation at the rate π^0. The capital stock associated with the equilibrium is k^0. We note that the equilibrium is contructed for given fiscal and financial policy. Accordingly, we can express the equilibrium inflation rate and capital stock in terms of the policy parameters:

$$\pi = \pi(v, g, t), \quad k = k(v, g, t). \tag{12}$$

19.2 Comparative Steady States

The long-run equilibrium of the model is determined by fiscal and financial policy. In this section we address the question of how changes in these parameters affect long-run inflation and capital intensity. Since it will turn out that the answers, even in this very simple model, are ambiguous, some emphasis will be given to a discussion of the key parameters that determine the sign and magnitude of comparative steady-state questions.

Consider first the effects of an increase in government spending. At the

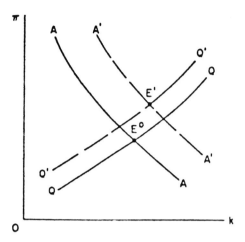

Figure 19.2
Effect of increased government spending

initial equilibrium inflation rate and capital stock there will be an excess demand. Accordingly, to restore goods market equilibrium, capital would have to be lower, remembering that $\alpha \equiv y_k - c_k < 0$, or inflation would have to be higher, thereby lowering wealth and consumption. It follows that, in figure 19.2, increased government spending causes the goods market equilibrium schedule QQ to shift up and to the left.

With respect to the budget, a higher level of government spending implies the need for additional financing. Such financing would come either from a higher stock of capital and thus a higher tax base or else from a higher rate of inflation that raises the real value of proceeds from money and debt creation. It follows that the budget schedule AA shifts up and to the right in figure 19.2.

It is immediately apparent from figure 19.2 that the new equilibrium at point E' must involve a higher rate of inflation. The effect of increased spending on the capital stock is ambiguous, since it depends on the relative shifts of the schedules.

It is worth identifying the separate forces that determine the new equilibrium. From a perspective of the budget the financing of higher real government spending requires higher inflation and or higher real capital and therefore a higher tax collection. From the perspective of goods market equilibrium, the excess demand will be eliminated by a reduction in capital —and hence wealth and consumption—and/or by an increase in inflation.

Consider the case where the demand for real money balances is very insensitive to the rate of interest and hence to inflation. Under these conditions inflation exerts relatively little effect on wealth, and accordingly, a large increase in inflation (or shift in the QQ schedule) is required to restore goods market equilibrium. By contrast, budget proceeds from money and debt creation will be highly responsive to inflation (with little reduction in real balances to offset the effect of higher inflation), and accordingly, only a small increase in inflation is required from a budgetary point of view. In these circumstances a reduction in the capital stock becomes likely. The interest elasticity of money demand, therefore, is a critical determinant of the behavior of the capital stock in response to increased government spending. With a low interest elasticity, increased government spending is accommodated by a relatively large increase in inflation combined with a reduction in capital. According, wealth and therefore private consumption decline. By contrast, a high interest response of money demand implies the possibility of an increase in capital, combined with a smaller reduction in consumption.

In fact, one can go a step further and note that if the interest elasticity of the ratio of money to capital, $\varepsilon = -ix_i/x$, is equal to unity, the relative shifts of the goods market equilibrium and budget schedules will depend just on the difference between the marginal propensity to consume out of wealth c_w and the real rate of interest.[5] Specifically, if the marginal propensity to consume out of wealth exceeds the real rate of interest, the AA schedule will shift up relative to the QQ schedule, as shown in figure 19.2, and accordingly, both capital and inflation will increase. Since there is no presumption concerning the relative magnitude of c_w and r, we conclude that in this case ($\varepsilon = 1$) the principal effect of an increase in government spending is on the rate of inflation with only little, if any, effect on the stock of capital.

Next we study the effects of a shift in the financing of the deficit. Specifically, consider the case where a larger fraction of the deficit is financed by debt creation. Such a shift in financing exerts effects because it changes the steady-state ratio of debt to money and wealth to capital. We note from (6) that an increase in v raises the ratio of debt to money and from (8) that wealth rises at each level of the capital stock and inflation rate. The latter result is due to the fact that a substitution of debt for money on the asset supply side reduces the equilibrium price level and thus raises real wealth.[6]

The increase in wealth, at each level of the capital stock and inflation rate, that is implied by an increase in v will raise consumption and thereby create an excess demand for goods. Accordingly, a reduction in the capital stock and/or an increase in inflation is required to restore goods market equilibrium. It follows that the goods market equilibrium schedule shifts upward, as in figure 19.2.

The shift in financing also affects the inflation rate required to finance the budget deficit as expressed in the AA schedule. Here the effect is of considerable ambiguity, depending as it does on the initial deficit, the tax rate, and the initial fraction of the budget financed by debt creation v.[7] The ambiguity arises for the following reason. As of a given inflation rate money rises relative to capital, thereby yielding a higher real revenue flow from asset creation and thus suggesting that a reduction in inflation is called for. At the same time, however, real debt rises relative to capital and, accordingly, debt service increases at each level of the capital stock. This latter effect potentially outweights the increased real revenue from asset creation and thus gives rise to the ambiguity. Assuming that the net effect is to give rise to excess revenue at the initial inflation rate and capital stock, a reduction in inflation and/or capital is required to maintain the balance between the budget deficit and its financing. In this event, the budget schedule in figure 19.2 would shift down and to the left (not drawn). The net effect would therefore be a reduction in the capital stock with an ambiguous effect on inflation.

The case where a shift toward debt finance reduces the equilibrium capital stock is more likely to arise the smaller the initial share of debt in budget financing and the larger the initial deficit. Specifically, this result must arise if initially government spending exceeds tax collection and $v = 0$. It is interesting to note that the criteria that determine whether debt finance displaces real capital are not those encountered in the discussion of "crowding out" in the short run or the intermediate run where interest and wealth elasticities of aggregate spending and money demand are relevant. By contrast, here the characteristics of the budget function specifically determine the long-run consequences of debt finance.

A shift toward debt finance has an ambiguous effect on the equilibrium rate of inflation. This fact is interesting because it implies that the converse, a shift toward money finance, is not necessarily inflationary. It is obviously true that the long-run rate of inflation is equal to the growth rate of money. However, the growth rate of money itself is endogenous and is not necessarily raised by a shift toward money finance.

The endogeneity of the inflation rate is likewise emphasized by a disturbance that arises from the private sector. Consider a permanent shift in the consumption function that raises consumption at each level of wealth. In terms of figure 19.1 this implies an up and leftward shift of the goods market equilibrium schedule and, accordingly, a reduction in the equilibrium capital stock along with an increase in the rate of inflation. An increase in consumption is inflationary because it reduces the capital stock and thereby the tax base so that the emerging budget deficit has to be financed by creation of nominal assets.

19.3 Concluding Remarks

This chapter has addressed the question of what determines long-run inflation, real capital and the composition of assets. The determinants are shown to be the requirements of budget finance, together with fiscal and financial policy. The introduction of debt, debt service, and deficit finance via debt creation introduces considerations in the discussion of "crowding out" that are altogether different from the relevant determinants in conventional aggregate demand oriented formulations. Further, even in a model as simple as the one considered here, the determinants of long-run capital intensity are sufficiently ambiguous not to warrant very strong results.

19.4 Appendix

This appendix investigates some dynamic aspects of the model with deficit financing under the assumption of long-run equilibrium expectations with respect to inflation. At any point in time the yield on real capital is determined by the capital stock:

$$r = r(k). \tag{A1}$$

The expected rate of inflation is equal to the long-run equilibrium rate of inflation π. Accordingly, the nominal interest rate is

$$i = r(k) + \pi, \tag{A2}$$

and therefore is given at a point in time along with the stock of capital.

In the short run, given the nominal quantity of debt and money and the real stock of capital as well as expected inflation, a price level is determined that will clear the asset market

$$\frac{M}{P} = \sigma(i)\left(\frac{M}{P} + \frac{B}{iP} + k\right). \tag{A3}$$

From (A3), which is the money market equilibrium condition, the price level is a function of the stock of capital, expected inflation, and the two nominal asset supplies, being linear homogeneous with respect to nominal asset supplies

$$P = P(k, \pi, M, B), \quad P_k < 0, P_\pi > 0, P_M > 0, P_B < 0. \tag{A4}$$

From equation (A4) it follows that real money, real debt, and real wealth can be written as functions of k, π, M, B:

$$m = m(k, \pi, M, B), \quad m_k > 0, m_\pi < 0, m_M < 0, m_B > 0, \tag{A5}$$

$$b = b(k, \pi, M, B), \quad b_k > 0, b_\pi < 0, b_M < 0, b_B > 0, \tag{A6}$$

since from (A4) the elasticity of the price level with respect to nominal money is larger than unity, and with respect to debt is negative. For real wealth we have

$$w = w(k, \pi, M, B), \quad w_k > 0, w_\pi < 0, w_M < 0, w_B > 0. \tag{A7}$$

The dynamic equations describing the equilibrium path of the model concern capital accumulation and asset creation in the process of deficit finance:

$$\dot{k} = y(k) - c(w) - g = \dot{k}(k, M, B; g, \pi), \tag{A8}$$

$$\dot{M} = (1 - v)P\theta(k, M, B; t, \pi) = \dot{M}(k, M, B; t, \pi, v), \tag{A9}$$

$$\dot{B} = iPv\theta(k, M, B; t, \pi) = \dot{B}(K, M, B; t, \pi, v), \tag{A10}$$

where the real budget deficit θ is given by

$$\theta \equiv g + \frac{(1 - t)B}{P} - ty = \theta(k, M, B; g, t, \pi). \tag{A11}$$

Stability of the system of equations (A8) through (A10) is not automatically ensured because of the problem created by debt service. An increase in debt outstanding lowers the price level and raises the dollar flow of debt service; accordingly, real debt service increases and so does the real budget deficit and therefore the financing requirement. The stability problem that emerges can be offset by a sufficiently high share of money creation in the financing of the budget deficit. That point can be appreciated by noting that for $v = 0$ we deal with the subsystem of (A8) and (A9), which is stable in the neighborhood of a balanced budget.

If stable, the system will converge to a stationary capital stock and a common growth rate for nominal money and debt, which is the rate of inflation. For money and debt to grow in nominal terms at the same rate, we require from (A9) and (A10) that

$$\frac{\dot{M}}{M} = (1 - v)\frac{P\theta}{M} = \frac{viP\theta}{B} = \frac{\dot{B}}{B}, \tag{A12}$$

or

$$b = \frac{vmi}{1 - v}. \tag{A12'}$$

Once a stationary capital stock is attained and money and debt attain the relationship in (A12'), the system is in a steady state with an inflation rate and capital stock determined by the policy parameters v, g, t.

Notes

1. The dynamics are sketched in the appendix.

2. The public debt takes the form of consols promising to pay a dollar a year indefinitely. With B the number of consols outstanding, i the nominal rate of interest, and P the price level, we have as an expression for real debt, $b = B/iP$. Public debt is included in wealth without any offsetting present value of tax liabilities. The reason is in part that the present model does not possess sufficient micro foundations to warrant consideration of future taxes. More important, the public debt service need not come out of taxes but can be provided by inflationary money and debt issues so that a simplistic discounting of taxes is inappropriate.

3. The assumption that $\alpha \equiv y_k - c_k < 0$ is adopted here as holding in the neighborhood of long-run equilibrium. The assumption is adopted because it tends to be part of the stability conditions that are not given explicit consideration here. The restriction is familiar from the monetary growth literature. See, for example, Dornbusch and Frenkel (1973).

4. The reader will appreciate that these restrictions are not entirely unambiguous. The reason is that changes in the capital stock and in the inflation rate affect the composition of portfolios and thereby affect the stock of real debt and money, which serves as basis for the inflation tax, as well as real debt service.

5. The interest elasticity of the ratio of money to capital ε is related to the interest elasticity of money demand η by the formula $\varepsilon = \eta w/k$. Accordingly, a value for ε of unity is compatible with an interest elasticity of money demand $\eta \equiv -i\sigma'/\sigma$ that is significantly less than unity.

6. See the appendix on the relationship between the price level, nominal asset supplies, and real wealth.

7. The effect of a change in v on the budget is given by $A_v = \pi k x_v + \theta - i(1-t)xk - iv(1-t)kx_v$, where $x_v > 0$.

References

Blinder, Alan, and Solow, Robert. 1973. "Does Fiscal Policy Matter." *Journal of Public Economics* 2, 319–337.

Brunner, Karl, and Meltzer, Allan. 1975. "Fiscal Policy, Inflation and the Price Level." Unpublished manuscript. University of Rochester.

Burmeister, Edwin, and Phelps, Edmund. 1971. "Money, Public Debt, Inflation and Real Interest." *Journal of Money, Credit, and Banking*, 3 (May), 153–182.

Christ, Carl. 1968. "A Simple Macroeconomic Model with a Government Budget Restraint." *Journal of Political Economy* 76 (January/February), 53–67.

Dornbusch, Rudiger, and Frenkel, Jacob A. 1973. "Inflation and Growth: Alternative Approaches." *Journal of Money, Credit, and Banking*, 5 (February), 141–156.

Foley, Duncan, and Sidrauski, Miguel. 1971. *Monetary and Fiscal Poicy in a Growing Economy*. New York: Macmillan.

Mundell, Robert, A. 1971. *Monetary Theory*. Pacific Palisades: Goodyear.

Stein, Jerome, L. (ed.). 1976. *Monetarism*. Amsterdam: North-Holland.

20

Inflation Stabilization and Capital Mobility

The problem of stabilization policy in high-inflation countries has, over the last ten years, undergone a substantial development. The traditional view takes stabilization policy to be primarily a fiscal issue. Although recognizing, and indeed emphasizing, that stabilization involves a cut in the standard of living, this view attaches no great transition costs to stabilization. It hardly perceives stabilization as a macroeconomic issue. The view is even carried to the point of arguing that disinflation has been made to look more painful than the historical record will bear out.[1]

The new elements in thinking about inflation stabilization in high-inflation countries, whether they be industrialized or semi-industrialized, include the following: First, although fiscal policy certainly sets the trend rate of inflation when there is deficit finance, inflation may be quite independent of the budget in the short run and enjoy a life of its own. Second, reinforcing the first observation, stabilization encounters the serious obstacle of inflation inertia. Inflation, other things equal, is what it was, and fiscal stabilization, or expectations thereof, will not lead to a collapse of the prevailing rate of inflation. Third, managed real appreciation of the exchange rate may prove a tempting tool in the stabilization process. Fourth, capital flows, responsive to international interest differentials, may become at various stages of the cycle both an aid and a burden to the stabilization effort. Fifth, expectations prove substantially more important in the capital account of the balance of payments than in the labor market. Sixth, there exists a possibility that monetary restriction induces, in the short run, an adverse effect on inflation.

The first part of this chapter sketches a simple version of the traditional model and draws the principal lessons. The discussion is followed by two points of qualification. One concerns the question of whether the system is

Originally published as NBER Working Paper No. 555, September 1980.

overdetermined—essentially the structuralist view of fiscal policy. The other concerns the question of terms of trade shocks and inflation. In the second part, the stabilization problem is approached from the perspective of macroeconomic dynamics. Emphasis is placed there on the inertia of the inflation process and on the interaction between stabilization rules for money, interest rates, and exchange rates and the resulting paths for output, real exchange rates, and the balance of payments.

20.1 Inflation, Fiscal Policy, and Terms of Trade Shocks

Fiscal Policy and Inflation

A first model of the open economy focuses on the goods market and the current account. Two key variables are highlighted: the real exchange rate $\theta \equiv EP^*/P$ and the budget deficit ratio ϕ, expressed as a fraction of GDP.

In the goods market full-employment equilibrium obtains when the demand for home output, determined by the deficit ratio and the real exchange rate, equals the available supply, $\overline{y}$:

$$\overline{y} = J(\theta, \phi), \quad J_\theta, J_\phi > 0. \tag{1}$$

In figure 20.1 we show the goods market equilibrium schedule II along which internal balance prevails. The schedule is negatively sloped since a real depreciation raises demand for home output so that for full employment we require an offsetting deflationary cut in the budget. Points above the schedule correspond to overemployment and points below to unemployment.

Along FF the current balance is in equilibrium. A real depreciation improves the current balance (given elasticity conditions). To maintain external balance, a real depreciation must be offset by a demand expansion through an increased budget deficit.

The budget deficit is financed by money creation, or by the "inflation tax." With the demand for real balances, x, a function of the rate of inflation, $\dot{p}$, the budget financing implies

$$\dot{p}x(\dot{p}) = \phi\overline{y} \tag{2}$$

With an inflation elasticity of less than unity, the equation implies that an increased deficit ratio calls for a higher inflation rate to finance the budget. This relation is shown in the lower panel of figure 20.1

Equilibrium obtains at point A where the economy is fully employed with a balanced current account or a current account financed by exogenous flows of lending, direct investment, and aid. Corresponding to the equilibrium of the real economy is an inflation rate $\dot{p}_o$.

What precepts does this model yield? The model has three implications:

1. Inflation is a purely *fiscal* phenomenon.

2. Trade problems require for their cure *both* a real depreciation and fiscal restraint.

3. With trend inflation, as an implication of the fiscal situation, the appropriate exchange policy is to have mini-devaluations that stabilize the real exchange rate.

Suppose past policies had moved the economy to a position of full employment with an external deficit at point A'. The conventional advice is to reduce the budget deficit, and hence absorption, and to generate an increase in net exports through a real depreciation. This would restore internal and external balance at point A. The policy mix would also lead to a reduction in the rate of inflation. In particular, with a highly nonlinear inflation–budget relation, the gain in terms of reduced inflation may prove substantial, especially if the government collects only a minor fraction of the seignorage.[2]

The Overdetermined System

A first complication to the program of stabilization is the recognition of further constraints. The model is not only one of internal and external balance and of budget finance, it also includes constraints on policies imposed by social relations. These may take any of a variety of forms: rigid real wages and hence a constraint on the real exchange rate, a distribution of income, or a relation between the real exchange rate and the budget. A broad characterization of these constraints is shown in figure 20.1 as the schedule cc. The schedule suggests that a real depreciation, because it lowers the standard of living, must be offset by an increased budget deficit that provides a real income supplement to some sector, such as food or credit subsidies.

It is apparent that the further constraint makes it impossible, except by good fortune, to attain internal and external balance. Typically, the real exchange rate consistent with full balance leaves the public with a standard of living below the level acceptable, and hence there is pressure to fiscalize the aspirations by moving to a deficit point such as A'', with occasional return to external balance whenever external financing crises come to dominate.

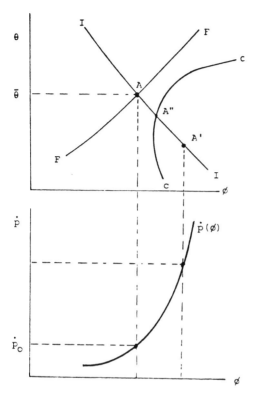

Figure 20.1

It is apparent that under these conditions, stabilization policy is not only a technical issue of restoring the right real exchange rate and stopping deficit finance. More likely some structural policies such as tariffs or employment subsidies are required to help reconcile the overdetermined system.

Terms of Trade Shocks and Inflation

The inflation stabilization problem is frequently rendered more difficult, and indeed obscured, by the presence of high underlying inflation combined with terms of trade shocks. These complications make it essential to introduce the distinction between services and manufactures where wage-price formation is "macroeconomic" and commodities (beef, coffee, oil) whose prices are susceptible of shocks. Changes in the world prices of commodity exports or imports, relative to those of manufactures, exert important effects on the inflation process through several channels:

1. Direct input cost effects.

2. To the extent that the commodities are wage goods, the required real wage in terms of manufactures rises. With home manufactures priced by a markup on wages, this implies a pressure for a real appreciation to compensate for the loss of real income in commodities by increased purchasing power in manufactures imports. This is of course a real wage-resistance argument. It is particular forceful when the price shock occurs in commodity exports because then the economy can actually afford, from a current account point of view, the real appreciation. Of course, for manufactures it represents a loss in competitiveness.

3. Closely related to the preceding argument, changes in commodity prices, in the presence of sticky *relative* sectoral wages, can lead to a rise of wages in industry. Again with markup pricing, inflation and real appreciation will result.

4. Changes in the real price of commodities affect real income and hence aggregate demand for industrial output. A rising real price of commodity exports lead to real appreciation for manufactures and conversely for an increase in real commodity import price.

In the remainder of this chapter I will abstract from these commodity inflation issues. They are introduced here mainly because in recent history they may have been an important aspect of the stabilization problem.[3]

20.2 The Dynamics of Inflation Stabilization

In this part we investigate the dynamics of inflation stabilization. We start with a brief discussion of our macroeconomic model and then sketch alternative policy arrangements. After identifying three key problems in the stabilization effort we discuss the adjustment process under alternative rules.

The Model

We consider an economy that produces and exports a single commodity, facing a downward sloping demand curve in the world market. Demand for domestic output depends on income, the relative price of competing importables in terms of domestic goods, θ, and of the real rate of interest, r. Output, y, is demand determined. Equilibrium in the home goods market requires the equality of output and demand, or in reduced form,[4]

$$y = a\theta - br. \tag{3}$$

Monetary equilibrium, in the manner of the standard LM curve, determines the interest rate, i, as a function of real balances and real income:

$$i = cy - dx, \tag{4}$$

where x denotes the log of real balances, $x = m - p$, with m and p the logs of nominal money and prices.

The balance of payments depends, via the current account, on real income and the real exchange rate and, via the capital account, on the international interest differential adjusted for anticipated depreciation, $\dot{e}$:[5]

$$B = f\theta - gy + h(i - \dot{e}). \tag{5}$$

Noting the definition of the real exchange rate, $\theta = e - p$, we can rewrite the capital account as a function of the real interest rate, $r = i - \dot{p}$ and the real depreciation rate, $\dot{\theta} = \dot{e} - \dot{p}$:

$$B = f\theta - gy + h(r - \dot{\theta}). \tag{5'}$$

In defining the capital account of the balance of payments, we have already imposed the perfect foresight assumption in that we identify expected inflation and depreciation with the actual rates.

The model is as yet incomplete in that neither the inflation process nor the monetary and exchange rate policies have been specified. Even so we can look at equilibrium of the goods market and the balance of payments, to gain some understanding of the real interest rate–real exchange rate relations. In figure 20.2 we plot as the II schedule the combinations of real interest rates and real exchange rates compatible with full-employment internal balance. Higher real interest rates reduce demand and thus must be compensated by a real depreciation that shifts demand toward domestic goods. Hence II is upward sloping.

The schedule FF shows external balance. The schedule is drawn for a zero rate of real depreciation. A higher level of the real exchange rate (a real depreciation) improves the current account and thus must be offset by a capital account deterioration due to lower real interest rates. Thus FF is negatively sloped. Points to the right of FF correspond to external balance with a depreciating real exchange rate, and points to the left to an appreciating real exchange rate. Long-run equilibrium obtains at point A where internal and external balance obtain, combined with a constant real exchange rate.[6] We observe that the long-run real equilibrium in figure 20.2 is independent of the rate of inflation. In the short run, though, inflation

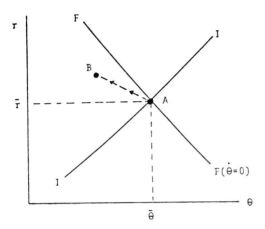

Figure 20.2

stabilization typically involves a move from a point like *A* to *B*: a reduction in demand below potential output, due to both real appreciation and increased real interest rates, and a payments surplus.[7] Beyond the real interest–real appreciation feature that needs explanation, stabilization policies have typically encountered three specific difficulties:

1. *The velocity problem.* In the transition to a permanent reduction in the rate of inflation, the demand for real balances rises. If the price level is not instantaneously flexible, this required gain in real balances must be borne in mind in designing stabilization rules. In particular, a fixed money growth rate rule imposes unnecesssary costs in terms of output lost.[8]

2. *The real appreciation problem.* In the early stages of a stabilization program real appreciation is often welcomed as supporting directly the disinflation effort through a "cooling" of the home inflation process.[9] What is neglected is the fact that across steady states the equilibrium real exchange rate remains unchanged. Any short-term gain through real appreciation is only borrowed and must be repaid later when the real exchange rate depreciates.

3. *The stubborn inflation problem.* Because of a lack of credibility, because of long-term contracts, and/or because of real wage resistance, the inflation process is stubborn. The price level is not instantaneously flexible, nor is even the rate of inflation.

There is a wide variety of policy mixes that can be used to stabilize inflation. Possibilities range from fully flexible nominal exchange rates with a constant money growth rate rule to a constant real interest rate with a managed real exchange rate, an intermediate case being a constant real exchange rate combined with constant money growth. We limit our analysis to only a few regimes, trying to highlight the interaction of the inflation process and the policy rules.

A Monetary Rule and a Constant Real Exchange Rate

In this section we assume that the government sets a fixed growth rate of nominal money, $\dot{m}$, and that the exchange rate is pegged along purchasing power parity lines so that $\dot{e} = \dot{p}$, or $\dot{\theta} = 0$. These assumptions describe the policy regime. We further need to specify the inflation process. As our first example, we take an inflation process that highlights the sluggishness with which expectations of trend inflation adjust to actual changes in monetary growth. Specifically, we assume that inflation is determined by exchange depreciation, expected trend inflation, z, and the output gap,

$$\dot{p} = \pi \dot{e} + (1 - \pi)z + \sigma y, \tag{6}$$

where z is anticipated trend inflation that is formed adaptively on the basis of observed money growth:

$$\dot{z} = \phi(\dot{m} - z). \tag{7}$$

The model of course implies that a sustained reduction in monetary growth will ultimately be reflected in lower actual and trend inflation.

Our assumption about the exchange rate rule, $\dot{p} = \dot{e}$, implies that inflation just depends on trend inflation and the gap:

$$\dot{p} = z + \frac{\sigma}{1 - \pi} y. \tag{6'}$$

From the definition of the real interest rate $i - \dot{p}$, and equations (3), (4), and (6'), it is readily shown that output is an increasing function of real balances and trend inflation, whereas the real interest rate is a decreasing function of these variables, as is the balance of payments:

$$y = y(x, z), \quad r = r(x, z), \quad B = B(x, z; \theta). \tag{8}$$

In figure 20.3 we show the schedule II along which output is at the full-employment level and the external balance is in equilibrium, given the purchasing power parity exchange rate rule. The schedule is negatively sloped since an increase in real balances lowers real interest rates, thus

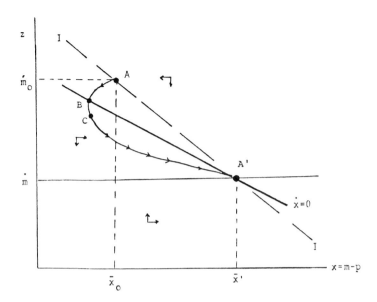

Figure 20.3

raising output and deteriorating the balance of payments. To restore balance, a reduction in expected inflation is required.

Figure 20.3 also shows the schedule $\dot{x} = 0$ defined by the equation

$$\dot{x} \equiv \dot{m} - \dot{p} = \dot{m} - z - \frac{\sigma}{1 - \pi} y(x, z). \tag{9}$$

The position of the schedule is explained as follows: if actual money growth falls short of trend inflation, real balances are falling unless a sufficently low level of activity helps dampen the inflation rate. The arrows in figure 20.3 define the adjustment of real balances and trend inflation, the latter being determined by (7).

Suppose now that the authorities permanently reduce money growth from an initial level at point A to the lower rate, $\dot{m}$, indicated by the line through point A'. How will employment, inflation, and the balance of payments respond to the stabilization? When money growth is first reduced, there is no impact effect at all. Real balances start declining, as money growth now falls short of trend inflation expectation and thus of actual inflation. Only as real balances actually have declined, do we start having an effect. The real interest rate is rising and hence output starts falling. Together with the fall in output, which improves the current account, the rise in real interest rates improves the capital account. There is

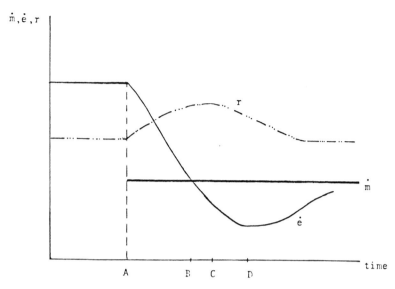

Figure 20.4

accordingly a balance of payments improvement or net reserve inflows. Inflation is decelerating.

As trend inflation is revised in the light of actual money growth, this, in combination with the inflation dampening of the recession, helps stop the decline in real balances. From here on, actual inflation further declines, and real balances grow.

The inflation trend is being revised downward in the light of actual money growth. The output gap dampens inflation and the combination of the two effects tends to lower inflation to the level of money growth. Real balances at first attain a point of constancy and then start rising. Only after real balances start rising, at a point like C, do real interest rates stop increasing and then start falling. The turning points for output and the balance of payments thus occur after point B, the turning point for real balances. The turning point for inflation and depreciation, finally, follows that of output and real income. These relations are shown in figure 20.4.

The exercise shows some of the principal lessons of the stabilization problem. First, inflation stabilization will involve transitory unemployment. Second, in the adjustment process real interest rates rise which, in combination with the decline in output, leads to a balance of payments surplus. Third, in the transition, inflation and depreciation decline below the new rate of monetary expansion so as to raise real balances and accommodate the change in desired velocity.

An Alternative Inflation Model

The preceding analysis captured the stickiness of inflation by the assumption of a slowly adjusting expectation of trend inflation. An alternative assumption is that inflation is what it was, except for the accelerating effects of real depreciation or overemployment:

$$\ddot{p} = v(\dot{e} - \dot{p}) + \mu y. \tag{10}$$

In this formulation, compatible, for example, with indexation, real depreciation exerts upward pressure on inflation because it raises input costs and cuts real wages. Conversely, real appreciation exerts a dampening influence on inflation. Domestic cyclical considerations affect inflation in that unemployment leads to a deceleration of inflation, whereas overemployment promotes an acceleration. What is special about this formulation of inflation is that only a period of *sustained* unemployment or real appreciation will achieve a reduction in inflation.

Managed Nominal Exchange Rates and Real Interest Rates

The next exercise considers the inflation model in (10) and a policy regime where the nominal exchange rate is decelerating according to a pre-set table. The real rate of interest and, hence, nominal money growth are managed so as to maintain balance of payments equilibrium. The model is difficult to present, but it is sufficiently important as a policy setting to deserve spelling out.

The exchange rate rule is specified in (11) as a rate of deceleration of the depreciation rate proportional to the discrepancy from the long-run target, $\dot{e}'$:

$$\ddot{e} = -k(\dot{e} - \dot{e}'). \tag{11}$$

Balance of payments equilibrium, from (5') and (3) specifies the real interest rate as a function of the level and rate of change of the real exchange rate:[10]

$$r = \alpha\dot{\theta} - \beta\theta, \quad a, \beta > 0. \tag{12}$$

Figure 20.5 illustrates the stabilization process in this model. We show the internal balance schedule II and the external balance schedule FF corresponding to a constant real exchange rate. We also show the schedule $\ddot{p} = 0$. The schedule lies in between the FF and II schedules—to maintain inflation constant real depreciation (to the right of FF) must be offset by unemployment. Whether the schedule is positively or negatively sloped

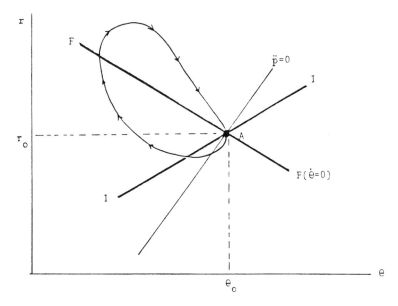

Figure 20.5

depends on the relative effects of depreciation and employment on the
acceleration of inflation. The case shown in figure 20.5 reflects a relatively
strong employment effect. (see the appendix).

The arrows in figure 20.5 indicate the adjustment path under a policy
that implements a deceleration on inflation starting from full equilibrium at
point A. We note that as the policy is first set up, inflation does not, as yet,
respond. The rate of nominal exchange depreciation starts declining, thereby causing the real exchange rate to start appreciating. The tendency for
the real exchange rate to start appreciating in turn requires policymakers to
offset the balance of payments improvement by lowering the nominal and
real interest rates. The first effect then is an appreciating real exchange rate
and a declining real interest rate. In terms of figure 20.5 it is apparent that
the initial real appreciation and real interest decline may be such that
output rises and inflation accelerates. This need not, however, be the case.

The subsequent path of the real interest rate and the real exchange rate
involve continuing real appreciation, as inflation deceleration lags the deceleration of exchange depreciation. But now the worsening of the current
account requires a rising real interest rate. After the path crosses the FF
schedule, the real exchange depreciation starts being undone. Inflation
deceleration continues, supported by the high level of unemployment but

gradually peters out. The real depreciation now improves the current account and thus allows real interest rates to be lowered.

The stabilization problem differs here from the preceding analysis in three respects: First, there is throughout balance of payments equilibrium. Second, because monetary policy maintains payment equilibrium, it is possible that inflation in the first instance accelerates. Third, in the transition process the real rate first appreciates and then depreciates. It is important to recognize that the cumulative change in the real exchange rate is zero and that, accordingly, by (10) the cumulative disinflation is entirely due to an output level that is on average below potential.

Fixed Real Interest Rates and Managed Real Exchange Rates

The last application of our model looks at the case of a pegged real rate of interest, $r = \bar{r}$, combined with an active real exchange rate management. The real rate of exchange is managed so as to reduce inflation. The particular rule for the exchange rate is to depreciate at the rate of inflation, but with an adjustment for the discrepancy between actual inflation and target inflation, $\dot{p}'$,

$$\dot{e} = \dot{p} - k(\dot{p} - \dot{p}') \quad \text{or} \quad \dot{\theta} = -k\dot{p}, \tag{13}$$

where we have assumed that the target rate $\dot{p}' = 0$. According to (13), the nominal and real exchange rates are actively managed to achieve disinflation.

Combining the exchange rate policy with the inflation model in (10) and the output equation in (3) yields an equation for acceleration of inflation:

$$\ddot{p} = -vk\dot{p} + \mu(a\theta - b\bar{r}), \tag{14}$$

where $\bar{r}$ is the given real rate of interest.

In figure 20.6 we show the schedule $\ddot{p} = 0$ along which inflation is constant. A real depreciation, by raising output, leads to an acceleration of inflation. To maintain inflation, the level of the inflation rate must be higher so as to induce a more vigorous real appreciation. Points to the left of $\ddot{p} = 0$ correspond to declerating inflation.

We also have in figure 20.6 the schedule II that shows the real exchange rate at which full employment prevails (given the real interest rate). The schedule FF, finally, shows the combination of inflation rates and real exchange rates that ensure balance of payments equilibrium. Higher inflation, via the exchange rate policy, implies a more rapid rate of real appreciation and therefore a higher return on domestic assets. To maintain payments balance, the favorable capital account must be offset by a current

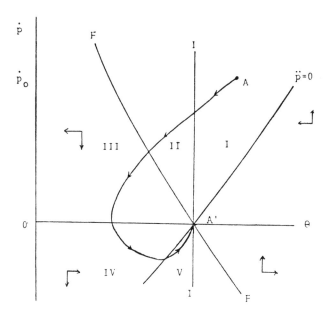

Figure 20.6

account deterioration through a real appreciation.[11] Points to the left of *FF* correspond to a payments deficit and points to the right to a surplus.

Suppose now that the stabilization program is implemented from an initial position at point *A* where there is overemployment (following a demand expansion) and the inflation rate is $\dot{P}_0$. The excessive rate of inflation leads the government to start appreciating the real exchange rate by depreciating the nominal rate below the prevailing rate of inflation. The balance of payments immediately shows a surplus as the real return on home securities, compared to foreign securities, $r - \dot{\theta}$, rises.

Over time, as the real appreciation gradually builds up, the declining competitiveness starts reducing output, while the current account deterioration begins to reduce the payments surplus. Entering into region II, output has fallen below potential as a consequence of real appreciation. Now the external balance approaches equilibrium, but the policy of real appreciation continues because inflation, though declining, still remains excessive. In passing to region III we arrive in the policymaker's trouble zone. Output has fallen substantially below normal through deliberate appreciation. The current account has deteriorated and is no longer offset anymore by capital inflows. Inflation has declined a lot, although it has not yet reached the zero target. If policies are continued, we now see in region

IV an undoing of the real appreciation. With unemployment now dampening the inflationary impact of the real depreciation, the real exchange rate reverts to its equilibrium value. Of course, to make this possible, inflation must fall below the target level. The early disinflationary effects of real appreciation are thus repaid in regions IV and V.

Again, as in the earlier examples, unemployment is the channel through which disinflation is achieved. What is special here is the balance of payments and real exchange rate cycle. The model highlights the stabilization problem in region III and IV where unemployment and a deficit make it hard to believe that real appreciation is the appropriate policy. It is important to recognize that an attempt to return to A' through rapid real depreciation, or a devaluation might cause a sharp acceleration of inflation. At the same time such a move would lead to dramatic capital outflows (the FF schedule would shift to the right) as the public recognizes the possibility of large capital losses on home assets. This point emphasizes the link between the capital account and actual and prospective policy rules.[12]

20.3 Concluding Remarks

This chapter has analyzed inflation stabilization policy by studying a number of alternative policy mixes. We started off with the recognition that the important issue in stabilizing inflation is not only the inevitable fiscal sanitation but more specifically the macroeconomic dynamics. With inflation stubborn or with inflation inertia—be it because of contracts, relative wages, real resistance, or credibility—reducing inflation involves *inevitably* a protracted recession.

The fact that inflation stabilization poses inevitably the need for a protracted recession raises some issues. The first is how to avoid any excess cost that arises from the velocity problem or from an overappreciation of the real exchange rate. This suggests that a purchasing power parity exchange rate policy might be preferable, although it may imply a slower process of disinflation. The velocity problem in turn suggests that anything in the nature of a constant money growth rule is particularly undesirable.

The chief concern of course remains the proposition that inflation stabilization involves inevitably a protracted recession. All the evidence suggests that there is not sufficient inflation flexibility to allow for a collapse of prevailing inflation rates simply because money growth has fallen. Because the costs of a protracted recession are vast compared to the allocational costs of policy activism, one cannot but return to the suggestion that an effective stabilization program, along with fiscal sanitation and *some* contraction of demand, should include wage controls and real interest rate ceilings.[13]

20.4 Appendix

In section 20.2 we discuss the turning points of real balances, real interest rates, and the rate of depreciation. The discussion is based on the following equations: from the definition of the real interest rate, $i - \dot{p}$, the interest rate equation (4), the income equation (3), and the inflation equation (6'), we have

$$r = \frac{va\theta - dx - z}{1 + bv}, \quad v = \left(c - \frac{\sigma}{1 - \pi}\right) > 0 \text{ by assumption.} \tag{A1}$$

Differentiating (A1) with respect to time, and using (7) and (9), yields

$$\dot{r} = -\frac{d\dot{x} + \phi(\dot{m} - z)}{(1 + bv)}. \tag{A2}$$

Since $\dot{m} - z$ is negative, the real interest rate is still rising at the point $\dot{x} = 0$, attaining its maximum level only after real balances have started already rising. Real income and the balance of payments, given the real exchange rate, share the turning points of the real interest rate. The inflation and depreciation rate, from (6') has the following acceleration:

$$\ddot{p} = \dot{z} + \frac{\dot{y}\sigma}{1 - \pi} = \varphi(\dot{m} - z) - \frac{b\sigma\dot{r}}{1 - \pi}. \tag{A3}$$

Now using (A2) to substitute for $\dot{r}$, we have

$$\ddot{p} = \dot{z} + \bar{b}d\dot{x} + \bar{b}\dot{z}, \quad \bar{b} = \frac{b}{1 + bv}, \tag{A4}$$

$$= \dot{z} + \bar{b}(d\dot{x} + \dot{z}).$$

Thus inflation initially decelerates. Comparing (A2) and (A4), when the real rate is constant, inflation is still decelerating. Only after the real rate starts falling, so that the term in brackets becomes sufficently positive, does inflation stop decelerating and turn around toward the target level.

In section 20.2 we introduce the $\dot{p} = 0$ schedule. From the balance of payments equation we can solve for $\dot{\theta}$, and substituting from the goods market equation in (3) yields the slope of the schedule:

$$\left.\frac{dr}{d\theta}\right|_{\dot{p}=0} = \frac{v(f - ga) + ah\mu}{v(gb + h) - \mu bh}; \tag{A5}$$

the slope is positive as assumed if $(vg - \mu h) \geq 0$.

Differentiating (12), using (10) and (11), we obtain the evolution of the real interest rate:

$$\dot{r} = -\alpha k(\dot{e} - \dot{e}') - (\alpha v + \beta)\dot{\theta} - \alpha\mu y, \quad \frac{d\dot{r}}{d\dot{e}'} = \alpha k. \tag{A6}$$

At the initial equilibrium, with $y = 0$ and $\dot{\theta} = 0$ at point A, the real interest rate is being lowered. Then, as unemployment develops and real appreciation proceeds, interest rates start being raised.

Notes

1. See Harberger, A. "The Inflation Syndrome," in Flanders, J. and Razin, A. (eds.), *Inflation in Developing Countries* (Academic Press, 1980).

2. See Mundell, R. A. *Monetary Theory* (Goodyear, 1971); Fischer, S. "Seignorage and the Case for a National Money," Massachusetts Institute of Technology, 1983; and Dornbusch, R. "Inflation, Capital and Deficit Finance," *Journal of Money, Credit and Banking* (February 1976).

3. See Banco Central de la Republica Argentina, *Anticipio Memoria Anual 1979, Mercado* (Argentina) January 10, 1980, pp. 20–27 and, for theoretical issues: Buiter, W. "Short Run and Long Run Effects of External Disturbances under a Floating Exchange Rate," *Economica* 45 (1978); Cardoso, E. "Oferta de Alimentos e Inflação," *Pesquisa e Planejamento* 10 (1980); and Flood, R. and Peregrim Marion, N. "The Transmission of Disturbances under Alternative Exchange Rate Regimes with Optimal Indexing" (National Bureau of Economic Research, 1980).

4. Here y and θ are the logs of output and the real exchange rate. Furthermore by choice of units, y can be interpreted as the deviation of output from the full-employment level $\bar{y} = 0$.

5. Note that for simplicity the foreign nominal interest rate is set equal to zero. With e the nominal exchange rate, $\dot{e}$ represents the rate of depreciation and $i - \dot{e}$ the interest differential in favor of the home country.

6. We entirely abstract from the effect of current account imbalance on asset accumulation. For references to the extensive literature on this question, see Dornbusch, R. *Open Economy Macroeconomics* (Basic Books, 1980).

7. There is now an extensive literature on this question. See in particular Martirena Mantel, A. "Devaluacion, Inflacion Y Desempleo," *Economica* (August 1968) and "The Argentina Experience with the Crawling Peg," in Williamson J. (ed.), *The Crawling Peg: Experience and Prospects* (Macmillan, 1981); Carlos Rodriguez, "El Plan Argentino de Estabilizacion del 20 de Diciembre," CEMA (July 1979); Calvo, G. "Stabilization Rules and the Managed Float: A Search for Essentials," (Columbia University, 1979); Díaz-Alejandro, C., "Stabilization Policies in the Southern Cone" (Yale University, 1979); Nissan Liviatan, "Anti-inflationary Monetary Policy and the Capital Import Tax" (Hebrew University, 1979); Mathieson, D. "Financial Reform and Capital Flows in a Developing Country," *IMF Staff Papers*, No. 3, 1979; and Krugman, P. "Speculation and Inflation with a Crawling Peg," MIT, 1979.

8. This problem is well familiar from Chicago prelims. For a recent discussion, see Simonsen, M. "Rational Expectations and Inflation Stabilization," Fundaçao Getulio Vargas, 1980; and Khan, M. and Knight, M. "Stabilization Programs in Developing Countries: A Formal Framework," International Monetary Fund, 1980.

9. Real appreciation is of course being used in the U.K. stabilization effort. See the discussion in House of Commons, *Enquiry on Monetary Policy*, H.M.S. Stationary Office, July 1980.

10. From balance of payments equilibrium in (5'), we obtain an equation for the real interest rate: $r = i - \dot{p} = -[(f - ga)\theta - h\dot{\theta}]/(h + gb)$, where $(f - ga)$ is assumed positive, thus giving us (12). We can also translate the real interest rate required for external balance into a real balance requirement by solving for the real interest rate from (3) and (4) to obtain $i - \dot{p} = (ca\theta - \dot{p} - dx)/(1 + bc)$, and equating the two real interest rate expressions to ensure goods and money market equilibrium as well as payments balance, we solve for real balances, $x = x(\theta, \dot{\theta}, \dot{p})$. The real money stock required for external balance will be an increasing function of the real exchange rate and a declining function of the rate of real depreciation and the rate of inflation.

11. Combining (13) and (5'), and setting the balance of payments equal to zero yields $\dot{p} = -[(f - ga)\theta + (bg + h)\bar{r}]/kh$, where $(f - ga)$ is assumed positive.

12. The discussion here alludes to the "peso problem"—the possibility of a change in rules which is taken into account in speculators' calculation of the prospective return. See Salant, S. and Henderson, D., "Market Anticipation of Government Policies and the Prices of Gold," *Journal of Political Economy* 4(1978); Krasker, W. "The Peso Problem in Testing the Efficency of Forward Exchange Markets," *Journal of Monetary Economics* (April 1980); and Lizondo, J. S. "Precios a Futuro de Divisas bajo Taxas de Cambio Fijas y com Expectativas de Devaluation," unpublished manuscript, ITAM, Mexico, March 1980.

13. Real interest rate ceilings are required to avoid the inflationary effects of tight money. See Cavallo, D. "Stagflationary Effects of Monetarist Stabilization Policies in Economies with Persistent Inflation," in Flanders, J. and Bazin, A. (eds.), *Inflation in Developing Countries* (Academic Press, 1980).

21

Lessons from the German Inflation Experience of the 1920s

Hyperinflations are laboratory experiments of monetary economics. In the presence of these extreme rates of inflation and depreciation, all other considerations that might normally obscure linkages between money and prices fall into the background so that these linkages emerge strongly and obviously, beyond discussion or controversy. Stabilization of inflation proceeds if and only if the source of inflation, money creation, is brought under control. This is the traditional view endorsed by Keynes (1923) and particularly developed by Cagan (1956) in his classic essay on the German hyperinflation.

The central emphasis on money creation as the exogenous variable in the inflation process has not gone unchallenged. Already during the hyperinflation experience there was a controversy between the "Quantity Theory School," which took this view, and the "Balance-of-Payments School," which held the view that balance of payments difficulties, associated with reparations payments, gave rise to exchange depreciation, which in turn led to inflation and monetization. Not suprisingly the government strongly endorsed this view. The special role of money in the hyperinflation process, and particularly in the stabilization phase, has also been reconsidered in a best-selling essay by Sargent (1982). In Sargent's work primary emphasis is placed on budget stabilization rather than on money growth per se. Indeed, he draws attention, as Keynes and other authors had before, to the very large rates of monetary growth following the actual stabilization.

Sargent's message is that *credible* fiscal stabilization is the sine qua non for stopping inflation. This is definitely not viewed as being in conflict with the monetary hypothesis, but it does represent a shift of emphasis. Here is how Sargent (1982, p. 89) puts his findings:

Originally published in R. Dornbusch and S. Fischer (eds.), *Macroeconomics and Finance. Essays in Honor of Franco Modigliani* (Cambridge, MA: The MIT Press, 1987), pp. 337–366.

The essential measures that ended hyperinflations in each of Germany, Austria, Hungary, and Poland were, first, the creation of an independent central bank that was legally committed to refuse the government's demand for additional unsecured credit and, second, a simultaneous alteration in the fiscal policy regime.... We have further seen that it was not simply the increasing quantity of central bank notes that caused the hyperinflation, since in each case the note circulation continued to grow rapidly after the exchange rate and price level had been stabilized. Rather it was the growth of fiat currency which was unbacked, or backed only by government bills, which there never was a prospect to retire through taxation.

The two views are not strictly identical. We can imagine that a deficit persists for some time but does not give rise to money creation because it is entirely financed by external loans. This was, for example, the case in the Austrian stabilization (see Dornbusch and Fischer 1986). An alternative possibility is the persistence of a deficit, for some time, financed by domestic borrowing. Finally, it is possible that the deficit is eliminated altogether but that money creation associated with private credit creation persists vigorously. It is therefore useful to separate the point of emphasis of the two hypotheses even though they may overlap in practice.

In this essay we draw attention to three further aspects of the stabilization of the hyperinflation, namely, the exchange rate and wages, interest rates, and the increase in the real yield of taxation deriving from the mere fact of price stability.

The central weakness of the Sargent position is to present "credibility" as some objective, unquestionable fact—as if passing a budget law or instituting an independent central bank is by itself enough to ensure that these institutions will in fact become what they represent on paper. Even though a government may intend or even initiate all the right measures in terms of budget stabilization and brakes on money creation, there remains still the problem of making these measures work once the costs of implementation become apparent (and hence actually being able to sustain them). This is of course the central issue in the transition to accomplishing a successful stabilization. Since policies are not in fact exogenous, in that the government creates an act on which it cannot, under any and all conditions, go back, the issue of credibility is paramount. In fact the scene is littered with failed stabilization policies, many of which faltered not from inception but on the way.

We argue that exchange rate and interest rate policy in the transition have traditionally formed the vehicle for establishing that credibility by a de facto stabilization. De facto stabilization in turn pays an immediate dividend via the recovery of the real tax yield, thereby creating the potential for a virtuous cycle. The improving budget situation in turn may attract capital flows that reinforce the stabilization. We develop these arguments by discussing the detailed events of the German hyperinflation.

In the German case at least the stabilization was a much more diffuse, accidental matter than a reading of the classics reveals. Exchange rate policy definitely played a key role. Well beyond the early stages of stabilization immensely high interest rates in the face of a sharply appreciating free market exchange rate wiped out adverse speculation, thus helping to establish stabilization until fundamentals—fiscal stabilization and foreign loans—could be brought into place.

The discussion also draws attention to the behavior of the real exchange rate and real wages during stabilization. The real exchange rate sharply appreciated in the final stage and persisted at an appreciated level well into the poststabilization phase. This may well have facilitated the political economy of the stabilization because of the implicit rise in real wages. It reflects the reverse of the coin of real depreciation in the capital flight phase.

21.1 Some Theoretical Considerations

The conventional or monetary model of hyperinflation centers on the money market. Rational expectations are assumed, and the rate of money creation is determined by the requirement of budget financing.

The budget deficit is a given fraction λ of real output. Deficit finance then implies that the real value of money creation equals the deficit:

$$\frac{\dot{M}}{P} = \mu m = \lambda y, \tag{1}$$

where

μ = the growth rate of money,

λ = the deficit as a share of output,

y = real output,

$m = M/P$ = real balances.

Assume now a linear velocity equation with π denoting the rate of inflation:

$$\frac{y}{m} = \alpha + \beta\pi. \tag{2}$$

Substituting (2) into (1), and assuming that in steady state equilibrium money growth equals inflation, $\mu = \pi$, yield

$$\pi = \frac{\lambda\alpha}{1 - \beta\lambda}. \tag{3}$$

The equilibrium rate of inflation thus depends positively and in a very nonlinear fashion on the budget deficit as a fraction of output, λ. It also depends on the parameters of the velocity equation. In particular, an exogenous flight from money (a reduction in α) raises the equilibrium inflation rate.

This model leaves out several important features of a hyperinflation process. Two of these relate to the budget. The first is a point emphasized in particular by Bruno and Fischer (1985), namely, that for many functional forms of money demand there is a Laffer curve of inflation tax revenue. Accordingly, there will be more than one inflation rate that can finance a given budget deficit. This raises the question of inflation dynamics. Which equilibrium will the economy move to? How is this path influenced by expectations and policies? What happens, as is possible, if the required inflation tax revenue exceeds the maximum rate that can be raised given the demand for money?

The second point concerns the link between the budget, inflation, and real exchange rates. The inflation rate will affect the budget deficit because it affects the real revenue of tax collection that can be realized from a given tax structure given the inevitable lags in tax collection. These lags can be shortened or their effect can be dampened by indexation. But there remains, in hyperinflations, an inevitable erosion of real tax revenue that is more substantial the higher the rate of inflation. It is worth separating here short-run and long-run effects: In the short run an acceleration of inflation, given lags, will inevitably reduce the real value of tax collection, and thus it widens the deficit, raises money creation, and thereby increases inflation. Over time the government may offset at least in part the erosion by shortening delays for tax collection. The dynamic influences then involve a race between the acceleration of inflation with its tax erosion effects and the acceleration of tax collection, or increased indexation, which exerts stabilizing effects.

But the deficit will also be affected by the real exchange rate. This is particularly the case if service of an external debt or reparation payments denominated in foreign exchange appears as a significant government outlay. With these two points in mind, the budget deficit in (1) now becomes

$$\mu m = \lambda(\pi, \sigma) y, \tag{1a}$$

where σ denotes the real exchange rate.

The introduction of the real exchange rate in (1a) raises the question of exchange rate determination in a hyperinflation economy. The tradition has been to emphasize PPP because a hyperinflation was viewed as the ultimate, pure case of a monetary experiment. But it is quite apparent from the facts that real exchange rates varied widely, certainly in the short run. But if PPP is not a satisfactory model of exchange rate–price relationships, then a more complete model of portfolio choice and real exchange rates needs to supplement the monetary model described here.

A related point concerns financial markets. The monetary model cuts this topic short by viewing the inflation process from a money–goods margin of substitution. But clearly financial markets did exist, and part of the reason for inflation, along with deficit finance, was the creation of credit for the private sector. Money creation therefore depends not only on the budget but also on the policy defining discounting of private paper. The behavior of real interest rates therefore appears to be an important feature of hyperinflation processes.

The final point concerns dynamics of wages, prices, and the exchange rate. Escalation of inflation, from moderate rates to a hyperinflation— defined by Cagan (1956) as an inflation rate in excess of 50 percent per month—involves systematic shifts in the timing relationships. We can imagine an economy where initially wages are adjusted in a backward-looking fashion at infrequent intervals, say every six months. Prices are adjusted more frequently and exchange rates perhaps weekly. As the inflation rate increases these lags shorten until ultimately all pricing takes place on the basis of the exchange rate. The shift to hyperinflation may be associated with the move from backward-looking wage adjustment to exchange-rate-based wages. The analysis is further complicated by the role of expectations, specifically expectations regarding such fundamentals as the budget, which is at best only partially exogenous.

To formulate a realistic model of hyperinflation, taking account of the issues raised here, is clearly beyond the scope of this paper. The purpose here is to look at the details of the German hyperinflation to point out that each of these complications was in fact an important part of the story, so that a simple budget-money-credibility story is not enough, even if in the final analysis stabilization cannot take place without them. They are necessary, but it is not apparent that they are also sufficient conditions.

21.2 Inital Conditions

In the immediate aftermath of World War I, Central Europe resembled Latin America of the past twenty years: political turmoil mixed with economic inequality, precarious democracy, and financial instability. Although the German hyperinflation stands out, problems of high inflation or even hyperinflation prevailed in many countries, including Russia, Austria, Poland, and Czechoslovakia. In fact, it is doubtful that there was any country that escaped altogether a significant increase in prices during World War I. Even in Switzerland the price level doubled during the war. The main difference is how various countries coped with the subsequent stabilization effort.

It is interesting to start our analysis well before the hyperinflation got underway and compare Germany with other major countries. Table 21.1 offers a comparison focusing on the price level and the dollar exchange rate. The bench-mark is the United States, and the comparison countries are France and the United Kingdom.

The central point emerging from table 21.1 is the large wartime price increases everywhere, including the United States. In the war years prices more than doubled in the United States and in the United Kingdom. In Germany and France the increases were much larger, more than 200 percent, and nearly 300 percent. But in this respect Germany was not much different from France.

The large change occurs between 1920 and 1922: the United States and the United Kingdom experience a sharp deflation as prices *decline* nearly 50 percent; in France prices fall less than 40 percent, and in Germany they

Table 21.1
Comparative price levels and exchange rates (indexes 1974 = 1, annual average)

	United States	United Kingdom		France		Germany	
	P	P	e	P	e	P	e
1914	1	1	1	1	1	1	1
1919	2.6	2.5	1.1	3.4	1.4	3.9	7.8
1920	2.6	3.1	1.4	4.9	2.8	14.1	13.5
1921	1.4	2.0	1.4	3.4	2.6	18.1	10.2
1922	1.3	1.6	1.3	3.1	2.4	323.3	101.8

P denotes the Wholesale Price Index, and e the index of the local currency price of the U.S. dollar.

increase by a factor of 23, or 2,200 percent. The United Kingdom returned to gold at the prewar par in 1925. France stabilized in 1926 to 1928, with a large depreciation and a much higher level of prices, seven times the 1914 level. Germany, by contrast, suffered a hyperinflation before prices were stabilized in a new currency. Clearly one decisive point is 1921, when other countries moved to *de*flation while Germany went into inflation.

Germany emerged from World War I with significant losses of territory and with a burden of reparations to be determined by an Allied Commission. The immediate postwar years were overshadowed by expectations of the reparation payments and by domestic political turmoil. There were revolutions and revolts, ranging from Soviet Republics in various states, including Bavaria, to right-wing activity of the demilitarized professional army. It was said that $100 could buy you a minor revolution. Uncertainty about the political and economic future is reflected in the erratic behavior of the exchange rate (marks/U.S. dollars) shown in figure 21.1

In the brief period from October 1919 (the Treaty of Versailles had been concluded in June 1919) to March 1920, the price of the dollar tripled. The

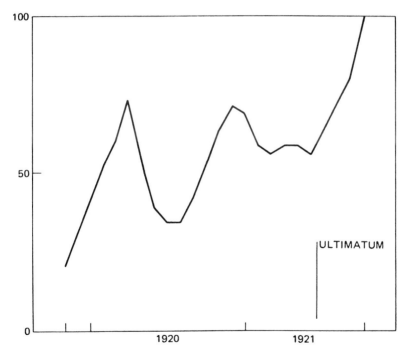

Figure 21.1
The nominal exchange rate (Reichsmarks/dollar)

depreciation was a reflection of the uncertainty in Germany, but it fed back to prices and fueled the turmoil. The sharp collapse in the spring of 1920 was one of the few points of potential return. Several factors helped create a moment of stability. The Erzberger fiscal measures strengthened the budget, the right-wing Kapp Putsch had been suppressed, and many other countries perhaps did not look that much better. But these improvements did not last, in part because of a sharp deterioration in the external balance.

A definite deterioration in the inflation outlook occurred in late spring of 1921 and relates to reparations. The terms fixed by the Reparations Commission required Germany to pay 2 milliard (2 billion in U.S. terminology) gold marks a year, plus 26 percent of German exports in addition to occupation expenses. The London Ultimatum of May 1921 required a front end payment of 1 milliard gold marks by August 1921 in foreign exchange, and a second slice of 500 million gold marks by November 15 of that year. The 1.5 milliard payment amounted to about half of total tax revenue. Using 1925 data, a payment of 2 milliard gold marks plus 26 percent of exports would amount to about 6 percent of GNP. The payment of reparations was associated with the massive exchange depreciation in the second half of 1921.

Further complications of political climate arose when the League of Nations imposed the separation of Upper Silesia from Germany. Germany's foreign policy with respect to reparations and other peace terms was a "policy of fulfillment." At least as a matter of policy, if not in the full delivery, Germany sought to implement the terms of the London Ultimatum. Although the 1921 payments were in fact met in early 1922, Germany protested its inability to fulfill these stiff terms and in June 1922 suspended all payments.

A commission of experts, including Keynes and Cassel, was invited to consider stabilization. The experts reported at the end of November 1922 to the German government, arguing three points (an excerpt from the report of the experts is reproduced at the end of the chapter): They were satisfied that the budget was balanced under conditions of reasonable price stability and excepting reparations and that stabilization could not proceed if reparations were to be continued. But they also made this observation (*Gutachten* 1922, p. 14): "We conclude that, in the conditions we postulate [suspension of reparations] an immediate stabilization is possible by Germany's own efforts.... At the rate of 3500 marks to the dollar the gold in the Reichsbank now amounts to about twice the value of the note issue.

This is an unprecedented situation. No other currency has fallen into decay with so great a potential support still unused."

But for the moment the possibility of stabilization disappeared as French and Belgian troops, in response to the suspension of reparations payments, occupied the Ruhr area. The occupation was met by German "passive resistance," the financial costs of which completely outstripped any chance of price stability.

21.3 The Hyperinflation

The prelude to the hyperinflation was the first part of 1923, when, in the face of the Ruhr occupation, the government attempted to stabilize the exchange rate. Figure 21.2 shows the official dollar exchange rate. Following the collapse in January, at the time of the occupation, the rate recovered and was stabilized between mid-February and mid-April. Inflation that had run at 28 and 89 percent per month in December and January rose to 111 percent in February and March. After the stabilization of the exchange rate, there is actual deflation of 17 percent and only 7 percent inflation in April. As soon as the exchange rate support was abandoned, because of huge reserve losses, the hyperinflation got underway.

Table 21.2 shows the dollar exchange rate (paper marks per dollar or gold mark) as well as the monthly rates of depreciation and of inflation for the critical period in 1923. During the Ruhr occupation in January and February 1923, prices had doubled each month, as did the dollar rate. But from the middle of February to the middle of April there was a brief reprieve, with falling prices and currency appreciation. The episode is explained by significant Reichsbank intervention in the exchange market.

By May inflation and depreciation accelerate, and for the rest of the year the German economy disintegrates as inflation rates reach at their peak 30,000 percent per month, or just above 20 percent *per day*. At 20 percent inflation per day, the price level doubles in less than four days!

The stories of life in the most dramatic stages of hyperinflation are well known. Keynes reports how people would order two beers at a time because the beer would grow warm and stale more slowly than the price was rising. Taxis were preferred to streetcars because one paid at the end of the trip. Other accounts include stories on how firms made payments to workers by furniture van. Schacht (1927) reports that the demand for notes was so immense that 133 printing firms produced notes for the government on more than 1,783 machines with 30 factories working full time to supply the paper.

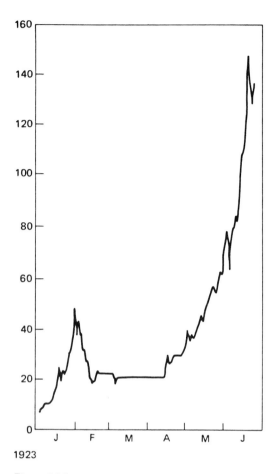

1923

Figure 21.2
The exchange rate (thousands of Reichsmarks/dollar)

Table 21.2
The German hyperinflation in 1923 (percentage change from previous month)

	Wholesale prices	Exchange rate
February	55	101
March	−13	−24
April	15	7
May	57	95
June	137	131
July	286	221
August	1,162	1,307
September	2,432	2,035
October	29,586	25,957
November	10,133	8,462

Source: *Wirtschaft und Statistik.*
Note: Stabilization occurred on November 15, 1923.

In July the inflation rate was still 3.5 percent per day. In August it rose to 6.5 percent per day, in September to 11.2 percent, and finally to an average of 20.9 percent in November. In the final stages of the inflation, prices and exchange rates became closely tied because even weekly reports on the cost of living or wholesale prices were far out of line with current developments. Quotations of the exchange rate, and thus of the gold mark, became the central pillar for calculating prices. The government had throughout resisted a dollarization of the economy, but in the middle of the year could no longer prevent much of pricing from shifting to gold or the dollar, even though German money continued to be used as required by law. The shift to the gold mark or foreign-exchange-based pricing led in July–August to a big upsurge in inflation via the once-and-for-all elimination of lags. Perhaps it is this shift to foreign-exchange-based pricing that is the ultimate element in the shift toward hyperinflation. Clearly, in September–November prices were changed more than once a day, and ultimately all inertia disappeared in a process that Pazos (1978, p. 93) has described as follows: "The reduction of intervals [for setting wages and prices] to their shortest possible duration and the pegging of wage adjustments—both upward and downward—to the freely fluctuating quotation of foreign currency give hyperinflation a mechanism different from that of intermediate inflation. The day to day adjustments of all contracts puts an end to all connections between the value of transactions in successive periods...."

21.4 The Stabilization

Elements of the stabilization occurred even before the extreme explosion got underway. As early as August 1923 the government had issued a loan of 500 million gold marks, in part in small denominations. These bonds had started circulating and had come to be accepted as hard currency even though they carried no backing other than the government's promise to redeem in gold. When the political improvement offered the prospect of budget improvement the acceptance of the gold mark bonds (for which convertibility in gold was certainly not assured) had paved the way for a new monetary instruments. In fact, the gold mark loan bonds served as backing for gold mark liabilities issued by municipalities and other government bodies.

But the deciding event was clearly political stabilization. On the political front the Streseman government, formed in August 1923, put an end to passive resistance in October. On the threat of resolution of parliament, an "empowering law" was enacted that allowed the government to pass regulations and laws, even suspending the constitution wherever the national economic interest so required.

Plans for stabilization focused on two alternatives: a Gold Bank or a Roggenbank (Rye Bank). In the end the idea of a Roggenbank won out, although in a somewhat different form, as the Rentenbank (Mortgage Bank). The key institutional elements of the stabilization were three:

• Legislation in mid-October introduced the Rentenbank as a semi-public body with capital represented by fictious claims on industry and land. The assets of the bank were to be claims on the government and credit to the private sector. The total loans were not to exceed 2,400 million Rentenmarks or gold marks, half to the government, half to private borrowers. Of the government part 300 million were to be set aside to retire the government floating debt held by the Reichsbank.

• The liabilities of the Rentenbank were the Rentenmark. They had a convertibility feature that linked them to the successful gold mark loan: upon request 500 Rentenmarks could be converted into a bond having a nominal value of 500 gold marks, thus establishing the 1 : 1 link between the Rentenmark and the circulating gold mark loan certificates. Because these certificates were accepted as hard currency, the convertibility linkage of the Rentenmark could readily be exploited to enhance the new money. But the paper mark remained legal tender, and the Rentenmark had only the claim that it had to be accepted by government agencies in payment.

• The same legislation instituted the rule that the Reichsbank would no longer be entitled to discount government bills. Reichsbank note issue had to be backed at least one-third by gold and the remainder by commercial paper. But the Reichsbank remained entitled, subject to the gold-backing requirement, to discount commercial paper.

On November 15 the Rentenbank came into operation, and issue of the Rentenmark started. Prior to the actual issue the government had already placed at the end of October of small denomination gold mark loan. The loan was issued to cope with the *cash crisis*, namely, the fact that the real money supply had declined to levels so low that the payments mechanism had substantially collapsed. Queues at the commercial banks and the Reichsbank trying to obtain paper money grew longer, and more and more of the demand for paper money went unsatisfied. Depreciation and inflation wiped out the real value of money much faster than the government, municipal authorities, and practically anyone could create paper money (see Yeager 1966, p. 271).

Within a month price and exchange rate stability had been restored. Extra taxation, and even more so the sharply increased real value of tax collection in January 1924 and beyond, eliminated fiscal difficulties as a source of inflationary deficit finance. But there remained a different threat, namely, Reichsbank commerical lending. During December 1923 and in early 1924 credit expanded so rapidly that a risk of renewed inflation and depreciation in March 1924 had to be checked by a credit crunch.

One of the striking features of the stabilization that is often emphasized is the comparative stability of prices and exchange rates. Monetarists are fond of quoting a well-known remark of Havenstein, the president of Reichsbank, to the effect that the arrival of new, high-speed printing presses would cope with the cash crisis. The remark is construed as reflecting complete ignorance of the source of inflation and the inflation-induced adjustment in velocity. But it may well reflect a more sophisticated model of inflation in which in fact, real balances were inadequate rather than burning holes in pockets. This is brought out in table 21.3. Between the date of stabilization, November 15, and the end of the year, Reichsbank credit increased fourfold. Over the same period the quantity of Reichsbank notes outstanding nearly doubled.

Another important feature of the stabilization that needs comment is the behavior of unemployment and of real wages. Figure 21.3 shows that the German real wage increased strongly in the stabilization. The real wage gain (relative to 1922–23, not 1913) persisted. The increase in unem-

Table 21.3
The aftermath of the stabilization (index December 1923 = 100)

	Money stock	Wholesale prices
1923		
November 15	20	22[a]
November 20	41[b]	118
November 30	70	119
December (end)	100	100
1924		
June	138	92
December	188	104

Source: *Wirtschaft und Statistik*, various issues.
a. November 13.
b. November 23.

ployment was dramatic, but it did come down from the record levels of December 1923. Of course, tight money and the overvalued exchange rate set the stage for the "Stabilisierungskrise"—the decline in activity that follows successful stabilization.

21.5 Why Did Stabilization Succeed?

There is no single obvious explanation for the successful stabilization of the German currency. The standard explanations are five, involving in each case a combination of a gain in confidence based on one or more of the following fundamental factors:

• Monetary stabilization via the discounting restraints imposed on the Reichsbank and the Rentenbank.

• Fiscal stabilization.

• Exchange rate stabilization.

• Political stabilization through the end of passive resistance and the appointment of an expert group of the Reparations Commission.

• The reduction in the real money supply prior to stabilization.

The question of how stabilization was achieved is not exactly the same as that of why hyperinflation occurred in the first place. But the latter question provides a good starting point. There are broadly two schools of thought: One emphasizes the budget and money creation as *active* sources of the hyperinflation. Adherents of this theory would make exchange rate

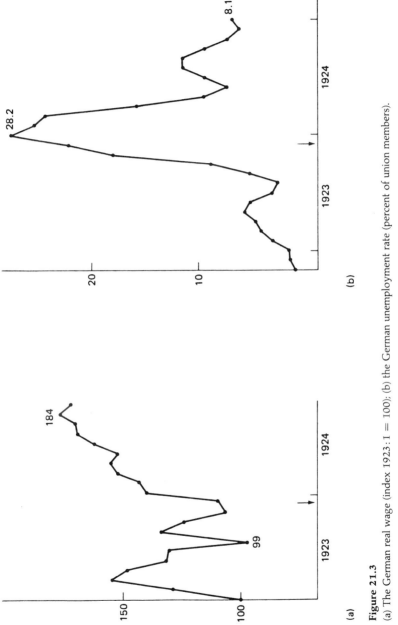

Figure 21.3

(a) The German real wage (index 1923 : 1 = 100); (b) the German unemployment rate (percent of union members).

adjustments passively respond to the domestic inflation developments along purchasing power parity (PPP) lines. The alternative theory is the balance-of-payments approach. This theory claims that adverse balance-of-payments developments force exchange depreciation, which then deteriorates inflation and, with that, budgetary performance. In a setting of passive money, exchange rate disturbances then *cause* inflation. Political disturbances fit in either setting as the proximate sources of disruption. For the monetary-fiscal approach they initiate deficit finance. For the balance-of-payments approach reparation payments are the source of extraordinary foreign exchange demands, which force depreciation of the currency, which then spreads to domestic inflation and a widening of the budget deficit.

For either of these schools the consolidation of the political events via an an end of passive resistance and the improved prospect of stabilization loans was thus an important ingredient. But beyond that there are differences on what is *the* essential element in gaining stability.

Sargent (1982, p. 83) attributes the stabilization to the institutional limit on monetization of deficits and the resulting need for fiscal correction. The limit on government credit from the Rentenbank and the prohibition of discounting of government debt by the Reichsbank combined to separate completely deficit finance and the monetary system. He notes that the government was forced into budget balance, and thus the objective conditions for inflation were removed "by a series of deliberate, permanent actions to raise taxes and eliminate expenditures." He refers in particular to the cuts in employment in the public sector. The proposed cuts were in fact very substantial: a reduction of 25 percent in government employment to be implemented in several stages. Of course, the data show that the gain in tax revenue was much more important for budget stabilization than the cut in spending.

The success of fiscal stabilization is seen in the budget shown in table 21.4. There is no question that Germany in fact moved to a balanced budget and beyond. GNP data for the early 1920s appear to be unavailable and hence it is difficult to express the budget relative to GNP. But an estimate for 1925 is possible. For that year budget receipts represent 10.4 percent of GNP.

Figure 21.4 shows the value of tax receipts in gold marks. The figure makes apparent the erosion of tax revenue in the hyperinflation and the very rapid recovery of real revenue once price stability returns.

The monetary-fiscal view would certainly be reinforced by the change in personnel, when in December, Schacht, a self-confessed gold standard man, replaced Havenstein as president of the Reichsbank. Graham (1930) is

Table 21.4
The budget (millions of gold marks, fiscal year April–March)

	1922	1923	1924	1925
Expenditure	3,951	8,979	7,220	7,444
Receipts	1,508	2,620	7,757	7,334
Budget deficit	2,442	6,359	−537	110

Source: *Wirtschaft und Statistik*, various issues.

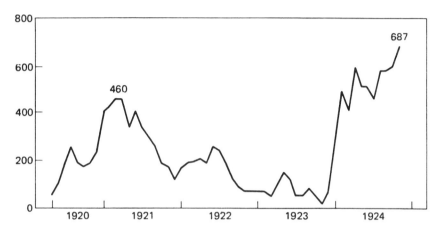

Figure 21.4
Tax collection (millions of gold marks)

quoted by Yeager (1981, p. 59) as writing of Havenstein's death as "a demise which cannot be thought of as other than opportune."

The Reichsbank effectively withstood the pressure to resume monetization of budget deficits. As already noted, the Reichsbank was prohibited from discounting government paper. When the Finance Minister turned in December to the Reichsbank for a bridge loan, he could not secure credit and had instead to raise emergency taxes, anticipate taxes, and issue gold mark bonds.

Table 21.5 shows that most of the monetary expansion that does occur in the early phase of the stabilization is in fact in the form of small denominations of the gold loan and Rentenmark, not Reichsbank money. An institutional feature worth recording is the extreme difficulty of putting Rentenbank notes into circulation: a printer's strike was taking place at the very time the Rentenmark was to be issued. As a result the printing was delayed, and the note issue proceeded very slowly. Accordingly, at no time in the early stabilization did the Rentenmark lose scarcity.

Table 21.5
Composition and level of the norminal money stock (millions of gold marks)

	Reichsbank	Rentenbank and gold loan	Emergency money	Coin	Total
1923					
November 15	155	286	18	—	459
December 31	497	1,666	111	—	2,274
1924					
March	690	2,081	28	26	2,833
June	1,097	1,837	—	139	3,073
December	1,941	1,835	—	383	4,159

The monetary-fiscal control is, of course, a central part of the stabilization and indeed the fundamental factor. But this does not really answer the more basic question: *How does a government that plans to do all the right things and, indeed, puts them on paper secure the credibility that then makes it possible to live with the policies?* It surely is not the case that there is an objective way of doing things right that, when hit upon, always and invariably yields instant public recognition and success. Observers of the time (as opposed to, say, Sargent's analysis) recognized this deeper problem. They were sensitive to it because they had seen earlier attempts in Germany and in other countries that started off right, but then fell apart because they were not supported by stabilizing speculation. A case in point might be the first Poincaré stabilization of 1924, which evaporated while the second, in 1926, stuck. Where is the difference?

Students of the German stabilization were keenly aware of the issue. Bresciani-Turroni (1937) refers to the stabilization as a "miraculous event" and notes (p. 355), "The stabilisation of the German exchange showed, as did that of the Austrain crown, this characteristic: The exchange was stabilized *before* there existed the conditions (above all the equilibrium of the Reich Budget) which alone could assure a lasting recovery of the situation."

Of course, one might argue today that the fact of stabilization is immaterial; what counts are the fundamentals, the firm expectation of stabilization. With the expectation of reduced money creation and inflation, there is growth in real money demand, which will be split between the transitory blip due to the Rentenmark issue and a fall in prices. But that, once again, begs the question of the certainly about the budget. Various observers note that it was the very fact of the cessation of inflation that provided the stabilization of the budget via increased real values of tax collection. This argument makes the termination of inflation a precondition for fiscal stabilization rather than the other way round. That argument, however, is not completely right. The fiscal stabilization had, in fact, four elements:

• The increase in the real tax collection that came from the end of inflationary erosion of the tax yield caused by collection lags.
• The elimination of the real value of the long-term government debt in the hands of the public via the hyperinflation.
• The elimination of part of the floating debt in the hands of the Reichsbank by the substitution of the (interest-free) Rentenmark credit.
• The creation of new taxes and cuts in outlays.

The important part, in respect to timing, concerns the long-term public debt. The service of the debt amounted at the end of the war to more than half the budget outlays. By 1924 it was less than 3 percent. To achieve that result there was a need for a sufficiently large cumulative increase in prices before the other three factors could complement the real debt reduction to stabilize the budget. In this sense the timing of the stabilization is not altogether indeterminate. This point is certainly reinforced by the fact that the reduction in outlays associated with the end of passive resistance was a precondition for financial stability.

A very interesting suggestion comes from the analysis of Keynes (1923, pp. 46–48) and Bresciani-Turroni (1937). The argument is that the rise in velocity, because of hyperinflation, ultimately reduces the real value of cash balances to so negligible a level that two factors are at work. First, *any* sort of external loan will be sufficient to place the entire currency outstanding on a gold cover, making it possible to implement convertibility. Second, the extreme rise in velocity is not sustainable (furniture vans delivering daily payments). As Keynes (1923, p. 47), writing before the actual stabilization, puts it,

... a minimum is reached eventually from which the least favorable circumstance will cause a sharp recovery.... When the overvalue of the currency has fallen to a very low figure, it is easy for the government, if it has any external resources at all, to give sufficient support to prevent the exchange from falling further for the time being. And since by that time the public will have carried their attempts to economise the use of money to a pitch of inconvenience which it is impracticable to continue, even a moderate weakening in the degree of their distrust of the future value of money will lead to some increase in their use of it; with the result that the aggregate value of note issue will tend to recover.

Comparison of a number of stabilization programs highlights this critical aspect of exchange rate stabilization. It appears invariably as *the* key step in a program. It is not sufficient by itself—this is shown by the February–March 1923 attempt to stabilize—but it is the critical step that coordinates expectations, at least temporarily, around a new trend of prices and thus gives a chance to fiscal stabilization via the revenue effects. It might be argued that stabilizing private speculation, in the face of the right kind of objective evidence, would perform the same function. It might well, but it would be difficult to disagree that enticing private speculators to perform the stabilization might require even more monetary-fiscal overkill than if the government itself takes the steps.

It is quite clear that the government was aware of the need to establish a sound base of departure for the stabilization. Schacht (1927) makes a point that between November 14, when the Rentenmark was about to be issued, and November 20 the government devalued by 333 percent so as to raise the value of reserves relative to the quantity of Reichsmarks outstanding. With money issue practically ceasing, at least for a while, this meant a huge contraction of the money stock in terms of foreign exchange and also in terms of domestic prices. The devaluation was also designed to move the official rate more in line with the free market rate observed in the occupied territories. The quotations for the official rate in Berlin and the free Cologne rate are shown in table 21.6. Figure 21.5 shows the same fact using the Berlin and Amsterdam rates.

The exchange rate data make the point that the stabilization was not an immediate, obvious set of measures reflected instantly in the exchange rate

Table 21.6
Official and Cologne exchange rates (billion of marks/U.S. dollar)

	Official	Cologne
November 12	0.630	3.90
November 13	0.840	6.85
November 14	1.26	5.80
November 15	2.52	6.50
November 20	4.20	11.70
November 30	4.20	7.80
December 6	4.20	4.90
December 10	4.20	4.20

Source: Schacht (1927).

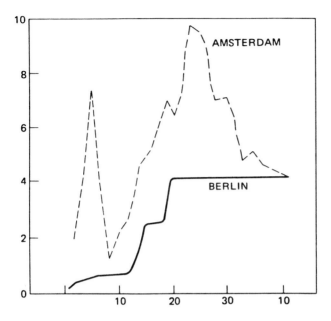

Figure 21.5
The Reichsmark/dollar exchange rate (billions of Reichsmarks/dollar)

in the free market. Even by November 30, when prices had stopped rising, the free market rate still exceeded very significantly the official now fixed rate of 4.2 gold marks per U.S. dollar. Only toward the middle of December, a full month after stabilization, did the market accept the policy. And as early as February–March 1924, because of excessive commercial credit expansion of the Reichsbank, a new depreciation of the free rate ensued.

The exchange market was perhaps slow in recognizing the viability of the policies merely because they could prove themselves only over time. The request of the Finance Ministry for accommodation, in late December 1923, really shows that there was at best a potential stabilization, with institutions that were there on paper and on probation.

Quotations from the weekly report of the *Economist*'s reporter in Berlin read as follows:

The currency question continues to be in a mixed condition and it is very dangerous to predict how things will develop. (November 27, 1923)

The finances continue to be in a hopeless condition and as the provisional Renten mark currency reform, which is at best doubtful, cannot possibly succeed without budget balancing the general situation is gloomy. (December 4, 1923)

The currency condition has distinctly improved, owing to the price-fall now followed by a relative stability which creates the impression in the public mind that the Renten mark, gold loan currency and even the paper mark are, for some reason not known to the science of currency, really stable. This view cannot be held. The dominating influence is that for the moment the same views seem to be held abroad (as far as there is any dealing in German currency) and that so long as foreign Bourses do not depress the mark, causing a paper mark price-rise ... the stability will be maintained. (December 16, 1923)

In that perspective a major credit for de facto stabilization must go to the actual fixing of the official exchange rate combined with supertight credit. The view that emerges from this perspective does recognize the importance of institutions (no government discounting, fiscal correction, printer's strike), but goes further to argue that these measures must, in fact, be made sustainable by actual success. Huge real interest rates and a stop to capital gains on the exchange market are a way, though a very expensive one, to bring hyperinflation to a screeching halt.

We now turn to the interest rate question, which seems a strikingly neglected factor in the literature.

21.6 The Real Interest Rate Problem

A fact that has recieved no attention at all in the literature (with the exception of Prion 1924 and Pfleiderer 1976) is the striking behavior in interest rates. Table 21.7 shows the interest rate *per day* quoted on the Berlin stock exchange for overnight loans (*Tagesgeld*).

To place these interest rates in perspective, we need to remember that prices were actually falling over the period and that the free market rate for foreign exchange was collapsing. Thus a *daily* interest rate of 0.5 percent, or nearly 500 percent per year, combined with falling prices implies a fantastic real interest rate. An interest rate of 3 percent per day, as prevailed in November–December, after the stabilization, amounts to a monthly cost of credit of nearly 150 percent. In the face of an official exchange rate that remained fixed, the mere postponement of a resumption of hyperinflation and hyperdepreciation by a few days meant dramatic capital losses for foreign exchange speculators. The fact of a depreciation of the dollar by nearly 100 percent, combined with the huge cost of credit, operated as a forceful stabilizing device. This was in fact the strategy of consolidating the stabilization success. Schact in particular makes much of the fact that in November–December the main game was to ruin speculators ("to serve them with their tail in their mouth").

Table 21.7
Interest rates in the aftermath of the stabilization (percent per day)

November 19	8–4%	December 3	1–3–1/2%
November 22	5–8–15–20%	December 4	2–1/4%
November 26	5–10–5%	December 5	1/2–2%
November 27	5–6–10–14%	December 7	2%
November 28	10–15–10%	December 8	1–1/2%
November 29	5–8–4%	December 10	1/4–1.5%
November 30	5–2%	December 11	1/2%
		December 12	1/2%
		December 13	1/6%
		December 17	1/2%
		December 18	1/4–1/2%
		December 19	1/4–3/4%
		December 20	1–1.5%
		December 21	6.5%
		December 22	2.5–3/4%

Source: *Berliner Borsen Courier.*

This regime of extremely high real interest rates carried through for more than half a year. This is apparent from the dollar exchange rate, the price level, and money market interest rates reported in table 21.8.

Note that the day-to-day money, for lack of a daily price index, is not indexed, but monthly loans are indexed. The large difference between the rates in January 1924, a full month after the stabilization, reflects the ongoing possibility of a resumption of depreciation and inflation.

One might ask how, conceivably, interest rates can be so high. Who would borrow and who would not lend? The active margin in all likelihood is foreign exchange. Given earlier experience with stabilization, and especially in the period February–April 1923, the public had every right to expect that from one day to the next, because of political events, the exchange rate could collapse and hyperinflation might resume. But even the indexed rate is extremely high; in fact it is Latin American. The difference here reflects, in part, the fact that indexation is stated in terms of prices and not the exchange rate. To the extent that a collapse would start with the exchange rate, the indexed rate should in fact also reflect somewhat the risk of renewed depreciation.

Table 21.8 also brings out the renewed credit squeeze in April 1924. Following a substantial credit expansion, the exchange rate in the free

Table 21.8
Interest rates, the dollar, and prices in 1924

| | Interest rate (percent per year) | | Dollar[a] | Prices[a] |
	Day money	Month money		
January	87.6	28.3	99.6	92.9
February	34.9	22.6	104.1	92.5
March	33.1	30.0	103.2	95.5
April	45.9	44.5	103.2	97.3
May	27.8	44.3	99.5	95.0

Sources: *Wirtschaft und Statistik*, 1925, p. 276, and Board of Governors.
a. Index December = 100.

market (i.e., abroad) weakened and confidence in the sustainability of the reforms softened. The Central Bank reacted by a complete freeze on money creation, which proved effective in reversing the adverse expectations. With prices falling and the stabilization established, the nominal rate now falls below the indexed rate. Table 21.8 thus suggests that only a few months after the stabilization, and after repeated demonstrations of the new rules, was the reform in fact established. In the meantime, of course, realized real interest rates had been very high, thereby creating a burden on real activity that was reinforced by the strong real exchange rate.

The real interest rate problem can easily be understood in terms of the standard model of interest rate determination. It is an issue that Mundell (1971) has particularly emphasized. Now we present the condition of monetary equilibrium in terms of the nominal interest rate, i,

$$\frac{M}{P} = L(i, \ldots), \tag{4}$$

which yields the equilibrium nominal interest rate

$$i = h\left(\frac{M}{P}\right), \quad h' < 0. \tag{4a}$$

The stabilization program involves policies that stabilize the price level via exchange rate fixing and a stop to (or drastic slowdown in) money printing. Through the combined channels, M/P is more or less frozen at a level close to the hyperinflation low. Therefore the equilibrium nominal interest rate, which now is also the real rate, stays extraordinarily high. This fact persists because M can only rise to the extent that the Renten-mark is issued or the Reichsbank discounts commercial paper and monetizes reserve inflows. Discounting of private bills, although clearly taking place, was still limited in the first six months, and the reflow of capital that did occur was not monetized but rather used to satisfy foreign exchange demand at the rationed rate. Reserves actually did not rise until late 1924. Prices did fall some, but the fixed exchange rate certainly precluded a massive deflation.

It is clear therefore that even with a 600 percent increase in nominal money, real interest rates still remain exceptionally high. The surprising fact is that capital inflows should not have occurred on a much more dramatic scale. It is worth noting that exactly the same problem of high real interest rates (or insufficient capital inflows) is now occurring in the Argentine stabilization. The problem is reinforced in Argentina because the central bank is not even expanding commercial credit so that capital inflows are the only way for money creation.

21.7 Exchange Rates and Inflation

The discussion of the German hyperinflation, and other inflation explosions, invariably brings up the question of whether the exchange rate depreciation is the "source" of inflation. The argument is immediately rejected on the ground that without validating monetary policy, the depreciation could not be sustained. But that argument may be too simple once it is recognized that money creation is endogenous via the budget and that the budget may be affected by the rate of inflation and by the real exchange rate.

Consider figure 21.6, where we show at ten-day intervals the prices of domestic goods and of imports in gold marks, that is, paper mark prices translated into foreign exchange at the going offical exchange rate. A rise in the gold mark price of domestic goods thus represents a rise in inflation relative to depreciation, and conversely for a decline in the gold mark price. It is quite obvious from the figure that there are huge shifts in the relative prices. During periods of exchange rate stability, in early 1923 and in late 1923, prices are stable or declining. By contrast, following an exchange rate collapse, as in April 1923, July 1923, and August 1923, there is an outburst of inflation. It is this sequence, running from exchange rate collapse to domestic inflation, that motivates the balance-of-payments approach.

The exchange rate issue enters the analysis in still another way. One of the striking features of many stabilizations is the sustained real appreciation. Figure 21.7 shows the real exchange rate in Germany. One explanation is that the exchange rate is driven by the portfolio holders' decision to

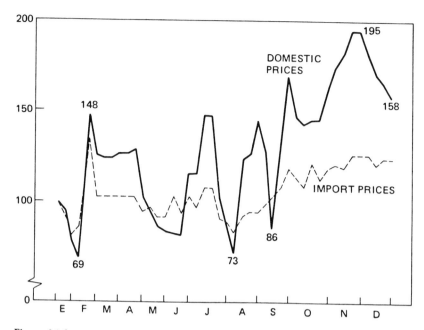

Figure 21.6
Import and domestic prices in gold (index 1923 : 1 = 100)

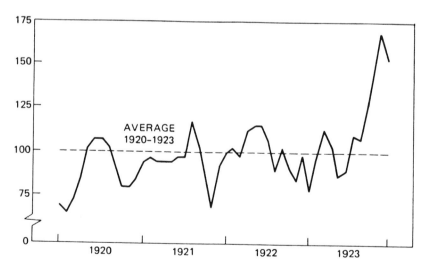

Figure 21.7
The German real exchange rate

move out of or into a currency. In the face of economic and political instability there is capital flight, which leads to real depreciation (and hence sharply accelerating inflation). In the stabilization phase there are net capital inflows and stabilization loans that allow current account balances or deficits, and hence a real appreciation. This fact is important because it helps explain, in part, the success of stabilization since it raises real wages.

21.8 Concluding Remarks

The detailed description of events in the German stabilization draws attention to the fact that stabilization appears a much more diffuse, multifaceted issue than a simple monetary model would predict. Two points, in particular, stand out: the government defended a fixed exchange rate, following an initial sharp depreciation, and extremely high real interest rates were maintained for more than half a year, even after actual budget balancing was in sight or even achieved. Were these steps essential? Could the hyperinflation have been stopped as effectively, or even at lower costs in terms of unemployment, if the government had on November 15 simply withdrawn from the foreign exchange market, allowing a flexible exchange rate without any controls on transactions? And, second, were extremely high interest rates required to establish the credibility of the reform? Could the government have got by with a larger issue of Rentenmarks and with lower interest rates? Finally, what role did expectations about relief from reparations and/or foreign loans play in supporting the government's monetary and fiscal policy? Had the Dawes loan not arrived in 1923, would the government have had to maintain huge real rates, and could it have afforded to do so?

None of these issues arises in the simple monetary model, but each is crucial in real life stabilization contexts. Only a broader model of the hyperinflation economy that models real exchange rates, portfolio balance, and credibility can hope to answer these questions. In the meantime exchange rate fixing (and wage–price controls) seem an effective means of giving the economy both guidance as to the equilibrium price level and an initial dose of inertia.

21.9 Appendix: Extract from the Report of the Group of Experts

II. Outlines of a Plan for Stabilising the Mark.

I. In return for a suspension of payments under the Treaty of Versailles for a period of two years, the German Government should offer to the Reparation

Commission in the following definite guarantees:

a) That an independent Board of Exchange Control would be constituted as a special department within the organisation of the Reichsbank and that the Reichsbank would hold adequate gold from their reserves at the service of the Board.

b) That so long as any part of such gold is unpledged, paper marks shall be purchased by the Board of Exchange, on demand, at a fixed rate to the dollar; this fixed rate to be determined on the principles outlined in the first part of our Report.

c) That the aggregate value of the net floating debt shall not be increased beyond a defined figure; all other government requirements for credit to be covered by funded loans.

No modification to be made in the above without the permission of the Reparation Commission.

It would be necessary, further, for the Reparation Commission on the one hand and the German Government on the other to exempt the resources of the Board of exchange from interference.

2. On the consent of the Reparation Commission being obtained to the above, the following measures to be taken:

a) The financial cooperation and support of an International Financial Consortium to be invited.

b) A foreign currency reserve, on such scale as may be required, to be created on the basis of the gold at the disposal of the Board of Exchange, in conjunction with the credits which may be negotiated with the International Consortium from time to time on such security as may be acceptable.

c) The abolition of all exchange regulations and the restoration of free and un-restricted dealings in exchange and foreign securities.

3. The Board of Exchange to buy and sell foreign exchange on demand (on gold-exchange standard principles) against paper marks at fixed rates, the selling rate being not above 5 percent dearer than the buying rate in the first instance.

4. The Bank Rate to be raised to a high rate and dear money to be maintained until stabilisation is quite secure; but discounts and advances to be made freely at this rate for regular trade transactions against all normally approved security.

5. In order to concentrate into its foreign-currency reserves as large an amount as possible of the free foreign assets of German nationals, under conditions which would inspire confidence:

a) The Board of Exchange would issue gold bonds, guaranteed by the Reichsbank, at an adequate rate of interest, repayable in gold in one or two years, in exchange for foreign bank notes, bank balances etc.

b) The Board of Exchange would buy foreign exchange spot and sell it forward at appropriate corresponding rates for various periods.

6. The additional notes required to carry on the business of the country, as it returns to more normal conditions, would be issued,

a) By trade discounts and trade advances by the Reichsbank and

b) The sale of marks by the Board of Exchange against the receipt of foreign currency; and, to the least possible extent and for a period not exceeding six months, against further Treasury Bills issued to cover the budgetary deficit during the transitional period before the budget can be balanced.

Berlin, November 7th 1922.

Signed: R. H. Brand,
    „   Gustav Cassel,
    „   Jeremiah W. Jenks.
    „   J. M. Keynes.

Note

I am indebted to Olivier Blanchard, Vittorio Corbo, and Stanley Fischer for helpful comments.

References

Angell, J. W. 1929. *The Recovery of Germany.* Yale University Press.

Bresciani-Turroni, C. 1937. *The Economics of Inflation.* Allen and Unwin.

Bruno, M., and Fischer, S. 1985. "Expectations and the High Inflation Trap." Unpublished manuscript, Massachusetts Institute of Technology.

Busch, O., and Feldman, G. (eds.). 1978. *Historische Prozesse der Deutschen Inflation.* Colloquium Verlag.

Cagan, P. 1956. "The Monetary Dynamics of Hyperinflation." In Friedman, M. ed., *Studies in the Quantity Theory of Money.* University of Chicago Press.

d'Abernon, V. 1926. "German Currency: Its Collapse and Recovery: 1920–26." *Journal of the Royal Statistical Society,* 90, pt. I.

Deutschlands Wirtschaft, Wahrung und Finanzen. 1924. Im Auiftrag der Reichsregierung. Zentral Verlag, Berlin.

Dornbusch. R., and Fischer, S. 1986. "Stopping Hyperinflation: Past and Present." *Weltwirtschaftliches Archiv,* April.

Graham, F. 1930. *Exchange, Prices and Production in Hyperinflation Germany.* Princeton University Press.

Gutachten der Internationalen Finanzsachverstandigen uber die Stabilisierung. 1922. Published by the German Foreign Office.

Guttman, W., and Meehan, P. 1975. *The Great Inflation.* Saxon House.

Haller. H. 1976. "Die Kriegsfinanzierung und die Inflation." In Deutsche Bundesbank, *Wahrung und Wirtschaft in Deutschland, 1876–1975.*

Holtfrerich, C. L. 1980. *Die Deutsche Inflation.* de Gruyter.

Keynes, J. M. 1923. *A Tract on Monetary Reform.* Macmillan.

Laursen, K., and Pedersen, J. 1964. *The German Inflation: 1918–1923.* North-Holland.

League of Nations. 1944. *International Currency Experience. Lessons of the Inter-War Period.*

League of Nations. 1946. *The Course and Control of Inflation.*

Mundell, R. 1971. *Monetary Theory.* Goodyear.

Pazos, F. 1978. *Chronic Inflation in Latin America.* Praeger.

Pfleiderer, O. 1976. "Die Reichsbank in der Zeit der Grossen Inflation, die Stabilisierung der Mark und die Aufwertung von Kapitalforderungen." In Deutsche Bundesbank, *Wahrung und Wirtschaft in Deutschland: 1876–1975.*

Polak, J. 1943. "European Exchange Depreciation in the Early Twenties." *Econometrica* 11, 151–162.

Prion, W. 1924. "Zinspolitik und Markstabilisierung." In *Schmollers Jahrbuch* 48, 843–868.

Sargent, T. 1982. "The Ends of Four Big Inflations." In R. E. Hall, ed., *Inflation.* University of Chicago Press and National Bureau of Economic Research.

Sargent, T. 1984. "Stopping Moderate Inflation: The Methods of Poincaré and Ms. Thatcher." In R. Dornbusch and M. H. Simonsen, eds., *Inflation, Debt and Indexation.* MIT Press.

Schacht, H. G. 1927. *The Stabilization of the Mark.* Allen and Unwin. Reprinted by Arno Press, 1978.

Statistisches Jahrbuch for das Deutsche Reich. 1923, 1924/25, 1926.

Williamson, J. (ed.), 1985. *Inflation and Indexation.* MIT Press.

Wirtschaft und Statistik. various issues.

Yeager, L. 1966. *International Monetary Relations.* Harper and Row.

Yeager, L. 1981. *Experiences with Stopping Inflation.* American Enterprise Institute.

Young, P. 1925. *European Currency and Finance.* U.S. Government Printing Office.

22

Inflation Stabilization: The Role of Incomes Policy and of Monetization

(with Mario H. Simonsen)

In 1985 to 1986 Argentina, Bolivia, Brazil, and Israel experienced extremely high rates of inflation and responded with a new kind of treatment: heterodox stabilization (see table 22.1). Among the key features of the stabilization programs in all instances (except Bolivia) were the use of wage–price controls, a fixed exchange rate, and fiscal correction as well as a significant expansion in the nominal quantity of money. A conversion table was introduced to adjust existing contracts to the disappearance of inflation. The combination of fiscal correction and incomes policy has come to be known as "heterodox" stabilization policy, thus opposing it to the conventional IMF programs which emphasize tight monetary and fiscal policies as the exclusive instrument of stabilization.

This chapter investigates two issues arising in the context of stabilization: what is the role of incomes policy and what role is played by monetary reform. In chapter 21 the discussion of the 1923 monetary reform in Germany highlighted the central role of fixing the exchange rate as a means of signaling a period of price stability. In the context of the programs in Israel, Argentina, and Brazil (though not Bolivia) inflation had not been as extreme and hence special problems and opportunities arose for incomes policy and monetary policy which are the topic of this chapter.

Table 22.1 shows averages of monthly inflation rates for the countries that undertook stabilization (Israel and Argentina, respectively, in June and July 1985, Bolivia in August 1985, and Brazil in February 1986) and for Mexico where so far inflation stabilization has not been tried. As the table makes clear, the programs failed utterly in Brazil and relatively in Argentina. In Israel and Bolivia price stability has been sustained.

The challenge is to understand the institutional features of the high inflation process and to isolate the precise role the heterodox aspects

Abridged and adapted from *Inflation Stabilization with Incomes Policy Support*, Group of Thirty, New York, 1987.

Table 22.1
Recent high inflation experiences
(annual and quarterly averages of monthly inflation rates)

	Argentina	Bolivia	Brazil	Mexico	Israel
1980	6.0	3.3	5.0	2.0	7.2
1981	6.2	2.2	6.2	2.0	6.6
1982	8.5	7.4	6.0	3.9	6.8
1983: I	13.4	7.1	8.3	7.0	6.7
1983: II	11.7	7.3	8.8	4.8	7.5
1983: III	17.0	17.6	10.2	4.0	7.5
1983: IV	17.9	20.6	8.4	4.5	16.0
1984: I	16.6	17.9	10.0	5.3	12.5
1984: II	17.8	37.9	9.2	3.7	16.1
1984: III	22.9	19.2	10.2	3.0	16.7
1984: IV	18.0	50.5	9.9	3.7	15.9
1985: I	24.1	92.4	12.0	5.1	10.3
1985: II	28.4	42.0	8.2	2.7	13.7
1985: III	3.6	63.1	11.5	3.9	11.5
1985: IV	2.5	6.0	12.3	5.1	2.1
1986: I	3.1	13.7	10.1	6.0	0.6
1986: II	4.4	2.9	0.8	5.7	2.2
1986: III	7.6	1.6	0.8	6.3	1.0
1986: IV	5.4	0.3	3.5	6.8	2.2
1987: I	7.4	1.6	14.1	7.3	1.5
1987: II	5.2	0.6	24.6	7.8	1.3
1987: III	11.9	0.5	5.1	7.6	1.0
1987: IV	11.1		15.0	10.0	1.5

of stabilization programs can play. Unlike traditional programs, heterodox stabilization programs do provide an immediate, temporary opportunity for basic policy reform. Even if they do not afford a magic relief from the necessity of fiscal correction, they surely represent a significant oportunity to try to achieve policy reform where before, in innumerable cases, that proved impossible or was overly delayed because of the perception of immense political costs associated with the large unemployment and slow disinflation.

Stabilization has two dimensions: whether or not the program includes fiscal correction or austerity and whether the program has an incomes policy (wage, price, and exchange rate freezing together with remonetization to be explained shortly). The standard program is the IMF approach, which consists of fiscal austerity but does not make incomes policy a key instrument. It is true that orthodox programs favor wage restraint, but price controls are not typically, or ever, an item on the conditionality list. On the contrary, price liberalization tends to appear in these programs. Heterodox programs, by contrast, combine an incomes policy with fiscal austerity.

Stabilization without austerity, relying merely on incomes policy, is not a viable approach. The most common form is to attempt stabilization by controls only, without paying attention to the sine qua non of fiscal correction. But history is crowded with many thousand years of failed experiments. Inevitably these programs come to an end after a more or less brief period of effectiveness. They fail when shortages become a sufficient political headache. Ultimately the patient, often too late, is rushed to the IMF.

There is another dimension along which programs might be distinguished in four-way classification. Programs might be orthodox or heterodox, and they can involve gradualism or shock treatment. In this distinction the present programs are classified as "heterodox shocks." An example of a heterodox-gradualist program would be the Brazilian Campos-Bulhoes stabilization of 1964–1967. An orthodox-gradualist program might be the case of Chile. It is more difficult to remember an orthodox-shock example, perhaps because of a lack of survivors to recount the episode.

We first discuss the inflation process and the role of incomes policy and then turn to the issue of monetary reform and monetization.

22.1 Incomes Policy and Stabilization

In this section we discuss the inflation process and the analytical case for wage-price–exchange-rate controls. Wage-price controls are understood here as an essential, but transitory, complement to the fiscal stabilization which is the sine qua non of successful anti-inflation policy.

That aggregate demand discipline is a necessary condition for sustained price stability has long been known by economists and by well-advised policymakers. Yet it may not be sufficient to stop inflation, or at least it may fail to work under conditions of tolerable unemployment. This is demonstrated by the failure of a number of IMF-supported programs that ignored the problem posed by inflationary inertia. As result IMF programs often lead to dismal stagflation and ultimately to a resumption of expansion and little or no success at definitely reducing inflation. Not surprisingly, countries like Argentina, Israel, and Brazil recently decided to focus on the supply side of inflation, attempting to stabilize prices by combining incomes policy with "monetary reforms."

Whether these experiments will ultimately yield success stories depends on a number of factors, including especially aggregate demand management. The overriding lesson from the ongoing experiments certainly includes the need for sound respect for fiscal discipline and the need to recognize that a good dose of initial overkill may be an inevitable ingredient for subsequent success.

One interesting issue is that such experiments were inspired by a sound game-theoretic approach to inflation. It can be argued, as we do below, that an incomes policy is necessary to coordinate individual behavior in a way not recognized by oversimplified versions of a rational expectations economy. The central question is to understand what causes inertial inflation and how incomes policy can break the dependence of the inflation rate on its past behavior.

Inertial Inflation

The starting point for the discussion is the recognition that a large part of a high inflation is essentially *inertial*. This observation applies equally to the United States, Europe, or Latin America. Inertial inflation means that inflation today is approximately equal to what it was yesterday. Let π be the current inflation, π_{-1} last years inflation and "gap" denote the economy's cyclical position. The actual rate of inflation would then be

$$\pi = \pi_{-1} + \alpha\text{Gap} + e, \tag{1}$$

where e denotes current period supply shocks. The essential point of modern inflation theory is the recognition that inflation is linked to the past through a variety of channels. It is not only "too much money chasing too few goods," which is the second term, or supply shocks like oil or agricultural price increases, or real depreciation, but also the sheer fact that inflation yesterday means inflation today.

The reason for this persistence or inertia is primarily formal or informal indexation interacting with staggered wage setting. This may take the form of a legally imposed wage rule, according to which wage adjustments today are based on the inflation over the past year or the past six months. It may also be that much more informal wage bargaining may lead to the same result. Other than through wage indexation the same mechanism also works via expectations. In setting their prices, firms will have to estimate their own cost increases and the price increases of competing firms. The best guess is that, cyclical and supply shock factors aside, inflation today will be approximately what it was yesterday.

Because everyone believes that inflation will in fact be approximately what is was yesterday, the public acts on these expectations and will therefore set the prices accordingly and will not hesitate to give wage concessions matching these inflation expectations. It is much easier to give wage increases in line with expected inflation than go through the risk of a strike. If everyone acts in this manner, then in fact the expected inflation turns out to be the actual inflation—and if yesterday's inflation is the bench-mark, then today's inflation will come out to be much the same as it was in the past.

Cyclical factors and supply shocks, including the need to depreciate exchange rates to cope with the debt crisis, are the chief reasons why inflation has exploded in many countries. The inertial part of inflation, other things equal, would tend to make for very stable inflation, at some particular level. But the extra elements can cause inflation to move, and often to move sharply. The cyclical factor is quite obvious in that it is simply demand inflation or cooling down of inflation due to slack in activity and employment. But it is worthwhile to recognize an asymmetry. There is no upper limit for firms' price increases in response to excess demand, but in reverse the argument does not apply. Stopping inflation of say 400 percent by slack is very difficult. Even as restrictive policy cuts nominal spending, firms are forced in the labor market to make wage concessions based on past inflation. Their cost increases thus might be of the order of 400 percent, and it is quite inconceivable that simply by reducing profit margins they would be able to reduce inflation significantly.

In the same way a cut in wage settlements below the prevailing rate of inflation will not make much of a difference to high inflation. Giving wage increases of 360 instead of 400 percent would mean a very large cut in the real wage (8 percent!) but a very minor reduction in inflation.

The idea of fighting inflation by slack thus applies only to an economy where wage reductions of 2 or 3 percent or cuts in profit margins of that order mean cutting inflation in half. When inflation is very high and very inertial, then demand policies have a hard time making a rapid and large impact. Because a rapid and large impact is the only way that is politically acceptable, governments in high inflation countries see little hope but to try to stem further inflation deterioration, though they do not see room for actually ending inflation.

The new stabilization programs recognize this problem in a way that IMF programs do not. They recognize the need for an incomes policy as a means of suspending the inertial forces, thus shifting the economy instantly from a high inflation state to a low one. This incomes policy should be understood in two ways. One is political. To stop inflation, someone must start offering cuts in either profit margins or real wages in order to introduce disinflation. The initial disinflation can then be passed along through indexation into a gradual path of further disinflation. Realistically, there will be no volunteers for such an approach. We each would like to jump to a low inflation state together, but no one will jump unless others also do. That means we each want to see the fact of zero inflation before we ourselves will set our own price or wage increases at zero. But if each of us adopts a "wait and see" attitude then, of course, inflation will continue. All attempts to restrict demand would translate almost entirely into reduced employment and practically not at all into lower inflation. The dismal performance of the economy and the lack of success at inflation fighting would make any such campaign short-lived.

The Pazos-Simonsen Mechanism

Institutional wage-setting mechanisms often rely on a fixed contract length, with wage adjustments occurring at specified intervals. The adjustment will be based on the accumulated increase in prices since the last adjustment. A good example is the Brazilian wage mechanism: wage earners receive full compensation for past actual price increases at regular intervals: yearly, until 1980, and at six month intervals since then. The interesting question is what happens when the frequency of adjustment increases. This point has been developed especially by Simonsen (1984) and Pazos (1978). It is of interest here because it highlights the characteristics of an accelerating inflation and the place of exchange depreciation in that context.

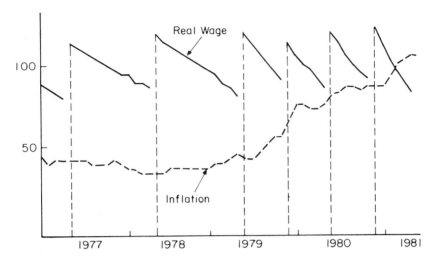

Figure 22.1
The real minimum wage and inflation in Brazil (1977–78 = 100 for wages; inflation in percent per annum)

With periodic wage adjustments the real wage follows the sawtooth pattern shown in figure 22.1. On each adjustment date, the real wage is increased by the cumulated inflation since the preceding adjustment, say 50 percent. Over the next adjustment interval it declines as the ongoing inflation erodes the purchasing power of the constant nominal payments. By the end of the adjustment interval, the real wage has declined below its period average. The higher the rate of inflation, moreover, the lower the average real wage, given the interval of adjustment.

In a system of full, but lagged, indexation, the real wage can be cut only by moving to a higher rate of inflation. Thus once-and-for-all depreciation of the currency immediately raises the rate of inflation and erodes existing contracts. But the catch-up through indexation ensures that inflation must be pushed to an even higher rate so that there is always some group of wage earners that is still lagging on the increasing rates of price increases. The same principle applies to the removal of subsidies undertaken to correct the budget. Measures undertaken to correct competitiveness or the budget can be effective only if they achieve a cut in the real wage, but that cut can take place only if inflation is allowed to run at a higher rate, because of full indexation. This mechanism often sets the stage for inflation explosions.

Consider a country that requires adjustments in the budget and external competitiveness. Suppose too that the government does not have the political force to suspend full indexation so that the removal of subsidies or exchange depreciation will speed up the inflation rate. Workers in the middle of their contracts or three-quarters toward the next adjustment will find that their real wages fall below what they consider a minimum standard of living. They cannot borrow, even in perfect capital markets. Hence they will call for a shorter interval between wage adjustments in order to recover the real wage losses imposed by inflation. They will ask for an advance of what they think is due. If the economy does in fact shift from, say, six- to three-month indexation intervals, as is likely to happen in Brazil today, the inflation rate will simply double.[1] But once the inflation rate has moved to a three-month scheme, two facts are clear. First, it is exceptionally unlikely that indexation will return spontaneously to a longer interval, even if shocks are favorable. Second, there is nothing to make the three-month interval more stable than the six-month interval that was just abandoned. Renewed shocks will shift the economy to even more frequent adjustments and hence to correspondingly higher rates of inflation. At this stage the exchange rate becomes critical.

In his seminal study of the inflation process in Latin America, Pazos (1978, pp. 92–93) has described the dynamics as follows:

When the rate of inflation approaches the limit of tolerance, a growing number of trade unions ask for raises before their contracts become due. And management grants them. These wage increases give an additional push to inflation and bring about a further reduction of the adjustment interval. Probably the interval is initially shortened to six months, and then, successively, to three months, one month, one week, and one day. At first the readjustment is based on the cost-of-living index; but since there is a delay of one or two months or more in the publication of this index, it must soon be replaced by another. The best-known and more up-to-date of the possible indicators in Latin America is the quotation of a foreign currency, generally the U.S. dollar.

This description of the inflation process makes clear that the dramatic escalation of inflation, seemingly disproportionate to the disturbances, arises from the endogeneity of the adjustment interval. This is due not so much to the direct impact on inflation of corrective exchange rate or price policies: it occurs because minor increases in inflation, being as highly visible as a 10 percent devaluation over and above a PPP rule or a removal of bread subsidies, are the straws that break the camel's back. They lead to an increase in the frequency of wage adjustments which brings on much higher inflation. The endogeneity of adjustment intervals is the mechanism that connects small inflation disturbances with the shift from 50 to 100 percent inflation, and beyond, to hyperinflation as we see in table 22.1.

The exact modality of the shift to increased frequency will differ from one experience to another: the government may cave in under the impact of a strike, business may find it is easier to give an "advance" on the real wage adjustment rather than risk labor unrest in the middle of a recovery or boom, or a planning minister may seek the popularity that comes from a wage policy apparently favoring labor. One way or another, the frequency will increase, and once it happens in a large part of the economy, it cannot fail to become generalized.[2]

It is immediately clear from the Pazos-Simonsen mechanism that the optimal incomes policy in this context is one that monitors above all the frequency of adjustments. An entirely different view emerges with respect to exchange rate and budget policy. As long as indexation remains full, even seemingly small corrections are a dramatic threat to the stability of the inflation rate and hence may not be worth undertaking.

Game Theory and Incomes Policy

The scenario thus described puts inflation fighting squarely in the area of game theory. When economic agents interact strategically in the fashion described earlier, coordination becomes essential to achieve good results. A system of wage–price–exchange-rate controls is the coordinating device that establishes the fact that the economy left to itself cannot establish zero inflation quickly except at extreme costs. It might be argued that if the government does undertake to produce the right kind of monetary and fiscal policy, then the public cannot escape the conclusion that in fact inflation has been left dead in its tracks. Unable to escape that conclusion, everyone will act on it and hence inflation will be dead.[3]

But there are two separate and crucial slips in this argument. One concerns the government's inability to credibly precommit to future policies. The other, which is more novel, concerns the problem of coordination in a world of price setters. We review these in turn.

The government cannot commit itself definitely, credibly, and beyond doubt. The institutional setting for such a precommitment does not exist (one thinks of constitutional amendments, the gold standard, and what not). Because the government cannot lock away beyond doubt its policies, the public always recognizes that there is some possibility that policy will not change to a noninflationary stance. Specifically, if, on average, agents do not quite believe that policy will change, then they each will behave somewhat defensively, charging some wage and price increases which then force the government to suspend the policy. The expectation that this is indeed the policy persuades the average agent to disbelieve the possibility of an instant end to inflation.

These ideas can be interpreted in a game-theoretic perspective, assigning the government a double task: to ensure credibility of the aggregate demand policy consistent with disinflation and to coordinate the expectations and actions of individual wage and price setters. Assume that after a prolonged inflation, the Central Bank announces that it will stop printing money and the Treasury announces that the budget deficit will be eliminated as a result of inceased taxes or expenditure cuts. Even if the general perception is that nominal GNP will be stabilized immediately, prudent price setters should not take the lead in stopping sectoral price increases, as long as they consider the possibility of further price increases in other sectors. In a noncooperative or noncoordinated game with many players, each individual player has little information on other players' payoffs. As a result there is no reason to believe that all players will hit the zero-inflation–full-employment equilibrium in the first move of wage and price setting. The uncertainty about the behavior of other players persuades the individual price setter to adopt a very cautious pricing policy.[4] How many moves it takes or how long it takes for the economy to reach the equilibrium is an open question, depending in part on the learning mechanism used by individual agents.

The convergence speed may be painfully slow after a prolonged period of high inflation. The more prolonged the period of learning, the higher is the unemployment rate that results from excessive prices confronted with a given nominal income target sustained by the stabilization policy. The higher and the more persistent is unemployment, the more agents will be inclined to believe that the authorities' determination may falter. Accordingly, rather than speeding up their price responses, they may persist even longer in their overly prudent disbelief.

The foregoing discussion provides the rationale for an incomes policy: if governments play transitorily the role of the Walrasian auctioneer, they can speed up the location of a zero-inflation–full-employment equilibrium. From this point of view incomes policy may be necessary to make economic agents behave in line with rational expectations models. It should be stressed that the central function of controls is not to constrain individual decision making but to tell each agent how other actors will play, clearing potential externalities in an imperfect information game. This role for controls, incidentally, dismisses a traditional argument against incomes policy, namely that governments are not better equipped than the private sector to discover the equilibrium. In fact the central problem is not to identify the equilibrium but to orchestrate the simultaneous playing of wage and price setters to reach the equilibrium.

A more fundamental contention is that the temporary success of an incomes policy may lead policymakers to forget that price stability can only be sustained with aggregate demand discipline. The temptation is to misread the price stability and produce a boom. The misleading signals are a true risk as is known from uncountable examples in history. Yet the converse is also true. Trying to fight a big inflation from the demand side may only lead to such dismal stagflation that policymakers may conclude that life with inflation is less uncomfortable than life with an IMF-supported program. Worse yet, they often reach that conclusion only after a prolonged period of recession.

Of course, the chances of hitting instantly a zero-inflation, zero-unemployment, and zero-shortage equilibrium via an incomes policy are remote. Wage-price controls will almost inevitably lead to some shortages unless there is a generalized recession that cuts demand. The central question is, What is worse in terms of social welfare—a few product shortages that may eventually be overcome by imports or a generalized shortage of jobs? From this point of view objections to an incomes policy should be balanced against the extreme costs of recession and unemployment. This is especially the case when the problem is to fight a big inflation with strong inertial roots. One reason to prefer an incomes policy is that it can be managed with appropriate flexibility, across sectors and across time, moving gradually from price freezes to price administration.

The case for a coordinating role for an incomes policy because of information externalities arises only when macroeconomic noise and uncertainty are large relative to the microeconomic uncertainties in each individual market. This explains why, in a second stage of the stabilization program, removing wage-price controls gradually, in successive sectoral steps, will result in less uncertainty and lower subsequent inflation than removing controls in one shot. The one-shot approach would simply bring back the uncertainty of individual players as to what every other player will do. As a result at the stage of liberalization there would be defensively large price increases which might well wreck the inflation stabilization.

Incomes Policy Matching

We conclude this section by noting that the various instruments of an incomes policy—exchange rates, wages, public sector prices, and the nominal money stock—must be carefully matched. Failure to align these policy instruments can easily lead to dramatically poor performance.

The clearest example of a poorly aligned policy might be the Chilean stabilization of the late 1970s. The budget had been moved to balance and, indeed, to a surplus. Money was under tight control, and inflation was gradually declining, though very slowly. To speed up disinflation, the government opted to stop the exchange rate depreciation that had previously been used to avoid loss of competitiveness in the face of continuing inflation. But the government failed to recognize that wage indexation, geared to the past inflation, implied cost increases for firms without providing offsetting relief on prices. The exchange rate soon became grossly overvalued, leading ultimately to the worst kind of speculation and financial instability.[5]

The need for a matching of instruments applies also to the money stock. As we will discuss in the next section, successful disinflation requires determined (though careful and limited) monetization of the economy.

22.2 Monetary Reform and Monetization

The stabilization program had as an important and highly visible component a monetary reform. We review here briefly the essential features of such a reform. They are mainly two. The first, which is crucial, is to shift contracts from those appropriate to an inflationary economy to those appropriate in a zero-inflation environment. The second, and less significant, component is the introduction of a new monetary unit, the main purpose of which, other than cutting zeros, is to increase confidence and consolidate expectations.

Contracts

In an inflationary environment with large uncertainty, contracts will have a very short maturity. Long-term capital markets will dry up. But even so contracts will be for a month or even six months. These contracts will specify nominal interest rates or implicit prices that are a reflection of the inflationary expectations prevailing at the time the contracts are concluded. For example, with an inflation rate of 10 percent per month, a one-month loan contract will carry an interest rate of at least 10 percent per month. Rent contracts entered into at any time will involve nominal payments over, say, six months that reflect the assumption of increasing prices. Wage contracts will be indexed in a formal or informal manner so that when they come up for renegotiation, they are adjusted for past or future inflation. A major problem for inflation stabilization is to recognize the presence of such contracts and institutions that are in force at the time of stabilization. If the economy were to move from one day to the next from high inflation to zero inflation, outstanding contracts and institutions would give rise to major problems.

It is immediately obvious that debtors can service loan contracts involving very high nominal interest rates only if in fact the inflation expected at the time of contract actually materializes. A six-month loan concluded with an inflation expectation of 10 percent per month would carry a 77 percent interest rate for six months. If inflation disappears, the nominal interest rate of 77 percent becomes the real interest rate, and hence the debt service burden would be extraordinarily large. An adjustment in all loan contracts is required to avoid a massive, unintended and unfair redistribution from debtors to creditors and the attendant risk of pervasive bankruptcy and financial instability.

For wage contracts the problem is perhaps even more complicated. Suppose, as is realistically the case, that wages are readjusted every three or six months. Every time a contract comes up for renewal, the money wage over the next three months is adjusted upward for the inflation that actually occurred over the past three months. With such a pattern of wage contracting, an instant end to inflation is nearly impossible. Just as the government seeks to impose zero inflation, some wage contract is coming up for renewal, and workers will ask to be compensated for *past* inflation. The wage increase in turn creates cost increases, and hence inevitably inflationary pressure.

Accordingly, the transition to zero inflation needs to be accompanied by some restructuring of wage contracting to avoid this inertia effect. At the time of stabilization some wage earners will just have recieved their adjustment, and hence will find themselves in the high real wage position of their three-month cycle, while others will be almost at the bottom. Freezing wages in this situation would be perceived as extraordinarily inequitable, and hence would serve as an impediment to stabilization.

Monetary reform is the broad term that characterizes the rewriting of contracts and the reform of institutions to make them compatible with the zero-inflation target. In the case of wages monetary reform requires that those who had recent increases, and hence have high real wages, must see their wages rolled back, whereas those who are in the low real wage phase need upward adjustments. This reform could, in principle, be achieved by money wage adjustments in the old currency. The confusion of a new money may, though, help achieve the transition in a simplified manner. Note too that a new money provides an important instrument to avoid legal complications, uncertainty, and challenges to the restructuring of contracts. Similarly, for contracts involving future nominal payments, a new money is a means of aligning the real value of payments with the expectations implicit at the time contracts were concluded. A conversion scale that sets the terms for translating the old money into the new according to a set timetable of depreciation is the practical means of achieving this end.

Often monetary reform also encompasses a capital levy on the public in the form of a write-down of monetary assets. Interestingly, in none of the recent stabilizations has this been attempted. This fact is all the more noteworthy in that, unlike in the 1920s, government debts remained very large, and hence made the idea of budget balancing via a capital levy particularly interesting. In the same way in Brazil, where domestic public debt accounts for nearly 20 percent of GNP, the idea of a capital levy remains attractive.

Real Interest Rates and Monetization

Monetary reform also often includes a change in the monetary institutions. Along with the change in the monetary unit, the change in the institutional arrangements is meant to dramatize the end of inflationary finance. But there is also a very difficult and central problem involving the need to reliquify the economy so as to reduce real interest rates. In the aftermath of stabilization, real interest rates are likely to be extraordinarily high. Failure to take them down by a policy of easy money threatens the stabilization through a variety of channels. The only way such a monetization can be achieved consistently with disinflation is of course by a commitment to fiscal correction that is altogether uncompromising.

The traditional way to signal new rules of the game is to announce the independence of the central bank and an end of automatic financing of the budget by the printing press. But it is important here to read the fine print. In the 1920s the stabilizations did, indeed, involve institutional changes and limitations on the access of the government to the printing press, but that did not imply an end to money creation for two reasons. One was that in some cases the transition was characterized by a large, once-and-for-all issue of money. It is instructive to review the stabilization experience in Germany in 1923 to 1924 to lay out the issue of high real interest rates in the aftermath of stabilization.

The German Experience with Monetization

An outstanding research issue is whether high realized real interest rates reflect primarily a shortage of liquidity, credibility, or else crowding-out. One argument is that real interest rates remain high unless monetization or deflation raise real balances back to noninflationary levels. The other is exactly the opposite. In this view nominal rates are high because of a lack of confidence in the program and an expectation of a collapse with a return of depreciation and inflation. Only by demonstrating monetary control can the authorities achieve a reduction in nominal and real interest rates.

It is apparent that the conflicting prescriptions pose an extraordinary policy dilemma. Even if steadiness in denying monetization is the right answer, there is still an overwhelming obstacle. Failure to bring down real interest rates rapidly leads ultimately to a debt problem in the way described by Sargent and Wallace (1982). In this scenario high real rates lead to debt accumulation, private and public, that ultimately may lead to repudiation or inflationary liquidation.

The German currency was stabilized on November 15, 1923.[6] The central fact of the stabilization was an increase in tax collection. To a lesser extent expenditure cuts helped eliminate the deficit. The fiscal part of the stabilization was reinforced and made possible by the establishment of a new monetary regime and a fixed exchange rate. Especially important was the creation of a new monetary institution in the form of the Rentenbank as well as the restriction on the Central Bank prohibiting the discounting of any government paper. Money issue therefore was limited to the monetization of foreign exchange inflows and credit creation through expansion of private credit.

In addition there was a fixed issue of Rentenmark and an issue of coin. The maximum issue of Rentenmark was 2,400 million gold Marks. Half of that amount was to be available for the government to bridge the gap between stabilization and the establishment of fiscal balance, the other for private credit creation. It is interesting to note at the outset that the 2,400 million gold Mark ceiling on the issue of Rentenmark amounted to fully five times the money stock in existence at the time of stabilization. It amounted to one-third of total government spending in the year 1924.

Table 22.2 shows the evolution of the German nominal money supply and of prices in the period following stabilization.

The table brings out an immediate and large monetization within the first month and a half. Since there was a printers' strike, this issue was not primarily in the form of the new Rentenmark but rather in small denominations of the gold loan issue. Later the main vehicle became the disburse-

Table 22.2
The German money stock and prices (millions of goldmarks)

Date	Reichsbank	Rentenbank and gold loan	Emergency money	Coin	Total	Prices[a]
1923						
November 15	155	286	18	—	459	100
December 31	497	1,666	111	—	2,274	89
1924						
March	690	2,081	28	26	2,833	87
June	1,097	1,837	—	139	3,073	84
December	1,941	1,835	—	383	4,159	89

a. November 20, 1923 = 100.

ment of the Rentenmark issue. Reichsbank liabilities in this period tripled, but they amounted to only a small part of the total money issue. The other point to note is the withdrawal from circulation of emergency money, and an offsetting issue of coin. It is not clear whether the coin issue (*Rentenpfennige*) was part of the one-time issue or a separate and unrestricted seignorage of the Treasury. The latter seems to have been the case.

In the immediate aftermath of the stabilization nominal interest rates were astronomical. Bresciani-Turroni comments on these high real rates, linking them to the expectation of depreciation:[7]

In December 1923 complete confidence in German money was not yet reestablished and the premium for the risk of depreciation remained, although it was lower. In the same month ... on day-to-day loans in papermarks an interest rate not lower than 3–5 percent per day was paid on the average. On the other hand, for Rentenmark loans with a clause which guaranteed the lender against the risk of the depreciation of the Rentenmark itself, interest of 1 to 1.5 percent per month was asked.

Newspaper quotations show that the interest rates on stock market loans were 2 to 5 percent per day in late November, declining to 0.75 to 2.5 percent by the middle of December.[8] At the same time that these rates prevailed, goods prices were falling and the black market rate of the dollar was collapsing. Hence real interest rates were extraordinarily high.

Complete series for asset yields are available on the basis of weekly averages for 1924. Table 22.3 shows the overnight rate, the one-month rate, and the yield on 5 percent gold bonds. For comparison, we also show the ninety-day bankers' acceptance rate in New York. Note that the three

Table 22.3
Interest rates and asset yields in Germany in 1924 (percent per year)

Week of	Day money	Month money	Gold bond	New York rate
12/31–1/5	113	—	7.5	4.13
1/7–1/12	134	30	7.19	4.13
1/14–1/19	101	36	7.37	4.06
1/21–1/26	50.3	30	7.5	4.06
1/28–2/2	25.9	21	7.4	4.0
2/4–2/9	28.1	16.5	7.39	4.0
2/11–2/16	36.8	21.0	7.64	4.13
2/18–2/23	46.2	21.5	8.15	4.1
2/25–1–3	31.1	27	8.2	4.1
3/3–3/8	34.5	27	8.7	4.1
3/10–3/15	44.4	30	9.0	4.1
3/17–3/22	30.1	30.3	9.4	4.0
3/24–3/29	23.6	32.5	9.6	3.9
3/31–4/5	45.0	38.8	9.8	4.0
4/7–4/12	47.3	43.8	10.1	4.0
4/14–4/19	39.7	42.4	10.6	4.0
4/21–4/26	49.9	46.8	10.9	3.9
4/28–5/3	41.4	51.1	11.6	3.6
5/5–5/10	43.1	53.8	12.1	3.5
5/12–5/17	19.9	43.5	12.9	3.4
5/19–5/24	16.0	39.6	12.8	3.0
5/26–5/31	24.3	31.4	13.1	3.0
6/2–6/7	36.7	44.7	13.3	2.9
6/9–6/14	23.9	36.2	13.8	2.6
6/16–6/21	19.8	27.3	13.5	2.4
6/23–6/29	15.9	25.4	12.9	2.2
6/30–7/5	16.8	25.0	11.9	2.0
12/21–12/26	8.0	10.4	8.0	3.0

Sources: *Wirtschaft und Statistik* 65(22), p. 339, and Board of Governors of the Federal Reserve *Banking and Monetary Statistics; 1914–1941*, 1943, p. 454.

German assets differs in the form of *indexation*. Overnight money is in Reichsmarks, one-month money is indexed to the price level, and the gold bond is indexed to foreign exchange. But there is of course also a difference in *maturity*. In particular, the gold bond is a long-term asset so that the return is the yield to maturity rather than a short-term rate.

Several points are of interest. Note first that the interest rates on overnight and one-month money start at extraordinary levels. Gradually they decline until March 1924. The reason is undoubtedly the substantial credit expansion that was taking place.

The second point of interest is the sharp increase in *all* yields in the period March to June 1924. This is the consequence of a credit tightening by the Reichsbank. A weakening of the Reichsmark against the dollar in February to March 1924 caused the Reichsbank to make a dramatic move in rationing the expansion of credit.

Here is how Reichsbank President Schacht (1978, pp. 164–165) comments on the events:

The restriction of credits swept like an autumnal storm through this garden of surface blossoms. The rate for one-month money rose from about 30 percent, to almost 45 percent ... But in the first half of May the culminating point was reached, and in the following weeks and months the money rates sank very rapidly indeed, in proportion as the crisis in trade and production made itself felt ...

I believe the Reichsbank is in a position of Odysseus, when he had to sail between the monster of Scylla and the whirlpool Charybdis. Charybdis is the whirlpool of a new currency inflation, and Scylla is the monster of economic paralysis which snatches the crew from the ship of the national economy and swallows them in her maw. I believe the Reichsbank can make no other choice than that which Odysseus made: that is to say, it must seek to avoid the Charybdis of inflation and steer close to Scylla, who may indeed snatch and swallow a certain number of the crew, but will allow the rest to pass unscathed.

In the period of credit restriction the yields on all assets rise. Thus it is apparent that these high rates reflect tight credit rather than a lack of confidence in the continuance of the fixed exchange rate. Precisely because a tightening of credit is used to defend the fixed rate, the yield on gold bonds rises along with indexed and nonindexed bonds. Here there is clearly a difference between, say, January 1924 and May 1924. In the former period the yield on gold bonds is very low, and that on overnight money is high. The difference may reflect to some extent the confidence factor.

The yield differential between one-month bonds, indexed to the price level, and day money reflects both the front end of the term structure, with rapid credit expansion seen to push down rates, and the risk premium associated with a return of inflation. One would think, though, that the chief factor must be the term structure since the day-to-day probability of a return of high inflation might be judged small.

The differential between one-month money and long-term gold bonds reflects both the term structure of interest and the differential between inflation and depreciation, should a collapse occur.

What can be learned from the German experience? Against a background of a sharp improvement in the budget, actually moving for a while to a surplus, monetary policy aggressively supported the restoration of real balances. That policy was pursued pragmatically with a large provision for government money issue to bridge the gap to fiscal stabilization. The limit on the monetization was not some rule for the quantity of money, but the exchange rate. As long as the exchange rate remained stable, monetization was allowed to continue. Long after price stability had been attained, in the second half of 1924, money was still growing at 50 percent per year for half a year. But at this stage the money creation no longer financed the government but rather was the counterpart of private credit creation and monetization of capital inflows.

Theory and Literature
The question of high real interest rates has been explored in the literature on ending inflation. It is well understood that in the transition from high to low inflation, real balances must rise. The problem is how to bring about that increase consistent with confidence and without a deep recession.

Monetary equilibrium is set out in equation (2) which states that the money market clears when real money supply equals the demand for real money balances:

$$\frac{M}{P} = L(i, \dots),\tag{2}$$

where M/P denotes the real money stock and i is the nominal interest rate. The equation can be inverted to yield the equilibrium nominal interest rate as a function of the stock of real balances and other determinants of real money demand:

$$i = h\left(\frac{M}{P}, \dots\right); \quad h' < 0.\tag{3}$$

Figure 22.2 shows the money market. During a high inflation the economy will move to a point like A, where the nominal interest rate is high,

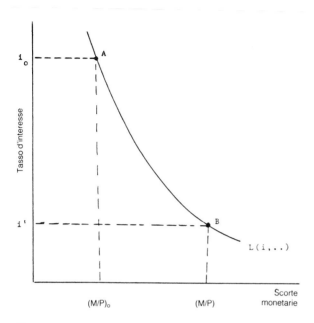

Figure 22.2
Real balances and equilibrium interest rates

reflecting more or less completely fully the rate of inflation. Now suppose a stabilization occurs, including a promise to restrict money creation and a fixing of wages, prices, and the exchange rate. The fact of stabilization means that the *real* money stock is roughly frozen at its prestabilization level M_0/P_0. The reason is that nominal money M_0 cannot increase because of the government commitment not to print money, and prices are unlikely to fall from their prestabilization level P_0, at least not precipitously. Accordingly, by this simple reasoning, the moment after stabilization the economy is still at point A with the initial stock of real balances.

The equilibrium *nominal* interest rate, determined by real money demand and the existing stock of real balances, is unchanged. But now inflation has disappeared, in terms of fundamentals or because of price controls. Hence the nominal rate of interest of the prestabilization becomes the *real* rate of interest after stabilization. The economy is stuck at point A rather than able to move to a position like B where real balances are higher, and thus the equilibrium interest rate is lower.

There is another point to be made. Suppose real money demand depends not only on the nominal interest rate but also on the expected rate of inflation, x:

$$i = h\left(\frac{M}{P}, x\right), \quad h_x > 0. \tag{2b}$$

In this case the equilibrium interest rate must actually rise. With the de facto stabilization of inflation, real money demand will now increase. The $L(i, \ldots)$ schedule would shift to the right, raising interest rates yet further.

There is accordingly a quite tight theoretical argument to say that real interest rates following a high inflation experience will be very high unless either the price level collapses, thus raising real balances, or else in one way or another the stock of nominal balances is allowed to increase.

The high real interest rate pattern in the aftermath of stabilization is familiar from any number of stabilization episodes. In the literature the issue is addressed as the "velocity problem."

Mundell pointed out that perhaps the most difficult part of stabilization is precisely this aftermath when velocity declines. His recommendation (Mundell 1971, p. 73) is to taper off monetary growth gradually. He notes:

Application of this rule for reducing the rate of monetary expansion stops inflation without causing deflation, although prices are stabilized, the monetary expansion continues at a (declining) rate just sufficient to offset changes in velocity. The new equilibrium level of the money supply will be higher than the level at the time of stabilization, and the price level will be constant throughout.

Milton Friedman (1983) has addressed the same issue in the following terms:

If a reduction in monetary growth leads to a decline in inflation, and that decline is embedded in anticipated inflation, the resulting lower cost of holding money will produce an increase in the quantity of real balances demanded. Velocity, which rises because of the reverse effect when inflation accelerates, and stabilizes when inflation stabilizes, will tend to decline when inflation declines. An ideal policy would therefore involve an initial decline in monetary growth, a subsequent rise when declining inflation reduces velocity, and a final decline in to the desired long-run level when velocity stabilizes.

Such a policy, while ideal in a world of perfect information and control, seems to me undesirable in actual practice. First, authorities never have the information required to approximate the correct pattern, except perhaps in cases of hyperinflation. Second, the authorities tend to be deceived by the decline in velocity when it comes, regarding it as more than a one-shot affair, and hence the danger—which has been realized more than once—of reigniting inflation and having to start all over.

It is worth recognizing the hyperinflation qualification in the Friedman quote. It is there presumably because of the massive decline in real balances during extremely high inflation, and hence the unquestionable need for *some* monetization.

The League of Nations, in reviewing the Austrian stabilization which was conducted under a program comparable to present-day conditionality under an IMF agreement, commented favorably on a policy of poststabilization money creation:

The net result of the increase in velocity during hyperinflation was that the currency in circulation when the League plan was started was quite inadequate to what were bound to be normal needs of the country.

This was recognized and turned to good account. "Unregulated issue was stopped on November 18th 1922; but as there was a difficult time ahead and it was known that expanding needs would absorb and demand extra currency, a considerable number of notes was printed just before November 18th and kept in hand to be used in succeeding months.

This provided an invaluable resource, capable of employment without in any way depreciating either the external or internal value of the crown. It was a bold expedient, fully justified by the results."

International Aspects

Monetization of the economy is one means to restore real balances; international capital flows are another. Here, it is interesting to observe the significant lag with which capital inflows respond to significant and persistent interest differentials. The experience seems far away from the world of perfect capital mobility which is the present-day bench-mark in international finance.

Portfolio theory for a world of capital establishes a link between home and foreign nominal interest rates consistent with *world* portfolio balance:

$$i = i^* + d + R(\ldots). \tag{4}$$

According to (4) the home nominal interest rate, i, is equal to the foreign rate, i^*, plus the expected rate of depreciation, d, plus a risk premium, R. Interpreting table 22.2 in terms of this equation suggests that either the anticipated depreciation was exceptionally high or the risk premium was large. Risk here concerns both uncertainty about exchange rate policy and also political risk. But when we go to the securities denominated in gold, exchange rate risk disappears and we are still left with significant differentials. These now must be thought of as one of three elements: transfer risks, risk of suspension of gold payments on a gold bond, or lack of international capital mobility.

How can we think of a lack of international capital mobility? Certainly investors take advantage of safe excess returns that are clearly, demonstrably available. The immediate implication of the large yield differentials in the case of Germany, as well as in other cases, shows that the major issue is uncertainly about what precisely the risks are. Is a gold bond in fact a gold bond? The only answer to that question is to wait and see. But if the international capital market takes a "wait and see attitude," then of course yield differentials can persist even at extreme levels. Because they do persist, financial difficulties in the high interest rate country can become more acute so that in the end financial stability is impaired.

Here is a link between stabilization and external support. The more strongly a government works on the fundamentals, in the form of fiscal correction, the more credible the policy of stabilization and the less uncertainty there is for the world capital market. With fiscal correction domestic monetization is not risky, but it is even unnecessary because capital inflows would ensure that interest rates come down as the central bank monetizes the resulting payments surplus. In Germany the period after June 1924 corresponded to this scenario.

Financial Institutions

A major issue in the sudden end to a high inflation is the fate of financial institutions, and specifically that of commercial banks and financial intermediaries. During inflation the public seeks to avoid holding money because of the depreciation of the purchasing power of money in terms of goods. The higher the rate of inflation, the larger is the implicit tax on money, and hence the larger the resources people are willing to devote to avoiding this tax. The natural consequence is the emergence of an industry that makes it possible to live with a minimum of real balances or, equivalently, to speed up the circulation of money.

Commercial banks and other financial intermediaries are the natural agents in promoting the moneyless economy. Credit cards are among the vehicles. They will surround potential customers with branches and attempt to attract deposits by paying some interest, thus helping their customers to avoid a complete loss of the purchasing power of their monetary assets. The proceeds of deposits in turn are re-lent at the high nominal interest rates commensurate with the prevailing rate of inflation. Differentials between deposit and lending rates leave ample room for the costs associated with an expansion of the banking system. The common observation, then, is that during inflation bank branches and bank employment mushroom.

When stabilization occurs inflation disappears and so does the absolute size of the deposit–loan rate spread. There is then an extraordinary profit squeeze which forces banks to close down branches and sharply curtail employment. The effect is totally predictable, and it is very serious not only from point of view of labor relations but, more important, from the perspective of financial stability. A successful monetary reform must take into account the fact that the financial industry is hurt by the end of inflation. Mergers, employment cuts, and a shift to fee for service banking will generally occur in the immediate aftermath of the stabilization.

22.3 Concluding Remarks

The new stabilization programs represent a critically important, viable alternative to traditional, orthodox, IMF-style programs. They grasp a central economic fact, the need for coordination rather than sheer slack, as an essential part of stabilization. From a political point of view they are dramatically successful, at least in the first stage, and as such they are feasible.

These new programs represent an important advance in macroeconomic policy, but even so they do not afford miracles. There is no substitute for a correction of fiscal disorder, the orthodox part of stabilization. But the success in Israel where such a program was implemented demonstrates that it is possible to stop inflation without a significant, protracted recession. That is a striking innovation, even if the examples of Brazil and Argentina show that success is rare. But then there is also no precedent of stopping inflation without recession using simply demand policies.

Somewhat surprisingly, governments seem to be unwilling to use the very strong increase in their political standing to follow up on the initial stabilization with a program of enduring, substantial improvement in public finance. This unwillingness is very shortsighted because any program will ultimately buckle under as boom and shortages force a return of inflation. There may be no outright collapse, at least for a long time, but gradually the program will tend to melt away for lack of sustainability, credibility, and confidence. As a result political support will inevitably fall off. And with the loss of support will fall the chances of achieving important changes in public finance. The chance of turning from stabilization to growth thus is missed.

Notes

Adapted from a paper with the same title, prepared jointly with Mario Simonsen for the Group of Thirty.

1. See the discussion in Simonsen (1983) on this point.

2. It is interesting to note that the dynamics of transition between intervals have not been modeled. Schelling's (1978, chap. 3) analysis of group choices placed in a macroeconomic setting might be a start.

3. How do we know that the economy cannot? That too is an issue in game theory. Schelling (1982) has written extensively on how to make threats stick. Ideas involve poison-pill strategies. Governments instinctively shy away from poison-pill strategies of no-return. As a result the public does not believe the fierce anti-inflation rhetoric, and the government in turn cannot afford to implement it. The late William Fellner (1976) developed these themes with great authority. See too "Anti-Inflation Policies and the Problem of Credibility" (1982).

4. See Simonsen (1986a, b) for a game-theoretic formulation that shows how players using maxmin pricing lead to an equilibrium different from the Nash equilibrium assumed in full-information rational expectations models.

5. See Dornbusch (1986a).

6. See Sargent (1982), Schacht (1978), Bresciani-Turroni (1937), Dornbusch and Fischer (1986), and chapter 21 in this book.

7. See Bresciani-Turroni (1937, p. 360).

8. See Dornbusch (1987).

References

Arida, P., and Lara Resende, A. 1985. "Inertial Inflation and Monetary Reform in Brazil." In J. Williamson (ed.), *Inflation and Indexation*, Institute for International Economics.

"Anti-Inflation Policies and the Problem of Credibility: Symposium." 1982. *American Economic Review* (May).

Baer, W., and Kerstenezky, I. (eds.). 1964. *Inflation and Growth in Latin America*. Yale University Press.

Bresciani-Turroni, C. 1937. *The Economics of Inflation*. Allen & Unwin.

Cardoso, E. 1986. "What Policy Makers Can Learn from Brazil and Argentina." *Challenge* (September–October).

Díaz-Alejandro, C. 1982. "Southern Cone Stabilization Plans." In W. Cline and S. Weintraub (eds.), *Economic Stabilization in Developing Countries*. Brookings.

Dornbusch, R. 1982. "Stabilization Policy in Developing Countries: What Lessons Have We Learnt?" *World Development*, no. 9.

Dornbusch, R. 1985a. "The Larida Proposal: Comment." In J. Williamson (ed.), *Inflation and Indexation*. Institute of International Economics.

Dornbusch, R. 1987. "Stopping Hyperinflation: Lessons from the German Experience in the 1920s." in R. Dornbusch, S. Fischer, and J. Bossons (eds.), *Macroeconomics and Finance: Essays in Honor of Franco Modigliani*. MIT Press.

Dornbusch, R., and Fischer, S. 1986. "Stopping Hyperinflation: Past and Present." *Weltwirtschaftliches Archiv* (April).

Fellner, W. 1976. *Toward a Reconstruction of Macroeconomics*. American Enterprise Institute.

Fischer, S. 1982. "Seignorage and the Case for a National Money." *Journal of Political Economy* 2. Reprinted in his *Indexing, Inflation and Economic Policy*. MIT Press, 1986.

Foxley, A. 1983. *Latin American Experiments in Neoconservative Economics*. University of California Press.

Friedman, M. (ed). 1956. *Essays in the Quantity Theory of Money*. University of Chicago Press.

Friedman, M. 1983. "Monetarism in Rhetoric and Practice." In Bank of Japan, *Monetary and Economic Studies* (October).

Graham, F. 1928. *Exchange, Prices and Production in Hyperinflation Germany*. Princeton University Press.

Heyman, D. 1986. *Tres Ensayos Sobre Inflacion y Politicas de Estabilizacion*. CEPAL, Buenos Aires, Doc. no. 18.

Keynes, J. M. 1923. *A Tract on Monetary Reform*. Reprinted by the Royal Economic Society, 1971.

League of Nations (Sir Arthur Salter). 1926. *The Economic Reconstruction of Austria*. Geneva.

Mundell, R. A. 1971. *Monetary Theory*. Goodyear.

Melnick, R., and Sokoler, M. 1984. "The Government Revenue from Money Creation and the Inflationary Effects of a Decline in the Rate of Growth of GNP." *Journal of Monetary Economics* (March).

Pazos, F. 1978. *Chronic Inflation on Latin America*. Praeger.

Okun, A. 1983. *Economics for Policy Making*. Brookings.

Ramos, J. 1986. *Neoconservative Economics in the Southern Cone of Latin America, 1973–83*. Johns Hopkins University Press.

Sargent, T. 1982. "The Ends of Four Big Inflations." In R. Hall (ed.), *Inflation*. NBER and University of Chicago Press.

Sargent, T., and Wallace. N. 1981. "Some Unpleasant Monetarist Arithmetic." Federal Reserve Bank of Minneapolis, *Quarterly Review* (Fall).

Schacht, H. 1927. *The Stabilization of the Mark*. Reprinted by Arno Press, 1978.

Simonsen, M. 1985. "Indexation: Current Theory and the Experience in Brazil." In R. Dornbusch and M. H. Simonsen (eds.), *Inflation, Debt and Indexation*. MIT Press.

Simonsen, M. 1986a. "Incomes Policy as Game Theory." Unpublished manuscript. Fundaçao Getulio Vargas.

Simonsen, M. 1986b. "Keynes Versus Expectativas Racionais." Unpublished manuscript. Fundacao Getulio Vargas.

Schelling, T. 1982. *Micromotives and Macrobehavior*. Norton.

Tobin, J. 1980. "Stabilization Policy Ten Years After." *Brookings Papers on Economic Activity*, no. 1.

Tobin, J. (ed.). 1983. *Macroeconomics, Prices and Quantities: Essays in Memory of Arthur M. Okun*. Brookings.

Yeager, L. 1981. *Experiences with Stopping Inflation*. American Enterprise Institute.

Index